Elementary Methods

Elementary Methods
An Integrated Curriculum

Donna M. Wolfinger
Auburn University at Montgomery

James W. Stockard Jr.
Auburn University at Montgomery

An imprint of Addison Wesley Longman, Inc.

New York • Reading, Massachusetts • Menlo Park, California • Harlow, England
Don Mills, Ontario • Sydney • Mexico City • Madrid • Amsterdam

Elementary Methods: An Integrated Curriculum

Longman, 10 Bank Street, White Plains, N.Y. 10606

Acquisitions editor: Virginia L. Blanford
Associate editor: Arianne Weber
Production editor: Linda Moser
Production supervisor: Edith Pullman
Cover design: Joseph DePinho
Compositor: ExecuStaff

Library of Congress Cataloging-in-Publication Data

Wolfinger, Donna M.
    Elementary methods : an integrated curriculum / Donna M. Wolfinger,
and James W. Stockhard, Jr.—1st. ed.
        p. cm.
    Includes bibliographical references and index.
    ISBN 0-8013-1609-X
    1. Interdisciplinary approach in education—United States.
2. Education—United States—Curricula. 3. Elementary school
teaching—United States. 4. Group work in education—United States.
I. Wolfinger, Donna M. II. Title.
LB1570.S76 1997
372.19—dc20
                                    96-12108
                                    CIP

3 4 5 6 7 8 9 10-MA-0099

CONTENTS

CHAPTER 3   INTEGRATED CURRICULUM AND EDUCATIONAL BASICS   51

CHAPTER 4   DEVELOPING AN INTEGRATED CURRICULUM   77

PREFACE

A curriculum that is based not on subject matter areas but on themes or problems requires a different type of organization and a different type of classroom pattern. The purpose of this text is to assist the elementary teacher in developing the skills needed for organizing an integrated program, for teaching within an integrated program, and for assessing children's progress in ways appropriate to an integrated program.

Any program for the elementary school should have a firm foundation in research. In the case of elementary school children, that research basis should begin with an understanding of the nature of the children who will be the recipients of the program. For this reason, this text is based in developmental theory, particularly that of Jean Piaget and his followers but also giving attention to the work of Lev Vygotsky. This foundation in developmental theory leads to a consideration of the kinds of themes, problems, and issues that will be appropriate to the elementary school child at the various grade levels. However, in our selection of themes, problems, and issues, the nature of children is not the only source of information. Learned societies and research literature also give a basis for the selection of appropriate areas for study. And finally, the foundation in developmental theory leads to teaching strategies and assessment techniques that are appropriate not only to the integrated curriculum but also to the children learning through the integrated approach.

AUDIENCE

The intended audience for this text is the undergraduate student preparing to work in the elementary school, the graduate student extending his or her knowledge of ways of organizing the elementary school curriculum, and the administrator seeking a means for developing an integrated program in the elementary school.

ORGANIZATION

The authors of this text believe that the following five areas are crucial to a successful integrated program. First, the teacher and administrator must understand the nature of an integrated program as well as its strengths and weaknesses. Second, the teacher and administrator must understand the nature of the children who will be taught within the integrated curriculum. This means an understanding of the cognitive and social development of the average child as well as of the child who may experience learning difficulties or the child who may excel in learning. Third, the teacher and administrator must understand methods that can be used to develop an integrated program: the use of themes or problems, integration through the various subject matter areas, integration through issues. Fourth, the teacher and administrator must understand the kinds of teaching strategies that are most effective within the integrated program. He or she must be familiar with what kinds of projects are appropriate, with discovery-oriented teaching strategies, with expository teaching strategies, and with the unit plan as a means for organizing both the content and the types of activities and projects in which students will engage. And finally, both teacher and administrator must be familiar with the kinds of assessment appropriate to the integrated curriculum. The chapters of this text are organized so that these five elements follow one after the other and are organized into four parts:

Part 1: Curriculum includes chapters 1 through 4. In this part is information on the nature of integrated curriculums and the nature of children at the elementary level as well as how the integrated curriculum assures basic knowledge. The final chapter of this section introduces the basic concepts of developing an integrated curriculum.

Part 2: Approaches to an Integrated Curriculum includes chapters 5 through 8. Each of these chapters deals with a method for integrating the curriculum: integrating through disciplines (chapter 5), through language (chapter 6), through themes (chapter 7), and through issues (chapter 8).

Part 3: Approaches to Instructional Delivery includes chapters 9 and 10. Chapter 9 deals with planning for teaching, while chapter 10 deals with instructional delivery strategies, that is, with the teaching methods most appropriate to the integrated program.

Part 4: Approaches to Assessment includes chapters 11 and 12. Chapter 11 deals with methods for assessing the children involved in the program, while chapter 12 deals with methods for assessing the effectiveness of the teachers and the program.

Instructional Aids

Aids to learning in this book include a variety of illustrative diagrams, chapter objectives at the beginning of each chapter so that major points are stated prior to reading or discussion, study questions at the conclusion of each chapter so that material may be reviewed and applied, and a complete bibliography for each chapter.

Acknowledgments

The authors are indebted to their colleagues at Auburn University at Montgomery for their help in identifying sources of information and for their assistance during the writing process. Special thanks go to graduate and undergraduate students who were involved in the testing of the content in their classes. The authors are grateful to the following individuals who reviewed the manuscript and provided helpful suggestions:

Gloria Boutte, University of South Carolina

Kriner Cash, Howard University

Joanne Frey, Northeastern Illinois University

Jann James, Radford University

Carole Murphy, University of Missouri, St. Louis

P. Maureen Musser, Portland State University

Tony Sanchez, Indiana University Northwest

M. Kay Stickle, Ball State University

Susan Trostle, University of Rhode Island

Finally, the authors are indebted to their families, who provided the support needed to begin and complete a project like this.

INTRODUCTION

One of the most disconcerting questions children can ask a teacher is: Why are we learning this? All too often, the answer to that question is one of the following:

You'll need this when you get to sixth grade (generally told to students in fifth grade).

It's in the book and we need to cover the book.

You'll need to know this when you get out in the real world.

You'll need this for the test (generally referring to some standardized test).

What would happen if, instead of a curriculum geared toward the development of skills and knowledge for some later time or for some test, classrooms were organized so that knowledge and skills were important then, right then, as children learn? What would happen if students learned because the information was inherently interesting to the learner as a child? What would happen if the textbook became a small part of the educational experience rather than a major classroom force? What would happen is that integrated programs would be found in many classrooms.

The integrated approach to curriculum allows students to develop skills and concepts in a way that shows their importance to the children learning those skills and concepts and so allows them to learn in a meaningful manner. Rather than considering isolated skills in artificial contexts, an integrated approach engages students in meaningful learning in authentic situations. Children learn to communicate effectively because they have a need to communicate the results of research and projects. Children learn to compute effectively and accurately because mathematics contributes to the development of new information, new concepts. Children learn the facts, laws, and theories of science because they are needed to solve problems, real-world problems, which have meaning for the children. Children learn historical, social, anthropological, and economic information because it contributes to their understanding of an issue or theme.

Within the integrated curriculum, learning becomes a cooperative effort as students and teacher plan together for a unit of study, as children work cooperatively in planning and carrying out projects, and as students share their new knowledge with other students, parents, and the public. Such cooperative efforts in planning help children learn to work together, to plan and carry out projects, and to become responsible for their own learning.

And within the integrated curriculum the relationships among and between subject area disciplines are shown and enhanced. Science uses mathematics to collect data, language to report that data and to draw conclusions from it, and art to illustrate the findings and the principles learned. Reading becomes a tool for gaining information in social studies rather than an end in itself, and literature a means of conveying historical, mathematical, social, and scientific concepts as well as an end in itself. Because problems and issues found in society rarely keep to the confines of a particular subject matter area, students become better able to solve problems because they are able to integrate concepts and skills from a variety of subject matter areas. Students are more able to see and understand why they are learning particular information because that information is used in context, in an authentic manner, in a way useful in the present as well as in the future.

The purpose of this book is to help the teacher and curriculum planner develop an integrated program for the elementary school level. To accomplish this purpose, the nature of the integrated curriculum is considered, followed by a discussion of the nature of the children who will learn through an integrated program. Then various means for organizing an integrated approach are discussed: integrating through disciplines, through themes, through problems and issues, as well as others. Finally, teaching strategies appropriate to the integrated curriculum are discussed, followed by means for assessing the effectiveness of the program in terms of both learner outcomes and teacher effectiveness.

CURRICULUM

CHAPTER 1

THE INTEGRATED CURRICULUM

CHAPTER OBJECTIVES

After reading this chapter you should be able to:

1. Define the term *integrated curriculum*
2. Discuss the strengths of an integrated approach to curriculum
3. Discuss the weaknesses of an integrated approach to curriculum

Memories of school usually include going to algebra class or writing essays in English, sitting in reading groups or working problems from a mathematics text, waiting for graded papers to be returned or report cards to be handed out. Many people recall particular teachers and identify those teachers with a certain subject matter area: Mrs. Jones was a great science teacher; Mr. Greye cared more about the spelling errors in an essay than the content; Ms. Brown was the most creative art teacher ever. Whether they are painful or pleasant, our memories of school generally are memories of subject matter areas. The traditional approach to organizing the **curriculum** is oriented around subject matter areas. Although this traditional approach to subject matter has worked effectively for many years, it generally gives little attention to the fact that problem solving in one subject matter area often requires information from another; that communicating the results of a science activity requires the use of writing or artistic skills; and that many subject matter areas are artificially separated in order to allow for ease of scheduling. Recognition that subject matter from different areas overlaps, that reading, writing, and mathematics skills are useful in all areas, and that problem solving is interdisciplinary in nature has resulted in consideration of other ways of organizing and presenting the curriculum to children at the elementary school level. One such way of organizing the curriculum is known as **curricular integration.**

THE INTEGRATED CURRICULUM

The following schedule hangs on the wall of a third grade classroom in a local elementary school:

8:15–8:30	Morning Routine and Class Meeting
8:30–10:30	Block One
10:30–11:30	Block Two
11:30–12:00	Lunch
12:00–2:30	Block Three
2:30–3:00	Class Meeting

Looking at the schedule, the visitor to the class wonders exactly what the children do all day. Where is the spelling? What happened to mathematics and science? When do they learn to read? There is no indication that these children are being expected to accomplish any of the traditional school subject areas, and yet they are active, busy learners. Rather than following a tight schedule of subject matter areas, learning for these children is organized within large **blocks** of time during which a variety of different subject matter areas is considered within the framework of a particular topic. Rather than organizing the schedule around the discrete subject matter areas, the class and teacher together organized learning around an integrated theme: "the role of plants in the environment."

The schedule posted reflects the way teaching and learning are approached within the integrated curriculum. In Block One students work in small groups to plan a series of field trips to various locations to see how farms, a state park, a logging company, and a planned community use plants. In Block Two children pursue their own interests, creating reports and projects on a variety of individually selected topics related to the overall theme. And in Block Three students are investigating various kinds of plants they are growing in the classroom: measuring and graphing the growth of bean plants, drawing pictures to show the stages in germination of a variety of seeds. They are using reference books to identify seeds found on a field trip, writing about the field trip, including thank-you notes to the guide, and planning how they will develop a wildflower garden for the school using the seeds they collected along with purchased seeds and seeds donated by a local gardening club.

Within the four planned blocks there are no special time periods for mathematics, science, language arts, or reading. Instead, children utilize important skills from a variety of subject matter areas within their investigations. In this integrated program conceptual development, understanding, and application of subject matter skills and concepts take precedence over discrete subject matter areas that may not be related to one another in authentic and purposeful ways.

Within each large block of time a variety of activities takes place. Some activities are independent, such as drawing pictures of germinating seeds. Some will be more teacher directed, such as reviewing how to write a thank-you note. Some activities will be remedial, as when the teacher reteaches graphing techniques to children who are having difficulty graphing the growth of their bean plants. Some activities, such as measuring bean plants, will be individual, while others, like planning and planting a garden, will involve the entire class.

DEFINITION

For purposes of this text, **integrated curriculum** is defined as an approach to curricular organization in which the lines separating subject matter areas from one another are erased, and distinct and discrete subject matter areas disappear. The integrated curriculum utilizes a conceptual or life-problem-oriented approach to organization in which skills are utilized in appropriate contexts, in which new skills are taught as the need arises, and in which students have the opportunity to select from or develop independently a variety of project and investigation options all within the context of the study area. Children in an integrated curriculum have an opportunity for significant input into the learning experience in which they will be involved, including not only the kinds of projects and activities in which they will be engaged but also the concepts that will be developed. Finally, the integrated curriculum utilizes authentic forms of assessment in which the individual child's growth is charted rather than measured against an external, established standard.

STRENGTHS OF THE INTEGRATED CURRICULUM APPROACH

No matter what the curricular pattern selected for use within a school, its success or failure will lie within the degree of organization it brings to the educational program. **External organization** refers to the manner in which the traditional curriculum is implemented at the classroom or district level; **internal organization** refers to the organization of the subject matter within the total curriculum. The integrated curriculum brings to the school great strength in both internal and external organization.

External Organization.   Within the integrated curriculum, external organization focuses on providing time for in-depth study, for active involvement in learning, and for discussion. When limited time periods are designated for study of discrete subject matter areas, often only 45 minutes for science or 30 minutes for social studies, children are generally unable to consider a topic in more than a superficial manner and must stop work before completion, often until the next day. The enthusiasm, intensity of concentration, and internal motivation the child brought to the task is likely to be lost. Organization around large blocks of time frees both the teacher and the student from the domination of the clock. If children become involved in a writing project, the use of blocks of time allows them to see that project to completion rather than being forced to halt work because they must move on to a different subject matter area. Large blocks of time also allow children to pursue more in-depth investigations. Students often become interested in particular questions or ideas resulting from their investigations. They want to discuss those topics of interest *then,* not tomorrow or the day after tomorrow, when the schedule allows for such a discussion. The use of large blocks of time rather than smaller periods of time permits the teacher and students to pursue the discussion rather than put it off until another time.

Internal Organization.   Equal in importance to the external organization of the integrated curriculum is the internal organization. This internal organization consists of two facets: authentic integration of subject matter areas and developmental appropriateness.

Integration of subject matter is, of course, the focus of the fully integrated curriculum. Rather than begin with distinct subject matter areas, the integrated curriculum begins with a topic or real-life problem. Within the fully integrated curriculm, no consideration is given to the separate subject matter areas and their inclusion or noninclusion. Instead a broad area is selected for investigation and study, and the various subject matter areas and skills develop as a result of the topic selected. Within the fully integrated curriculum, the inclusion of traditional subject matter is authentic rather than contrived.

Authentic inclusion occurs when the concepts and skills of science, mathematics, language arts, reading, social studies, art, or music are used as a means of gathering, presenting, or understanding information. Authentic inclusion means that students are able to see how subject matter is related to their present search for knowledge and will be related to their future lives. In the real world mathematics problems are not generally worked in isolation, sentences are not constructed simply to practice a particular grammatical form or type of punctuation, and chemical formulas are not memorized for the joy of memorizing chemical formulas. The mathematician, grammarian, or scientist has a purpose for learning certain information. So should the child have a purpose for learning information. Divorcing subject matter from purpose only results in memorization of bits of isolated information soon forgotten or perpetuates the myth that one studies mathematics or French or chemistry simply to get a grade so one can move on to yet another subject and so "finish" school.

The focus of attention within the integrated curriculum on authenticity and purposeful inclusion of subject matter areas does not mean, however, that the subject matter areas are never approached individually. For example, students at the sixth grade level may be working with the concept of prehistoric cultures. As they research this area of study they discover that neolithic people used tools made of stone but that there were a wide variety of these stone tools. The students begin to ask how those tools were made and, more importantly, how archaeologists know which tool was used for which task. This is an appropriate time to invite an archaeologist to the classroom for a "social studies lesson" dealing with the answers to those questions. Similarly, if students are having difficulty making accurate measurements of the weight gained by developing silkworm larvae, the teacher may present a lesson on how to use a balance accurately. So, within the integrated curriculum, already developed skills and concepts are used in new investigations while direct teaching strategies impart new information and reinforce previously learned skills. Which skills or concepts are taught directly to the children by the teacher depends not on some previously determined scope and sequence document but on the actual needs of the children as they learn.

The internal organization that erases the lines of demarcation between subject matter areas within the integrated curriculum also provides for a more developmentally appropriate program. Young learners, particularly those in kindergarten through third grade, do not view the world as divided into discrete bits of information. Rather, their viewpoint is global. They see language as a whole rather than separated into reading, writing, spelling, speaking, and listening. They see no divisions between science and social studies, between mathematics and art. Consequently, a curriculum pattern that differentiates between subject matter areas is contrary to the perspective of young learners. It is only when young children experience a differentiated approach to subject matter that they learn to view each area as distinct. After years of exposure to the traditional subject-matter-oriented approach to curriculum children are surprised that spelling counts in science, that mathematics has applications in social studies, that music and art can enhance reading. Because the integrated curriculum naturally maintains the global approach to understanding, it helps maintain the concept that subject matter areas are interrelated and aids students in conceptualization.

Conceptualization.   Very often the curriculum of schools appears to be oriented more toward the memorization of names, dates, definitions, and procedures than the development of in-depth understanding of the major **concepts** of the various subject matter areas. Ideas learned through memorization and in isolation are soon forgotten; ideas interrelated through concepts are remembered and applied. The integrated curriculum focuses on **conceptualization** rather than on memorization. Consider, for a moment, learning new vocabulary. One way is through word lists, in which the new vocabulary is coupled with definitions. The usual strategy for learning is to memorize the word and the definition. Learned in this way, that is, out of context, those new vocabulary words are retained for the test and quickly forgotten, rarely making it into the common speech of the learner. If, instead of memorizing words in a list with their definitions, vocabulary is learned through use, in context, then those new words are likely to be retained and used. As an example of learning within context consider a group of three- and four-year-old children in a preschool setting. They were collecting "creepy crawlies," mainly insects, and making a zoo so that they could watch the creatures in their classroom before returning them to the outdoors. As a part of this study, a guest speaker brought in large photographs of insects and asked the children what they saw. The butterfly was blue and had wings, feet, legs, hair, a skinny body, and two straws on its head. The grasshopper had feet, legs, a body, eyes, and two straws on its head. After the second mention of the "straws" the guest speaker said, "Right, they have antennae that look like straws." The next photograph was of a locust. Included in the list of characteristics: two antennae. This inclusion came from the children, not from the speaker. They had picked up on the appropriate term because they had developed meaning for that term through context and examples.

Within the integrated curriculum, this kind of contextual learning becomes the norm rather than the exception. As children pursue their studies and investigations, appropriate terminology develops as a natural outgrowth of learning. Terms are learned in context rather than in isolation, and conceptualization occurs. As study gains greater depth, more connections are made between previously learned information and new information, thus assuring understanding and retention of content. The more connections that can be made within the cognitive schema developed by the students, the more likely understanding will develop and retention will occur.

Autonomy.   Within some curricular patterns, children have little say as to what they will study, which projects they will complete, or how long they will spend in an area of study. This leads to dependency on the teacher for instruction and direction. This dependency is often termed **heteronomy.** Within the integrated curriculum, **autonomy** rather than heteronomy is fostered. With this autonomy, children develop the ability to think for themselves and to guide their own learning. Although this may sound as if the teacher relinquishes his or her role within the classroom, this is not so. Within the integrated approach, the teacher is still of great importance to the success of the program, but he or she holds the reins of the curriculum less tightly. Large blocks of time and in-depth study frequently lead to questions from children, questions that can lead to further investigation and study. As children gain in skill and maturity they begin to plan with the teacher, therefore bringing their ideas and interests to the topic from the very beginning. Within the integrated curriculum, the children have an opportunity to develop self-determined projects and to pursue those projects in self-determined ways. Having the freedom to pursue areas of interest, the child becomes more autonomous in his or her learning, especially if given the opportunity to decide for himself or herself how to pursue those interests.

Problem Solving.   Consider for a moment a fifth grade mathematics class studying the topics of area and perimeter. The children come into the classroom, participate in individual activities in which they find the perimeter of various objects in the classroom using string and meter sticks, then use paper squares to cover various surfaces to determine the area. From these hands-on activities, the children are helped to understand the formulas used to calculate perimeter and area. They then go to their mathematics texts to work the problems on pages 135 through 137. At the end of the unit is a section entitled "Solve It!" in which students are presented with a problem to solve. The teacher knows his students can solve perimeter and area problems, but when he looks for their work on the problem-solving page, few children have even attempted the problem.

Now consider a second classroom, also fifth grade and also working with area and perimeter. The difference is that the second group has been studying about plants and has decided to grow a vegetable garden on a plot of land next to the playground. They need to know how big their garden is so that they can decide how many plants to grow. They discuss various methods they could use to find the answers to their problems and find they need some additional help. The teacher then helps them to find both the perimeter and the area of the garden. With that additional information, the students return to their group and begin to work out how many plants they can grow and how they will be spaced.

In the first example, the students learn skills without purpose. No one really needs to know the perimeter or area of his or her desk. Because the information has not been related to real problems, the "Solve It!" exercise is unsolved. In the second example, the students are learning the same information, but they are learning that information in the context of problem solving. They identified the problem of needing to know the size of their garden and discussed a variety of ways of finding that size. When they were unable to solve the problem satisfactorily, they went to the teacher for asssistance. The teacher gave them the information, then allowed the students to decide how they would use that information in the solution of their problem.

Within the integrated curriculum, such authentic problem-solving situations are common. Students work in small groups on a particular project, identifying and solving problems as a part of their learning experience.

Interpersonal Skills. A common view of the classroom has children sitting at individual desks placed in orderly rows. Each student works with an individual book, completing each assignment on his or her own. The classroom is quiet as the children work without interacting. When all of the lessons are finished, each student completes a test. This sort of individual work is found in schools, but rarely found outside of the school; in the worlds of work and play, teamwork and cooperation are far more common than individualized work. Schools, therefore, need to give more attention to providing opportunities for students to work cooperatively.

Within the integrated curriculum, much work is done in small groups rather than individually. As students work together in developing their projects and solving problems, they must interact with one another. Through this interaction, students learn to communicate their ideas effectively to one another. They learn to disagree with one another and to argue without fighting. They learn to compromise. Their interpersonal skills develop along with their knowledge.

Learning Styles.   Just as children do not all learn the same things at the same time, they do not learn the same things in the same way. Some children learn best when they can interact directly with materials, while others learn more effectively by watching that interaction. Some children find it easier to organize their ideas in words while others are far better at organizing through drawings. Some children learn best when they can involve their bodies fully in learning, while others prefer to remain quiet and watch. Some children are report writers, some are model builders, some are song writers, and some are story tellers. Children learn in a variety of ways and show their learning in a variety of ways. The integrated curriculum provides opportunities for children with different **learning styles** to pursue their learning through their strengths.

In many subject-centered classrooms, students may select the topic they wish to study but are assigned the mode in which the collected information will be presented. For example, students studying ancient Greece may select a topic from the following list: schools in ancient Greece, Athens's rise to power, Greek architecture, and clothing worn in ancient Greece. However, they must present the results of their investigation in a research paper following a specified style and format. In the integrated curriculum, the topics for study may be the same, but the means of presentation vary according to the topic or the students. Going to school in ancient Greece may be presented as a play written, staged, and costumed by a group of five. Greek architecture may become a soap carving replicating a not entirely fictional "downtown Athens." Clothing styles may be presented through a fashion show of dolls dressed in various styles. And, yes, the rise of Athens still may be presented as a neatly printed paper proudly presented by a budding historian.

Within the integrated curriculum, students have the opportunity to present information in ways appropriate not only to the topic, but also to the students. Students have the opportunity to work in small groups, in teams, or alone. They have the opportunity to utilize their strengths rather than being forced to display their weaknesses.

Assessment.   Within the majority of classroom settings, assessment is generally in terms of specified objectives which are then measured through teacher-made or standardized testing procedures. The child is, therefore, measured against the curriculum. In the integrated approach, assessment of progress is measured in terms of the accomplishments of each child. The integration of subject matter areas requires that evaluation procedures be holistic. To teach in an integrated manner and then test in a subject-matter-specific manner is unfair to the students and counter to the aims of the integrated curriculum. Although specific information can be assessed, it is assessed as a part of the total package of study. For example, a student who prepares a report on the planet Venus provides opportunities for the teacher to assess progress in writing skills, researching skills, art work, and organizational abilities.

The use of products such as reports to evaluate student progress is vital to the integrated curriculum and to the authentic evaluation of the students involved. In using such reports and projects for assessment, however, a second concept about **authentic assessment** should be considered. Students should be measured against themselves rather than against some predetermined standard. The gain made by the individual child from the start of an area of study to the end, from the start of a grading period to the end, from the start of the school year to the end, is of greater importance than a comparison of that child to others in the school, class, or nation.

As an example, consider two students at the fifth grade level. They enter into a cooperative project to study simple machines. At the start of the effort, Jenny can name five of the six categories of simple machines and can create models of three of those five. By the end of the project, she knows all six categories, can make models of all six, and has worked with Lara to create a complex machine that will pick up pencils from the floor. Lara, on the other hand, began the project with the concept that a bicycle was a simple machine and a truck was a complicated machine. By the end of the project, she had differentiated between simple and complex machines, knew all of the categories of simple machines, and could draw pictures of each showing how it is commonly used. She worked in equal partnership with Jenny in creating their invention. Which of these students learned more? If a simple test asking for names and examples of simple machines is used as an assessment, then both girls learned equal amounts. But if one considers the starting level of knowledge, Lara probably learned a great deal more than Jenny because she started with a lower level of knowledge. Authentic assessment gives attention both to the starting level of the student and to the final level.

WEAKNESSES OF THE INTEGRATED CURRICULUM APPROACH

The integrated curriculum provides a powerful tool for the development of educational programs, but, as with any approach to curriculum development, there are weaknesses as well as strengths.

Internal Organization.   While conceptual development is facilitated by the integrated approach, the sequencing of skills and concepts within the total curriculum is less systematic than in other organizational patterns. The integrated curriculum is built around topics or real-life problems rather than around specific subject matter areas. New skills are introduced as they are needed within the projects developed rather than as separate entities divorced from their use within the curriculum. As a consequence, there is no standard sequence for the introduction of particular skills and concepts. Some adherents to more structured models for curriculum development fear that vital skills will be omitted from the curriculum, leaving children without necessary skills. The possibility does exist that children may not learn certain areas of the traditionally defined curriculum. However, if those skills do not arise in authentic situations during in-depth study, there is the distinct possibility that the skills or concepts may be of no real value to the student or to the adult that student will become. It is highly unlikely that vital skills will be omitted from the curriculum. Children will learn to read, to write, to use mathematics. They will learn science and social studies concepts that are necessary to the solution of real-life problems. What they will not learn is the disjointed, often outdated and useless information that has caused the curriculum at the elementary school to be overstuffed and superficial.

Coordination.   A second problem with the integrated curriculum is that without close coordination from grade level to grade level it is possible for the same topic or theme to be repeated again and again. When I was working with a school moving from an interdisciplinary approach to an integrated approach, I asked the teachers at each grade level to list the themes or topics used at that level. Each had included a unit on the human body. Although there were differences in the way the topic was handled at each grade level, there were two areas included at every level: the five senses and care of teeth. By the time the children in this school reached sixth grade they had learned how to brush their teeth properly at every grade level and had been thoroughly versed in identifying objects through smell, taste, touch, sound, and hearing. No wonder the fourth grade teachers reported a lack of interest and the sixth grade teachers reported groans! The topics and problems selected for the integrated curriculum should be coordinated so that different grade levels are not considering the same problems with pollution, rain forests, brushing teeth, or anything else.

Documentation.   A third weakness of the integrated approach is in the paperwork involved in documenting the skills, concepts, and projects developed by each child and used at each level. This **documentation** is far more extensive than the usual grades posted in a grade book. The accomplishments of each child must be shown, and each child may be showing that progress in a different way. And, while documentation is necessary to record each child's progress, it is also needed to record the curriculum achievements at each level of the integrated program. This second need for documentation is required so that need-less repetition is avoided and so that gaps in the program can be identified and remedied.

Transition.   Making the transition from a subject-matter-oriented curriculum to an integrated curriculum is not easy and can result in some weaknesses. First, it requires a total reorganization of the school program, which, even though it can be accomplished in steps, is a difficult and time-consuming endeavor. Second, the integrated curriculum requires that all teachers be firmly committed to the concept and the practice of integration. Without this commitment, the program may deteriorate into pockets of integration within a subject-matter-oriented program or pockets of subject matter orientation within an integrated program. Articulation then becomes extremely difficult. Third, the move to integration may be viewed by some teachers as an opportunity to focus on *their* strengths and *their* interests, rather than as an opportunity to engage the children in learning that is meaningful to them.

Assessment.   Assessment within the integrated curriculum, usually a strength, can also become a weakness. Teachers are held accountable for the education of their students. That **accountability** is frequently determined by scores on standardized tests administered nationally. While it is true that there is great variability among school systems in terms of what is taught at each grade level, a subject matter orientation within most approaches to curriculum development allows for some standardization, especially as textbooks become the driving force for the subject-oriented curriculum. The integrated curriculum, however, does not necessarily conform to standard subject matter sequencing. Therefore the integrated curriculum may fare poorly on standardized tests even though children are learning a great deal.

An additional weakness of the integrated curriculum in terms of evaluation is in the necessity for evaluating each child as a distinct, continuously developing individual to be assessed on the basis of individual growth rather than against a predetermined measure of learning. Such individual assessment requires more differentiation of evaluation and so more documentation, more paperwork for the teacher often already immersed in paperwork.

SUMMARY

The integrated curriculum is an approach to curriculum development that involves the teacher and the student in development, implementation, and assessment of the educational program. Its strengths lie in its organization, authenticity of subject matter and assessment, attention to conceptualization rather than memorization, student autonomy, attention to problem solving, development of interpersonal skills, and attention to the variety of learning modalities among children.

But, just as any organizational pattern has strengths, so does it have weaknesses. The weaknesses of the integrated curriculum pattern lie in its internal organization, particularly in the development of sequential learning, in the difficulty of coordinating the program from grade level to grade level, in the amount of paperwork necessary to document the education program and progress of the children, and in the implementation of the program.

ACTIVITY ONE

PURPOSE

The purpose of this activity is to present a persuasive argument to parents for an integrated curriculum model.

PROCEDURE

The school in which you teach has decided to move to an integrated curriculum approach. Because the school knows the importance of parental support, you have been selected to inform parents of the reasons for making a change to an integrated model and of the benefits for their children. You have decided to use a newsletter to inform parents. Write a newsletter article to persuade parents that the new approach to curriculum will be beneficial to their children.

ACTIVITY TWO

PURPOSE

The purpose of this activity is to role-play an interaction between a teacher and a parent in which the parent voices concern about the appropriateness of the integrated approach to curriculum for his or her child.

PROCEDURE

1. One person should be selected to play the role of the teacher and a second person to play the role of a parent.
2. The person who is selected to play the parent should select one of the following roles to play:
   a. The parent of a child who is gifted, either academically, artistically, athletically, or in some other way
   b. the parent of a child from a culture different from the mainstream culture of the school
   c. the parent of a disabled child
   d. the parent of a child who is capable of learning but who has little interest in academics
   e. a parent with either a highly conservative or liberal orientation who is concerned about the content his or her child will learn
   f. a parent who is more concerned with whether his or her child will be able to get into a "good" college than with what the child does in the present
   g. a single parent who is concerned about his or her child's preparation for a job

3. Once the role has been selected, the parent should make a list of questions to ask the teacher, focusing on concerns specific to the parent and his or her children.
4. Parent and teacher then role-play an encounter in which the teacher attempts to respond to the parent's concerns.

STUDY QUESTIONS

1. Discuss the strengths and weaknesses of the integrated curriculum. How can the classroom teacher help to eliminate the weaknesses of the integrated program?
2. On parents' night, you discover that many of the parents are concerned their children will not learn to read, write, spell, or compute because the schedule for the day does not show these subject matter areas. How would you answer these parents to allay their fears about their children's learning?
3. Think back to your own elementary school days. Compare and contrast your elementary school program with the kind of program described in an integrated curriculum approach.
4. You have been asked to serve on a committee to help move the elementary school where you teach from a subject matter approach to an integrated approach. What suggestions would you make to the committee about how to proceed in this change of curriculum?

BIBLIOGRAPHY

Ackerman, D. (1989). Intellectual and practical criteria for successful curriculum integration. In H. Jacobs (Ed.), *The interdisciplinary curriculum, design and implementation* (pp. 25-37). Alexandria, Va.: Association for Supervision and Curriculum Development.

Beane, J. A. (1993). Problems and possibilities for an integrative curriculum. *Middle School Journal, 25,* 1, 18-23.

Beane, J. A. (1995). Curriculum integration and the disciplines of knowledge. *Phi Delta Kappan, 76* (8), 616-622.

Caine, R. N., and Caine, G. (1990). Understanding a brain-based approach to learning and teaching. *Educational Leadership, 48* (2), 66-70.

Cardellichio, T. L. (1995). Curriculum and the structure of school. *Phi Delta Kappan, 76* (8), 629-636.

Cummings, R. J. (1989). The interdisciplinary challenge: Connection and balance. *National Forum: The Phi Kappa Phi Journal, 69* (2), 2-3.

Gaff, J. G. (1989). The resurgence of interdisciplinary studies. *The Phi Kappa Phi Journal, 69* (2), 4-5.

Gibbons, J. A. (1979). Curriculum integration. *Curriculum Inquiry, 9,* 321-332.

Hamilton, D. (1973). The integration of knowledge: Practice and problems. *Journal of Curriculum Studies, 5* (2), 146-155.

Hayes, H. J. (Ed.). (1989). *Interdisciplinary curriculum: Design and implementation.* Alexandria, Va.: Association for Supervision and Curriculum Development.

Jacobs, H. (1989). The growing need for interdisciplinary discipline content. In Jacobs (Ed.), *The interdisciplinary curriculum, design and implementation* (pp. 1-11). Alexandria, Va.: Association for Supervision and Curriculum Development.

Kolde, R. F. (1991). Integrated learning for a competitive work force. *Phi Delta Kappan, 72* (6), 453-455.

Maute, J. (1989). Cross-curricular connections. *The Middle School Journal, 20* (4), 20-22.

Panaritis, P. (1995). Beyond brainstorming: Planning a successful interdisciplinary program. *The Phi Delta Kappan, 76* (8), 623-628.

Relan, A., & Kimpston, R. (1993). Curriculum integration: A critical analysis of practical and conceptual issues. In R. Fogarty (Ed.), *Integrating the curricula: A collection* (pp. 31-48). Palantine, Ill.: RI/Skylight Publishing.

Shoemaker, B. J. (1989). A comparison of traditional and integrative approaches. In R. Fogarty (Ed.) (1993), *Integrating the curricula: A collection* (pp. 111-120). Palantine, Ill.: RI/Skylight Publishing.

Shoemaker, B. J. (1991). Education 2000 integrated curriculum. *Phi Delta Kappan, 72* (10), 793-797.

Webster, T. (1990). Projects as curriculum: Under what conditions? *Childhood Education, 67* (1), 2-3.

CHAPTER 2

CHILD DEVELOPMENT AND THE INTEGRATED CURRICULUM

CHAPTER OBJECTIVES

After reading this chapter you should be able to:

1. Discuss the cognitive and social characteristics of elementary grade children as identified by Piagetian psychology

3. Compare the cognitive and social characteristics of primary and intermediate grade children as identified by Piagetian psychology

4. Discuss the effect on the integrated curriculum of cognitive and social development as identified by Piagetian psychology

5. Discuss the application of Vygotsky's theory of learning on curriculum and teaching

6. Discuss the characteristics of special needs children on the integrated curriculum

7. Discuss the effect of special needs children on the integrated curriculum

According to many parents and other individuals concerned with education, classrooms should be quiet, orderly places in which children follow a set curriculum while sitting at desks in neat rows, books open, mouths closed unless answering questions posed by the teacher, and pencils ready. Children should be "on-task" from the beginning of the school day to the break for lunch and from the end of lunch to the end of the day. On-task frequently means using a textbook, pencil or pen, workbook or worksheet, notebook paper or other type of paper. The effectiveness of instruction can be determined through tests, teacher made or standardized, that measure children against a predetermined standard and against other children. The underlying philosophy is that all children of a particular age should learn the same things at the same time, in the same way, and to the same extent. The teacher, the established curriculum, and the textbook are the focal points of instruction throughout the day.

Walk into a typical elementary school classroom and you will get a different picture of how children and teachers interact during the day. Some children pay attention, some do not. Some children have pencils and paper ready, while some are unprepared for the task. Paying attention does not necessarily mean attention to the teacher or the lesson and certainly is not nonstop from morning to lunch or lunch to day's end. The teacher has a thousand little tasks to attend to as well as the designated task of presenting lessons to the children. And, while some children do learn the designated content, others are bored and still more have tuned out completely. Tests indicate that children are not learning and so teachers are blamed for not teaching the material.

Bringing the reality of education closer to the desired image often results in more stringent rules, more tests, and, unfortunately, more failure. Teachers become more frustrated because the children are not learning. Parents become more frustrated because the children are not learning. And children become more frustrated, more turned off to education.

Why is it that the public's image of the classroom so rarely translates into reality? What are reasonable expectations for children at the various grade levels in the elementary school? How does the variety of children one sees in the classroom affect what occurs within the classroom? In essence, how do children affect the curriculum?

In order to answer this final question, it is necessary to explore the cognitive characteristics of children at the various grade levels. For purposes of this exploration, the developmentalist perspective as developed by Jean Piaget and his followers will be considered.

PRIMARY GRADE CHILDREN

How can a child get 7+5=12 correct and miss 5+7=12? They're the same problem!

In science we were discussing living and nonliving things. My class thinks clouds are living and trees are nonliving. Where do they get these ridiculous ideas?

One of the topics in social studies is how the movement of the Earth around the Sun causes the seasons. This isn't that hard, but my third graders had no idea of what I was talking about.

My students can't find the cause and effect in a sentence. In their workbooks they just underline the first part of the sentence and call it the cause and the second part of the sentence and call it the effect.

I asked my kids how they thought the little girl in the story felt about her puppy running away and they told me about their puppies. Not one of them could put himself or herself in the place of the girl in the story.

My first graders talk all the time but when I try to lead a discussion, they have a hard time keeping on the topic. Most of the comments they contribute have nothing to do with the lesson.

The teachers who shared these incidents were amused and frustrated at the same time. What seemed so straightforward to them as adults was difficult for the children. What seemed logical to them as adults was not so logical to the children they taught. How can we explain these all too frequent occurrences?

In one statement: Children at the primary grades do not think like adults, they think like children—preoperational children.

A Definition of Preoperational Thought

The term *preoperations* defines the stage. According to Piaget, an **operation** is an action carried out and reversed mentally rather than physically. At the **preoperational stage,** children have not yet developed this ability to use operations. They are, however, beginning to develop the ability to use symbols such as words, gestures, signs, and images to stand for objects that are not physically present. This growing ability to use symbols for objects will eventually result in the ability to think through words and symbols rather than through actions. Preoperational children tend to think globally, not differentiating their learning along traditional subject matter lines but rather seeing all areas as one.

Cognitive Development in Preoperational Children

In considering preoperational thought processes in children, the following areas will be discussed:

1. one-to-one correspondence
2. seriation and ordering
3. classification
4. centration
5. egocentricity
6. conservation
7. cause and effect
8. reasoning
9. language use
10. reversibility
11. concrete materials

One-to-One Correspondence.   In essence, **one-to-one correspondence** is the ability to match one object in a set of objects to one object in a second set of objects. Giving out cupcakes so that each child receives one cupcake is an example of one-to-one correspondence. Early in the preoperational stage of development, children have some difficulty with one-to-one correspondence when it occurs outside of familiar situations. Four-year-old children may be able to hand one cupcake to each child but will probably have difficulty constructing a one-to-one correspondence between two rows of coins. Children of five years of age tend to be able to make a one-to-one correspondence between sets of objects without difficulty. Two variations on one-to-one correspondence which are slightly more difficult are **many-to-one correspondence** and **one-to-many correspondence.** In the former, the task is to match a variety of objects to a single object, as when setting the table by putting all of the items necessary for a place setting at a single place. In the latter, one object is matched to a variety of objects, as when a single ball is used by a group of children in a game of dodgeball.

The use of one-to-one correspondence, many-to-one correspondence, and one-to-many correspondence is important not only in daily experiences but also in the development of mathematical concepts. Counting is based on the development of a one-to-one correspondence between a number name and an object. Place value is based on the many-to-one correspondence, as when ten ones are regrouped as one ten, and on the one-to-many correspondence, as when one ten is regrouped as ten ones.

Seriation and Ordering.   **Seriation** is most easily defined as placing objects in order on the basis of some characteristic. See Figure 2.1 for an example of a **single seriation.** For example, toy cars can be seriated from smallest to largest in overall size. Such a seriation of toys would be considered a single seriation. In a **double seriation,** the objects of one set are matched to the objects of a second set so that the object in the first set having the greatest amount of a given characteristic is matched to the object in the second set having the least of the given characteristic. For example, the longest fork in a series is matched to the shortest spoon and so on until the shortest fork in the set is matched to the longest spoon. See Figure 2.2 for an example of a double seriation.

For the preschool child the concept of seriation is a global one. Children at the preschool level can describe a single seriation or a double seriation but are unable to construct such seriations for themselves. Between five and seven years of age, children begin to construct both single and double seriations, but they do so through a trial-and-error method rather than through a concerted plan of attack.

Classification.   **Classification** is defined as placing objects into groups or sets on the basis of one or more characteristics. Until about five years of age, the idea of classifying is not present in children. Younger children will make interesting patterns or pictures rather than group objects. At about five years of age, children begin to classify, but the five-year-old child is most likely to match

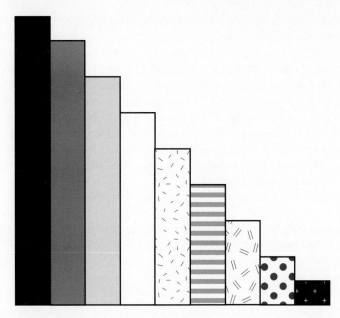

FIGURE 2.1 Single seriation

FIGURE 2.2 Double seriation

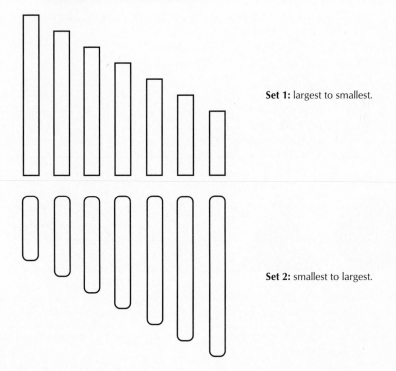

Set 1: largest to smallest.

Set 2: smallest to largest.

two objects on the basis of a characteristic, then select a third object with a different characteristic but one present in the second object, then select a fourth object because it is somehow similar to the third object but not necessarily to the first or second. This matching of two objects is known as *resemblance sorting;* see Figure 2.3 for an example. In addition to resemblance sorting, many preoperational children will group only as many objects as they care to group and then conclude the task. This decision to stop at a particular point without necessarily classifying all of the available objects is known as a lack of **exhaustive sorting.**

Later in the preoperational stage, as children reach about six years of age, they become better able to classify in a manner similar to that of adults. At about six years of age children are able to classify exhaustively according to a single characteristic such as color, shape, smell, or taste.

Centration.   **Centration** is the tendency to consider a single characteristic to the exclusion of all others; it is typical of preoperational thought in children through about five years of age. Children who center may see that an object is red but not that it is fuzzy until their attention is turned away from the color of the object. They may see that an object is round without seeing that it is easily deformed. The tendency to centration means that children may draw conclusions on the basis of a characteristic that is of little importance to the stated conclusion.

Egocentricity.   **Egocentricity** is the tendency on the part of the young child to see all things from his or her own point of view, to be unable to consider other points of view, and to be certain everyone knows what he or she knows.

FIGURE 2.3   Example of resemblance sorting

The diagram shows a square paired to a striped square, the striped square paired with the striped rectangle, the striped rectangle paired with the dotted rectangle, the dotted rectangle paired with the dotted circle, the dotted circle paired with a shaded circle, the shaded circle paired with a shaded triangle, a shaded triangle paired with a striped triangle, a striped triangle paired with a striped rectangle.

Egocentric children think the Sun follows them down the street. Egocentric children will often talk to or for themselves, finding it unnecessary for another person to participate in the conversation. In fact, conversations with egocentric children are often difficult for adults to follow because the child assumes the adult knows everything he or she knows.

Conservation.   **Conservation** is the understanding that when the appearance of an object changes, the quantity of the object does not also change. For example, if given an orange to eat, the child who does not conserve may see an orange in segments as being greater in quantity than an orange that is whole. Preoperational children do not conserve. Consequently the preoperational child will see little meaning in formal consideration of number; measuring liquid or solid volume—for example, pints and quarts or pounds and ounces; determining weight through use of a scale; finding length with formal measuring devices, such as rulers, or area through computation; and learning how to tell time. Children who do not conserve see four quarts as more than one gallon, 36 inches as more than one yard, two dimes and a nickel as greater in value than one quarter. Until children have developed the ability to conserve, formal consideration of related mathematical concepts is meaningless to them.

Cause and Effect.   **Cause and effect** is simply the ability to attribute to some event a certain result and to determine a cause for a particular event. If I push a toy truck, it moves. The concept of cause and effect is found in nearly all subject matter areas: science, social studies, language arts, reading, mathematics. The basic problem is that the young child, the preoperational child, has little concept of cause and effect, with the exception of a single area. When the cause and the effect are immediately related in space and time and the child is the cause, then the child understands causal relations. For example, preoperational children riding tricycles can conclude that the harder they work at turning the pedals the faster they will move. On the other hand, preoperational children who are asked to identify cause and effect from written or oral materials will find the task virtually impossible. Trying to develop cause-and-effect relationships for events that are abstract or for which they have no experience is equally impossible.

The difficulty children have with cause and effect also results in problems in three closely related ideas: making inferences, drawing conclusions, and making predictions. All three of these thought processes are based on the ability to relate ideas, objects, or phenomena in a causal format.

Reasoning.   **Reasoning** requires the use of past information in a logical manner. Preoperational children by definition are not yet able to manipulate mental structures. Instead, they rely on the use of concrete materials in their thinking. The preoperational child's thinking can be quite logical provided the experience is concrete and appropriate in terms of cognitive skills such as cause and effect, reversibility, or egocentricity. In less concrete situations, preoperational children utilize a less logical form of reasoning known as **transductive reasoning**. Transductive reasoning is present when a child draws a conclusion from something connected perceptually to the occurrence. For example, a child using transductive reasoning may decide flowers in a vase wilted because they were near a chair that was brown. Transductive reasoning is also at work when a child reasons from specific to specific without drawing a generalized conclusion. For example, after looking at a series of numbers, such as 3, 5, 7, 9, 11, the child may state that 3 is odd and 5 is odd and 7 is odd and 9 is odd, and 11 is odd, rather than saying they are *all* odd numbers.

Language Use. Children at the preoperational stage of development use language well in terms of vocabulary and sentence structure. They can use a word or symbol to represent something that is no longer present. Their facility in learning new words often leads adults to think they use language more fluently than they do. However, the preoperational child's use of language is not as effective as it appears to be. Early preoperational children, as previously mentioned, are egocentric in their world view. Consequently their language skills are also egocentric. Young preoperational children talk to themselves and frequently for themselves. Conversations prior to the age of five are generally dual monologues rather than true interactions. For the child of six or seven, soliloquies are frequent, even when they are in the company of others. However, children at the first and second grade level do indeed talk to one another and attempt to make themselves understood rather than assume understanding. In speaking with adults, the six- or seven-year-old is helped by the adult who truly wants to understand. A problem that arises here is that because the adult understands, he or she assumes the child also understands. Consequently children develop a variety of ways of pretending to comprehend when they do not. Ask a six-year-old whether he or she understands and the answer will be a consistent yes. Until about seven or seven and a half, children generally will not ask for clarification if they do not understand. Another characteristic of the use of language among preoperational children is the tendency for these children to understand but to pretend they do not. Finally, genuine collaboration and true argument do not develop until the late preoperational stage. Children may begin to work together but decide they would rather work alone or simply may think that working together means working side by side. They find collaborating closely on a project difficult because of their egocentricity. Prior to the age of seven, children's arguments tend to be simple clashes of words without any attempt to justify or support a point of view; arguments of "do, too" and "do not" are most frequent then.

The lack of justification or support for a point of view is perhaps understandable when one realizes that prior to seven years of age children do not make any effort to stick to a single point of view. They adopt successive opinions about the same topic. Toward the end of the preoperational stage, however, children are better able to present a point of view and to justify it. For the first time, discussions become a possibility for children in the classroom.

Reversibility.   **Reversibility** is most easily defined as the ability to follow a process in both the forward and reverse directions. For example, a child who has not yet attained reversibility of thought will find it difficult to understand that John is his brother and, conversely, that he is John's brother. Difficulty with reversing thought processes means that the child involved in learning will need to experience both the forward and the reverse of a process rather than experiencing the forward process and being expected to reason out mentally the reverse process.

Concrete Materials.   The child who is preoperational in thought processes needs to have concrete materials if he or she is to comprehend ideas, processes, or events. For the preoperational child, **concrete objects** are the real objects rather than a pictorial or model representation of the actual object. Therefore, concrete objects do not include worksheets, workbooks, color sheets, textbooks, or other pencil-and-paper types of learning materials. Because these children need concrete materials to learn, verbal explanations and written materials are not effective in helping them develop an understanding of their world.

The need for concrete materials in learning points to three requirements for appropriate kinds of concepts and materials for the preoperational child. First, children need to have the real object. Preoperational children are so tied to their perceptions that they consider models to be the real object. Consider the following: A teacher of kindergartners brought scale models for a new playground into her classroom. In the models the sliding board was about three inches high and the rest of the playground equipment was shown proportionally. The children viewed the models and the teacher talked about how nice it would be to have a new playground. At the end of her presentation she asked if the children had questions. One child raised his hand and asked: "Who's going to play on that playground? Ants?" To these children the model was exactly what the real playground would be like.

Second, the need for concrete objects points out the need for children to be able to see rather than imagine. Children in the preoperational stage find it difficult to imagine objects they cannot see—for example, atoms and molecules. Third, their need for concrete objects explains the fact that young children have difficulty imagining events they have not experienced. It is difficult for a child living in the heart of Kansas who has never traveled beyond his hometown to imagine the ocean; similarly, it is difficult for a child in Maine to imagine herself in the tropics. If they are to comprehend new information, children first need to have experienced related ideas and events.

SOCIAL AND MORAL DEVELOPMENT

Because the integrated approach to curriculum can utilize as a basis problems showing the connection of the curriculum to the real world, it is important to understand what can be expected of the preoperational child in terms of social and moral development.

Social Development. For the early preoperational child, group activity is becoming more possible and yet is still developing. Very young children enjoy planning together for activities. However, they do not see the necessity for completing the activities they have planned. The young child finds satisfaction in planning and in beginning but does not necessarily find satisfaction in attaining adult-specified closure. When planning and beginning to work, children will work cooperatively in groups, but they also need to be able to withdraw from the group and work alone if they wish. Young preoperational children are not yet ready to work continually in groups. For preoperational children competition is not important. Games are played for the sake of playing a game and not for the sake of winning the game. In fact, preoperational children will often withdraw from a situation that becomes too competitive and simply choose not to play.

As children move from the early phase of preoperations into later preoperations, peer groups begin to gain importance. The peer group provides young children with a way of sharing interests, developing new skills by imitating others in the peer group, demonstrating increasing autonomy, and practicing language skills. Early peer groups are generally based on mutual interests and change as the interests of the children change. By second grade, however, peer groups are more stable and are more likely to be based on gender rather than on interests.

In terms of responsibility, preoperational children are becoming more responsible. They want to help with home and classroom chores. However, responsibility is not a consistent behavior at this point, and children sometimes forget their chores or begin without completing the task assigned. Preoperational children often benefit more from being given a choice of tasks to be completed at a particular time or on a particular day than from being required to complete the same task every day. It should always be remembered that preoperational children are just developing the ability to be responsible and should not be expected to act in a fully responsible manner all of the time.

Moral Development. In terms of moral development, children at the preoperational stage tend to be in Kohlberg's **prenormative stage**. Their moral reasoning is based on obedience to authority out of fear rather than on obedience based in mutual respect. For children at the preoperational stage, rules are fixed and absolute. Contradictory to this perceived nature of rules, preoperational children may not see any necessity for adhering to rules in playing games. In fact, even though children are aware of the rules of a game, they may not all understand them in the same way. Consequently preoperational children may spend more time arguing over the rules for a game than actually playing the game.

Preoperational children also have difficulty understanding the differences between intentional acts and accidents, between honest mistakes and lies. When an accident occurs, young children often retaliate against the child who caused the accident. A child who accidentally splashes water on another child's finger painting may get pushed or hit in return. Although adults may see this as an overreaction, the preoperational child considers the accident to be intentional and punishment therefore necessary.

Lying is a difficult behavior for the parent or teacher of a young child to deal with. However, the preoperational child's concept of a lie is different from that of an adult. For the preoperational child lies are any statements that are naughty or untrue. They include even honest errors, as when a child says he thinks his brother is 16 when the brother is only 15.

For preoperational children, lying, like other wrong acts, is something that should be punished. But just as the child's concept of lying is different from that of the adult, so is the child's concept of punishment. For the preoperational child punishment is considered expiatory; this means that the child believes the punishment should be strong but not necessarily related to the "crime" committed. To the preoperational child it is perfectly understandable that spilling paint be punished by standing in a corner. For children at the preoperational stage of development, punishment is a way of stopping rule breaking, and the stronger the punishment, the more likely it is that the rule will not be broken again.

INTERMEDIATE GRADE CHILDREN

My fifth grade kids are so interested in rain forests and endangered species. I never knew kids that age were interested in anything outside themselves.

These fourth graders just don't pay attention. I've taught them about volume for three days and they still can't figure out what to do to solve a problem in math that has to do with volume.

I give up. My science book says these sixth graders should write hypotheses, develop experiments, and draw conclusions. These kids couldn't write a hypothesis if you offered them a million bucks, and as for controlling variables in an experiment . . . you've got to be kidding!

One of the things my third grade textbook for social studies wants me to do is teach children the difference between a right and a privilege. It also wants these kids to compare the government of Mexico to the government of the United States. I have yet to have a class that can understand either of those topics. Why do they put them in the third grade books?

These teachers are asking questions about the curriculum of their schools and why the children they teach have such difficulty in understanding topics that are included in their textbooks. In many cases, they work hard at trying to help children understand but find themselves faced with blank stares and poor test grades. They are discovering that some of the topics commonly taught are not as easy for children as they might be for adults. As with primary grade children, the cognitive characteristics of intermediate grade children can help to determine the topics they will understand. In general, children in the third through sixth grades vary greatly in their cognitive-developmental level. Some children at the third grade level may not yet conserve number and so will still be considered preoperational in their thought patterns; many will be in the **concrete operational stage** of development, and, at the sixth grade level, some will be making or will have made the transition to formal operational thought.

COGNITIVE DEVELOPMENT

Conservation.   As previously stated, conservation is the understanding that when the appearance of an object changes, the quantity of the object does not also change. There are a variety of types of conservation that affect the child's ability to comprehend concepts and topics included in the curriculum. The development of the ability to conserve in a variety of situations is indicative of the child's development of operations, that is, of thought processes that can be reversed and can be integrated with other actions.

Conservation of Number.   Conservation of number is the underlying concept for an understanding of mathematical computation. The attainment of conservation of number also signals the transition from preoperational thought to concrete operational thought. In general, conservation of number is attained between six and a half and seven years of age, but one cannot assume that all children of seven will be conservers of number.

Conservation of number simply means that a child who is presented with two identical stacks of coins and then sees one of the stacks stretched out in a row will know that there is no difference in quantity simply because the appearance has changed. In essence, the child who conserves number has developed a sense of the constancy of quantity. Conservation is attained for a variety of different concepts, including substance, length, area, weight, time, and volume. These various types of conservation occur during the concrete operational period of development, with conservation of number generally attained first and conservation of volume last. Indeed, conservation of volume indicates the transition from concrete operational thought to formal operational thought. The attainment of the various types of conservation gives an indication of when the child is ready to comprehend ideas from mathematics such as length, weight, volume, area, time, and number.

Egocentricity.   The concrete operational child is generally no longer egocentric. He or she is increasingly able to understand that a variety of points of view exist, to consider those points of view without automatically changing his or her mind, and to defend his or her own point of view. At the onset of formal operational thought, however, the child returns to an egocentric point of view, although not with the same severity as at the preoperational stage of development. The formal operator is able to consider differing points of view but may choose not to do so.

Classification.   Classification develops rapidly as the child enters the concrete operational stage of development. By about eight years of age, the groupings made by a child are stable so that the same characteristic can be applied to all objects and so that all objects are classified. From the age of 8 until about 11 or 12 years of age, the child grows in ability to classify by increasing the number of characteristics used in classification. A child of eight may choose to classify a group of blocks by color alone. A child of nine may use both size and color in constructing groups, while a child of ten may use size, color, and thickness. This growing ability to use a variety of traits in classification possibly results from the disappearance of centration in concrete operational children.

At about 11 or 12 years of age, children develop the ability to use a highly complex form of classification known as *hierarchical classification.* This is the form of classification used in the biological classification system, in which a single category is used inclusively and then each successive category is a subset of the prior category. The use of hierarchical classification requires the development of the ability to classify on the basis of a variety of traits as well as the use of class inclusion. The use of logical thought processes combined with the ability to consider many characteristics at the same time are required for the development of hierarchical classification.

Cause and Effect.   Cause and effect still presents problems for the intermediate grade child who is at the concrete operational stage. Although the understanding of cause and effect has developed so that children realize there must be a reason for an event, they still find it difficult to understand the reason, that is the cause, if it is not readily apparent. The most appropriate kinds of cause-and-effect activities for intermediate concrete operational children are those in which the child is able to cause the effect or is able to infer the cause of an event from his or her actions or those of objects. For example, children at the intermediate grades are able to carry out an activity in which they give plants varying strengths of fertilizer and then draw conclusions as to the effect of fertilizers on plant growth. Although the cause and the effect are separate in time, they are able to make the inference that, since the factor changed was fertilizer strength, it is the cause of growth differences. Concrete operational children, however, are still not able to comprehend that unequal heating of the Earth's surface causes differences in air masses and so differences in weather conditions. In this example, not only are the children unable to act on objects to cause changes, but they must imagine events they have never experienced and which are not visible except as images constructed from collection of data on temperature and air pressure.

The intermediate grade child who has entered into formal operations, however, has a mature grasp of cause and effect and is no longer tied to the production of the cause to understand causal relations.

REASONING

The reasoning ability of the concrete operational child is reflective of his or her growing ability to use cause and effect, a reduction in egocentricity, and growth in use of language. Reasoning is more logical than at the preoperational stage and generally does not involve the use of transductive reasoning. However, the concrete operational child, as the name implies, is still able to reason most effectively when concrete materials are available for use. In addition, reasoning from a premise is not yet available to the concrete operational child, and the interpretation of proverbs is difficult. For example, concrete operational children find it difficult to answer questions like: What would South America be like today if the Spanish had not conquered the native populations? They also have difficulty in interpreting proverbs like: Don't cry over spilt milk.

Formal operational children are able to reason logically both on the basis of direct experience and on the basis of a premise. The formal operational thinker is able to envision a variety of possible interpretations of a set of data and then to determine through experiments or logical thought which of those interpretations hold true. Rather than being tied to concrete materials, the formal operational child can operate on ideas, therefore statements form the basis for formal thought processes. Rather than being tied to concrete-based images of the world, the formal operator can engage in thoughts and reasoning over a wide range of time; past, present, and future become a part of thought. And because students are able to think abstractly, they can now consider abstractions. Reasoning from a premise and interpreting proverbs are no longer difficult for the formal operational child. Such abstract concepts as death, love, hope, and democracy become understandable.

LANGUAGE USE

The intermediate grade child uses language for communication rather than simply for the sake of language. Conversations with peers and with adults are meaningful and frequent. Group discussions are possible and children enjoy being able to present their points of view along with the reasons they hold those particular views. This ability does, however, develop through the grades, with sixth grade children far more able to communicate views and reasoning than fourth grade children. By the sixth grade level, children are engaging in debate. Because egocentricity is at a low point, children in the intermediate grades are interested in other points of view and in other ways of doing things. They are, therefore, interested in other parts of the country and other parts of the world.

SOCIAL AND MORAL DEVELOPMENT

Children in the concrete operational stage of development differ from preoperational children in their social and moral characteristics just as they do in their cognitive characteristics.

Fairness.   Concrete operational children are generally in Kohlberg's second stage in moral reasoning: What is right is determined by what is fair. If a child misbehaves on the school bus it is fair that he or she not be allowed to ride the bus, but it is not fair for everyone on the bus to be punished because of that one child. The concept of fairness is also applied to adults but with the realization that adults do have different privileges. It is fair for an adult to go to bed later than a child but not for a child of the same age to go to bed at a later time. This concept of fairness also has a role to play in deciding how to react when certain events occur. If someone hits you, it is only fair to retaliate by hitting back. If someone ruins your homework paper, it is only fair to ruin his or her homework paper.

Although fairness is a major factor in determining right and wrong, another factor also comes into play. If an action causes harm, it is considered wrong. And harm occurs only when something hurts. Therefore, it is wrong to hit someone but it may not be wrong to cheat on a test; the former causes pain, the latter does not.

Rules.   Concrete operational children begin to follow rules voluntarily rather than because of fear of punishment. This change in behavior results from a developing understanding that rules can be developed and changed by mutual consent, by individuals living under those rules. This further results in greater understanding of laws and the development of laws within society.

Lying.   Just as the child's view of rules changes, so does the child's view of lying. At the start of the concrete stage, children tend to view lies as anything that is not true. As the concrete stage progresses children separate the message from the intent. Lies become intentional untruths told with intent to deceive, rather than simple errors of fact.

Punishment.   Rather than view punishment as expiatory, children in the concrete stage see punishment as reciprocal. Concrete operational children, generally those children found in the third through sixth grades, develop an understanding that punishment should be related to the crime and that sometimes simply telling a person not to repeat the action is enough to stop the inappropriate behavior.

Social Development.   During the concrete operational period a major shift occurs in how the child views himself or herself within society: Concern for the interests of individuals shifts to concern for one's group and society. This shift in moral reasoning reflects the child's growing awareness that he or she can empathize with others and others can empathize with him or her. Children at the concrete operational level develop the idea that moral behavior involves doing what is accepted, desired, or approved by one's social group, and so the child comes to conform to the order of the society in which he or she lives. Rewards for appropriate behavior, especially from one's peers, become important, and the child begins to place emphasis on what a good person would do in a particular situation.

As the concrete operational child develops, the peer group takes on great importance. While early concrete children are influenced by their peers, late concrete children are pressured by their peers and place more importance on the opinions of the peer group than on adult opinion. Peer group acclaim can help the child develop self-esteem, while peer group rejection can cause self-doubt. Although the peer groups of younger children tend to be highly fluid, by the end of the concrete operational stage the peer group is generally stable and cohesive, with a formalized structure.

In their traditional form, Piagetian stages of development are invariant and sequential. It was long thought that the preoperational child (generally preschool to grade three) would be preoperational in all thought processes, the concrete operational child (generally grades three through six) concrete in all thought processes, and the formal operator (late sixth grade and above) formal in all processes. The evidence, however, now shows that this is not a valid picture of thought processes in children. Children who are concrete operational in some situations may utilize preoperational thought in others, particularly in situations new to them. Formal operational individuals frequently use concrete operational thought processes when learning new ideas, new concepts. In fact, every adult is familiar with this tendency to revisit former stages of cognitive development. In learning to ski, adults do not generally sit down with a book on skiing, read about how to ski, then take to the advanced slope. Although capable of gaining a great deal of information from written materials, adults will usually begin in a far more concrete mode: skis, rope tow, beginners' slope. Gradually, the adult gains in skill through use of the real objects (skis, boots, poles, snow) and eventually reaches the advanced slope. At that point, reading about new techniques will be effective.

The stages in cognitive development, therefore, give clues as to what a child can or cannot comprehend, and why a child has difficulty with a particular concept. The cognitive abilities of children at various levels can also inform the curriculum planner as to appropriate topics, strategies, and organizational principles. The stages should be used to point out the basic differences between child and adult thought, to aid in the selection of appropriate content, and to allow for the development of teaching strategies appropriate to the level of the child rather than to categorize children of a particular age into a particular mode of thought.

THE IMPACT OF COGNITIVE DEVELOPMENT ON THE CURRICULUM

Traditionally, the curriculum for the elementary school has been divided along subject matter lines. Reading, language arts, science, mathematics, social studies, art, music, and physical education each are allotted a certain number of minutes per day or per week. Textbooks by their very nature further reduce the curriculum into subject matter areas: spelling book, science book, mathematics book. The traditional curriculum is based on a view that the various subject matter areas can be separated along distinct lines and that the content within that subject matter can be organized from simple to complex.

This view of the curriculum functions well in terms of organization. Specialists in subject matter can determine which concepts build on other concepts and which skills are necessary before other skills can be developed, but only from the view of an adult specialist. The consequence is that children may be required to learn information for which they are not yet cognitively ready.

In order to develop a curriculum that is cognitively appropriate for children, both the content selected and the cognitive ability of the children taught must be taken into account. At the elementary education level, the cognitive nature of the child is of greater importance in determining subject matter than is the nature of the subject matter.

For example, within the science curriculum a conceptual theme of great importance deals with matter and the molecular nature of matter. One generally begins by considering solids, liquids, and gases, then moves on to elements, compounds, solutions, and mixtures, and finally into molecules, atoms, and the particles comprising the atom: protons, neutrons, and electrons. For the young child, solids and liquids are appropriate topics but gases, because of their invisibility, generally are not understood by young children. Cognitively it would be more appropriate to move from a consideration of solids and liquids to mixtures and solutions; solids and liquids can be easily combined and separated, combined and recombined by the young child. For middle grade children, the study of changes in matter, both physical and chemical (in a descriptive manner, without causality or use of formal chemical equations), along with a beginning consideration of gases would be more appropriate. In the upper grades, students are able to comprehend elements and compounds and their properties as well as the kinds of elements that combine to form compounds. The atomic structure of atoms and molecules, the nature of chemical bonds, and the internal structure of the atom are incomprehensible to children who think in a concrete mode and who need real objects for understanding; this aspect of matter is best left for the high school.

The cognitive level of children is extremely important in the selection of topics for the integrated curriculum. This importance does not stop at the average child in the classroom but extends to the child who is at risk for academic failure or who is gifted.

PIAGET AND VYGOTSKY

During the past few decades the work of Jean Piaget has been highly influential in elementary education. However, Piaget is not the only theorist to consider the cognitive development of children. Of growing influence is the work of Lev Semenovich Vygotsky, whose work differs somewhat from that of Piaget and therefore adds another dimension to the understanding of children. In essence, Vygotsky's work considers three areas. The first emphasizes the influence of social, cultural, and historical aspects on cognitive development. The second area emphasizes the relationship between thought and language and presents the greatest area of difference between Vygotsky and Piaget. The third area considers how learning and instruction contribute to the advancement of cognitive development.

CULTURAL AND HISTORICAL CONTEXT

According to Vygotsky, the world of a child is a world of social institutions, cultural mores, and historical influences. The child's cognitive development is a result of an increasing understanding and an increasing mastery of that world. This cognitive development is enhanced through interactions with adults who help the child to master the language and customs and even the games and toys of their culture. From this point of view, language and culture play a highly important role in the child's development.

THOUGHT AND LANGUAGE

The role of language in cognitive development is the area of greatest difference between Piaget and Vygotsky. To Piaget the **egocentric speech** of young preoperational children is an expression of their egocentric thought; young children talk to themselves and for themselves because they view the world egocentrically. Egocentric speech, therefore, disappears as the child outgrows his or her egocentrism. To Vygotsky, egocentric speech plays a crucial role in development by providing coordination between thought and action.

Investigating egocentric speech in young children, Vygotsky discovered that egocentric speech increased when children encountered problems and that the increase was directly related to the difficulty of the problem. From this he concluded that speech is not simply an accompaniment to thinking, but an overt indication of the thought processes being used. The child uses egocentric speech to direct attention to aspects of the problem, to plan for problem solution, to form concepts, and even to gain self-control. In essence, egocentric speech helps to regulate the developing child's behavior.

According to Vygotsky, egocentric speech, rather than disappearing with the disappearance of egocentricity, gradually becomes the instrument of thought as it is typically used by adults in planning and solving a problem. In essence, the overt egocentric speech of the young child becomes the silent, mental speech of the adult solving a problem. This transition from audible egocentric speech to silent, internally directed speech is a fundamental process in cognitive development.

LEARNING AND INSTRUCTION

While the application of Piagetian developmental theory to the classroom has been left to the educator, application of the work of Vygotsky has been elucidated by Vygotsky.

According to Vygotsky, at any point in the child's development there are certain problems the child is on the verge of solving. If left alone to solve the problem, the child will probably be unable to do so, but with the assistance of an adult or an older child, he or she can solve the problem. This "area"—where a child can solve a problem with help but not alone—is called the **zone of proximal development**. Vygotsky defines the zone of proximal development as "the distance between the actual developmental level as determined by independent problem solving and the level of potential development as determined through problem solving under adult guidance and under the direction of more capable peers" (1978, p. 86).

This concept of a zone of proximal development can be applied in the classroom and in curriculum development in order to assist the child in developing new concepts and skills. In order to apply this concept, children are placed into a learning situation where they must reach to understand. It is not enough, however, simply to arrange a learning environment in which children can learn on their own. Instead, students should be guided by explanations, demonstrations, and work with other children. Indeed, the most effective teachers may be other children who have just learned how to accomplish a particular task. In any learning situation, children should be encouraged to use language to organize their thinking, to talk about what they are trying to accomplish, and to communicate to themselves and others their successful and unsuccessful strategies in learning.

Vygotsky's concept of teaching as presenting children with tasks somewhat beyond their current abilities and then providing assistance, particularly from other students, supports the use of an integrated approach to curriculum. In particular, support is given to the use of group projects because of the opportunity for children to interact with and teach one another. Support is also given to children's contributing suggestions for areas of study to a particular theme or problem. Often children will ask questions or suggest areas of study that are just beyond their current levels of ability or knowledge; this places them into the zone of proximal development.

The work of Vygotsky adds another dimension to the concept of cognitive development in children. His attention to the role of language, culture, and interaction with others provides support for the school as an important institution for cognitive development.

SPECIAL NEEDS CHILDREN IN THE REGULAR CLASSROOM

Between 1975 and 1990, three federal laws were passed to assure that children with handicapping conditions receive a free and appropriate public education. As a consequence of these laws, individuals with disabilities are assured of the availability of appropriate public education in the least restrictive environment and at no cost to parents.

Two concepts become important in considering the disabled child in the regular classroom. The first is the concept of **mainstreaming**. A child with a disability is mainstreamed if he or she spends any part of the day in the regular classroom setting. This includes a physically challenged student who attends all academic classes with his or her peers and has a special physical education class, and a learning disabled child who spends the majority of his or her time with peers but also receives additional assistance from a resource teacher. The second concept is that of **inclusion**. Inclusion, according to a policy adopted by the Council for Exceptional Children at the 1993 convention, means that children with disabilities are to be served within regular classroom settings whenever possible. Specially trained individuals are available to assist the regular classroom teacher in providing for the individual needs of included children. Inclusion is in essence a more comprehensive form of mainstreaming.

Children who were formerly excluded from the regular classroom were generally known as *special students,* a term that includes any child who may require special attention or special programs in order to succeed in school. The major criterion for classification as a special student is that the child's condition or background place him or her in a position where academic success is in jeopardy. The definition, therefore, includes not only children with disabilities but also children with exceptional abilities: the gifted and talented.

CHILDREN WITH DISABILITIES

Disabled children are those who have special learning needs because of mental, physical, language, or emotional disabilities. In the following sections, the needs of students with learning disabilities, mild retardation, communication disorders, sensory disorders, and physical or health handicaps will be briefly considered.

Because they are often of average or higher ability, working with children with learning disabilities can be confusing to the teacher and the curriculum planner. These children learn some subject matter areas easily but have great difficulty with others. Problems in learning occur, not because of some deficiency, but because of difficulty processing information. Learning disabled children may have difficulty with attention or with perception, memory, or expressive language. They may use poor strategies for learning. Because their ability is generally average or above, learning disabled students may fall short of teacher or parental expectations or may experience high levels of success in one area while simultaneously failing in another. The achievement of the learning disabled student is often erratic, with high levels of success one day and failure the next, high retention at one time and recall of nothing the next.

Reading, language, and mathematics are most frequently areas of difficulty for the learning disabled student. At the preschool and kindergarten levels, learning disabled children often have poor listening or speaking skills. In the primary grades, these difficulties result in difficulty in learning to read or spell. Mathematics and handwriting are also areas where young learning disabled students experience great difficulties. In the upper elementary grades, academic difficulties may be coupled with inability to work independently because of poor organization skills.

However, academic difficulty is not the only problem area for learning disabled children. Many learning disabled children show high levels of activity in the classroom and may have difficulty sitting still, listening, or paying attention during the school day. Learning disabled children may also be easily distracted by those around them and so have difficulty focusing their attention on specific lessons and activities.

Two recent additions to the terminology of learning disabilities are attention deficit disorder (**ADD**) and attention deficit hyperactivity disorder (**ADHD**), a learning disability affecting about 5 percent of children in the United States. ADD and ADHD children are characterized by inattention, distractibility, impulsivity, and hyperactivity. Children who show these characteristics should not automatically be labeled ADD or ADHD; in some cases, these traits are indicative of environmental factors or of children resisting a particularly inappropriate learning experience. Young children who are expected to sit still and quiet for long periods of time while working on pencil and paper tasks will often show the characteristics of inattention, distractibility, and hyperactivity, while children from backgrounds where they are not expected to sit quietly may not have gained the skills needed to conform to school rules.

Academically Challenged Children.   Children who are mildly retarded may be considered as **academically challenged** because they have learning problems that affect academic learning in a variety of subject areas. These children generally enter school at an academic and developmental level lower than that of their chronological peers. This means that academically challenged children will acquire basic educational skills at a later age than average children and that they will attain those skills more slowly. However, by the conclusion of their academic careers, most academically challenged children will have attained upper elementary level skills in reading and mathematics.

Certain areas are particularly challenging for the academically challenged child: focusing attention, remembering information, and transferring skills and concepts learned in one situation to another. Tasks that involve abstract reasoning are of particular difficulty for the academically challenged child because these children do not reach the level of formal operational thought. Problem solving and creative tasks are also highly challenging.

Sensory Disabled Children.   Glasses to correct vision and aids to enhance hearing are not unusual in the elementary school. It is only when treatment of visual or hearing problems does not correct the problem that children are considered **sensory disabled**. Those who still experience visual or hearing problems after correction make up a very small group of elementary school children.

Among sensory disabled children with visual difficulties those who receive so little information through their sense of sight that they must use other senses in their learning are considered *blind*, while those who can use residual vision to learn are considered *visually impaired.* Children with visual problems may need assistance in learning to move about the classroom and school and, depending on the degree of the disability, may need to be taught to read and write through Braille. Often these children need encouragement to interact with others in the classroom.

The two terms generally used to describe individuals with hearing impairments are *deaf* and *hard of hearing.* Hard of hearing individuals can generally understand speech, usually with the assistance of a hearing aid. But deaf children receive so little information through their sense of hearing that they are unable to comprehend speech. Children with hearing losses may be academically delayed in subjects related to language, such as reading, spelling, and written expression.

Physically Disabled Children.   Although less than 1 percent of students in the school age population are **physically disabled**, it is an exceptionally diverse group. It includes children with functional limitations in areas such as body control, hand use, or mobility; children with medical conditions that affect strength and stamina; and children with missing limbs, spinal cord injuries causing paralysis, and muscular dystrophy. In addition, health disorders such as diabetes, heart conditions, asthma, hemophilia, cancer, and **AIDS** may also cause children to be physically disabled.

In the regular classroom, students with physical or health disorders may encounter few if any academic problems. When academic problems do occur, they are generally due to missing school because of health problems rather than due to slower learning ability. If the classroom and the school can accommodate the child's physical needs, there should be little if any difficulty including the physically disabled child in the classroom.

CURRICULUM AND THE DISABLED CHILD

As children with varying disabilities are included in the classroom, the need for an integrated approach to curriculum becomes clearer. Children with varying disabilities will need to have activities and projects adapted to their needs. This type of adaptation is easily accomplished when the curriculum is developed through interaction between the teacher and the children. The variety of activities and projects that are inherent in the integrated curriculum allows students and teacher to select those most appropriate to the child. Since social interaction is often an area of difficulty for the mainstreamed or included child, the opportunities afforded for social interaction by group projects and planning sessions within the integrated curriculum are particularly appropriate to integrating the disabled child into the regular classroom. Finally, because evaluation is designed to measure the child against himself or herself, the integrated curriculum is particularly appropriate for the disabled child whose academic progress may be slower than that of the average child. A more realistic picture of the child's progress can be gained through authentic assessments rather than through assessment according to standards developed for the average child.

GIFTED CHILDREN IN THE REGULAR CLASSROOM

THE EIGHT INTELLIGENCES AND GIFTEDNESS

The usual image of a gifted student is that of a child who reads at 2, takes algebra in second grade, and graduates from Harvard Medical School at 14. This is, of course, an extreme example, but giftedness and exceptional academic ability are often seen as synonymous. In 1985, however, the book *Frames of Mind: The Theory of Multiple Intelligences* by Howard Gardner added a breadth to the concept of giftedness it did not have previously. Rather than consider academic ability to be the sole indicator of giftedness, Gardner suggested that intelligence comes in many forms. In Gardner's view, eight intelligences, that is, eight ways of being gifted, exist. These intelligences are interpersonal, intrapersonal, linguistic, spatial, logical, bodily, musical, and mathematical.

Interpersonal Intelligence. **Interpersonal intelligence** is used to understand the feelings, desires, and ideas of others. Children gifted in interpersonal intelligence are able to interact with others in a variety of situations. They also excel in developing ways to solve conflicts that are nonthreatening to others. Children with high interpersonal intelligence will volunteer to work with children who are different, will include in games those who are not often included, and will be able to understand that differences in children do not mean inferiorities. Children of high interpersonal intelligence often learn information in the context of the persons involved in the events.

Intrapersonal Intelligence. While interpersonal intelligence is concerned with others, **intrapersonal intelligence** is more concerned with the self. Individuals of high intrapersonal intelligence are highly aware of themselves and often tend to be introspective. Intrapersonal intelligence not only allows a person to learn how he or she is similar to and different from others but also to understand the effect of one's own values and beliefs on how one behaves. Children of high intrapersonal intelligence tend to be self-starters who complete long-term projects with little or no supervision. They work independently without difficulty and usually know their own strengths and weaknesses. Consequently, children of high intrapersonal intelligence approach learning on an emotional and personal basis, often employing trial-and-error approaches.

Linguistic Intelligence. **Linguistic intelligence**, as its name implies, focuses on the elements of language: writing, reading, speaking. Stories and conversation are the mainstay of this type of intelligence. Linguistic intelligence, however, goes beyond simply learning to communicate through language. It involves enjoying the very sound of language, the playfulness and humor of language, and the ways in which various peoples communicate through language. The focus is on language itself rather than on the message conveyed by the language. High linguistic intelligence means a love of words and joy in finding, using, and playing with new words.

Linguistically intelligent children generally learn through narratives and stories, particularly those rich in colorful language, as well as through reading and writing.

Spatial Intelligence. Seeing, hearing, tasting, touching, and smelling are ways in which the spatially intelligent individual interacts with the environment. He or she is interested in the physical attributes of the world and often encodes memories in the form of images or pictures.

Spatial intelligence includes movement through the world in the manner of the geographer, visualization of spatial arrangements in much the manner of the chess player, use of visual symbols such as blueprints and graphs, and use of geometric concepts. In all four of these methods, the world is organized through spatial relations. Those gifted in spatial intelligence are often involved in the visual arts or in manual arts such as carpentry.

For the person of high spatial intelligence learning is generally visual and focuses on the development of relationships in space. The use of visual art in its various forms enhances learning on the part of the spatially gifted individual.

Logical Intelligence. Using reasoning, developing systems to organize and classify information, and developing logical conclusions according to a systematic set of rules are all part of **logical intelligence**. The use of a systematic set of rules in thinking results in the use of inductive or deductive logic by the individual of high logical intelligence. Logical intelligence also involves looking for the validity and reasonableness of connections between and among ideas, identifying patterns that connect different objects or events, drawing conclusions about the patterns, and making predictions about future events.

The individual of high logical intelligence will learn most effectively when his or her logical processes are used to develop classifications, illustrate relationships among ideas, and recognize patterns.

Bodily Intelligence. Individuals with high **bodily intelligence** are not simply aware of their bodies, as most people are, but rather live primarily through their bodies. These individuals are able to form mental images about how their bodies will feel when they are in motion or preparing for motion. The individual with high bodily intelligence can rehearse the movements of an activity mentally and benefit from this mental rehearsal.

For persons of high bodily intelligence, learning is enhanced through activities that allow them physically to involve their entire bodies.

Musical Intelligence. **Musical intelligence** is the ability to think in terms of musical properties: melody, harmony, countermelody, rhythm, pitch, key, and chord. Children from cultures where music is not written down easily learn the musical forms of the culture through listening and are able to pass on the sounds and rhythms to others through demonstration. Children in cultures where music is written in symbols find those symbols easy to comprehend and translate into sound. But it is not simply the reproduction of music that demonstrates high musical intelligence; these are individuals who are able to manipulate the aspects of the music they play and so create new musical forms and compositions.

Obviously, learning for the person of high musical intelligence will be enhanced through a musical context.

Mathematical Intelligence. Although **mathematical intelligence** is defined as thinking about the physical world and its properties, it is not the same as spatial intelligence. While spatial intelligence encodes information in terms of images, mathematical intelligence encodes in terms of numbers and symbols, which can then be manipulated according to established rules and procedures.

Mathematical intelligence goes beyond the simple ability to use mathematics in daily living to using mathematics to develop a model of the world. To the mathematically intelligent individual, mathematics possesses a beauty, an aesthetics, and a humor of its own.

The person with high mathematical intelligence will be especially involved in the learning of mathematics and will relate to other subject matter areas through mathematical means.

Although each of these intelligences can be separated out and discussed, they should never be considered mutually exclusive or fixed. Most individuals excel in more than one area. Many great mathematicians are also fine musicians. Great writers may also be superlative athletes. And as the child matures the area of greatest ability may change, so that the mathematically minded child in third grade may become the artist of the ninth grade.

A consideration of the various types of intelligence is not presented here to categorize children and so provide them with a single-faceted educational program. Instead, the concept of multiple intelligences should help us understand that academic giftedness is only one aspect of giftedness. The concept of multiple intelligences can also bolster the concept of an integrated curriculum, because it points out the fact that children bring various strengths to the classroom in the form of these different intelligences. Additionally, the concept of multiple intelligences indicates that the curriculum needs to have a wide variety of activities so that children of varying abilities can select from or develop activities appropriate to their ways of learning and encoding information.

SUMMARY

One of the strengths of the integrated approach to curriculum is that it takes into account the nature of the children in the classroom, especially their level of cognitive development. In children in the primary grades, the thought processes are generally preoperational in nature. These children have not yet developed a concept of cause and effect, view the world egocentrically, think through materials in ways that seem illogical to the adult, and tend to center on a single characteristic at a time. In addition, preoperational children have not yet developed the ability to conserve or to act on ideas through reversible operations. Children in the intermediate grades are most likely to be in the concrete operational stage of development. They have learned to conserve and to act on ideas through the use of reversible operations. Although egocentricity and centration are no longer characteristics of these children's thought patterns, concrete operational children still retain some of the preoperational child's difficulty with concepts of cause and effect. Also like the preoperational child, the concrete operational child still requires concrete objects for learning to be meaningful. At the sixth grade level, some children have made or are making the transition to formal operational thought and so will demonstrate the logical thought processes available to adults.

In addition to the average child found in the classroom, there are also children who are considered "special," a term that refers to their need for special services or adaptations if they are to reach their fullest potential. Children with visual or hearing impairments and physically and academically challenged children are often in need of additional help if they are mainstreamed into the regular classroom.

Gifted children are also a part of the regular classroom. The concept of giftedness has been extended beyond the narrow definition of academic giftedness to include interpersonal, intrapersonal, bodily, spatial, mathematical, musical, logical, and linguistic intelligence.

In the case of special children in the classroom, whether disabled or gifted, the integrated curriculum provides a highly appropriate educational setting. The use of a wide variety of projects and activities allows children to pursue concepts to the extent of their abilities, to select activities that play on strengths rather than weaknesses, and to learn in a setting appropriate to their needs rather than to the adult's conception of their needs.

ACTIVITY ONE

PURPOSE

The purpose of this activity is to do a systematic observation of children in a kindergarten, first, or second grade classroom (a total observation time of 90 minutes).

PROCEDURE

1. Select one child in a kindergarten, first, or second grade classroom to be the focal point of the observation. Observe the child for at least 30 minutes on three separate occasions.
2. As you observe the child consider the following:
   a. the child's location in the classroom
   b. the interactions that take place between the focal child and other children in the classroom
   c. the reactions of the child to the lessons presented by the teacher
      (1). What differences are there in various subject activities?
      (2). What differences are there in various teaching strategies?
   d. the interactions of the child with the teacher
   e. any conversations carried on by the child, either in soliloquy or with other children
   f. other occurrences during the day
3. As you record information be certain that you are recording what happens rather than an interpretation of what happens. For example, "Johnny threw the pencil on the floor, crumpled up his paper, and stopped working on arithmetic problems" is an observation, while "Johnny became frustrated with his arithmetic, threw his pencil on the floor and crumpled his paper" is an interpretation.
4. If the child who is being observed begins to realize he or she is under observation and becomes uncomfortable or distressed, *stop immediately.*

ACTIVITY TWO

PURPOSE

The purpose of this activity is to do a systematic observation of children in a third, fourth, fifth, or sixth grade classroom (a total observation time of 90 minutes).

PROCEDURE

1. Select one child in a third, fourth, fifth, or sixth grade classroom to be the focal point of the observation. Observe the child for at least 30 minutes on three separate occasions.
2. As you observe the child consider the following:
   a. the child's location in the classroom
   b. the interactions that take place between the focal child and other children in the classroom
   c. the reactions of the child to the lessons presented by the teacher
      (1). What differences are there in various subject activities?
      (2). What differences are there in various teaching strategies?
   d. the interactions of the child with the teacher

    e. any conversations carried on by the child, either with the teacher or with other children

    f. other occurrences during the day

3. As you record information be certain that you are recording what happens rather than an interpretation of what happens. For example, "Mary and Joan worked on their project for 15 minutes, deciding how they would design the cover, who would draw the pictures, and how the booklet would be assembled" is an observation, while "Mary and Joan work together with great camaraderie and with mutual respect for each other's talents" is an interpretation of the observations.

4. If the child who is being observed begins to realize he or she is under observation and becomes uncomfortable or distressed, *stop immediately.*

◤◢ ACTIVITY THREE

PURPOSE

The purpose of this activity is to interview a classroom teacher who is currently working with a class containing mainstreamed or included children.

PROCEDURE

1. Before conducting the interview, prepare a series of questions to ask the teacher. As you prepare your questions, consider the following areas:

    a. the disabling conditions of the children mainstreamed or included in the classroom

    b. the effect of those disabling conditions on how the children learn

    c. the changes the teacher needs to make to accommodate the disabling conditions

    d. the benefits of having children mainstreamed or included in the classroom

    e. the difficulties encountered in having mainstreamed or included children in the classroom

    f. sources of information used by the teacher

2. Record the teacher's responses in writing or by using a tape recorder. Before using a tape recorder be certain to get the permission of the teacher.

3. Use follow-up questions to help clarify any of the answers given by the teacher.

4. Do not use the teacher's name or the names of any children in your written report.

ACTIVITY FOUR

PURPOSE

The purpose of this activity is to organize a teaching strategy that will allow children of different intelligences to learn effectively.

PROCEDURE

1. Choose one of the following concepts:
   a. The kind of clothing worn changes from one culture to another.
   b. New inventions change how people do things.
   c. Plants and animals become endangered when their habitats change.
   d. Different forms of language can be used for the same purpose.
   e. Art can be used for many different purposes.
   f. Mathematics is used by people in many different professions and jobs.
2. Describe a lesson teaching the concept to children.
3. Show how the lesson could be extended so that it would be appropriate for children possessing high levels of each of Gardiner's eight intelligences: interpersonal, intrapersonal, linguistic, spatial, logical, bodily, musical, mathematical.

STUDY QUESTIONS

1. Define each of the following terms: one-to-one correspondence, seriation, centration, egocentricity, conservation, reversibility, concrete material, zone of proximal development, mainstreaming, inclusion, ADD, ADHD, multiple intelligences, interpersonal intelligence, intrapersonal intelligence, linguistic intelligence, spatial intelligence, bodily intelligence, musical intelligence, mathematical intelligence, logical intelligence.
2. Compare the cognitive development of the preoperational child to the cognitive development of the concrete operational child.
3. Describe how Piaget and Vygotsky each viewed speech in children, then discuss the implications of both of these views for classroom teachers.
4. Cause and effect is a difficult concept for children to understand. Discuss the development of an understanding of cause and effect from the preoperational through the concrete operational stages of development.
5. A first grade teacher is very surprised to find that her students are having little difficulty with the integrated topic "machines in our world." Using what you know about children at the first grade level, explain why this topic would cause little difficulty for children at that level.

6. In a third grade social studies program, two of the topics considered are "wants versus needs" and "rights versus privileges." The third grade teachers complain to one another that the students simply do not understand these ideas. Using what you know about the cognitive development of children, why would these topics be so difficult?

7. How can the work of Vygotsky be used in planning teaching in the elementary school classroom?

8. Your fifth grade classroom has mainstreamed children with academic, physical, and sensory disabilities. Using the topic "plants in the environment," discuss the kinds of adaptations that might be necessary to assure the success of disabled children.

9. You have decided to develop the integrated topic "life in the future" with a class of elementary students. What activities might be included in order to work with the multiple intelligences found within your classroom?

10. Using what you know about the cognitive and social development of children in the elementary school, list one topic that would be appropriate and one topic that would not be appropriate at the preoperational stage of development, and one topic that would be appropriate and one topic that would not be appropriate at the concrete operational stage of development. Discuss why each topic is or is not appropriate.

BIBLIOGRAPHY

Affleck, J., Lowenbraun, Q. S., & Archer, A. L. (1980). *Teaching the mildly handicapped in the regular classroom* (2nd ed.). Columbus, Ohio: Merrill.

Allen, K. E. (1980). *Mainstreaming in early education.* Albany, N.Y.: Delmar.

Anderson, J. R. (1985). *Cognitive psychology and its implications.* New York: Freeman.

Andre, T., & Phye, G. D. (1986). Cognition, learning, and education. In D. D. Phye & T. Andre (Eds.), *Cognitive classroom learning* (pp. 79–93). New York: Academic Press.

Barone, T. (1989). Ways of being at risk: The case of Billy Charles Barnett. *Phi Delta Kappan, 71,* 147–151.

Baska, L. K. (1989). Characteristics and needs of the gifted. In J. Feldhusen, J. Van Tassel-Baska, & K. Seeley (Eds.), *Excellence in educating the gifted* (pp. 138–156). Denver: Love.

Bauer, A. M., & Shea, T. M. (1989). *Teaching exceptional students in your classroom.* Boston: Allyn and Bacon.

Beckman, P. J., & Burke, J. P. (1984). Early childhood special education: State of the art. *Topics in Early Childhood Special Education, 1,* 19–23.

Bivens, J. A., & Berk, L. E. (1990). A longitudinal study of elementary school children's private speech. *Merrill-Palmer Quarterly, 36,* 443–463.

Blankenship, C., & Lilly, M. S. (1981). *Mainstreaming students with learning and behavior problems.* New York: Holt, Rinehart, and Winston.

Bredekamp, S. (Ed.) (1987). *Developmentally appropriate practice in early childhood programs serving children from birth through age 8.* Washington, D.C.: National Association for the Education of Young Children.

Bryan, T. H., & Bryan, J. H. (1977). The social-emotional side of learning disabilities. *Behavioral Disorders, 2,* 141-145.

Buhker, C. (1983). The social behavior of children. In C. A. Murchison (Ed.), *A handbook of child psychology* (pp. 238-257). New York: Russell and Russell.

Campione, J. C., Brown, A. L., Ferara, R. A., & Bryant, N. R. (1984). The zone of proximal development: Implications for individual differences and learning. In B. Rogoff & J. V. Wertsch (Eds.), *Children's learning in the "zone of proximal development"* (pp. 52-75). San Francisco: Jossey-Bass.

Cartwright, G. P., Cartwright, C. A., & Ward, M. E. (1989). *Educating special learners* (3rd ed.). Belmont, Calif.: Wadsworth.

Cartwright, S. (1988). Play can be the building blocks of learning. *Young Children, 43* (5), 44-46.

Coie, J. D., Dodge, K. A., & Coppotelli, H. (1982). Dimensions and types of social status: A cross age perspective. *Developmental Psychology, 18,* 557-570.

Cowen, E. L., Pederson, A., Babigian, H., Izzo, L. D., & Trost, M. A. (1973). Long-term follow-up of early detected vulnerable children. *Journal of Consulting and Clinical Psychology, 41,* 438-446.

Cuban, L. (1985). The "at-risk" label and the problem of urban school reform. *Phi Delta Kappan, 70,* 780-784, 799-801.

Damon, W. (1984). Peer education: The untapped potential. *Journal of Applied Developmental Psychology, 5,* 331-343.

Davis, G., & Rimm, S. (1990). *Education of the gifted and talented* (2nd ed.). Englewood Cliffs, N.J.: Prentice-Hall.

deGrandpre, B. B., & Messier, J. M. (1979). Helping mainstreamed students stay in the mainstream. *The Directive Teacher, 2* (2), 12.

DeVries, R., & Kohlberg, L. (1987). *Constructivist early education.* Washington, D.C.: National Association for the Education of Young Children.

Dodge, K. A. (1983). Behavioral antecedents of peer social status. *Child Development, 54,* 1386-1399.

Dodge, K.A., Petit, G., McClaskey, J., & Brown, M. (1986). Social competence in children. *Monographs of the Society for Research in Child Development, 51,* 2, serial number 213.

Eaton, J. F., Anderson, C. W., & Smith, E. L. (1983). When students don't know they don't know. *Science and Children, 20,* 6-9.

Ennis, R. H. (1973). On causality. *Educational Researcher, 2,* 4-11.

Ennis, R. H. (1982). Abandon causality? *Educational Researcher, 11,* 25-27.

Fauvre, M. (1988). Including young children with "new" chronic illnesses in an early childhood education setting. *Young Children, 43,* 71-77.

Feldhusen, J. F. (1989). Thinking skills for the gifted. In J. F. Feldhusen, J. Van Tassel-Baskra, & K. Seeley (Eds.), *Excellence in educating the gifted* (pp. 72-96). Denver: Love.

Forster, P., & Doyle, B. A. (1989). Teaching listening skills to students with attention deficit disorders. *Teaching Exceptional Children, 21* (2), 20-22.

Gallagher, J. J. (1988). National agenda for educating gifted students: Statement of priorities. *Exceptional Children, 55,* 107-114.

Gardner, H. (1985). *Frames of mind: The theory of multiple intelligences.* New York: Basic Books.

Gardner, H. (1987). Developing the spectrum of human intelligences: Teaching in the eighties, a need to change. *Harvard Educational Review, 57,* 2, pp. 187-193.

Gardner, H., & Walters, J. M. (1985). The development and education of intelligences. In F. R. Wink (Ed.), *Essays on the intellect* (pp. 1-21). Alexandria, Va.: Association for Supervision and Curriculum Development.

Genishi, C. (1987). Acquiring oral language and communicative competence. In C. Seefeldt (Ed.), *The early childhood curriculum: A review of current research* (pp. 136-151). New York: Teachers College Press, Columbia University.

Glazzard, P. (1980). Adaptations for mainstreaming. *Teaching Exceptional Children, 13,* 26-29.

Goffin, S. G., & Tull, C. Q. (1988). Encouraging cooperative behavior among young children. *Dimensions, 16,* 15-18.

Goldston, D. B., & Richman, C. L. (1985). Imagery, encoding specificity, and prose recall in 6-year-old children. *Journal of Experimental Child Psychology, 40,* 395-405.

Hanline, M. F. (1985). Integrating disabled children. *Young Children, 40,* 45-48.

Hartup, W. W., & Moore, S. G. (1990). Early peer relations: Developmental significance and prognostic implications. *Early Childhood Research Quarterly, 5,* 1-17.

Hersh, R. H., Paolitto, D. P., & Reimer, J. (1979). *Promoting moral growth: From Piaget to Kohlberg.* New York: Longman.

Holtzman, M. (1983). *The language of children.* Englewood Cliffs, N.J.: Prentice-Hall.

Howley, A., Howley, C. B., & Pendarvis, E. D. (1986). *Teaching gifted children: Principles and strategies.* Boston: Little, Brown.

Howes, C. (1988). Peer interaction of children. *Monographs of the Society for Research in Child Development, 53,* 1, serial number 217.

Inhelder, B., & Piaget, J. (1964). *The early growth of logic in the child.* London: Routledge and Kegan Paul.

Ireland, J. C., Wray, D., & Flexer, C. (1988). Hearing for success in the classroom. *Teaching Exceptional Children, 20* (2), 15-17.

Johnson, D. W., & Johnson, R. T. (1980). Integrating handicapped students into the mainstream. *Exceptional Children, 47,* 90-98.

Jones, C. J. (1992). *Social and emotional development of exceptional students: Handicapped and gifted.* Springfield, Ill.: Charles C. Thomas.

Kitano, M. K. (1989). The K-3 teacher's role in recognizing and supporting young gifted children. *Young Children, 44* (3), 57-63.

Kitano, M. K., & Kirby, D. E. (1986). *Gifted education: A comprehensive view.* Boston: Little, Brown.

Klein, E. (1989). Gifted and talented. In G. P. Cartwright, C. A. Cartwright, & M. E. Ward (Eds.), *Educating special learners* (3rd ed.) (pp. 36-49). Belmont, Calif.: Wadsworth.

Kohlberg, L., Yeager, J., & Hjertholm, E. (1969). Private speech: Four studies and a review of theories. *Child Development, 39,* 691-736.

Kostelnik, M. J., Stein, L. C., Whiren, A. P., & Soderman, A. K. (1988). *Guiding children's social development.* Cincinnati: South-Western.

Kulik, J. A., & Kulik, C. C. (1984). Effects of accelerated instruction on students. *Review of Educational Research, 54,* 409-425.

Ladd, G. W. (1988). Friendship patterns and peer status during early and middle childhood. *Journal of Developmental and Behavioral Pediatrics, 9,* 229-238.

Ladd, G. W. (1990). Having friends, keeping friends, making friends, and being liked by peers in the classroom: Predictors of children's early school adjustment? *Child Development, 61,* 1081-1100.

Larkin, J. H. (1993) Learning through growth of skill in mental modeling. In *Proceedings of the third annual conference.* Berkeley, Calif.: Cognitive Science Society.

Laurendeau, M., & Pinard, A. (1962). *Causal thinking in the child.* New York: International Universities Press.

Lazear, D. (1991). *Seven ways of knowing: Teaching for multiple intelligences.* Palatine, Ill.: Skylight Publishing.

Lerner, J. W. (1989). *Learning disabilities* (5th ed.). Boston: Houghton Mifflin.

Lewis, R. B., & Doorlag, D. H. (1991). *Teaching special students in the mainstream.* New York: Merrill.

Linn, M. C. (1973). The effect of direct experiences with objects on middle class, culturally diverse, and visually impaired young children. *Journal of Research in Science Teaching, 20,* 183–190.

Miller, L. (1993). *What we call smart: A new narrative for intelligence and learning.* San Diego: Singular Publishing Group.

Miller, P. H. (1983). *Theories of developmental psychology.* New York: W. H. Freeman.

Murray, F. B. (1972). Acquisition of conservation through social interaction. *Developmental Psychology, 6,* 1–6.

Parke, B. N. (1989). *Gifted students in regular classrooms.* Boston: Allyn and Bacon.

Parker, J. G., & Asher, S. R. (1987). Peer relations and later personal adjustment: Are low accepted children at risk? *Psychological Bulletin, 103,* 357–389.

Parsons, A. S. (1988). Integrating special children into day care programs. *Dimensions, 16,* 15–19.

Pasche, C. L., Gorrill, L., & Strom, B. (1989). *Children with special needs in early childhood settings.* Menlo Park, Calif.: Addison Wesley.

Pelligrini, A. D. (1988). Elementary school children's rough-and-tumble play and social competence. *Developmental Psychology, 24,* 802–806.

Pendarvis, E. D. (1985). Gifted and talented children. In W. H. Berdine & A. E. Blackhurst (Eds.), *An introduction to special education* (2nd ed.) (pp. 223–241). Boston: Little, Brown.

Peterson, N. L. (1987). *Early intervention for handicapped and at-risk children.* Denver: Love.

Piaget, J. (1967). *The language and thought of the child* (3rd ed.). London: Routledge and Kegan Paul.

Piaget, J. (1972). *The child and reality.* New York: Grossman.

Piaget, J. (1972). *The child's conception of physical causality.* Totowa, N.J.: Littlefield, Adams.

Piaget, J. (1972). *Judgment and reasoning in the child.* Totowa, N.J.: Littlefield, Adams.

Piaget, J. (1973). *Psychology of intelligence.* Totowa, N.J.: Littlefield, Adams.

Piaget, J. (1975). *The child's conception of the world.* Totowa, N.J.: Littlefield, Adams.

Piaget, J., & Inhelder, B. (1958). *The growth of logical thinking from childhood to adolescence.* New York: Basic Books.

Poest, C. A., Williams, J. R., Witt, D. D., & Atwood, M. E. (1990). Challenge me to move: Large muscle development in young children. *Young Children, 45* (5), 4–10.

Putallaz, M., & Gottman, J. (1981). An interactional model for children's entry into peer groups. *Child Development, 52,* 986–994.

Reis, S. M. (1989). Reflections on policy affecting the education of gifted and talented students: Past and future perspectives. *American Psychologist, 44,* 399–408.

Renzulli, J. S. (1978). What makes giftedness? Reexamining a definition. *Phi Delta Kappan, 60,* 180–184, 261.

Rogoff, B. (1990). *Apprenticeship in thinking: Cognitive development in social context.* New York: Oxford University Press.

Slavin, R. E. (1989). Students at risk of school failure: The problem and its dimensions. In R. E. Slavin, N. L. Karweit, & N. A. Madden (Eds.), *Effective programs for students at risk* (pp. 60-66). Boston: Allyn and Bacon.

Stephens, T. M., & Wolf, J. S. (1978). *The gifted child.* In N. G. Haring (Ed.), *Behavior of exceptional children* (2nd ed.) (pp. 217-232). Columbus, Ohio: Merrill.

Sternberg, R. J. (1986). *The triarchic mind: A new theory of human intelligence.* New York: Viking.

Sternberg, R. J., & Davidson, J. E. (Eds.). (1986). *Conceptions of giftedness.* Cambridge, Mass.: Cambridge University Press.

Suter, D., & Wolf, J. (1987). Issues in the identification and programming of the gifted/learning disabled child. *Journal for the Education of the Gifted, 10,* 227-237.

Thomason, J. (1981). Education of the gifted: A challenge and a promise. *Exceptional Children, 48,* 101-103.

Trabasso, T., & van den Broek, P. (1985). Causal thinking and the representation of narrative events. *Journal of Memory and Language, 24,* 612-630.

Trawick-Smith, J. (1990). Give and take: How young children persuade their peers. *Dimensions, 19,* 22-24.

Vygotsky, L. S. (1962). *Thought and language.* Cambridge, Mass.: MIT Press.

Vygotsky, L. S. (1978). *Mind in society.* Cambridge, Mass.: Harvard University Press.

Walker, J. L. (1988). Young American Indian children. *Teaching Exceptional Children, 20* (4), 50-51.

Waters, E., & Sroufe, L. (1983). Social competence as a developmental construct. *Developmental Review, 3,* 79-97.

Webb, J., Meckstroth, E., & Tolan, S. (1982). *Guiding the gifted child.* Columbus, Ohio: Ohio Psychology Publishing.

Wertsch, J. V. (1984). The zone of proximal development: Some conceptual issues. In B. Rogoff and J. V. Wertsch (Eds.), *Children's learning in the "zone of proximal development"* (pp. 7-30). San Francisco: Jossey-Bass.

Wertsch, J. V. (1985). *Culture, communication, and cognition: Vygotskian perspectives.* Cambridge: Cambridge University Press.

Wheatley, G. (1989). Instructional methods for the gifted. In J. Feldhusen, J. Van Tassel-Baska, & K. Seeley (Eds.), *Excellence in educating the gifted* (pp. 252-265). Denver: Love.

White, B. P. (1986). It'll be a challenge! Managing emotional stress in teaching disabled children. *Young Children, 41,* 44-48.

Ziv, A., & Gadish, O. (1990). Humor and giftedness. *Journal for Education of the Gifted, 13* (4), 332-345.

CHAPTER

3

INTEGRATED CURRICULUM AND EDUCATIONAL BASICS

CHAPTER OBJECTIVES

After reading this chapter you should be able to:

1. Define the term *literacy* in relation to the integrated curriculum
2. Define the term *basic knowledge* in relation to the integrated curriculum
3. Discuss the role of foundation knowledge within the integrated curriculum
4. Discuss the role of basic knowledge within the integrated curriculum
5. Define critical and creative thinking in the context of the integrated curriculum
6. Discuss the roles of critical and creative thinking within the integrated curriculum
7. Discuss how literacy, basic knowledge, critical thinking, and creative thinking are included within the integrated curriculum

When the curriculum is fully integrated, subject matter areas are subsumed under the topic of study and so lose their identity. No longer does the teacher teach reading or science or mathematics or social studies. Instead, the classroom and the curriculum are organized around broad areas of study, themes, societal problems, or areas of personal concern. Because the subject matter areas no longer exist as distinct entities, there is often concern that children will not receive an education in the "basics," that is, in the various skills and concepts distinctive to the subject areas.

While it is true that the subject matter areas no longer exist as separate entities, it is not true that those subject areas are lost to the curriculum. Indeed, the skills and concepts of the various subject matter areas are enhanced as children learn in context rather than in isolation. Learning to add becomes learning when to use addition in solving real-life problems—rather than learning to compute isolated, numerical problems on a piece of paper with no purpose other than to complete the problems. Learning about plants becomes learning the role of plants within the ecosystem of the rain forest and the effect destruction of the rain forest will have on the Earth as a whole—rather than learning plant parts and classification for no reason other than to take a test. And language learning becomes a means for communication, oral and written—rather than a means for completing a workbook page or answering questions about a story in a basal text.

Integration of the curriculum, however, does result in certain losses within the subject matter areas. The first of these losses is the loss of meaningless learning. No longer will students be asked to learn information that is unconnected to their lives or to other learning. Studying mathematics without showing its connection to science, reading without showing its connection to writing, social studies without showing its connection to literature, music, art, or science, will no longer occur. Instead, the richness of a culture will be shown in all its complexity as the other subject areas are brought into play, or the scientific knowledge needed to solve a societal problem will be developed in depth as students bring that knowledge to the solution of a problem.

The second loss is the loss of isolated skill learning. No longer will students be subjected to memorizing lists of isolated spelling words, multiplication facts, or symbols for chemical elements. Instead, learning will be developed in context with spelling related to writing and reading, arithmetic facts learned to solve problems arising through study, and symbols for chemical elements acquired as a means for communicating simply and quickly.

The third loss is loss of boredom. No longer will students be asked to learn information for the sake of learning the information or, perhaps worse, because it will be needed in the next grade level or the next organizational level of schooling. No longer will teachers be filling time with meaningless worksheets and activities, ostensibly to practice skills but often to keep the children occupied. Instead, teachers and children will be challenged to bring together diverse areas of learning to projects, activities, and cooperative ventures that not only challenge the learner to learn and the teacher to find new and exciting ways of presenting information but also engage the learner in self-selected activities, interesting and pertinent to the child as a child.

While most of the losses are positive in their result, there is one additional loss that should be mentioned. When the switch from a subject-oriented curriculum to an integrated curriculum is made, there is sometimes a loss or drop in standardized test scores. One possible reason for this type of drop is that the curriculum no longer reflects the content information in the selected standardized test. A second reason may be that the developer of the integrated

opportunities for literacy development than does the traditional approach to curriculum. As a means for the development of literacy skills, a **whole language** approach to literacy is most compatible with the integrated approach to curriculum.

WHOLE LANGUAGE AND LITERACY

Within the integrated curriculum, the whole language approach to literacy is the most logical approach. In essence, whole language is based on six premises. First, whole language is based on the concept that learning is a social rather than an individual process. Collaboration is a means for helping students go beyond their individual limitations, to learn from one another, and to practice the communication skills that are a part of literacy itself. Second, the whole language approach is based on the concept that learning occurs in a context rather than as a hierarchy of isolated skills. A context for learning makes learning relevant, as students are able to identify personal reasons for learning particular skills. In addition, learning in context gives meaning to learning, as the skills are attained and practiced in a rich variety of situations and through a rich variety of subject matter. Third, the whole language approach is based on the concept that learning can best be achieved through direct engagement and experience. Rather than having children engage in isolated skill sheets or "lessons" predetermined by the teacher as necessary prerequisites for future lessons, children are engaged in the writing process as they seek to communicate with others, engaged in reading to find information relevant to a learning need, and engaged in speaking as they cooperate with other students to plan learning experiences or share the results of their activities and researches. Fourth, the whole language approach is based on a realization that learning is driven by the purposes and intentions of the learners. Children, like adults, learn more if they are interested in the subject matter, learn more if the information allows for personal development. The rate of learning is decreased when learning is based on teacher-developed exercises that have little meaning for children and for which they have no sense of ownership. Fifth, the whole language approach to learning involves students in approximation and revision. Rather than expect students to present fully correct examples of specific outcomes, the whole language approach helps students to develop the standard forms for writing, speaking, and spelling by providing opportunities to refine ongoing work. Finally, the whole language approach does not simply give children "right" answers, then wait for them to parrot back those answers. Instead, the whole language approach immerses children in learning so that they use information, revise that information, and finally develop a finished product.

These assumptions about whole language learning indicate that whole language is not a method for instruction but rather a philosophy of teaching that aids the teacher in developing learning materials, handling children's errors, and developing methods for presenting the conventions of language learning.

The key to a whole language approach is in the authenticity of the experiences presented rather than in the specific teaching strategies used.

STRATEGIES FOR A WHOLE LANGUAGE APPROACH TO LITERACY

Although discussing strategies may seem contrary to the concept of whole language as a philosophy rather than as a teaching strategy, there are certain strategies that are found in whole language classrooms.

Immersion.   Whole language classrooms **immerse** children in literacy by providing a classroom that is rich in literacy experiences and examples. Bulletin boards show student work. Library shelves are filled with books written by the children as well as those formally published. Walls are filled with charts, posters, song lyrics, poems, and labeled art works. Students are continuously interacting with written and oral language.

Engagement.   Students are engaged in meaningful learning experiences. They make choices as to what to do, with whom to do it, when to complete a project, and when to add to a project. In order to facilitate engagement, students are helped to see themselves as able to complete a particular activity or project, to see that project as "doable."

Interest.   The interests of the children are used to teach skills, concepts, and content. The use of student interests as the basis for teaching means that the learning will be highly motivational and that children will be making decisions and determining directions for their study. Because their interests are involved, children can be expected to develop links between past and current knowledge, which will allow them to retrieve information more easily and store it more effectively.

Enjoyment.   When learning is fun, stimulating, and active, students are more likely to be involved in their learning. Increased involvement leads to increased learning. Consequently, one is unlikely to see children seated in structured rows, all silently completing worksheets developed by the teacher. Instead, children are likely to be working in groups, sprawled on the floor, and enjoying themselves as they learn.

Reading and Writing.   In the whole language approach, children read real books and write from their own experiences and imaginations every day. Popular techniques are SSR (Sustained Silent Reading), STAR (Silent Time at Reading), and DEAR (Drop Everything and Read), in which time is set aside each day for reading and only reading. A daily time for writing, when children write on topics of interest in journals or other formats, allows children to play on their own experiences and imaginations. Some pieces of written work may be nurtured all the way through to the publishing process, while others may be for an audience of one: the child. The important factor in writing is that children edit their own work. Rather than the teacher grading papers so that errors are highlighted, teachers and children engage in conferences in which errors in conventional language use are discussed and corrected in cooperation.

Literature.   Finally, the whole language classroom uses literature. Real, unabridged works of children's literature and, when appropriate, adult literature are used in the classroom. Children rarely all read the same book but may be reading about the same topic. Teachers read to children on a frequent basis, exposing them to good oral reading strategies and to fine literature that may be beyond their current reading levels. Additionally, literature for the whole language classroom also includes class books written and illustrated by individual children or in collaborations.

In the integrated curriculum, the development of literacy comes as a natural part of the program rather than through skill hierarchies and artificial learning experiences designed to begin with the smallest possible fragments and work to the largest possible whole. The use of a whole language approach to literacy development can successfully develop literate students while integrating the teaching of reading, writing, listening, and speaking into the totality of the curriculum.

BASIC KNOWLEDGE IN THE INTEGRATED CURRICULUM

Literacy, of course, is basic to the integrated curriculum, but literacy takes place in context. That context is typically the science, mathematics, and social studies content of the curriculum. The whole language approach immerses children not only in the development of literacy skills but also in the development of the concepts of science, social studies, and mathematics.

Traditionally, these content areas have been separated from the rest of the curriculum, with science and mathematics more likely to be totally separated than social studies. Recently, however, the trend is to incorporate, that is, to integrate these subject areas into the rest of the curriculum.

INTEGRATING SCIENCE

In 1989, *Project 2061: Science for All Americans* from the American Association for the Advancement of Science (AAAS) made certain recommendations for the development of a scientifically literate populace. In particular, this report stressed:

> *Science for All Americans* is based on the belief that the scientifically literate person is one who is aware that science, mathematics, and technology are interdependent human enterprises with strengths and limitations. . . . (p. 4)

The emphasis on the interdependence of these areas in the sciences is the beginning of a call for integration of science into the curriculum rather than a separation of science from the rest of the curriculum. In addition, *Project 2061* recommended that students study fewer topics in greater depth but with a de-emphasis on specialized vocabulary and memorized procedures. Instead, students were to learn science as sets of ideas chosen to make sense at a simple level but also to provide a lasting foundation for learning more. Concepts and thinking skills were to be emphasized.

According to *Project 2061,* to select content for this more integrated approach to science as scientific literacy five criteria need to be considered:

1. *Utility.* Will the proposed content—knowledge or skills—significantly enhance the graduate's long-term employment prospects? Will it be useful in making personal decisions?
2. *Social Responsibility.* Is the proposed content likely to help citizens participate intelligently in making social and political decisions on matters involving science and technology?
3. *The Intrinsic Value of Knowledge.* Does the proposed content present aspects of science, mathematics, and technology that are so important in human history or so pervasive in our culture that a general education would be incomplete without them?
4. *Philosophical Value.* Does the proposed content contribute to the ability of people to ponder the enduring questions of human meaning such as life and death, perception and reality, the individual good versus the collective welfare, certainty and doubt?
5. *Childhood Enrichment.* Will the proposed content enhance childhood (a time of life that is important in its own right) and not be intended solely for what it may lead to in later life? (p. 21)

Each of these criteria indicates that science, mathematics, and technology are not to be viewed as ends in themselves, but rather as ways of assisting the learner in seeing science as an integral part of life and a tool for solving real problems and concerns. As such, science and technology are integrated into an understanding of society and human history, allowing for even greater integration into the total elementary school curriculum. Science in the integrated curriculum, therefore, becomes another source of information, another organizing theme that can be brought into play as children investigate the world around them.

The integration of science with other content areas requires that science be looked at in a way different from the traditional viewpoint. Rather than simply a collection of facts, laws, and vocabulary to be memorized by students in preparation for more complex courses, science is a way of viewing the world.

To look at science in this way, and as a set of beliefs and attitudes about the work of the scientist, consider these ten concepts:

1. The world is understandable; that is, events in the world occur in consistent patterns that are comprehensible through careful, systematic study. Science assumes that the universe is a vast single system in which the basic rules are everywhere the same.

2. Scientific knowledge is durable. Although scientists reject the notion of attaining absolute truth and accept some uncertainty as part of nature, most scientific knowledge changes little with time. Continuity and stability are as characteristic of science as change is, and confidence is as prevalent as tentativeness.

3. Science cannot provide complete answers to all questions. There are many matters that cannot usefully be examined in a scientific way. Beliefs, issues concerning good and evil, and the meaning of life are all areas in which science can provide no information.

4. Science demands evidence. Scientists are concerned with getting accurate data and with using that data to support their claims.

5. Science is a blend of logic and imagination. Although all sorts of imagination and thought may be used in coming up with hypotheses and theories, sooner or later scientific arguments must conform to the principles of logical reasoning.

6. Science explains and predicts. Scientists strive to make sense of observations of phenomena by inventing explanations for them that use, or are consistent with, currently accepted scientific principles. The credibility of scientific theories often comes from their ability to show relationships among phenomena that previously seemed unrelated.

7. Scientists try to identify and avoid bias. When faced with a claim that something is true, scientists respond by asking what evidence supports it. Bias attributable to the investigator, the sample, the method, or the instrument may not be completely avoidable in every instance, but scientists want to know the possible sources of bias and how bias is likely to influence evidence.

8. Science is not authoritarian. It is appropriate in science as elsewhere to turn to knowledgeable sources of information and opinion, usually people who specialize in relevant disciplines. But esteemed authorities have been wrong many times in the history of science. There are not preestablished conclusions that scientists must reach on the basis of their investigations.

9. Science is a complex social activity. Scientific work involves many individuals doing many different kinds of work and goes on to some degree in all nations of the world. As a social activity, science inevitably reflects social values and viewpoints. The direction of scientific research is affected by informal influences within the culture of science itself, such as prevailing opinion on what questions are most interesting or what methods of investigation are most likely to be fruitful. Because of the social nature of science, the dissemination of scientific information is crucial to its progress.

10. Science is organized into content disciplines. Organizationally, science can be thought of as the collection of all of the different scientific fields or content disciplines. They differ from one another in many ways, including history, phenomena studied, techniques and language used, and kinds of outcomes desired. The advantages of having disciplines is that they provide a conceptual structure for organizing research and research findings. The disadvantage is that their divisions do not necessarily match the way the world works, and they can make communication difficult.

These basic concepts about the nature of science point out that science is not merely a collection of facts about various parts of the universe. Rather, science is a way of thinking and of approaching the world; it is a way of learning and a way of reacting to what is learned. By focusing more on the nature of science one focuses on ways in which science can interact with the world. This still requires the development of content knowledge, but that content is related to problems and theories, to the search for the underlying regularities of the world inhabited by the students rather than to the accumulation of facts and especially of vocabulary. The facts, the laws, the principles, and the theories of science, if they are truly ways of viewing the world and explaining its phenomena, will be learned through application to problems. The vocabulary of science will be learned as students attempt to communicate their learning to others.

INTEGRATING MATHEMATICS

Like science, mathematics has often been viewed as a subject matter area so different from other areas that it must be separated from the remainder of the curriculum. This may have some validity if mathematics is considered computation rather than a combination of conceptualization and computation. However, this view of mathematics as computation is challenged in *Everybody Counts: A Report to the Nation on the Future of Mathematics Education* (1989), in which there is strong criticism of the emphasis on computation, that is, on the mechanics of mathematics over the conceptualization. This report recommends a shift from a mathematics program that strives for computational accuracy to one that helps students develop common sense about how to find answers and choose computational methods.

Additional emphasis on the conceptual rather than the computational nature of mathematics came from the National Council of Teachers of Mathematics (NCTM) in its 1989 document, *Curriculum and Evaluation Standards for School Mathematics*. Rather than emphasizing mathematical computation skill as evidence of mathematical literacy, NCTM states that mathematical literacy will be found through the following five goal for all students.

First, students should learn to value mathematics. NCTM suggests that students have "numerous and varied experiences related to the cultural, historical, and scientific evolution of mathematics so that they can appreciate the role of mathematics in the development of contemporary society and explore relationships among mathematics and the disciplines it serves: the physical and life sciences, the social sciences, and the humanities" (p. 5). This is a definite call for the integration of mathematics into the total curriculum, rather than isolating mathematics as solely computation skills.

Second, NCTM suggests that the curriculum for mathematics focus on helping children to become confident in using their growing mathematical abilities to "make sense of problem situations in the world around them" (p. 6). Closely related to this is the third suggestion, that students learn to become mathematical problem solvers with a focus on issues that will allow them to become productive citizens. The integrated curriculum, often based on problems within the child's world, allows for emphasis on both of these suggestions.

Fourth, the NCTM suggests that children learn to communicate mathematically. According to the NCTM: "The development of a student's power to use mathematics involves learning the signs, symbols, and terms of mathematics. This is best accomplished in problem situations in which students have an opportunity to read, write, and discuss ideas in which the use of the language of mathematics becomes natural. As students communicate their ideas, they learn to clarify, refine, and consolidate their thinking" (p. 6). Once again, there is a clear call for integration of mathematics in the curriculum as students use language skills to communicate mathematically.

Finally, students should learn to reason mathematically. Students should be involved in building arguments to support their ideas and in demonstrating good reasoning skills. The NCTM standards even go as far as to suggest that "a demonstration of good reasoning should be rewarded even more than students' ability to find correct answers" (p. 6).

In order to help students achieve these goals of mathematical literacy, the NCTM makes certain assumptions about the curriculum:

1. The mathematics curriculum should be conceptually oriented, with skills acquired after concepts are developed and in context.
2. The mathematics curriculum should actively involve children in learning mathematics. The use of concrete materials through which children can explore, test, develop, discuss, and apply ideas is vital to learning.
3. The mathematics curriculum should emphasize the development of children's mathematical thinking and reasoning so that the habits of thought they develop will be useful to them in the present as well as in the future.
4. The mathematics curriculum should emphasize the application of mathematics. Children should see mathematics as a useful subject that can be applied to a wide variety of real problems. Mathematics should help children to understand and interpret their world. Problem situations that establish the need for new ideas and motivate students should serve as the context for mathematics.

5. The mathematics curriculum should include a broad range of content. Children need to learn more than simple arithmetic computation to be mathematically literate. They should also have knowledge of measurement, geometry, statistics, probability, and algebra. They should see that mathematics is important in many occupations.

6. The mathematics curriculum should make appropriate and ongoing use of calculators and computers. Calculators and computers are a part of daily life and of most occupations. It is important that children learn how and when to use such technology.

If mathematics is not to be viewed as mere computation, then how is mathematics to be considered within the modern elementary curriculum? The NCTM suggests 13 strands that include mathematics as a thinking skill and mathematics as computation.

1. Problem solving should be the central focus of the mathematics curriculum. Students should use problem solving to investigate and understand mathematical content, to formulate problems from everyday mathematical situations, to develop and apply problem-solving strategies to a wide variety of problems, and to verify and interpret results with respect to the original problem.

2. Mathematics should be viewed as a means for communication, a language that must be meaningful if students are to communicate mathematically and apply mathematics productively. Students should be able to relate physical materials, pictures, and diagrams to mathematical ideas; reflect on and clarify their thinking about mathematical ideas and situations; relate their everyday language to mathematical language and symbols, including reading, listening, and viewing; and realize that representing, discussing, reading, writing, and listening to mathematics are a vital part of learning and using mathematics. Children should also learn to discuss mathematical ideas and make conjectures and convincing arguments as well as to appreciate the value of mathematical notation and its role in the development of mathematical ideas.

3. Mathematics should be viewed as a means of reasoning. A major goal of mathematics instruction is to help children develop the belief that they have the power to do mathematics and that they have control over their own success or failure. Students should learn to draw logical conclusions about mathematics, use models, known facts, properties, and relationships to explain their thinking, justify their answers and solution processes, use patterns and relationships to analyze mathematical situations, and believe that mathematics makes sense. Children should develop the ability to understand and apply reasoning processes with special attention to spatial reasoning and reasoning with proportions and graphs.

4. The mathematics program should emphasize mathematical connections. Children should be helped to see how mathematical ideas are related. This includes helping children to link conceptual and procedural knowledge, relate various representations of concepts or procedures to one another, recognize relationships among different topics in mathematics, use mathematics in other curriculum areas, and use mathematics in their daily lives. Students should learn to apply mathematical thinking and modeling to solve problems that arise in other disciplines, such as art, music, psychology, science, and business.

5. The mathematics curriculum should include estimation. Estimation presents students with another dimension of mathematics in which terms such as *about, near, closer to, between,* and *a little less than* illustrate that mathematics involves more than exactness. Students should explore estimation strategies, recognize when an estimate is appropriate, determine the reasonableness of results, and apply estimation in working with quantities, measurements, computation, and problem solving. The use of estimation should extend into the solving of proportions and to selecting and using appropriate methods for computing from among mental arithmetic, paper and pencil, calculator, and computer methods.

6. The mathematics curriculum should include whole number concepts and skills. Children must understand numbers if they are to make sense of the ways numbers are used in their everyday world. Students should construct number meanings through real-world experiences and the use of physical materials; understand our numeration system by relating counting, grouping, and place-value concepts; develop number sense; and interpret the multiple uses of numbers encountered in the real world.

7. The mathematics curriculum should include concepts of addition, subtraction, multiplication, and division of whole numbers, fractional numbers, decimal numbers, integers, and rational numbers. Understanding the fundamental operations of addition, subtraction, multiplication, and division is central to knowing mathematics. Children should develop meaning for the operations by modeling and discussing a rich variety of problem situations, relating the mathematical language and symbolism of operations to problem situations and informal language, recognize that a wide variety of problem structures can be represented by a single operation, and develop operation sense.

8. The mathematics curriculum should develop whole number, fractional number, decimal number, integer, and rational number computation so that students can use computation to solve problems. Children should be able to model, explain, and develop reasonable proficiency with basic facts and algorithms, use a variety

of mental computation and estimation techniques, use calculators in appropriate computational situations, and select and use computation techniques appropriate to specific problems and determine whether the results are reasonable. Students should understand and appreciate the need for numbers beyond the whole numbers, understand how the basic arithmetic operations are related to one another, and develop and apply number theory concepts such as primes, factors, and multiples and apply these in real-world and mathematical problem situations.

9. The mathematics curriculum should include 2- and 3-dimensional geometry. Geometric knowledge, relationships, and insights should be shown to be useful in everyday situations and connected to other mathematical topics and other subject areas. In particular, children should be able to describe, model, draw, and classify shapes; investigate and predict the results of combining, subdividing, and changing shapes; develop spatial sense; relate geometric ideas to number and measurement ideas; and recognize and appreciate geometry in their world. Children should also explore transformations of geometric figures, represent and solve problems using geometric models, understand and apply geometric properties and relationships, and develop an appreciation of geometry as a means of describing the physical world.

10. The mathematics curriculum should also include measurement. Measurement is of central importance to the curriculum because of its power to help children see that mathematics is useful in everyday life. Children should learn to understand the attributes of length, capacity, weight, area, volume, time, temperature, and angle; develop the process of measuring and concepts related to units of measurement; make and use estimates of measurement; and make and use measurements in problem and everyday situations. Students should extend their understanding of the concepts of perimeter, area, volume, angle measure, capacity, and weight and mass.

11. The mathematics curriculum should include experiences with data analysis and probability so that students collect, organize, describe, display, and interpret data as well as make decisions on the basis of that information. Children should collect, organize, and describe data; construct, read, and interpret displays of data; formulate and solve problems that involve collecting and analyzing data; and explore concepts of chance.

12. The mathematics curriculum should include fractions, decimals, integers, and rational numbers as well as ratios, proportions, and percents, as these represent a significant extension of children's knowledge about numbers. Children should develop concepts of fractions, mixed numbers, and decimals; develop number sense for fractions and decimals; use models to relate fractions to decimals

and to find equivalent fractions; use models to explore operations on fractions and decimals; and apply fractions and decimals to problem situations. They should investigate relationships among fractions, decimals, and percents and represent numerical relationships in 1- and 2-dimensional graphs.

13. The mathematics curriculum should include the study of patterns and relationships, including functions. Patterns are everywhere. Children who are encouraged to look for patterns and to express them mathematically begin to understand how mathematics applies to the world in which they live. Children should learn to recognize, describe, extend, and create a wide variety of patterns; represent and describe mathematical relationships; and explore the use of variables and open sentences to express relationships. They should also describe and represent relationships with tables, graphs, and rules; analyze functional relationships to explain how a change in one quantity results in a change in another; and use patterns to represent and solve problems.

Yes, computation is important to the mathematics curriculum, but as these standards make clear, computation is only one part of the total curriculum. Rather than continuing the view that mathematics is nothing but computation and that computational accuracy is the goal of the mathematics program, the NCTM standards focus on mathematics as thinking, problem solving, applicable to real-world situations, and as computation. The vision of mathematics as problem solving in real-world situations is particularly suited to the integrated curriculum approach.

INTEGRATING SOCIAL STUDIES

Social studies is already an **interdisciplinary** subject matter area, formed from the fusion of history, geography, economics, anthropology, political science, and sociology. As such, it is already well on the road to integration within the curriculum. As with science and mathematics, recent thinking on the social studies promotes an increased emphasis on the integration of the social studies with other subject matter areas.

In 1994, the National Council for the Social Studies voted to approve the following definition of *social studies.* This definition not only emphasizes the interdisciplinary nature of social studies but also the need for its integration.

Social studies is the integrated study of the social sciences and humanities to promote civic competence. Within the school program, social studies provides coordinated, systematic study drawing upon such disciplines as anthropology, archaeology, economics, geography, history, law, philosophy, political science, psychology, religion, and sociology, as well as appropriate content from the humanities, mathematics, and the natural sciences. The primary purpose of the social studies is to help young people develop the ability to make informed and reasoned decisions for the public good as citizens of a culturally diverse, democratic society in an interdependent world. (p. 157)

In 1994, the National Council for the Social Studies published its *Curriculum Standards for Social Studies: Expectations of Excellence.* According to these standards, social studies is distinguished from other fields of study by four factors, all of them pointing up the interdisciplinary nature of social studies and the emphasis on integration of social studies into other areas of the curriculum.

1. "Social studies programs have as a major purpose the promotion of civic competence—which knowledge, skills, and attitudes are required of students to be able to assume 'the office of citizen' (as Thomas Jefferson called it) in our democratic republic" (p. 3). This goal requires that students not only have knowledge about the community, nation, and world but also develop the skills of data collection and collaboration with others, decision-making and problem-solving skills and communications skills.
2. "K–12 social studies programs integrate knowledge, skills, and attitudes within and across disciplines" (p. 3). This is frequently addressed through the use of themes in teaching. Thematic teaching in turn requires that children utilize information from language arts, science, mathematics, and other skills in investigating the theme.
3. "Social studies programs help students construct a knowledge base and attitudes drawn from academic disciplines as specialized ways of viewing reality" (p. 4). This defining factor emphasizes social studies but also considers social studies an interdisciplinary approach including the disciplines of history, geography, political science, sociology, anthropology, and psychology. However, it also emphasizes the necessity for communication, including verbal and oral language, as well as the fine arts as means of communication.
4. "Social studies programs reflect the changing nature of knowledge, fostering entirely new and highly integrated approaches to resolving issues of significance to humanity" (p. 5). Social issues are now recognized as cutting across the boundaries of disciplines and requiring information from a variety of disciplines in order to provide solutions. The use of social problems as a means of integrating the curriculum is one of the long-standing techniques in social studies.

In addition to providing this view of the nature of social studies, the *Curriculum Standards for Social Studies* states that social studies teaching and learning are powerful when they are integrative and acknowledge that integration across the curriculum.

As previously indicated, the social studies curriculum often shows its integration through the use of **themes**. The *Standards* discusses ten themes that can serve as unifying concepts. As one can see, these themes cut across subject matter boundaries and provide a means for integrating the total curriculum.

Theme 1: Culture. The social studies programs should include experiences that provide for the study of culture and cultural diversity. Human beings create, learn from, and adapt to culture. Culture helps us to understand ourselves as both individuals and members of various groups. Human cultures exhibit both similarities and differences, with each system unique.

Theme 2: Time, Continuity, and Change. Social studies programs should include experiences that provide for the study of the ways human beings view themselves in and over time. Human beings seek to understand their historical roots and to locate themselves in time. Such understanding involves knowing what things were like in the past and how things change and develop. Knowing how to read and reconstruct the past allows one to develop a historical perspective and to answer questions about one's connection to the historical past.

Theme 3: People, Places, and Environments. Social studies programs should include experiences that provide for the study of people, places, and environments. Technological advances connect students at all levels to the world beyond their personal locations. The study of people, places, and human-environment interactions assists learners as they create their spatial views and geographic perspectives of the world.

Theme 4: Individual Development and Identity. Personal identity is shaped by one's culture, by groups, and by institutional influences. Examination of various forms of human behavior enhances understanding of the relationships among social norms and emerging personal identities, the social processes that influence identity formation, and the ethical principles underlying individual action.

Theme 5: Individuals, Groups, and Institutions. Institutions such as schools, churches, families, government agencies, and the courts all play an integral role in our lives. These and other institutions exert enormous influence over us, yet institutions are no more than organizational embodiments to further the core social values of those who comprise them. It is important that students know how institutions are formed, what controls and influences them, how they control and influence individuals and culture, and how institutions can be maintained or changed. This includes the study of sociology and anthropology as well as other disciplines.

Theme 6: Power, Authority, and Governance. Social studies programs should include experiences that provide for the study of how people create and change structures of power, authority, and governance. Understanding the historical development of structures of power, authority, and governance and their evolving functions in contemporary U.S. society as well as in other parts of the world is essential for developing civic competence. By examining the purposes and characteristics of various governance systems, learners develop an understanding of how groups of nations attempt to resolve conflicts and seek to establish order and security. Through study of the dynamic relationships among individual rights and responsibilities, the needs of social groups, and concepts of a just society, learners become more effective problem solvers and decision makers when addressing the persistent issues and social problems encountered in public life.

Theme 7: Production, Distribution, and Consumption. Social studies programs should include experiences that provide for the study of how people organize for the production, distribution, and consumption of goods and services. People have wants that often exceed the limited resources available to them. Unequal distribution of resources necessitates systems of exchange, including trade, to improve the well-being of the economy, while the role of government in economic policy making varies over time and from place to place. Increasingly these decisions are global in scope and require systematic study of an interdependent world economy and the role of technology in economic decision making.

Theme 8: Science, Technology, and Society. Social studies programs should include experiences that provide for the study of relationships among science, technology, and society. Technology is as old as the first crude tool invented by prehistoric humans, but today's technology forms the basis for some of our most difficult social choices. Modern life as we know it would be impossible without technology and the science that supports it.

Theme 9: Global Connections. Social studies programs should include experiences that provide for the study of global connections and interdependence. The realities of global independence require understanding the increasingly important and diverse global connections among world societies. Analysis of tensions between national and global priorities contributes to the development of possible solutions to persistent and emerging global issues in many fields: health care, economic development, environment quality, universal human rights, and others. Analyzing patterns and relationships within and among world cultures, such as economic competition and interdependence, age-old ethnic enmities, political and military alliances, and others, helps learners carefully examine policy alternatives that have both national and global implications.

Theme 10: Civic Ideals and Practices. Social studies programs should include experiences that provide for the study of the ideals, principles, and practices of citizenship in a democratic republic. An understanding of civic ideals and practices of citizenship is critical to full participation in society and is a central purpose of social studies. All people have a stake in examining civic ideals and practices across time and in diverse societies as well as at home, and in determining how to close the gap between present practices and the ideals upon which our democratic republic is based.

The ten themes of social studies provide a framework for making decisions about the major organizing conceptualizations and the factual information to be included within the integrated curriculum. They are not advocating "throwing out" the traditional content of the social studies program but rather a reorganization of that content around unifying concepts and themes. Such reorganization results in greater understanding and less memorization.

DEVELOPING CRITICAL AND CREATIVE THINKING

Within the typical elementary school, much learning is considered to be low level, that is, more concerned with the development of skills and facts than with the development of concepts. Children memorize vocabulary terms and multiplication facts, learn the dates of important Civil War battles, develop a list of grammatical and punctuation terms. Unfortunately, much of what is learned through memorization is retained only long enough to be demonstrated on a test. There is often little attempt to connect the bits and pieces of factual information to concepts, especially to concepts already known to the children.

Within the integrated curriculum, however, the focus is not simply on the acquisition of facts and skills, but on the application of those facts and skills to the solution of a variety of problems. As a consequence, children need to develop the ability to think critically and creatively.

DEFINITION OF THINKING

Thinking is frequently defined as a search for meaning within a set of information that apparently has no meaning. In searching for this meaning, students engage in decision making, problem solving, conceptualizing, analyzing, synthesizing, distinguishing the relevant from the irrelevant, and reasoning. Within the integrated curriculum, thinking should be a major aspect of learning simply because the integrated curriculum is geared toward increasing understanding through the utilization of appropriate subject matter. The use of real-life problems as a means of curriculum integration gives purpose to the search for meaning and so to thinking skills. In essence, teaching through the integrated curriculum is teaching through thinking. Teaching through thinking is more interested in how students approach subject matter, in how they use subject matter, and in how they react to a lack of information than in how many bits and pieces of information they can parrot back on a test.

Although thinking is an integral aspect of the integrated curriculum and should be taught at all grade levels, it should be remembered that thinking is a developmental process. The kinds of thinking skills used by children become more complex and more sophisticated as children move from the kindergarten to the sixth grade. This growth shows not only the increasing maturity of the children but also the changes occurring in developmental level and in experience. Therefore, thinking requirements should be geared to the developmental level and experiential background of the children.

Within the integrated curriculum, three assumptions should be kept in mind when teaching thinking. The first is that all children can learn to think, no matter what their age or background. In the past it was thought that children from impoverished backgrounds have such deficits in academic skills that their education should focus only on the acquisition of information. As a consequence, children were taught skills and lessons directed toward the knowledge level of learning. Teachers and curriculum planners erroneously thought that children from impoverished backgrounds could not be taught to think until they had acquired all of the knowledge children from affluent backgrounds had acquired. In reality, children from all socioeconomic and ethnic backgrounds need to learn thinking skills along with content information. Second, teachers should keep in mind that students can think better than they are inclined to do on their own. The complaint of teachers that children can't think is often correct, but it is not correct to think that they cannot learn to think. Just as children must be taught to read and write and multiply, they must be taught to think using appropriately developed lessons and appropriate teaching techniques. Closely related to the first assumption is the assumption that thinking is for children of all intellectual levels and not simply for those who have been identified as intellectually gifted. In the past, thinking development programs have been implemented only as a part of programs for the gifted child. These children were generally pulled out of the regular classroom, given specific lessons in critical thinking, problem solving, and **creative thinking**, and then returned to the classroom to continue the daily routine. Such an approach to teaching thinking is indefensible when it is acknowledged that children of all intellectual abilities are challenged to make decisions every day and so should be given the tools needed to make those decisions appropriately.

Although the integrated curriculum does focus on the teaching and use of thinking skills, it should not be assumed that thinking is a generic sort of skill. Instead, thinking skills can be differentiated in critical thinking and creative thinking.

CRITICAL THINKING

Critical thinking involves not only the production of ideas but also the evaluation of those ideas. It incorporates recognition and construction of sound arguments, application of principles of logic, and the avoidance of logical fallacies. Critical thinking includes analyzing arguments in the light of evidence and then judging the accuracy or worth of a particular idea or claim.

In considering critical thinking in the classroom, the emphasis should be on the evaluation of ideas based on factual evidence rather than on opinions.

Students in the integrated curriculum should be helped to develop the ability to provide reasons when presenting ideas, to analyze the sources of information for possible bias, and to consider the logic of arguments presented in sources of information. In particular, the integrated curriculum should develop in students the ability to bring to a situation accurate and unbiased information from a variety of sources and subject matter areas.

Within the integrated curriculum, the development of critical thinking skills should be an integral part of the curriculum rather than a body of knowledge and skills taught separately from the activities and problems presented within the curriculum. The teacher should continually guide students in developing critical thinking skills by asking questions such as: (1) What was your source of information? (2) When was the information published? (3) Who is the author of the source? and (4) Is the author an expert in the field?

We discuss critical thinking and methods for developing critical thinking skills in the classroom more fully in Chapter 10.

CREATIVE THINKING

While critical thinking tends to focus on a single outcome that can then be evaluated in light of factual evidence, creative thinking focuses on many outcomes. In general, critical thinking is convergent in nature while creative thinking is divergent.

Creative thinking begins with curiosity and a willingness to go beyond the usual limitations of an object or idea and goes on to generate something new. It is original, flexible, and diverse in nature. Because creative thinking tests limits, fear of failure may be a limiting factor. The more likely a person is to fear failure, the less likely he or she is to think creatively. Fear of failure inhibits creativity, and so creative ideas cannot be evaluated according to the same kinds of criteria used for evaluating ideas in critical thinking. In fact, creative thinking is enhanced when students can brainstorm a variety of possibilities without the threat of judgment.

Creative thinking differs from critical thinking in terms of the product. The product of creative thinking is original. It may be practical. It may be elegant. It may be esthetically pleasing. On the other hand, the result of creative thinking may also be impractical, inelegant, or esthetically unpleasing. The emphasis is on originality in the solution of a problem.

Creative thinking also differ from critical thinking in terms of approach to problem solving. Creative thinking depends more on mobility of thought than on fluency of thought. When difficulties arise in creative thinking, creative thinkers do not generally attempt to find more ideas but instead attempt to make the original problem more abstract or concrete, more general or specific, or more practical or fanciful; reformulating the problem is more common than **brainstorming** additional problem solutions.

And finally, creative thinkers accept confusion, uncertainty, and higher risk of failure as a part of the process of thinking and creating than do critical thinkers. Creative thinkers are able to consider different viewpoints, set final or intermediate products aside and come back to them later, to evaluate their products with distance, and to seek intelligent criticism. This ability to set products aside and to look at them objectively probably stems from the fact that creative thinking is more intrinsically motivated than is critical thinking. Creative people feel that they choose for themselves what to do and how to do it rather than relying on other people to choose for them. They tend to view the task they have undertaken as worthwhile in itself and not just as a means to an end; they enjoy the activity, the context, and the setting.

We discuss creative thinking skills and means for teaching creative thinking in the integrated classroom more fully in Chapter 10.

SUMMARY

The integrated approach to curriculum results in the loss of distinct subject matter areas, a fact that causes concern to those who are more used to the traditional curriculum. This concern frequently focuses on such educational basics as reading, writing, mathematics, science, and social studies. There needs to be an assurance that these areas will be included.

The development of basic literacy skills in the integrated approach is best illustrated through a whole language approach to literacy. In this approach learning to read, write, speak, and spell are intertwined so that literacy is the outcome. As with all aspects of the integrated curriculum, the use of a whole language approach to literacy is based on authentic activities and the authentic use of language. Children are immersed in literacy and so become literate.

The areas of science, mathematics, and social studies are considered basics in most educational programs. In the past all three of these areas have been distinct from one another, even though science overlaps social studies and mathematics is an integral part of any scientific experiment. Recently, the American Association for the Advancement of Science, the National Council of Teachers of Mathematics, and the National Council for the Social Studies have all made a stand for interdisciplinary and integrated study. In each of these content areas, the application of information in authentic situations is equally as important as or more important than the learning of isolated facts. Each of the three major areas of the curriculum, then, supports the trend toward the integrated curriculum.

ACTIVITY ONE

PURPOSE

The purpose of this activity is to interview a teacher who is using the whole language approach to literacy.

PROCEDURE

1. Before conducting the interview, prepare a series of questions to ask the teacher. As you prepare your questions, consider the following areas:
   a. how the teacher organizes the classroom space for use of a whole language approach
   b. what kinds of materials are used in teaching a whole language approach
   c. how the teacher organizes the materials used in the whole language approach
   d. the benefits of using a whole language approach in the classroom
   e. the difficulties encountered in using a whole language approach in the classroom
   f. the effect of a whole language approach on children with disabling conditions in the classroom
   g. how the whole language approach incorporates disciplines such as science, mathematics, social studies, and fine arts
   h. methods used to inform parents about the whole language approach
   i. sources of information used by the teacher
2. Record the teacher's responses in writing or by using a tape recorder. Before using the recorder be certain to get the permission of the teacher.
3. Use the follow-up questions to help clarify any of the answers given by the teacher.
4. Do not use the teacher's name or the names of any children in your written report.

ACTIVITY TWO

PURPOSE

The purpose of this activity is to critique a science textbook's or science curriculum guide's content information according to the criteria for selecting content outline in *Project 2061* of the AAAS.

PROCEDURE

1. Choose a science textbook for a single grade level or a single grade level of a science curriculum guide.
2. Review the criteria listed by *Project 2061* and in this chapter.
3. Critique the content found in the textbook or the curriculum guide according to the listed criteria. How well do the topics included fit the criteria suggested? What would need to be done to make the content more appropriate according to the listed criteria?

⚎ ACTIVITY THREE

PURPOSE

The purpose of this activity is to critique a mathematics textbook's or mathematics curriculum guide's content information according to the assumptions made in the NCTM's *Curriculum and Evaluation Standards.*

PROCEDURE

1. Choose a mathematics textbook for a single grade level or a single grade level of a mathematics curriculum guide.
2. Review the criteria listed by the *Curriculum and Evaluation Standards* and in this chapter.
3. Critique the content found in the textbook or the curriculum guide according to the listed criteria. How well do the topics included fit the criteria suggested? What would need to be done to make the content more appropriate according to the listed criteria?

⚎ ACTIVITY FOUR

PURPOSE

The purpose of this activity is to critique a social studies textbook's or social studies curriculum guide's content information according to the assumptions made in the *Curriculum Standards* of the National Council for the Social Studies.

PROCEDURE

1. Choose a social studies textbook for a single grade level or a single grade level of a social studies curriculum guide.
2. Review the criteria listed by *Curriculum Standards* and in this chapter.
3. Critique the content found in the textbook or the curriculum guide according to the listed criteria. How well do the topics included fit the criteria suggested? What would need to be done to make the content more appropriate according to the listed criteria?

⚎ ACTIVITY FIVE

PURPOSE

The purpose of this activity is to revise a typical textbook lesson to include more critical and creative thinking processes.

PROCEDURE

1. Select a textbook for a single grade level in one of the following subject matter areas: science, mathematics, or social studies.
2. Select one lesson from the textbook. Read the teacher's guide for the lesson and describe the teaching strategies suggested for the lesson.
3. Revise the lesson as taught through the teacher's manual to include more attention to critical and creative teaching strategies.

STUDY QUESTIONS

1. Although the integrated curriculum approach to organization should not result in a decrease in subject matter information, it does result in certain losses. What are these losses? How will they affect the learning of children in the elementary school?
2. How does the approach to literacy taken in the traditional elementary school differ from that taken in the integrated approach to curriculum?
3. What is meant by the term *whole language*? How does the whole language approach view the development of literacy in children?
4. Select three topics from an elementary science textbook. Using the criteria for integrating science into the curriculum, analyze the appropriateness of the topics for inclusion in the integrated curriculum.
5. Select and read a unit in an elementary school science textbook. Then, using the ten concepts related to science as a set of beliefs and attitudes, critique the presentation of the material.
6. The National Council of Teachers of Mathematics lists five goals for all students. What are those goals? How could they be used to organize mathematics content within the integrated curriculum?
7. Review an elementary school mathematics textbook. How well do you think the unit meets the 13 suggested strands of the National Council of Teachers of Mathematics?
8. In the *Curriculum Standards for Social Studies* ten themes appear. Review an elementary school social studies textbook. How well do you think the textbook covers those themes?
9. Compare and contrast critical thinking skills and creative thinking skills.
10. Select one of the following topics. How would you develop critical and creative thinking skills within the topic?
    a. Endangered species in the world
    b. Folk tales of the United States
    c. Mathematical probability
    d. Life in colonial America

BIBLIOGRAPHY

American Association for the Advancement of Science. (1989). *Project 2061: Science for all Americans.* Washington, D.C.: American Association for the Advancement of Science.

American Association for the Advancement of Science. (1993). *Benchmarks for science literacy.* New York: Oxford University Press.

Beck, I. L., & Dole, J. A. (1992). Reading and thinking with history and science text. In C. Collins & J. N. Mangieri (Eds.), *Teaching thinking: An agenda for the 21st century.* Hillsdale, N. J.: Laurence Erlbaum.

Beyer, B. K. (1987). *Practical strategies for the teaching of thinking.* Boston: Allyn and Bacon.

Brady, S. K., & Sills, T. M. (Eds.). (1993). *Whole language: History, philosophy, practice.* Dubuque, Iowa: Kendall-Hunt.

Caine, R. N., & Caine, G. (1991). *Teaching and the human brain.* Alexandria, Va.: Association for Supervision and Curriculum Development.

Cambourne, B. (1988). *The whole story: Natural learning and the acquisition of literacy in the classroom.* Auckland: Ashton Scholastic.

Clark, J. H. (1990). *Patterns of thinking: Integrating learning skills in content teaching.* Boston: Allyn and Bacon.

Collins, C. (1992). Thinking development through intervention: Middle school students come of age. In C. Collins & J. N. Mangieri (Eds.), *Teaching thinking: An agenda for the 21st century.* Hillsdale, N.J.: Laurence Erlbaum.

Collins, C., & Mangieri, J. N. (Eds.). (1992). *Teaching thinking: An agenda for the 21st century.* Hillsdale, N. J.: Laurence Erlbaum.

Costa, A. (1992). An environment for thinking. In C. Collins & J. N. Mangieri (Eds.), *Teaching thinking: An agenda for the 21st century.* Hillsdale, New Jersey: Laurence Erlbaum.

Costa, A. (Ed.). (1985). *Developing minds: A resource book for teaching thinking.* Alexandria, Va.: Association for Supervision and Curriculum Development.

Edelsky, C., Alwerger, B., & Flores, B. (1991). *Whole language: What's the difference?* Portsmouth, N.H.: Heinemann.

Eisner, E. W. (1994). *Cognition and curriculum reconsidered* (2nd ed.). New York: Teachers College, Columbia University.

Fogarty, R. (Ed.). (1993). *Integrating the curricula: A collection.* Palatine, Ill.: IRI/Skylight.

Fogarty, R., & Stoehr, J. (1995). *Integrating the curricula with multiple intelligences.* Palatine, Ill.: IRI/Skylight.

Harlin, R., Lipa, S. E., & Lonberger, R. (1991). *The whole language journey.* Markham, Ontario: Pippin Publishing.

Jones, B. F., Palincsar, A. S., Ogle, D. S., & Carr, E. G. (1987). *Strategic teaching and learning: Cognitive instruction in the content areas.* Alexandria, Va.: Association for Supervision and Curriculum Development.

Lapp, D., Flood, J., & Farnan, N. (Eds.). (1989). *Content area reading and learning: Instructional strategies.* Englewood Cliffs, N.J.: Prentice-Hall.

National Council for the Social Studies. (1994). *Curriculum standards for social studies.* Washington, D.C.: National Council for the Social Studies.

National Council of Teachers of Mathematics. (1989). *Curriculum and evaluation standards for school mathematics.* Reston, Va.: National Council of Teachers of Mathematics.

National Reseach Council. (1989). *Everybody Counts: A Report on the Future of Mathematics Education.* Washington, D.C.: National Academy Press.

Ruggiero, V. R. (1988). *Teaching thinking across the curriculum.* New York: Harper & Row.

CHAPTER

4

DEVELOPING AN INTEGRATED CURRICULUM

CHAPTER OBJECTIVES

After reading this chapter, you should be able to:
1. Describe an integrated approach to teaching in the elementary school
2. Distinguish between teacher-as-director and teacher-as-facilitator
3. Describe distinguishing characteristics of teacher-as-director classrooms
4. Describe distinguishing characteristics of teacher-as-facilitator classrooms
5. Compare and contrast discipline-based approaches with integrated approaches
6. Discuss the relationship of higher-order thinking skills to the integrated curriculum
7. Discuss the relationship of multiple intelligences to the integrated curriculum
8. Depict an approach to integration based on disciplines
9. Depict an approach to integration based on language and literature
10. Depict an approach to integration based on themes
11. Depict an approach to integration based on issues
12. Describe barriers and constraints to an integrated curriculum

CURRICULUM INTEGRATION AT THE CLASSROOM LEVEL

Real and meaningful curricular change can only occur in the classroom. No matter what philosophies, concepts, principles, theories, strategies, and viewpoints about curriculum are adopted by the school hierarchy (the principal,

---

Box 4.1   Typical Dictionary Definitions for *Director*

di-rec'-tor
Noun

One who:

- supervises, controls, governs, or manages
- keeps watch over and directs the work of others
- imposes tasks, especially burdensome or laborious ones
- is a source of burden or responsibility
- is in charge
- has administrative or managerial authority
- manages, officiates, conducts
- is an executive; an administrator
- is highest in rank or authority
- is head, leader, master, chief, boss, chieftain, director, supervisor, manager, superintendent, foreman, overseer, taskmaster

---

the superintendent, the school board, and the like), curricular implementation (and change) reside in the classroom, in the hands of the teacher and the students. It is the philosophy embraced and employed by the teacher that actually dictates the strategies for teaching and learning that emerge in the classroom. The classroom teacher, then, becomes the all-important focus in curriculum implementation and in curricular change.

In developing an integrated classroom, it is important for the teacher not only to understand, endorse, and embrace curricular integration, but to make a personal transition from teacher as director of instruction in the classroom to teacher as **facilitator** of learning in the classroom. The nouns *director* and *facilitator* represent entirely different concepts. In the *director,* we find a controlling manager who is often dictatorial and restrictive and imposes burdensome tasks in an authoritative, autocratic, and ironhanded way. Box 4.1 shows typical dictionary definitions for *director.*

A *facilitator,* on the other hand, assists, enables, and empowers, orchestrating things in a harmonious way. Typical dictionary definitions for *facilitator* are depicted in Box 4.2.

In making the transition from teacher-as-director to teacher-as-facilitator, the classroom teacher relinquishes the kind of control exercised by teacher as director of instruction in favor of the kind of control exercised by teacher as facilitator of learning. When a teacher makes the transition to facilitator of learning in the classroom, the characteristics depicted in Box 4.3 emerge. As a facilitator, a teacher models ongoing learning for children. Students see teachers who have become facilitators of learning themselves engaging in the activities

---

Box 4.2   Typical Dictionary Definitions for *Facilitator*

fa-cil'-i-ta-tor
Noun

One who:

- makes it easier to accomplish tasks
- makes things less difficult
- expedites things
- harmonizes in a common action or effort
- promotes naturalness and freedom from constraint
- causes a reduction in tension, pressure, or rigidity
- coordinates working together in harmonious fashion
- combines and adapts in order to attain a particular effect
- coordinates, accommodates, conforms, reconciles, attunes, articulates
- arranges, connects, links, integrates, unifies, blends, synthesizes, orchestrates

---

of ongoing learning, such as using problem solving, numeracy, literacy, creative processes, and the like.

Teachers who function as facilitators see learning more as a process than a product. Learning as a process involves the development of strategies for finding out about things we want to know about or to do. In process-based learning, it

---

Box 4.3   Characteristics of the Teacher as Facilitator

When teachers are facilitators of learning in the classroom, they are characterized by:

- sharing the responsibility for learning with the learners
- orchestrating groups of learners in the cooperative pursuit of skills and knowledge
- collaborating with individuals and groups of learners to successfully establish, pursue, and effect fulfillment of objectives
- expecting learning to occur with all children
- providing all children with opportunities to achieve success
- encouraging, promoting, and cultivating children's cooperative pursuits of learning

is natural for the learner to develop strategies for coming to know while engaged in meaningful, interesting, and authentic activities and events.

Teachers who function as directors see learning as a product or a behavior that can be easily measured. In such a **behaviorist**, product-based view of learning, there is a lockstep methodology of test-teach-test where children learn only what is taught directly by the teacher after it has been broken down into small bits and pieces for their consumption. In that regard, Stice, Bertrand, and Bertrand (1995) raise an important point: "If behaviorism is the most accurate explanation of how humans learn, why do we learn so many things—water skiing, riding a two-wheeler, or using a computer—without someone else organizing it for us, without direct teaching and testing by a teacher? Does learning in school have to be different and more difficult than learning outside the classroom?" (p. 10).

When teachers act as facilitators of learning, they provide students with opportunities for discussion, demonstration, and student-teacher **conferencing**, helping them become aware of their thinking processes in learning. Teachers as facilitators invite children to use a variety of sign and symbol systems, such as writing, math, music, art, drama, and discussion, to explore and learn and then to present their learnings to others.

TEACHER-AS-DIRECTOR CLASSROOMS

The teacher-as-director classroom follows a traditional curriculum organization that recognizes distinct divisions between the content areas. Language arts, science, social studies, and mathematics usually comprise the core subjects of the traditional curriculum, with music, art, and physical education included as well. In most cases, there is a sequencing of these school subjects around a rigid time frame required by either the state, county, or local school system. Figure 4.1 illustrates a typical segmented, rigid, daily time frame for the subjects in a traditional, teacher-as-director elementary school curriculum.

Language arts is usually allocated the longest period of time in the traditional elementary curriculum, generally 120 minutes each day. The language arts include the skills of listening, speaking, reading, and writing, the components of communication. Listening and reading are both decoding skills, and speaking and writing are both encoding skills. Decoding involves interpreting, either from aural input (listening) or from graphic forms (reading). Speaking involves encoding sounds that you make so that they are meaningful, and writing involves encoding the sounds in your head so that you can produce graphic (written) symbols. Often, language arts is broken into three segments of communication: **aural-oral** communication, reading communication, and written communication. In aural-oral communication, the skills of listening and speaking are addressed. In reading communication, the skills of word perception, reading comprehension, and vocabulary development are taught. And in written communication, the teacher addresses grammar and usage, handwriting, spelling, practical writing, and creative writing.

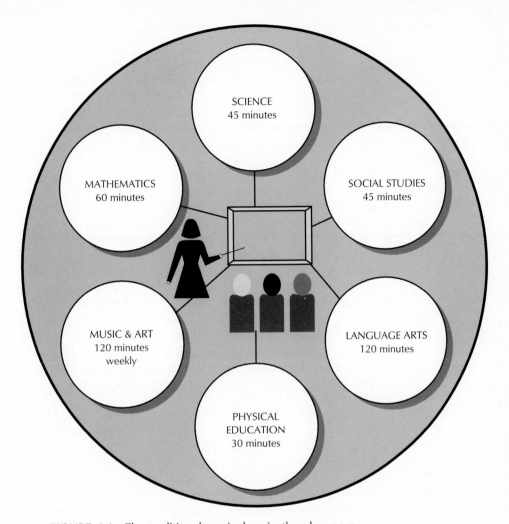

FIGURE 4.1 The traditional curriculum in the classroom

    Mathematics is usually allocated 60 minutes per day in the traditional elementary school curriculum and is concerned with addition, subtraction, multiplication, and division of whole numbers, common fractions, and decimal fractions. Geometric concepts are explored, and there is an emphasis on finding solutions in applications.

    Social studies and science are generally given 45 minutes each per day. Social studies involves the core disciplines of the social sciences—geography, history, sociology, political science, anthropology, and economics; current events in the world, including **media** influence and media ownership; vital **topics** of the day, such as establishing global perspectives, understanding the world of work, developing tolerance and understanding in a multicultural society, appreciating sexual equity, and becoming knowledgeable about AIDS, the environment, and similar societal concerns; and the development of an enlightened and informed citizenry. Science is concerned with investigations, with coming to know through participatory experiences. It is a hands-on, doing program with students actively involved in touching, manipulating, observing, experimenting, and the like. Both social studies and science are best taught by student-participatory activities, but unfortunately many teacher-as-director classrooms address these two vital content areas as textbook-as-the-only-resource, read-the-chapter, answer-the-questions sessions.

Physical education, usually allocated 30 minutes per day in the elementary school program, is often taught by a specialist who teaches large groups of children (two or more classes at a time) either outside or in a gym. Classroom teachers get planning time during the time their students are with the physical education teacher.

Music and art generally get 120 minutes per week in the traditional elementary school program. Often, one or both of these subjects are taught by a music or art specialist outside of the regular classroom. When this occurs, the classroom teacher gets planning time.

The physical setting in a teacher-as-director classroom is often revealing of the nature of the instructional program. The teacher's desk is usually centrally located and prominent. The students' desks are configured in a grid system of columns and rows. It is obvious from the arrangement of the chairs and desks and other furniture that the teacher teaches *to* the children rather than *with* the children. Figure 4.2 shows a typical arrangement often found in teacher-as-director classrooms.

In teacher-as-director classrooms that are self-contained, teachers have more opportunities to vary from the time frame, particularly if there are no mandates from the school system about strict compliance. Some teacher-as-director classrooms conform exactly to the time allocations for the various subjects and stop a lesson in one subject to start another lesson because the schedule calls for it. Other teachers, however, may choose to extend a "hot" lesson that is being very productive and carry it into the time allocated to another subject. Their thinking is that they will later make up the time in the subject that was slighted, and, over the long haul, the time allocations for the various subjects will be met. In a school with **departmentalized** or semidepartmentalized classrooms, this is not so easy to do; the departmentalized teachers usually follow time allocations more closely than their self-contained counterparts. In any event, teacher-as-director classrooms, whether self-contained or departmentalized, separate the school subjects so that they are taught more or less independently of one another.

TEACHER-AS-FACILITATOR CLASSROOMS

Teacher-as-facilitator classrooms are distinguished by a lack of separation of the school subjects. Instead, the subjects are largely integrated, often to the point of "blurring" the subject area distinctions so prominent in teacher-as-director classrooms. In the teacher-as-facilitator classroom, the teacher is a co-learner with

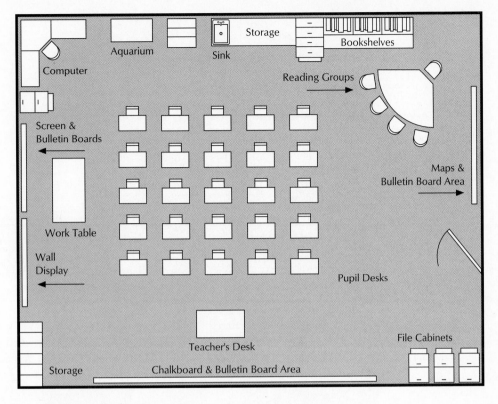

FIGURE 4.2   Teacher-as-director classroom

the students, coaching them, listening to them, observing with them (and observing them), encouraging them, participating with them, working cooperatively with them, and responding to them. Figure 4.3 shows the connections, interconnections, and linkages occurring when the curriculum is integrated in the classroom.

Charbonneau and Reider (1995) indicate that integrated classrooms are distinguished by characteristics similar to the following:

- Students act as researchers; particular emphasis is placed on student-designed and -executed projects. There are multiple resources available.
- Teachers act as coaches; that is, they serve as resources and challenge students to be responsible for their own discoveries.
- Less emphasis is placed on lecture and more emphasis is placed on students working together in cooperative, collaborative groups to do research projects.
- Students demonstrate their proficiency and understanding of subject matter by actually exhibiting their work.

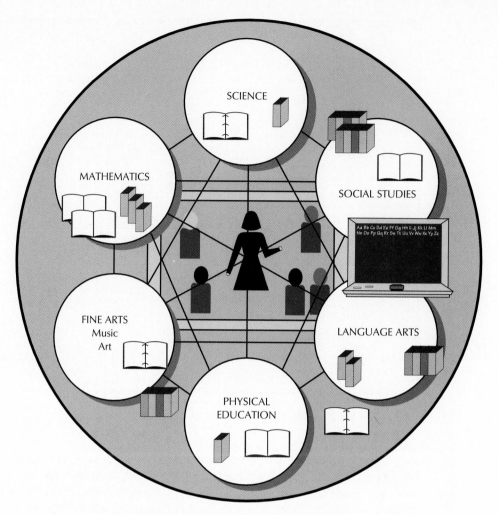

FIGURE 4.3 The integrated curriculum in the classroom

- "Less is more" because subject matter is explored in depth. Accumulating unrelated facts is less important than understanding a major concept.
- Less emphasis is placed on standardized time frames and more emphasis is placed on children learning according to their needs.
- Less emphasis is placed on right and wrong answers and standardized solutions and more emphasis is placed on continued learning, divergent thinking, and problem solving.
- Students are encouraged to believe that each individual should be treated with dignity and respect.

- Education is seen as partnerships that operate within the classroom, within the school, and between the school and the surrounding community.

In classrooms where the teacher serves as a facilitator of learning rather than as a director of learning, the subjects in the curriculum are melded, blended, and fused in meaningful ways so that related concepts are integrated. Learning coalesces and unifies around central themes, major ideas, important concepts, formidable **issues**, compelling problems, and the like. The pursuit of knowledge and understanding is a cooperative venture between the teacher and the students which, at appropriate times, combines, blends, and unites elements of language arts, social studies, science, mathematics, art, music, health, and physical education to form an integrated curriculum. Figure 4.4 shows the various subjects in the elementary school program being fused into a central aggregate, that is, an integrated curriculum.

The physical setting in a teacher-as-facilitator classroom is very different from the physical setting in a teacher-as-director classroom. The teacher's desk is usually off to one side of the room, often hard to find, and sometimes even nonexistent. It serves mostly as a place just to store things. Students sit and work in groups, and it is obvious from the arrangement and types of furniture that learning is a cooperative and collaborative enterprise. The teacher teaches *with* the children rather than *to* the children. There is an immersion in the learning

FIGURE 4.4 The integrated curriculum

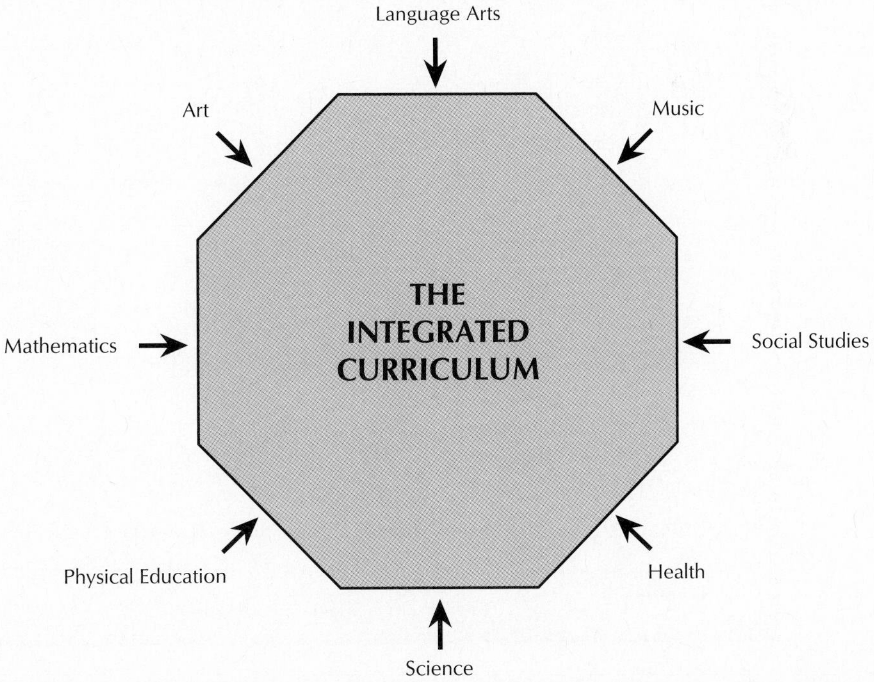

process that is rarely found in the teacher-as-director classroom. Expectations are high and learners are empowered with cooperative decision making with respect to the what, when, and how of their learning. And in teacher-as-facilitator classrooms learners share cooperatively the responsibility for their learning. Figure 4.5 shows a typical arrangement found in teacher-as-facilitator classrooms.

According to Canadian researchers Drake and Miller (in Willis, 1995), as teachers proceed into curriculum integration in the classroom, there is a move from a time-based, subject-based approach to an outcome-based approach. They emphasize that when curriculum integration becomes a reality in the classroom, three basic assumptions change:

1. Ensuring the success of all students takes priority over maintaining the status quo.
2. **Higher-order thinking** skills and interpersonal life skills are valued as much as content learning.
3. Traditional instructional delivery systems and transmission modes shift to an integrated, **constructivist approach** to teaching.

FIGURE 4.5 Teacher-as-facilitator classroom

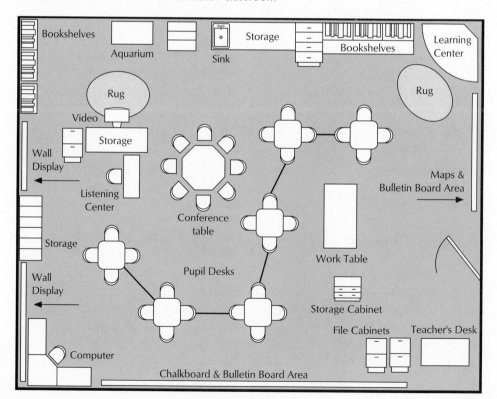

HIGHER-ORDER THINKING SKILLS AND CURRICULUM INTEGRATION

Drake (1993) writes that when students tackle real issues and problems that go beyond the boundaries of the standard **disciplines**, they are in a position to maximally develop, exercise, and enhance their higher-order thinking skills. The synthesizing and unifying brought on by curriculum integration gives relevancy to learning that takes students to higher levels of thinking.

The real strength of integrating the elementary curriculum is the potential it has for moving children beyond superficial knowledge to an in-depth, multidimensional understanding of a topic. The interdisciplinary nature of integrated education perceives the skills areas of the language arts as processes that evolve rather than as fixed products of literacy; it moves children into provocative discussions, problem solving, interpreting and reinterpreting, reading meaningful material for a real purpose, writing and rewriting, and experimenting with new and engaging ideas. The child's developing knowledge base is used to make applications, to analyze and synthesize data, and to make judgments and evaluations. Curriculum integration provides students with abundant opportunities to exercise higher-order thinking skills.

Curriculum integration allows more opportunities for exercising, practicing, and using multiple intelligences (see Chapter 2 and Figure 4.6) than a curriculum

FIGURE 4.6   Gardner's multiple intelligences

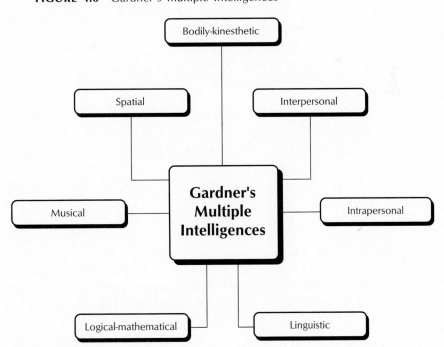

where there is distinct separation of the school subjects. Reporting on how the recognition of multiple intelligences and the application of multiple-intelligence theory at the New City School in St. Louis resulted in a revised curriculum, Hoerr (1994) writes, "We have found that multiple intelligences is more than a theory of intelligence; it is, for us, a philosophy about education with implications for how kids learn, how teachers should teach, and how schools should operate" (p. 29). Enthusiastic about the use of multiple intelligences in developing the integrated curriculum, Armstrong (1994) writes,

> At times, I almost think of Gardner as an archaeologist who has discovered the Rosetta stone of learning. One can use this model to teach virtually anything, from the "schwa" sound to the rain forest and back. The master code of this learning style model is simple: for whatever you wish to teach, link your instructional objective to *words, numbers* or *logic, pictures, music, the body, social interaction,* and/ or *personal experience.* If you can create activities that combine these intelligences in unique ways, so much the better! . . .
>
> When planning a lesson, ask the right questions! Certain questions help me look at the possibilities for involving as many intelligences as possible.
>
> *Linguistic:* How can I use the spoken or written word?
>
> *Logical-Mathematical:* How can I bring in numbers, calculations, logic, classifications, or critical thinking?
>
> *Spatial:* How can I use visual aids, visualization, color, art, metaphor, or **visual organizers**?
>
> *Musical:* How can I bring in music or environmental sounds, or set key points in a rhythm or melody?
>
> *Bodily-Kinesthetic:* How can I involve the whole body, or hands-on experiences?
>
> *Interpersonal:* How can I engage students in peer or cross-age sharing, cooperative learning, or large-group simulation?
>
> *Intrapersonal:* How can I evoke personal feelings or memories, or give students choices? (pp. 26–27)

APPROACHES TO CURRICULUM INTEGRATION

Approaches to integrating the elementary school curriculum generally fall into four categories: integrating through disciplines, integrating through language and literature, integrating through themes, and integrating through issues. (Each of these approaches is presented and explored in depth in Chapters 5–8.) Box 4.4 shows the four major approaches to curriculum integration.

**Box 4.4   FOUR MAJOR APPROACHES
TO CURRICULUM INTEGRATION**

- **Integrating through Disciplines**
  Integrating two or more fairly distinct bodies of knowledge; bringing several categories of knowledge together
- **Integrating through Language and Literature**
  Using rich literature as the vehicle for integrating in and among school subjects
- **Integrating through Themes**
  Integrating with a central theme around which the inquiry and learning will take place
- **Integrating through Issues**
  Integrating through investigating societal issues and problems

---

INTEGRATING THROUGH DISCIPLINES

Some school subjects, like social studies and science, may be called interdisciplinary because they integrate other fairly distinct bodies of knowledge. For example, social studies draws on history, geography, political science, economics, anthropology, sociology, and psychology, while science draws on biology, chemistry, physics, geology, and physiology. It is fairly common, for example, to see history, geography, and other social sciences intermingled, mixed, and blended during the teaching of social studies. In like manner, one commonly finds a fusion of biology, physics, chemistry, and geology during the teaching of elementary school science. Galda (1990) indicates how various kinds of trade books could be valuable in teaching science:

> Every year hundreds of nonfiction books are published. They cover topics ranging from the moon to turnips, from computers to medieval feasts. Some of the most beautiful illustrations in all of children's literature, as well as some of the liveliest prose, can be found in informational books. A good informational book is as artistically arranged as a good picture book, with text and illustrations working together to explain information, to distinguish between fact and opinion, to illuminate concepts, and to inspire young readers to explore some facet of their world. . . .
>
> In addition to nonfiction, [there are] examples of fiction and poetry that could accompany a study of the natural world. One of the nice results of building a topic-focused unit with children's literature is that you get the opportunity to approach the topic in a variety of ways. You

can read about the ecology of a meadow in a nonfiction text, share some poems about its inhabitants with your students, and visit a meadow through a story. Your students' sense of what a meadow is like certainly will be expanded by this multigenre approach to the topic. (p. 322)

This, however, is integrating instruction within a subject rather than between and among school subjects.

Integrating Classroom Instruction between and among School Subjects.
In the larger sense, an integrated curriculum means to integrate instruction between and among school subjects. It spawns the idea of cutting across all subject matter lines, creating a wholly unified program that integrates the various areas of the school curriculum. Jarolimek and Parker (1993) claim that the major strengths of an integrated curriculum lie in the potential for helping children move beyond superficial knowledge to higher-order thinking. Curriculum integration ". . . brings several categories of knowledge together for the purpose of helping children more fully understand the object of study" (p. 339). Maxim (1995) writes, "Elementary schools around the country are moving toward the idea of integrating the various subjects of the curriculum, and social studies appears to be the major area for blending subjects previously taught separately" (p. 23).

Also indicating the ideal nature of social studies as an umbrella for integrating the elementary school curriculum, Berg (1988) writes:

A major goal of the social studies is to help students understand the myriad interactions of people on this planet—past, present, and future. Making sense of the world requires using skills that allow one to read about the many people and places that are scattered about the globe; to use literature to understand the richness of past events and the people who are a part of them; to apply math concepts to more fully understand how numbers have enabled people to numerically manage the complexity of their world. The story of humankind well told requires drawing from all areas of the curriculum. (p. 1)

Already possessing a broad foundation of academic disciplines and already integrating these disciplines within its own content area, social studies is ideally suited to integrate the school subjects of the elementary school. Social studies forms a perfect umbrella for integrating the elementary school curriculum. Integrating traditional content areas under social studies provides students with a curriculum that can help them extend and refine their knowledge and skills in meaningful, connected ways rather than in fragmented pieces.

Social Studies as the Core of an Integrated Approach.   The National Council for the Social Studies is the largest association in the country devoted solely to social studies education. Founded in 1921, the NCSS serves as an umbrella organization for all who are interested in social studies. In 1995, the NCSS had more than 22,000 members in all 50 states, the District of Columbia, and 69 foreign countries. There are more than 110 state and local councils affiliated with the NCSS in their efforts to engage and support educators in strengthening and advocating social studies. The NCSS began publication of its journal, *Social Education,* in 1937 and introduced a journal for elementary grades, *Social Studies and the Young Learner,* in 1988. In addition, the NCSS publishes yearbooks, bulletins, leaflets, position papers, and other documents pertaining to social studies education. The address for the NCSS is:

National Council for the Social Studies
3501 Newark Street, NW
Washington, DC 20036

In late 1994, after a two-year period of intensive work, the NCSS released curriculum standards for teaching social studies. The standards, developed by the NCSS's National Task Force for Social Studies Standards, function as a guide for curriculum development in social studies from kindergarten through grade twelve. Box 4.5 depicts the ten thematic strands around which the social studies standards are based. The standards incorporate learning experiences from many disciplines and recommend a framework for social studies that is truly interdisciplinary and integrates the curriculum significantly.

The Oregon Trail, a microcomputer software simulation published by MECC (the Minnesota Educational Computing Consortium), provides a rich variety of higher-order thinking experiences in an interdisciplinary format. Students form small, cooperative teams to take wagons over the Oregon Trail from Independence, Missouri, to Oregon in the 1840s. Decision making enters the simulation early when the cooperative group must select a wagon leader and then decide during which season of the year the trip will begin. Next, decisions about which supplies to buy take the students into math applications as they use a fixed budget to purchase the supplies they deem appropriate and necessary for the journey. The journey itself is filled with real-life problems of the times and provides students with opportunities to decide on solutions and try them out in the simulation. Depending on the group's success and the amount of time devoted to the project each day, *The Oregon Trail* simulation can last for several days, even weeks, providing students with rich, interdisciplinary learning experiences that are highly integrative across several disciplines and skills areas. Chapter 5 presents an in-depth look at curriculum integration through disciplines.

INTEGRATING THROUGH LANGUAGE AND LITERATURE

No matter what approach is used in integrating the elementary school curriculum, the **subgenres** of children's literature will play a major role in the instructional design. That is especially true, of course, when one chooses to

Box 4.5   NCSS Ten Thematic Strands for Social Studies

Strand One: Culture

Social studies programs should include experiences that provide for the study of the culture and cultural diversity.

Strand Two: Time, Continuity, & Change

Social studies programs should include experiences that provide for the study of the ways human beings view themselves in and over time.

Strand Three: People, Places, & Environments

Social studies programs should include experiences that provide for the study of people, places, and environments.

Strand Four: Individual Development & Identity

Social studies programs should include experiences that provides for the study of individual development and identity.

Strand Five: Individuals, Groups, & Institutions

Social studies programs should include experiences that provide for the study of interactions among individuals, groups, and institutions.

Strand Six: Power, Authority, & Governance

Social studies programs should include experiences that provide for the study of how people create and change structures of power, authority, and governance.

Strand Seven: Production, Distribution, & Consumption

Social studies programs should include experiences that provide for the study of how people organize for the production, distribution, and consumption of goods and services.

Strand Eight: Science, Technology, & Society

Social studies programs should include experiences that provide for the study of relationships among science, technology, and society.

Strand Nine: Global Connections

Social studies programs should include experiences that provide for the study of global connections and interdependence.

Strand Ten: Civic Ideals & Practices

Social studies programs should include experiences that provide for the study of the ideals, principles, and practices of citizenship in a democratic republic.

<small>SOURCE:</small> Adapted from *Curriculum Standards for Social Studies: Expectations of Excellence,* 1994, National Council for the Social Studies. Used with permission.

integrate through language and literature. Figure 4.7 illustrates the subgenres of children's literature that are essential in all approaches to curricular integration.

In many ways, curriculum integration got its major impetus, if not, indeed, its initiation, from the whole language movement. The movement to a whole language philosophy in many elementary schools and classrooms served as a precursor to integrating the elementary school curriculum. Goodman (1986) indicates that whole language teaching comes out of a philosophy of education that provides children with authentic, content-rich reading experiences that integrate language and thinking. In this sense, authentic reading means reading about something, just as people do when they read in the real world and not just contrived, formula-driven basal reader selections. **Content-rich** reading means a wide variety of high-quality books, descriptive materials, and informational resources. Authentic, content-rich reading, thinking, and language experiences lead to learning events that necessarily cut across subject matter boundaries. "Teachers who believe that language is the foundation for all school and future learning, that children learn language by using it, and that language in use is always whole, meaningful, and purposeful tend to create learner-

FIGURE 4.7 The subgenres of children's literature

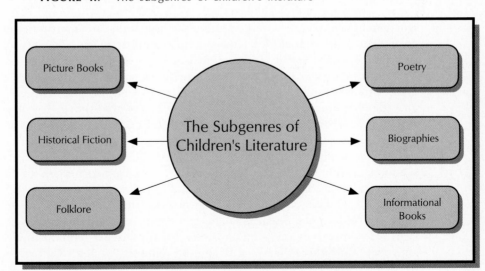

centered, literature-based, integrated classrooms" (Stice, Bertrand, & Bertrand, 1995, p. 94).

In the past few years the progress of whole language approaches in the curriculum of the elementary school has been remarkable. Implementation of whole language approaches has been extensive and has often been the precursor to more extensive curricular integration.

Whole language teaching emphasizes the integration of the skills taught in the language arts. Rather than teaching reading, writing, speaking, listening, and the subskills pertaining to language arts, such as spelling, handwriting, and grammar, separately and in isolation, they are integrated. Skills instruction in reading and writing, for example, incorporating the subskills of word perception, comprehension, vocabulary development, spelling, grammar, punctuation, capitalization, and handwriting, might be integrated through children's literature. Whole language is defined by Fredericks (1992) "as the integration of reading, writing, speaking, and listening into a context that is meaningful to the child" (p. 9). Bereiter and Scardamalia (1987) write that integrating the teaching of language arts skills has resulted in a new literacy **empowerment** for students which didn't exist before. Tchudi (1994) indicates that the whole language approach, emphasizing as it does the role of reading and writing throughout the curriculum and establishing relationships among and between all curriculum subjects, creates an integrated curriculum. Hennings (1986), too, writes that whole language instruction has a natural propensity for integrating the curriculum because it integrates thinking, listening, speaking, writing, and reading activities into communicating meaningful content from the social and natural sciences.

Integrating through Themes

A very promising format for integrating the subjects of the elementary school curriculum is the use of a central theme around which the inquiry and learning will take place. Theme studies and thematic units are instructional designs created around a central idea. Thematic units emphasize key concepts in language arts, mathematics, social studies, and science. Activities within units integrate skills from a variety of subjects and curricular areas. The integrated nature of theme studies brings relevancy and meaning to learning. The scope of activities in a thematic unit provides an accurate evaluation of student learning through authentic assessments with journals, **anecdotal records**, checklists, conferences, student self-evaluation, and portfolios (Meinbach, Rothlein, & Fredericks, 1995).

Theme studies are of rather short duration, perhaps just one period in a school day, while thematic units are extended over longer periods of time—days, weeks, and even longer. The thematic unit approach to teaching is not new, having had its inauguration during the days of John Dewey and the Progressive Education Movement. Figure 4.8 illustrates part of a unit plan from around the year 1928 which derives from an outline of the Project Method then in use by Miss Nell Curtis, teacher at the Lincoln School, Teachers College, Columbia

Reading

Reference materials pertaining to topics under discussion, found in school library or at home. Children's books on Leif and Thorkel, Viking stories, early sea people. Boat book prepared by other third grade; material prepared by student teachers.

Science

How can we tell if our boats will float and balance? Try out in delta table. Three experiments: Why do some objects float and why do some sink? How do people know how much to put into a boat before it will sink?

History

The *Half-Moon* directed interest to Hendrick Hudson and his ship. Historic ships: *Santa Maria, Mayflower.* Reference work, reading and discussion about: Vikings—color and kinds of clothing, what they ate, kinds of houses they had, what were their boats like?, story of Leif Ericson, the gods of the Vikings, Viking beliefs; Phoenicians—scenery, boats, people, trade, beliefs, clothing, cities, industries, etc.; Egyptians—scenery, country, boats, beliefs, tools, writing, etc.; Story of the building of *Solomon's Temple.* Early Mediterranean peoples.

Industrial Arts

Construction of boats: making pattern, shaping hull, making sail, making keel, casting weight for keel, making rack for boat, testing boat. How boats developed from early times. Difficulty of building a toy boat so it will balance in water. Kinds of sailboats. Need for different kinds of boats. Different methods of propelling boats. What makes boats float? Modern boat propulsion. Different uses of boats today.

Arithmetic

Measuring for boat patterns and measurements in boat making. Figuring the number of board feet used by class in building boat racks. Arithmetic problems in connection with science experiment of water displacement and floating objects. What is a gram? What is a cubit? Dimensions of Solomon's Temple compared with those of Lincoln School.

STUDY OF BOATS
Third Grade
The Lincoln School
Circa 1928

Dramatization-Music

Play-story of Leif Ericson, spontaneously prepared by class. Old Gaellic lullaby. "Volga Boat Song." "Sail, Bonnie Boat."

Geography

Pictures of boats from newspapers that interested children in world geography. Geography related to countries studied. Norway—country, climate, people and occupations; Phoenicia—country, climate, people, trading routes, daily life of early people compared with that of today; Egypt—country, climate, trading, etc. Map interest: Norway, showing ancient home of the Vikings. The Mediterranean countries. Globe in frequent use to locate places mentioned. Outline world map; locating countries. Interest in determining distances (reading scales on a map). How far from Norway to Phoenicia; from Norway to America? Building Lower Manhattan on floor with blocks to exhibit ships. Map drawn on floor showing buildings in New York City that helped most with sea travel.

Composition-Literature

Stories written about the trip to see *Half-Moon.* Stories of other trips by individual children. Original poems about boats and the sea. Labels and invitations for boat exhibit. Written and oral reports about boats, Vikings, Phoenicia, and Egypt. Stories for bulletin, room paper, council news, or absent class members, telling of class interest and study.

Fine Arts

Sketching and painting pictures of *Half-Moon.* Sketching and painting boat models. Drawing blackboard frieze showing history of boats. Ten easel pictures showing story of Leif Ericson. Cut paper pictures of boats. Painting Egyptian boats seen at museum. Painting Viking pictures showing clothing. Painting modern boats. Making clay tablet.

FIGURE 4.8 Excerpts from a unit plan, circa 1928

SOURCE: Adapted from H. Rugg and A. Shumaker (1928). *The Child-Centered School.* New York: World Book (pp. 100–101).

University, and reprinted on pages 100–101 in *The Child-Centered School* by Harold A. Rugg and Ann Shumaker, published in New York by World Book. The information on the chart outlines what Miss Curtis did in her units on the study of boats nearly 70 years ago! Note the similarity to present-day thematic units.

Today experienced teachers recall a time when the *unit method* was taught to them during their teacher preparation programs in college. In the 1980s, however, the unit approach was frowned upon and fell into disfavor when a fragmented curriculum became the vogue. But in the mid-1990s, integration across the curriculum became the trend, and thematic units began resurging as the focal point of bringing different content areas together (Maxim, 1995). Theme studies and thematic units are becoming the heart of approaches that result in rather extensive integration of the curriculum in the elementary school, significant curriculum integration at the middle school level, and some curriculum integration even at the high school level.

Many have suggested theme studies as an approach to interdisciplinary education. Viewing learning as interrelational, Taba (1962) sees a kinship between the elements of learning, defining those elements as (1) the materials of learning; (2) the abilities, interests, and nature of the learner; and (3) the sequence, form, and structure of the learning. Taba's curriculum development is designed around these seven steps:

1. Diagnosing needs
2. Formulating objectives
3. Selecting the content
4. Organizing the content
5. Selecting the learning experiences
6. Organizing the learning experiences
7. Determining what to evaluate and how to evaluate it

A four-step plan for developing theme studies suggested by Jacobs and Borland (1986) includes:

1. Selecting a theme
2. Brainstorming for topics and ideas to associate with the theme
3. Formulating questions that might guide the probe of the theme
4. Designing and implementing activities to aid inquiry into the theme

In greater detail, but similar in overall nature, Martinello and Cook (1994) suggest the following guidelines in planning and designing theme studies:

1. Select a theme topic in a cooperative manner
2. Use a web or graphic organizer to build an abundance of ideas
3. Develop questions that can be visualized through various subjects
4. Identify concepts associated with the theme
5. Meet guidelines established by the school, the district, and the state

6. Map the general investigative sequence to be used
7. Create and craft questions for student inquiry
8. Develop ideas for cooperative group activities
9. Specify content and process objectives
10. Plan and plot learning activities
11. Select and design culminating activities and projects
12. Utilize resources to investigate questions
13. Determine strategies for record keeping, reporting, and ongoing assessment

Meinbach, Rothlein, and Fredericks (1995), in similar fashion, suggest the following five areas for consideration in designing effective and successful thematic units:

1. Selecting the theme
2. Organizing the theme
3. Gathering resources and materials
4. Designing activities and projects
5. Implementing the unit

In *selecting theme topics,* teachers find that themes can come from a variety of sources. Some of the areas from which theme topics may be selected include curricular topics that frequently appear in textbooks or curriculum guides; issues and concerns that affect students and their families directly; **problems** that pervade and plague much of humankind; special events such as local, state, and national celebrations and holidays; student interests like hobbies and leisure-time pursuits; and literary interests that include studying related books, books by a particular author, and genres of children's literature.

Organizing for thematic teaching involves determining purposes and objectives for the unit, and it is at this point that aspects of the elementary curriculum are interrelated and integrated. Organization also encompasses developing the skills and activities that will be used to nurture and cultivate understanding and appreciation of the unit's substance. Chapter 7 presents specific and detailed strategies for organizing the theme, including **theme-webbing** and **bookwebbing**.

A host of *materials and resources* are gathered and utilized in thematic units to provide students with abundant opportunities for student-participatory learning. A primary consideration in gathering materials and resources is recognition of the types of literature that will be useful in the unit. In addition to the literature resources, other materials will include various printed resources (such as newspapers, magazines, journals, and maps), visual resources (such as videos, filmstrips, and CD-ROMs), and artifacts (the types of artifacts appropriate for a particular unit will be dependent on the topic of the unit; for example, a unit on simple machines might include pliers, screwdrivers, screws, and pulleys).

Designing activities and projects that are well orchestrated and designed to assist students in comprehending and developing appreciation for the specific topics and general ideas included in the unit is critical. It is important to recognize that thematic units are not arbitrary, indiscriminate collections of random activities. Indeed, activities and projects are included in the unit for specific reasons, such as for focusing on the interrelatedness of concepts; being both motivational and instructional for the student; providing revelations; and allowing for self-paced, cooperative, and **collaborative learning**. Chapter 7 contains a penetrating look at activity development in thematic units.

Implementing a thematic unit has several options that can take equally worthy avenues. For example, work on the unit may be done for part of each day over a period of several days; the unit may dominate the total day for one or more days; the unit may be pursued in two or more subject areas only (for example, science, social studies, and language arts) for a period of days; or the unit may be intermingled with the regular curriculum organization in an intermittent manner for a period of time. There are multiple options in both the design of thematic units and in the use of thematic units (Meinbach, Rothlein, & Fredericks, 1995). Chapter 7 presents an in-depth look at curriculum integration through themes.

INTEGRATING THROUGH ISSUES

"Give students a problem that really connects with their world, empower them to generate solutions, and watch the serious thinking that follows" (Savoie & Hughes, 1994, p. 54). Reporting on a two-week project that provided a real-world context for examining the issues involved in a problem their students found in the *Wall Street Journal,* Savoie and Hughes (1994) found that issues and problems provide a strongly motivating mechanism for having students come to grips with significant subject matter. They found problem-based learning to be particularly motivating and suggested the following procedures in pursuing an issues approach:

1. Begin with a problem.
2. Ensure that the problem connects with the students' world.
3. Organize the subject matter around the problem, not around the disciplines.
4. Give students the major responsibility for shaping and directing their own learning.
5. Use small teams as the context for most learning.
6. Require students to demonstrate what they have learned through a product or a performance. (p. 54)

Hartoonian (1992) reported on a long-term experiment called Project 2061, which places strong emphasis on an integrated curriculum through the inclusion of social and natural problems that persevere in the world, thus, an issues approach to integration. Project 2061 is designed to better educate twenty-first-century Americans in science, but is very integrational because of its strong emphasis on the nature of social and natural problems that persist in the world.

Significant issues and problems abound in our world. There are societal issues, scientific issues, environmental issues, medical issues, religious issues, legal issues, philosophical issues, moral issues, media issues, and more, and such problems in the world as AIDS, cancer, nuclear war, and pollution, which provide the gist for integral and consequential integration of the curriculum. For example, in looking at the issues revolving around media and their influence, including truth and veracity, the following two quotations, one by Mark Twain (from "How I Edited an Agricultural Paper," a short story that appeared in 1870) and the other from journalist Walter Lippmann (from his book, *The Public Philosophy,* chapter 2, 1955), could serve as a launching pad to all sorts of meaningful inquiry and investigation that would integrate the curriculum naturally and meaningfully. Mark Twain said:

> You try to tell me anything about the newspaper business! Sir, I have been through it from Alpha to Omaha, and I tell you that the less a man knows the bigger the noise he makes and the higher the salary he commands. (Twain, in Neider (ed.), 1957)

Walter Lippmann said:

> When distant and unfamiliar and complex things are communicated to great masses of people, the truth suffers a considerable and often a radical distortion. The complex is made over into the simple, the hypothetical into the dogmatic, and the relative into an absolute. (Lippman, 1955, Chapter 2, Section 3)

In studies of American history during the time of the Civil War and the presidency of Abraham Lincoln, the issue of slavery often becomes a focal point. In that regard, the following quotation by Abraham Lincoln regarding slavery could be a launching pad for significant curricular integration:

> As I would not be a slave, so I would not be a master. This expresses my idea of democracy.

And the following diametrically opposed remarks concerning the controversial issue of abortion present many implications for integrating the curriculum. From Pope John Paul II:

> The cemetery of the victims of human cruelty in our century is extended to include yet another vast cemetery, that of the unborn. (*Observer,* June 9, 1991)

From Mother Teresa, winner of the Nobel Peace Prize:

> The greatest destroyer of peace is abortion because if a mother can kill her own child, what is left but for me to kill you and you to kill me? There is nothing between. (Nobel Peace Prize Lecture, 1979)

From Ruth Bader Ginsberg, United States Supreme Court justice:

> The emphasis must be not on the right to abortion but on the right to privacy and reproductive control. (*Ms.*, April 1974)

Issues and problems can provide a platform where real and meaningful curricular integration can occur. It is an area where individual learners can collaborate with other learners and engage in a plethora of authentic activities and enterprises integrated across subject lines in pursuit and fulfillment of learning. Chapter 8 presents an in-depth look at curriculum integration through issues.

BARRIERS TO INTEGRATING THE CURRICULUM

Personal barriers and time barriers often hinder the launching of integrated curricula in the elementary school. Teachers develop personal barriers to integrating the curriculum when they become so identified with their current teaching assignment that they become locked into being a math teacher only, a language arts teacher only, a science teacher only. Teachers in such circumstances need to understand that integrating disciplines will not in some way taint or dilute the subjects they hold dear but, rather, will enhance relevancy and understanding for students.

Time can also be a significant obstacle when educators seek to initiate interdisciplinary approaches to education. Exuberant supporters of interdisciplinary education often want to jump right into curriculum integration and go full speed ahead. Often, however, full speed ahead turns into dead stop when exuberant interdisciplinarians run afoul of the time barrier. Rapid changes are not often well accepted in the education community. More success can be achieved when a course of gradual change is followed. Introducing change gradually makes the conversion more palatable to those who are dissenters and oppose the changes that interdisciplinary education will bring (Jacobs, 1991). Box 4.6 points out major barriers to establishing an integrated curriculum.

Acknowledging and applauding meaningful curriculum integration as an educational goal that is both admirable and worthy, Routman (1991) recognizes that curriculum integration is often difficult to achieve because of **constraints** related to theoretical understandings, time, administrative support, resources, and curriculum requirements. Routman elaborates on the constraints:

Box 4.6   Barriers to Establishing
            an Integrated Curriculum

- understanding the theory behind integrated curriculum
- need for long blocks of uninterrupted time
- gaining administrative support
- access to abundant resources and materials
- constraints often imposed by curricular guides

Constraints Based on Theoretical Understandings

Before integration can take place, we need an understanding of the theory underlying children's language acquisition, an in-depth knowledge of the literature and resources being used, and an understanding of the curriculum. Without this knowledge of theory and practice, teachers are likely to "basalize" units with only superficial interdisciplinary connections. With a large majority of teachers acting as scripted technicians managing preset commercial programs, we are still a long way from being curriculum decision makers. Ongoing staff development efforts need to include helping teachers to understand integration and develop meaningful integrated language units.

Constraints Based on Time

We need to work with our administrators to create uninterrupted blocks of instructional time in daily schedules. On the elementary level, self-contained classrooms—with no switching of rooms for various subjects—promote flexibility and offer opportunities for integration. Many teachers find the only way they can tie language arts and reading to the content areas and have time for both is through integration, made possible by large blocks of uninterrupted time.

Additionally, teachers must have release time to plan with colleagues, research topics, write and adjust curriculum, and gather resources. It is unrealistic to expect individual teachers to devote hours of planning on their own time. While common planning time across grade levels is a start, it is not sufficient. Teachers cannot be expected to implement an integrated curriculum without several hours a month of release time for planning. While I noticed that some administrators in Australia were willing to make such a time commitment, I have rarely seen it here in the States.

In one district teachers were expected to meet by grade levels after school every few months to share ideas and plan and write units. One angry teacher commented that because release time had not been provided, many teachers would continue to do "whatever is easier."

Constraints Based on Administrative Support

An integrated curriculum requires a fully committed administrator who values and understands the approach and is willing to give teachers time and funds to develop it. Teachers cannot get a budget for curriculum development and the purchase of resources and equipment without administrative support.

Constraints Based on Resources

Beyond collections of fiction, there is a need for in-class libraries with quality literature of all types. Nonfiction materials especially—magazines, newspapers, encyclopedias, information books—do not presently exist in most classrooms. There is also a need for flexible, open library times for students—not standard practice in many school libraries.

Constraints Based on Curriculum Requirements

Teachers and administrators are constrained by course objectives and state guidelines. Some of these are necessary to ensure that important concepts are developed in logical sequence at particular grade levels. However, many districts further constrain themselves by adopting basal texts and social studies and science textbooks using publishers' guidelines as a total program. These texts should be used as one of many resources—to be referred to, not adhered to.

Reflections

An integrated language curriculum focuses on important concepts through topic and theme development in a manner that is not contrived. Students come to understand their world better through engaging in relevant school experiences. While interdisciplinary integration is a desired long-range goal, we need to begin by working toward integration in smaller areas; we might begin with literature study and then add social studies, science, and math. We need to integrate the language arts and the visual arts—reading, writing, speaking, listening, art, music, drama, dance—into the various subject areas instead of trying to bring every subject into the language arts. The language arts can then be the medium for integrating the subject areas. Finally, as in all difficult transitions, we need to move slowly and allow ourselves time for continuous risk taking, reflection, and rethinking.[1]

Cullinan (1993) proposes a gradual curriculum integration by introducing literature as the major instructional resource in subjects like science and social studies. By making literature an integral part of the learning experiences in

---

[1] Reprinted by permission of Regie Routman, *Invitations: Changing as teachers and learners K-12* (Heinemann, A division of Reed Elsevier Inc., Portsmouth, N.H., 1991).

subjects like social studies and science, curriculum integration is begun gradually and accomplished without a great deal of added effort or disruption.

Using Caution in Making Curricular Changes

There are many favorable aspects to be realized in utilizing discipline approaches, language and literature approaches, theme approaches, and issue approaches to integrate the elementary school curriculum. But educators need to recognize some of the pitfalls that hinder undertaking innovative curriculum practices. Inexperienced teachers, for example, may find it difficult to know when to use integrated activities and when it is more fruitful to examine topics separately. Confusion is the result when teachers try to integrate curriculum areas when there is no meaningful interrelatedness among the concepts being pursued or when children are presented with activities for which they are unprepared.

Perhaps the best approach is for one to be eclectic. Don't choose only one method for instruction. Instead, exercise professional judgment and select the plan best suited for the job at hand. Sometimes an integrated approach will not fit the needs and purposes as well as a discipline-based plan, and in such instances the teacher should be wise enough to select the best strategy for the task at hand. It makes good sense, for example, to look at colonial American history through literature, but it may not be as wise to assume that map reading skills or mathematics skills are adequately taught while examining a map used by explorers in the Americas (Jarolimek & Parker, 1993). Map reading skills needed to understand the legends used and the other information that such a map would convey might best be taught as a distinct area of instruction. The same would be true for basic math skills needed to accurately measure distances on the map.

Jacobs (1991) points out that while the integrated curriculum often helps children acquire targeted skills and concepts from various disciplines in a more effective manner, "there are times when skills and concepts are best addressed through the singular focus of one discipline. In essence then, both perspectives are necessary" (p. 22). Such a dual emphasis differs from past attempts at curriculum integration, where the two approaches were seen as opposing points of view. Today, many teachers across the country carefully examine their curricular needs and provide students with integrated experiences when they are appropriate and best meet the needs at hand, and with a singularly focused, discipline-based experience when it is more appropriate.

Summary

While traditional plans partition school subjects into distinct divisions, curriculum integration merges, intermingles, blends, and fuses the content of different subjects in meaningful ways. This synthesizing often provides more opportunity for higher-order thinking among students, the use of multiple intelligences, and a reorganization of the physical setting to incorporate collaborative learning.

The whole-language movement served as precursor to integrated curricula, and approaches to integration rely heavily on language and literature, themes, issues, and content from the disciplines. Children's literature is a mainstay in all approaches to curricular integration.

In general, opportunities for both teachers and students are expanded by the holistic, multidimensional, collaborative, and cooperative environment of an integrated curriculum. But there are times when an integrated approach will not fit the needs and purposes of the job at hand, and a discipline-based plan might work best. In any event, remember that curriculum integration is not an "all or nothing" proposition. A teacher may very well be eclectic and use a variety of approaches but be wise enough to select the best strategy for the task at hand.

ACTIVITY ONE

PURPOSE

The purpose of this activity is to design a classroom that would support the teacher as a facilitator.

PROCEDURE

Divide into three groups. Each group is to work cooperatively and collaboratively to design a classroom where the arrangement of furniture and equipment is conducive to teaching in a facilitating way. The groups will use large posters or transparencies to present their work to the other groups. Discussion on each group's presentation should ensue regarding the pros and cons of the design.

ACTIVITY TWO

PURPOSE

The purpose of this activity is to present a panel discussion for the faculty in a school seeking to develop an integrated curriculum.

PROCEDURE

One person should be selected to be the moderator and panel members should be selected according to the following tasks:

- support an approach to integration based on disciplines
- support an approach to integration based on language and literature
- support an approach to integration based on themes
- support an approach to integration based on issues

Under the moderator's direction, each panel member will present information on the topic assigned. After all panel members have made presentations, there should be an opportunity for questions from the audience. Lively discussion should be encouraged.

STUDY QUESTIONS

1. Contrast the functioning of a teacher-as-director with the functioning of a teacher-as-facilitator. As a practicing teacher, describe how you might make a personal transition from being a director of instruction to being a facilitator of learning.
2. Describe how whole language teaching has often been a precursor to an integrated curriculum.
3. Using thematic units is not an "all or nothing" proposition, and there are several alternative possibilities for implementing thematic teaching that range from intermittent use to using themes all the time. Describe several possible alternatives in which you might use thematic units in a fifth grade classroom.
4. Using one of the ten thematic strands developed by the NCSS, create a scenario for an elementary class where that particular strand could serve as a focal point for integrating the curriculum.
5. Because you are an elementary teacher who has had significant success in teaching with thematic units, your school principal has asked you to speak at an upcoming faculty meeting about thematic teaching. What will you say?
6. What constraints and barriers may be encountered by those wishing to integrate the curriculum?

BIBLIOGRAPHY

Allen, H., Splittgerber, F., & Manning, M. (1993). *Teaching and learning in the middle level school.* New York: Merrill.

Armstrong, T. (1994). Multiple intelligences: Seven ways to approach curriculum. *Educational Leadership, 52* (3), 26–28.

Barr, I., & McGuire, M. (1993). Social studies and effective stories. *Social Studies and the Young Learner, 5* (3), 6–8, 11.

Bean, J. (1992). Creating an integrative curriculum: Making the connections. *National Association of Secondary School Principals Bulletin, 16* (11), 46–54.

Bereiter, C., & Scardamalia, M. (1987). An attainable version of high literacy: Approaches to teaching higher-order skills in reading and writing. *Curriculum Inquiry, 17* (1), 9–30.

Berg, M. (1988). Integrating ideas for social studies. *Social Studies and the Young Learner, 1 (2),* pull-out feature.

Charbonneau, M., and Reider, B. (1995). *The integrated elementary classroom: A developmental model of education for the 21st century.* Boston: Allyn and Bacon.

Chatton, B. (1989). Using literature across the curriculum. In J. Hickman & B. E. Cullinan (Eds.), Child*ren's literature in the classroom: Weaving Charlotte's web* (pp. 61–70). Needham Heights, Mass.: Christopher-Gordon.

Cheek, E., & Cheek, M. (1983). *Reading instruction through content teaching.* Columbus, Ohio: Merrill.

Cullinan, B. (1993). *Fact and fiction across the curriculum.* Newark, N.J.: International Reading Association.

Danielson, K., & LaBonty, J. (1994). *Integrating reading and writing through children's literature.* Boston: Allyn and Bacon.

Dobson, D., Monson, J., & Smith, J. (1992). A case study on integrating history and reading instruction through literature. *Social Education, 56* (7), 370–375.

Drake, S. (1993). *Planning integrated curriculum.* Alexandria, Va.: Association of Supervision and Curriculum Development.

Fogarty, R. (1991). Ten ways to integrate curriculum. *Educational Leadership, 49* (10), 24–26.

Fredericks, A. (1992). *The integrated curriculum.* Englewood, Colo.: Teacher Ideas Press.

Fredericks, A., Meinbach, A., & Rothlein, L. (1993). *Thematic units.* New York: HarperCollins.

Galda, L. (1990). Children's books: Our natural world. *Reading Teacher, 41,* 322–326.

Gamberg, R., Kwak, W., Hutchings, M., & Altheim, J. (1988). *Learning and loving it: Theme studies in the classroom.* Portsmouth, N.H.: Heinemann.

Gardner, H. (1993). *Multiple intelligences: The theory in practice.* New York: Basic Books.

Gehrke, N. (1991). Explorations of teachers' development of integrative curriculums. *Journal of Curriculum and Supervision, 6* (2), 107–117.

Ginsberg, R. B. (1991). *Ms. 1* (5), p. 86. New York: Communications, Inc.

Goodman, K. (1986). *What's whole in whole language?* Portsmouth, N. H.: Heinemann.

Hartoonian, M. (1994). *The knowledge connection.* Madison, Wisc.: Department of Public Instruction.

Hennings, D. (1986). *Communication in action: Teaching the language arts* (3rd ed.). Boston: Houghton Mifflin.

Hoerr, T. (1994). How the New City School applies the multiple intelligences. *Educational Leadership, 52* (3), 29–33.

Jacobs, H. (1989). The growing need for interdisciplinary curriculum content. In H. Jacobs (Ed.), *Interdisciplinary curriculum: Design and implementation* (pp. 1–12). Alexandria, Va.: Association for Supervision and Curriculum Development.

Jacobs, H. (1991). On interdisciplinary education: A conversation. *Educational Leadership, 49* (10), 24–26.

Jacobs, H., & Borland, J. (Fall, 1986). The interdisciplinary concept model: Theory and practice. *Gifted Child Quarterly, 30* (4), 159–163.

Jarolimek, J., & Parker, W. (1993). *Social studies in elementary education.* New York: Macmillan.

Lazear, D. (1994). *Multiple intelligence approaches to assessment: Solving the assessment conundrum.* Tucson: Zephyr Press.

Lippman, W. (1955). *Essays in the Public Philosophy* (p. 136). Boston: Little, Brown.

Lipson, M., Valencia, S., Wixson, K., & Peters, C. (1993). Integration and thematic teaching: Integration to improve teaching and learning. *Language Arts, 70* (4), 252–263.

Martinello, M., & Cook, G. (1994). *Interdisciplinary inquiry in teaching and learning.* New York: Merrill.

Maxim, G. (1995). *Social studies and the elementary school child* (5th ed.). Englewood Cliffs, N.J.: Merrill.

Meinbach, A., Rothlein, L, & Fredericks, A. (1995). *The complete guide to thematic units: Creating the integrated curriculum.* Norwood, Mass.: Christopher-Gordon.

Michaelis, J. (1992). *Social studies for children: A guide to basic instruction.* Boston: Allyn and Bacon.

Moss, J. (1984). *Focus on units in literature: A handbook for elementary school teachers.* Urbana, Ill.: National Council of Teachers of English.

Routman, R. (1991). *Invitations: Changing as teachers and learners K–12.* Portsmouth, N.H.: Heinemann.

Savoie, J., & Hughes, A. (1994). Problem-based learning as classroom solution. *Educational Leadership, 52* (3), 54–57.

Stice, C., Bertrand, J., & Bertrand, N. (1995). *Integrating reading and the other language arts.* Belmont, Calif.: Wadsworth.

Sunal, C. (1990). *Early childhood social studies.* Columbus, Ohio: Merrill.

Taba, H. (1962). *Curriculum development: Theory and practice.* New York: Harcourt Brace Jovanovich.

Tchudi, S. (1994). *Integrated language arts in the elementary school.* Belmont, Calif.: Wadsworth.

Twain, Mark (1870). How I edited an agricultural paper. In Charles Neider (Ed.), *The comic Mark Twain reader,* 1977 (pp. 20–32). New York: Doubleday.

White, E. B. (1952). *Charlotte's web.* New York: Harper & Row.

Willis, S. (1995). Making integrated curriculum a reality. *Association for Supervision and Curriculum Development Education Update, 37* (4), 4.

Zarnowski, M. (1990). *Learning with biographies: A reading and writing approach.* Washington, D.C.: National Council for the Social Studies and National Council of Teachers of English.

PART

2

APPROACHES TO
AN INTEGRATED
CURRICULUM

CHAPTER

5

INTEGRATING
THE CURRICULUM
THROUGH DISCIPLINES

CHAPTER OBJECTIVES

After reading this chapter you should be able to:

1. Describe how to integrate the curriculum through the use of the disciplines
2. Describe how to integrate the curriculum through the use of science and social studies
3. Describe how to integrate the curriculum through the use of mathematics
4. Describe how to integrate the curriculum through the use of the fine arts

The integrated curriculum focuses not on disciplines but on themes and problems. Consequently it seems contradictory to consider how to integrate the curriculum through the disciplines. The contradiction, however, is illusory. The themes or problems used to develop an integrated program must begin somewhere and that somewhere is within the disciplines. For example, students at the fourth grade level enter into the study of pollution within their community. The problem is rooted in the discipline of science although it easily incorporates social studies, mathematics, and language arts and could incorporate the fine arts through the creation of posters or the writing of songs and jingles. As a second example, consider a sixth grade class beginning its investigations into the ways in which individuals and peoples communicate with one another. Depending on the slant developed by the teacher and the students, the core discipline could be the social studies or the fine arts. From a social studies perspective students could look at the development of communications systems over history, at how languages relate to one another, and at how culture helps to determine how individuals within a society and how societies communicate with one another. From a fine arts perspective students can investigate various forms of music and their uses, visual arts from realism to cubism to illustrations and cartoons, and dance forms from classical ballet to country line dances to ritual dances in various cultures. Although the separate disciplines may no longer be kept as separate entities within the curriculum, they still form the foundation for the development of an integrated approach to curriculum.

The disciplines are important as a starting point for the selection of topics within the curriculum, but that is not their only importance. The disciplines are important as a source of security to the teacher in the midst of change from the traditional to the integrated curriculum.

Although junior and senior high school teachers are most frequently associated with a particular discipline, elementary school teachers also feel a certain identification with the disciplines. For the elementary teacher, the identification is generally with the discipline in which he or she has the greatest strength or feels the greatest competence. By selecting the themes or problems from a discipline of strength, elementary classroom teachers within the integrated curriculum are more likely to feel secure working with an integrated approach. And when teachers feel secure in a particular area, they are more likely to try a new approach, to allow students to develop individual interests, and to work with students in the development of an area of study. And teachers who feel secure integrating around one area are more likely to make the attempt to integrate in other areas.

In working with the integrated curriculum, both teachers and administrators need to make certain changes in their views of how planning and daily scheduling take place. First, although the teachers involved in the integrated approach do plan the theme or problem, much of the learning is planned through interaction between the students and the teacher. No longer is the teacher completely responsible for all planning relevant to the classroom.

Second, advanced planning in terms of specific lessons may be difficult. In the integrated curriculum, lessons dealing with specific skills are developed when necessity requires rather than when textbook scope and sequence dictate. As a consequence, the teacher may be required to develop a lesson almost instantaneously. Thus, the teacher must have a wide range of teaching strategies at his or her fingertips. For example, second grade students may be investigating a watermelon to determine its characteristics. They have little difficulty using a tape measure to measure the circumferences of the fruit: the distance around the thickest part and the distance around the longest part. They have no difficulty weighing the fruit on a bathroom scale and reading the digital readout. Then they decide to find out how much pulp there is in relation to the total weight. The only problem is that their subtraction skills are not yet ready to handle subtraction of two two-digit numbers. At this point, the teacher presents the children with a lesson on how to subtract. Advanced planning in this case is virtually impossible; instead, the teacher must rely on his or her professional knowledge.

Third, in school systems where teachers are required to hand in lesson plans at the start of a week, such extensive planning will not be possible. Far more flexibility in teaching is needed in the integrated curriculum than is allowed by such a practice. Fourth, scheduling of time no longer is based on individual disciplines but rather on large blocks of time in which children are involved in their interdisciplinary researches; many subject areas are covered during a single block. Finally, both teachers and administrators must accept the idea that skill-specific scope and sequence charts and timetables for skill development will no longer be appropriate for grade levels or school systems.

In the following section, integrating through science or social studies is used as a model for the development of an integrated approach to curriculum. These disciplines are considered together because they are similar in nature and because they frequently overlap in terms of concepts considered. On the other hand, the areas of mathematics and fine arts provide certain unique aspects that need to be considered separately.

PLANNING FOR INTEGRATING THROUGH SCIENCE OR SOCIAL STUDIES

Classrooms utilizing an integrated curriculum sometimes appear to be chaotic, with individual children working on some projects, small groups working on others, and the teacher conferencing with individual children or working with small groups to develop skills. This apparent chaos is only that: apparent. In reality, the use of a discipline-centered integrated approach requires a great deal of planning if the program is to function efficiently and effectively.

Planning for the discipline-centered integrated curriculum based on science or social studies follows certain steps: problem selection, grade level planning, teacher planning, teacher-student planning. The foundation for this planning is an agreement by the teachers and school administrators involved that integration is the best strategy for curriculum development within the school.

PROBLEM SELECTION

The discipline-based integrated curriculum begins with teachers **brainstorming**. The purpose of this brainstorming session is to develop a list of themes that can be used within the integrated curriculum. At the problem selection level, three steps are followed.

In step 1 of selecting the problem, the teachers involved in the planning must decide whether to focus on the discipline of science or the discipline of social studies. Once the discipline is selected, the teachers then brainstorm any possible themes or topics associated with that discipline. All suggestions are listed on large sheets of paper so that they can be in full view of the teachers. During the brainstorming session, no attempt is made to separate themes or problems from simple topics, to decide which are "good" and which are "bad," or to assign grade levels. If a more focused approach is desired, the discipline of science or social studies may be narrowed somewhat. In this case, teachers may consider biological science, physical science, or earth-space science or within the social studies consider history, economics, geography, anthropology, sociology, or political science. The problem with this narrowing is that it limits the range of brainstorming and so may result in a severely limited curriculum. However, when teachers have difficulty coming up with topics, they may be helped by a slightly narrower focus at the start of the brainstorming session.

In step 2 of selecting the problem, teachers begin to consider these lists and to separate topics from themes or problems. At this point, it may be beneficial for teachers to review what is meant by a topic, theme, or problem.

Topic.   A topic is generally a narrowly focused content area. For example, characteristics of vertebrates is a topic in science and the Battle of Bunker Hill is a topic in social studies. As can be seen, these are limited not only in scope but in subject matter areas. Topics are generally specific to the discipline and show little possibility for integrating the total curriculum.

Theme.   According to Walmsley (1994, p. 3), a theme is "something substantive and worth exploring; it provides teachers and students with a focus for their teaching and learning. A theme is composed of appropriate activities that explore topics that make up, relate to, or stem from the central idea. Thus, a theme comprises both meaning (the central idea) and structure (the way in which the central idea is explored)." Within a thematic topic, the skills of the discipline are secondary to the concepts of the theme. A theme such as "the westward expansion" can be used as an organizing base for activities dealing with history, art, physical education, science, mathematics, music, and geography. The theme becomes the focal point for study, but does not generally include a problem relevant to the present lives of the children in the class. In addition to providing a focal point for study, good themes allow for the development of cultural diversity and for a variety of viewpoints, thus raising the possibility of disagreement among students. Disagreement can then lead to investigation of the many sides of a single issue. Finally, good themes allow for interaction between students and teachers in developing the thrust of study.

Problem.   A problem is a real-world situation to which students must bring content information from a wide variety of sources to arrive at a solution. A problem differs from a theme in that the theme provides a framework about which to gather information while a problem requires that the information be used toward a solution. "Endangered species" can be a theme if learning revolves around investigating which species are endangered and why. This same area of study can be a problem in a community where an old zoo exists and the community wants to develop a more modern zoo where endangered species can be housed and bred for later release into the wild. The problem then is: How can the zoo be reconstructed to provide for endangered species?

In the following discussion themes as means of integrating the curriculum will be considered, followed by a consideration of problems as a means to integration.

Step 3 in selecting the problem begins once the list of brainstormed ideas has been narrowed by the deletion of topics. This does not mean, however, that topics should be deleted without discussion. It is quite possible that some of the topics may, through discussion, be expanded into themes or restated as problems. For example, the topic of the water cycle may be reworked into the theme "cycles," which could include not only the water cycle but also life cycles, the rock cycle, the oxygen-carbon dioxide cycle, and other natural cycles.

Once the list has been culled to delete simple topics or the topics have been rewritten into themes, then teachers should work together to decide which of the themes should be considered at the various grade levels. This is best done not by relying on traditional topics or teacher preferences, but rather by comparing the requirements of the topic to the developmental characteristics of children at the various levels within the elementary school. Young children will easily become involved in a theme dealing with plants in their environment but will be less likely to become involved with a theme dealing with rain forests. However, a theme can be approached from a variety of viewpoints, and often the point of view helps to determine the appropriateness of a topic. For example, a theme like "pollution" can be appropriate at a variety of grade levels depending on how that theme is handled. Primary grade children may consider the theme from the viewpoint of their school and home. Early intermediate grade children may become involved in problems of the community, while upper intermediate grade children, sixth graders, may consider national or world problems. When more than one grade level lays claim to a theme, discussion can help to elucidate the point of view being taken and may result in the same theme being considered at a variety of grade levels but in an ever-expanding manner. Once the grade levels have been established, then the teachers begin their work.

GRADE LEVEL PLANNING

In step 1 of grade level planning, the teachers at each grade level begin the task of selecting from the total list those themes that will be most effective with the children they teach. Not only do developmental characteristics need to be taken into account at this point, but also the backgrounds of the children, the location of the school, and the resources of the school and community.

Consider the theme "oceans," which can be studied from either a science or a social studies point of view. "Oceans" is broad enough that it can be easily used as an organizational pattern for a variety of activities in which skills from the various disciplines can be brought into play. For a group of fourth graders living in southern Alabama, not far from the beaches of the Florida Panhandle, this theme may be especially appropriate. Not only are the majority of the children likely to have gone to the beach and so to the ocean, but seafood is common, and there are oceanographic and fisheries research centers nearby for children to visit or that can provide guest speakers. The theme of "oceans" builds on the available backgrounds of the children and so provides for an appropriate organizing theme. But suppose the children live in rural Kansas. Most have never seen the ocean and so have little concept of it on which to build; seafood generally comes frozen and batter dipped and oceanographic research facilities are nonexistent. The "oceans" theme is probably not as appropriate to Kansas children as it is to Alabama children; a better strategy would be to begin with "prairies" and gradually move outward to more unfamiliar ecosystems.

Grade level teachers not only need to consider the themes in terms of their appropriateness, but also to make decisions as to which of the large number of possible themes will be used. In some cases, all teachers at a grade level may decide to use exactly the same themes, while in others teachers may pursue different themes as determined from the list. It should always be kept in mind that the teacher should be able to use his or her discretion in pursuing other themes during the year and that arise from the interaction of the students and the teacher. Whatever themes are chosen, they should provide for the authentic use of the various disciplines in the pursuit of knowledge, be important to the classroom community, and be broad enough to allow students to develop an understanding of the interconnectedness of the world.

In step 2 of grade level planning, the grade level teachers analyze the themes selected to be certain that a well-balanced program of study is developed. One way of looking at balance in the program is to consider each of the themes in a mapping strategy. The strategy is used to brainstorm the concepts associated with the theme.

When planning a theme, a semantic map provides a visual organizer for the theme. The semantic map is created in five steps. In step 1, the theme is identified, written in the center of a large sheet of paper, and surrounded by a box or circle. Step 1 serves to focus attention on the exact theme. Step 2 begins with brainstorming. The purpose of the brainstorming is to list the concepts students should learn about the topic. Any concept that comes to mind should be listed. No attempt is made at this stage to evaluate the concepts. Evaluation of the concepts is the major aspect of step 3 in the development of the map. Concepts are evaluated on their appropriateness to the grade level, the degree of relationship to the theme, and the importance to the theme. Concept appropriateness is evaluated according to the cognitive and developmental characteristics discussed in Chapter 2. Relationship to the theme is evaluated by looking at the closeness of the concept to the theme. In brainstorming, concepts may be listed which come to mind but which do not have a clear relationship to the theme. For example, a theme dealing with rocks and minerals might have a concept listed dealing with how various types of minerals form and a second concept dealing with collecting minerals as a hobby. The first concept, because it develops an understanding of minerals, would be considered more closely related than the second. And finally, the importance of the theme is evaluated by considering whether or not the concept is of primary importance to an understanding of the theme. For example, brainstorming about a theme dealing with rain forests might have one concept dealing with factors affecting the location of a rain forest on the Earth and a second dealing with how many square miles of the Earth are covered with rain forests. The first concept would probably be of more importance than the second. Eventually, four to six concepts should be selected as a starting point for the map. In step 4, the chart is once again used. The concepts are written on the chart and connected to the theme with lines. Finally, in step 5, each of the concepts on the chart is considered and specific ideas are listed with each of the concepts. The ideas listed should be directly related to the concept and should show the information that would be considered while studying the particular concept.

See Figure 5.1 for a sample map developed by brainstorming around the theme "oceans." Once the starting map has been developed, associated ideas may be added to further develop the topics that may be studied. Figure 5.2 shows the map as it has been further developed.

The theme is considered in terms of the concepts that are a part of the theme and in terms of the specific ideas that can be included within the concepts.

Step 3 in grade level planning begins with a consideration of the kinds of activities possible within the totality of the theme. The best themes allow for a wide variety of kinds of activities: library research, hands-on activities,

FIGURE 5.1   Semantic map of oceans

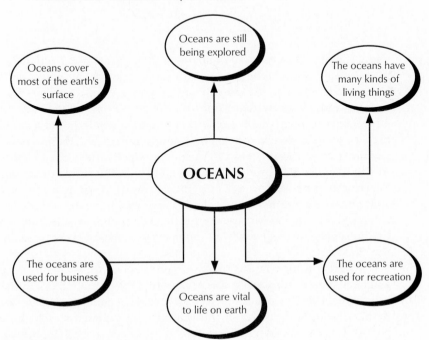

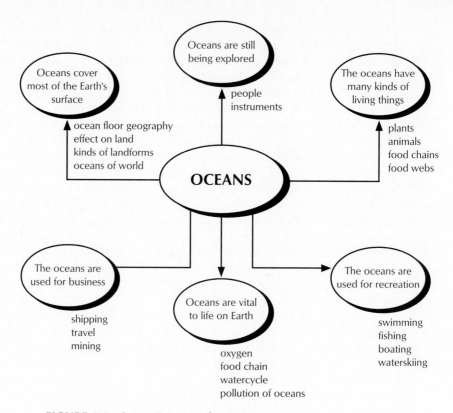

FIGURE 5.2   Semantic map of oceans

experiments, art activities, simulations, computer-based activities, games, skits, plays, guest speakers, field trips, and more. The variety of activities should also allow students to work individually, in pairs or small groups, in large groups, and as a class. A theme that allows information to be gained only through reading is probably too narrow. A theme that allows for only individual or whole group activity is also too narrow. Before scrapping such a theme, however, teachers should attempt to broaden it to include a wider variety of possible activity types. At this stage, it is helpful to keep in mind that the teachers are simply trying to determine whether or not the theme lends itself to a variety of learning strategies. They are not attempting to specify the strategies that will be used in teaching. The strategies that are actually used within the classroom are developed by the specific teacher with the input of the children who are to be investigating the theme.

When considering the theme or problem at this stage in development, the teachers should *not* look at the variety of subject matter disciplines included in the theme. It is *not* necessary to have every discipline included in every theme. Rather, during the course of the school year students should be involved with all disciplines. When teachers feel it is necessary to include every subject discipline in every theme or problem, then some disciplines begin to be included artificially, as when students study the theme of dinosaurs and artificially include music by singing "Ten Little Dinosaurs" or solve problems in mathematics using dinosaur-shaped counters. Although these can be fun for children to do, neither activity generally advances an understanding of dinosaurs, their characteristics, their habits, or their nature. The key to a fully integrated curriculum is to have the disciplines emerge naturally from the theme or to have the skills of the disciplines used naturally in research into the theme.

In step 4 of grade level planning, the kindergarten through sixth grade teachers again meet in group session. At this time, the themes selected by the various grade levels should be presented for a view of the total program. The teachers now should look for balance within the total program. For example, if the discipline of science was used as the basis for the original brainstorming, then teachers should look for how the scope of science is represented. Is the program balanced in terms of biological, physical, and earth-space science, or is one area predominating over the others? If one area predominates, then how can other areas be included within the program? Look also for the inclusion of technology within the program. Is the total program geared toward the consideration of science content without looking at the role human enterprise plays in that content or the way in which that content plays a role in society? If so, consider how the technological aspects may be more fully included. And finally, look to see whether the themes or problems selected are handled in a solid manner or in a trendy and superficial manner. Deciding to use a particular theme because it is based on a particular motion picture or television program is likely to result in a theme that is both trendy and superficial. However, developing a theme around cartooning or photography can result in an interesting and beneficial field of study.

INTEGRATING THE CURRICULUM THROUGH PROBLEMS

The use of problems as a means of integrating the curriculum poses certain challenges to the teacher that are not inherent in the use of themes in integrating the curriculum. Themes can be generated by teachers through brainstorming and can then be developed by the children. The teacher is able to do a great deal of the advanced planning and to build up background knowledge before tackling the theme. Problems, however, result more often from the interests of children and the current events of the day. Newspaper articles, television news programs or entertainment programs, films, books, experiences of the children, and many other occurrences can initiate a problem which is then used as a means for immersing children in an integrated study. For example, children at the sixth grade level hear a news report that the state legislature is going to reduce the amount of money it gives to schools in the state; parents express concern over what that could do to the quality of education. Students begin to discuss this issue and a problem for study arises: How will reductions in funding for schools affect school quality? This can necessitate a study of how schools are funded, where the money comes from and how it is spent, how one state compares to another, how funding of education differs from one nation to another, why legislators would want to reduce funding, how voters and others can influence legislators, and a wide variety of other possibilities.

Problems may also arise during the study of a particular theme. For example, in studying about oceans a student views a television program in which the statement is made that oceans are growing more and more polluted. The student shares that piece of information with others in the class and is immediately challenged by students who are certain the ocean is too big to be polluted; other students say the pollution would make no difference since they never go to the beach. From this discussion comes a problem: Does pollution of the ocean make any difference other than whether or not you can go swimming? Investigation of the ramifications of ocean pollution can lead children into concepts from both science and social studies as well as into problem solving, decision making, and consideration of ethical concepts.

Although the use of problems in integrating the curriculum is more difficult than the use of themes because there is little the teacher can do in advance, the use of problems is especially rewarding because children become fully immersed in the important events of their community, their state, their nation, and their world. They quickly see that the information they learn in school is applicable to the "real world" rather than simply being information that must be learned before something else is learned and before one can pass to the next higher grade.

Although there is often concern that the use of problems as the basis for a curriculum will result in gaps in knowledge, this concern is generally unfounded. Investigating and solving real-world problems results in the acquisition of knowledge that is important to the learner and to the adult he or she will become. Some of the more esoteric bits of information currently included in the curriculum may be omitted, but if those bits of information are so useless in the real world that they never come up, why bother with them in the first place?

But what about those pieces of information and those skills that are important but do not appear in the integrated curriculum? First, it is unlikely that vital pieces of information will not be used within a well-planned integrated approach. To ensure that such information is included the curriculum must be continually evaluated, both at the grade levels and at the school level. Classroom assessment of students during each unit and over each year will allow the teacher to pinpoint areas that are not receiving attention, not receiving enough attention, or receiving too much attention. Grade level discussion can then be used to modify the curriculum and the projects within each topic of the curriculum. Schoolwide discussions of weaknesses can allow the teachers and administrators to determine whether vital skills and information are being included over the course of the educational program.

Once the themes and problems for each grade level have been selected, the teacher begins planning for his or her classroom. The topic of teacher planning will be fully discussed in Chapter 9.

INTEGRATING THE CURRICULUM THROUGH THE DISCIPLINE OF MATHEMATICS

Integrating the curriculum through mathematics requires a change in the general concept of what mathematics is. For most teachers and curriculum planners, mathematics and arithmetic are interchangeable terms; however, there are distinct differences between them.

ARITHMETIC

Arithmetic is concerned with computation: addition, subtraction, multiplication, and division of whole numbers, common fractions, and decimal fractions. Also within the area of arithmetic are counting rotely, measuring in standard or metric measure, and determining the area, perimeter, and volume of objects through formulas. In arithmetic, the purpose of the numerical manipulations is to derive a particular answer that is deemed correct. All else is considered incorrect and subject to reconsideration. Arithmetic focuses on particular skills and on the acquisition of those skills at a particular level of mastery. It has traditionally been the focus of the program at the elementary school level. There is only one problem with a focus on arithmetic: It is not necessary to understand what one is doing or why one is doing it; it is only necessary to get the correct numeral as an answer.

MATHEMATICS

Mathematics is concerned with conceptualization rather than with computation. In mathematics one develops an understanding of the nature of addition, subtraction, multiplication, and division, develops concepts of fractional parts and of measurement, develops the ability to see and develop patterns, interprets the meaning of numerical data, develops problem-solving skills, and in general is not strictly concerned with manipulating numerals in a way that will result in a particular predetermined outcome.

In order to develop an understanding of the difference between these two aspects of quantitative thinking, consider the following lessons on measurement. Both took place at the fourth grade level.

In the first class, the teacher began the lesson by holding up a meter stick and telling the class it was 1 meter in length. She then wrote the word *meter* on the chalkboard. Then the teacher pointed out the places on the meter stick identified by numerals. She told the students there were 100 of these places and that each of them represented 1 centimeter. She related the word *centimeter* to the word *cent* and indicated that there were 100 cents in a dollar. The word *centimeter* was also written on the chalkboard. Then she pointed to the marks 10, 20, 30, 40, and so on. She indicated that each of these places was known as a *decimeter* because each of them contained 10 centimeters. She wrote the word *decimeter* on the chalkboard and then related the word to *decade,* meaning ten years. Once the children were shown the markings, they were divided into teams and given lengths of string. Each piece of string had a piece of tape on it identifying the string as string A, B, C, D, E, F, or G. The partners were to measure the length of each string in centimeters or in decimeters and to record the measurements on a worksheet. The groups were graded on the accuracy of their measurements. Any measurement more than 1 centimeter "off" was considered incorrect. Most of the measurements were correct. The next day the children were asked to measure certain objects in the room. They needed to be taught once again how to use the meter stick.

In the second lesson, the teacher began by telling the students that she had something in another room that she wanted to bring to their room. The only problem was that she was not certain whether the "something" would fit into the classroom. She wanted to determine whether or not the "something" would fit. How could she do it? The children moved into teams of four to brainstorm how they could determine whether or not the "something" would fit into the room. Once the small groups had their lists they shared them with the entire group, which then discussed and debated the possibilities, finally narrowing the list down to one item. They could measure their room, measure the "something," and then determine if it would fit. At this point the teacher brought in an additional difficulty: All of the rulers in the school had mysteriously disappeared. Now what were they going to do? The children quickly came up with a variety of possibilities for measuring devices. All were listed on the chalkboard and discussed. The good possibilities were identified and the teacher had the students try them out, measuring the distance between two lines drawn on the sidewalk outside of the school. Not only were all of the measurements different, but not one of the measuring devices fit the length exactly. They were always too short. A discussion then ensued as to what could be done to solve the problem of different measurements and too long lines. In the end, the students concluded that they would need to decide on one measurement and they would have to divide that one measurement up into smaller pieces so that they could say the lines were 10 chair lengths and 5 chair pieces long. Once the children had conceptualized the need for a standard way of measuring and for smaller pieces within the standard, the teacher "found" a meter stick and announced that they would be seeing how the use of meters and parts of meters would solve their problems of measurement.

In the first lesson, the teacher focused on the arithmetic side of the quantitative curriculum. The major purpose was to have children learn to measure accurately in centimeters and decimeters. The focus of the grading system was on the accuracy of the measurements. It made little difference whether the children understood the purpose for using the metric system or for having two different types of divisions. It was only necessary to match the stick to the string and find the appropriate number.

In the second lesson, the teacher focused on the mathematics side of the quantitative curriculum. The purpose of the activity was to develop a variety of concepts. First, the children developed the idea that measuring was a way of solving a particular problem. Second, they discovered that without a standard method of measuring, various answers to the distance between two lines could be obtained. Finally, they developed the idea that when measurements did not "come out even" they needed to divide the standard up into smaller pieces. With these mathematical concepts developed, these students would be ready to move into the use of metrics and use that system with understanding.

Arithmetic provides little opportunity for the integration of the curriculum. It is a skill that can be applied to a variety of areas of study, but its focus is so narrow that it does not allow for the integration of other subject areas into itself. Mathematics, on the other hand, develops conceptualizations and so can provide a foundation for the integration of the curriculum. Arithmetic is used in mathematics but as a tool for the application of mathematical concepts. The following list, based on the National Council of Teachers of Mathematics' *Curriculum and Evaluation Standards for School Mathematics,* identifies common mathematical concepts that are appropriate starting points for the integration of the curriculum.

1. *Geometry:* developing geometric relationships and spatial sense; a means for representing and describing in an orderly manner the world in which we live.
2. *Measurement:* developing an understanding of the attributes of length, capacity, weight, area, volume, time, temperature, and angle and their uses in describing, conceptualizing, and modeling the world.
3. *Problem Solving:* developing and applying strategies to solve a wide variety of problems, including verifying and interpreting results with respect to the original problem; includes reasoning through the use of models, known facts, properties, and relationships.
4. *Mathematical Communication:* mathematics as a powerful language that can be used to organize and communicate information effectively; using pictures, graphs, charts, and diagrams as well as the appropriate language of mathematics to communicate.
5. *Probability and Statistics:* collecting, organizing, describing, displaying, and interpreting data as well as making decisions and predictions on the basis of that information; constructing, reading, and interpreting displays of data; developing sampling techniques.
6. *Patterns and Relationships:* recognizing, describing, extending, and creating a wide variety of patterns; looking for regularities in events, shapes, designs, and sets of information.
7. *Comparing and Contrasting:* looking for similarities and differences within the natural world.

8. *Sorting and Classification:* looking for relationships among and between objects and phenomena within the natural world.
9. *Functions:* determining how changes in one quantity result in changes in another quantity.

As an example of the use of mathematics as an integrating force within the curriculum consider the theme "describing our world" as an exploration of statistics and their uses in decision making. Figure 5.3 shows the mapping strategy used to organize this theme.

As can be seen from the diagram, the use of statistics in describing the world begins with the simple and probably familiar concept that numerical information in the form of graphs, charts, and data tables can be used to describe many kinds of things. The basic information is then used to describe the school through statistical techniques, including sampling and the calculation of such averages as mean, median, and mode as well as the application of probability. This leads into how the local community can be described using statistical information and can include the investigation of changes over time. Once the school and community have been described students can move on to describing the natural

FIGURE 5.3   Using mathematics as an organizing theme

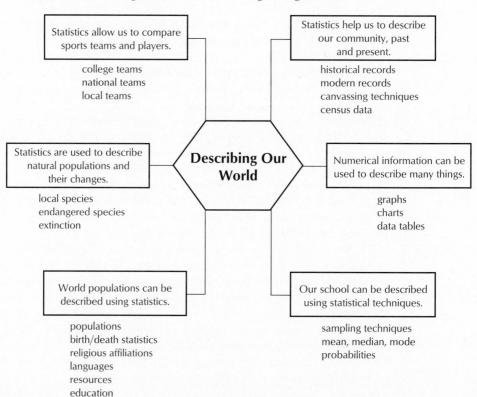

world, looking at plant and animal communities and their changes over time. They can compare the local community to the world community using statistical information. The example of sports teams can illustrate the use of statistical information in making decisions.

As can be seen from this brief description, the use of statistics and statistical data can result in an integrated approach that uses mathematics as a basis. At the same time, investigation of the community and the world involves students in the use of social studies skills; investigation of the natural world involves students in scientific information; and all of the topics involve students in reading and in presenting information in writing as well as through oral communication.

The key to the use of mathematics as an integrating framework is in viewing mathematics from a conceptual basis rather than from a computational basis. Addition may not be functional as the basis for an integrated curriculum theme, but statistics, patterning, and problem solving are.

INTEGRATING THE CURRICULUM THROUGH THE FINE ARTS

From a traditional point of view, the fine arts are painting, sculpture, architecture, and drawing; decorative arts, photography, and graphics, including computer graphics, can be added to the list. To further broaden the realm from which themes can be developed for use in an integrated program, the performing arts—dance, music, and theater—will also be included.

Like mathematics, the fine arts present certain challenges to the school, grade level, and teacher developing an integrated approach to curriculum. But in the case of the fine arts, it is not a problem of finding topics broad enough to serve as the focal point of integration, but rather one of narrowing topics from so wide a variety of possibilities. The first problem with the arts is to determine the perspective from which the art form will be considered:

1. A historic perspective considers the development of the art form over a period of time.
2. A cultural perspective considers how a particular art form manifests itself in various cultures.
3. A ritual perspective, although part of the cultural aspect, considers how an art form is used in religious and secular ritual.
4. A communications perspective considers how an art form is used to convey a particular message to an audience, including such areas as mass media, advertising, propaganda, and so on.

Once the perspective is chosen it is necessary to determine which of the art forms will be given attention. For a historical perspective, one might develop a theme around changes in sculpture from classical Greece to the modern period. For a cultural perspective, one might look at how traditional musical forms from the Far East, the Middle East, Africa, and North America are similar and how they are different. For a ritual perspective, one might consider how dance is used in religious and secular rituals. For a communications perspective, one might consider how graphics can be used to shape public perceptions.

Once the perspective and the art form have been chosen, there is an additional consideration. Art is both a product and a human enterprise. One needs to decide whether it is the product or the creator of that product that will be the focus of the integrated study. Although it seems that one equals the other, this is not necessarily so. Take Leonardo da Vinci: If the decision is made to consider only his paintings, then one omits his drawings, frescoes, anatomical studies, work as a military engineer, and inventions. However, by making the starting point of study Leonardo himself, all of his areas of endeavor can be considered.

Figure 5.4 shows a beginning **semantic map** used for developing an integrated theme dealing with Leonardo da Vinci.

Five areas of study are considered. As students look at the life and the times of Leonardo, they delve into history and in particular into the Renaissance period with its city-states, political families, and system of patronage in the arts. They can also look at other artists of the time, making comparisons among those who

FIGURE 5.4   Leonardo da Vinci

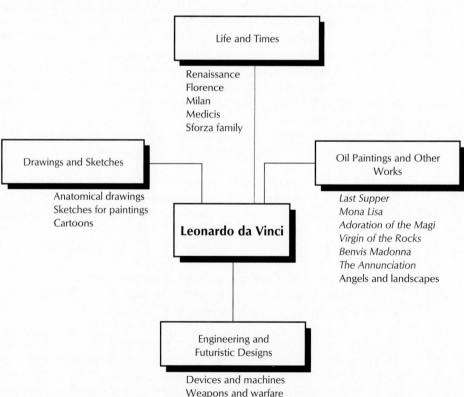

were the contemporaries and rivals of Leonardo. Students can look in depth at Leonardo's accomplishments—painting, sculpture, engineering, flying machine, weapons, and anatomical sketches and drawings—his work providing for diverse areas of interest and study. Looking at his painting techniques can lead to experimentation with various media; considering his futuristic designs can lead to model building, comparison with modern inventions, and invention contests.

The study of the fine arts, therefore, can lead students into a study of history, techniques, media, and human beings as artists. It can also demonstrate the role played by art in culture and in ritual.

Like the fine arts, the performing arts lead children into varied and interesting areas of study. A theme such as "putting on a play" offers a variety of possibilities for integrating all areas of the curriculum. Figure 5.5 shows a semantic map for this theme.

In this particular thematic approach, students may begin with brainstorming ideas for the play they wish to present. At this point the students who will be the authors of the play will be designated. As soon as the authors and the play itself are determined, the students choose an area of interest for developing: sets, makeup, costumes, incidental music, or advertising campaign. Students working on sets will need to create sketches and models to show what the stage setting

FIGURE 5.5 Putting on a play

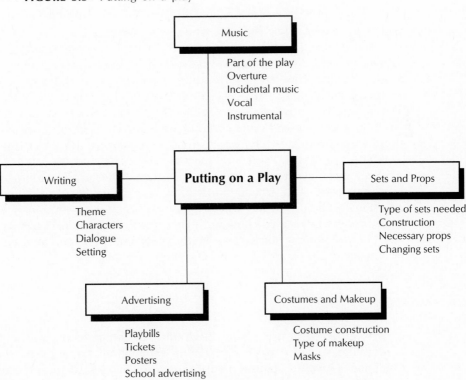

(whether classroom or school auditorium) will look like, and then will need to construct the actual sets for the stage, including any props needed for the action. Those who are working with costumes will need to develop their ideas, present drawings to show the costumes needed, and construct those costumes, while those working on makeup first will need to decide whether makeup is needed and what kind of makeup, or whether masks might be more appropriate; if masks are chosen, students will need to design and construct them. The group working on incidental music for the production will need to consider what type of music would be appropriate; rock music is probably not going to work for a play on colonial America, but folk songs may be fitting. They will also need to decide how that music will be provided: Is live music possible? Will they need to find recordings and, if so, is there a way to play the recordings? They may also need to decide on music that will be a part of the play itself. Will there be any need for characters to sing songs or dance?

The final group is not so concerned with the play itself but with the advertising for the play. How will they advertise? Where will the advertising be placed? What will the programs for the play be like? In the case of the advertising campaign and the programs, students will again need to provide sketches for approval before actually going ahead with the final products.

Even when the play is ready, there will still be other factors to consider. Where and how will rehearsals be conducted? Who will be the actors and who the stagehands, dressers, and technical persons? When will the play be given and for whom? It may also be appropriate to have a "critic" in the audience who will write a review for the play when it is performed.

In the theme "putting on a play" students are involved in language arts through writing and advertising as well as in presenting their ideas for costumes, advertising, music, and sets. They are involved in arts and music as they develop their sets, costumes, music, and perhaps dance. No matter what play they produce, they will also be involved in research into historical or contemporary music, art, dance, and clothing. And, they will most certainly be involved in group decision making as they work together to choose costumes, sets, music, and advertising.

With the arts as a basis for a thematic approach, students can develop insight not only into the art forms but also into their historical development, their use in ritual, their use in communication, and their basis in human activity. Additionally, the use of the arts as a thematic basis gives prominence to an area of the elementary school program that generally takes a backseat as something "fun" to do within a unit or as something separate from the total curriculum to be taught in a separate room by a separate teacher.

Summary

At first glance, the use of the disciplines to integrate the curriculum seems contradictory to the basic concept of curriculum integration. However, the disciplines provide a starting point for brainstorming ideas for integration as well as a place of security for the teacher only beginning to work with a thematic approach. In using the disciplines for integration, the school and grade levels should work together to develop a consistent and balanced program before the individual teacher begins his or her work. Always, in planning for integration, the teacher should leave much room for planning with the students.

The broad concepts in science and social studies provide a multitude of opportunities for curriculum integration. And, since many concepts are common to science and social studies, integration between these two areas is easy.

Mathematics provides more of a challenge to integration. To integrate the curriculum through mathematics, the teacher needs to observe the difference between arithmetic and mathematics. Arithmetic, with its emphasis on computation, provides little opportunity for thematic integration. However, mathematics, with its orientation toward conceptualization, provides ample opportunities for integration through topics such as probability, measurement, geometry, and problem solving.

The arts also provide opportunities for integration of the curriculum. Like mathematics, the arts are different in focus than social studies and science. Rather than simply focus on concepts, the arts can allow for integration from a variety of perspectives: historical, cultural, communications, and human. Each of these perspectives allows for the development of a thematic approach that will involve the students in a variety of investigations.

ACTIVITY ONE

PURPOSE

The purpose of this activity is to stimulate the planning that would occur in developing an integrated curriculum for an elementary school.

PROCEDURE

Preparation
1. The class will play the role of the faculty of an elementary school.
2. One person should be selected from the class to act as the school's principal and so lead the activity of the teachers.
3. The class members should be divided into grade level groups according to the levels they teach or the levels they want to teach. The groups should be about equal in size.

Activity
1. The "principal" should assist the "teachers" in deciding which discipline will be the focus for the activity: mathematics, science, social studies, or fine arts. Once the decision is made, the "principal" should lead the group in brainstorming possibilities for the

curriculum. The possibilities should be identified as problems, themes, or topics. Topics can then be expanded into themes or rewritten as problems.

2. Working as a group, teachers should divide the list of brainstormed themes and problems into grade levels.

3. After the grade levels have been determined, the grade level groups should meet to determine the following:
   a. which of the themes and/or problems are developmentally appropriate for the grade level
   b. which of the themes and/or problems are appropriate to the location of the school
   c. which of the themes and/or problems should be included in the grade level curriculum and which should be returned to the pool of possibilities for other grade levels to consider

4. The total group should meet again and review the curriculum that has been developed. At this time, all of the topics selected for a grade level should be chosen. The total group should then:
   a. critique the scope of the curriculum
   b. critique the sequence of the curriculum
   c. critique the entire curriculum for balance and make any necessary adjustments
   d. critique the entire curriculum for repetition and make any necessary adjustments

5. Grade level groups should meet again and from the themes and problems selected develop the following:
   a. a list of the concepts to be included in the theme or problem
   b. a list of the activities to be included in the theme or problem

6. Finally, each grade level group should present its theme or problem to the rest of the school and discuss the scope of subject matter areas considered in the total curriculum, as shown in one of the themes and/or problems.

ACTIVITY TWO

PURPOSE

The purpose of this activity is to develop a semantic map showing the development of a specific theme from science, mathematics, social studies, or fine arts.

PROCEDURE

1. Select one of the following disciplines: sciences, mathematics, social studies, or fine arts.

2. Brainstorm a list of five to ten possible themes or problems in the selected discipline.
3. Select two of the brainstormed topics and develop a semantic map for each topic. The semantic maps should be geared toward specific grade levels.
4. After the map has been developed, critique it in terms of subject matter areas outside the chosen discipline, developmental appropriateness of the theme or problem selected, the kinds of activities included, and the relationship of the kinds of activities included to Gardner's eight intelligences.

Study Questions

1. Four steps are generally used in planning for an integrated approach to the curriculum. List and define them.
2. Compare and contrast topics, themes, and problems as they are related to the integrated curriculum.
3. List four topics generally taught in social studies and four topics generally taught in science. Change each of those topics into a theme that could be used to integrate the curriculum. Discuss why the newly written form is a theme rather than a topic.
4. Select one theme from social studies and one from science. Develop a semantic map for each of the selected topics that shows the concepts and specific ideas that would be included under each concept. Brainstorm some activities for investigating each of the concepts.
5. How does integrating the curriculum through problems differ from integrating the curriculum through themes?
6. Discuss the differences between arithmetic and mathematics. Why is mathematics a more effective means for integrating the curriculum than arithmetic?
7. Select one of the mathematics concepts listed in this chapter. Develop a semantic map to show how it could be used to integrate the curriculum.
8. Four perspectives can be used to integrate the curriculum through the fine arts. List and define each perspective, then give an example of how each could be used with a fine arts concept.

Bibliography

Altwerger, B., & Flores, B. (1991). The theme cycle: An overview. In K. S. Goodman, L. B. Bird, & T. M. Goodman (Eds.), *The whole language catalog.* New York: American School Publishers.

Bambourne, B. (1988). *The whole story: Natural learning and the acquisition of literacy in the classroom.* Auckland: Ashand Scholastic.

Brady, S. K., & Sills, T. M. (1993). *Whole language: History, philosophy, practice.* Dubuque: Kendall/Hunt.

Edelsky, C., Altwerger, B., & Flores, B. (1991). *Whole language: What's the difference?* Portsmouth, N.H.: Heinemann.

Fogarty, R. (1991). *How to integrate the curricula.* Palatine, Ill.: IRI/Skylight.

Fogarty, R. (Ed.). (1993). *Integrating the curricula: A collection.* Palatine, Ill.: IRI/Skylight.

Fogarty, R., & Stoehr, J. (1995). *Integrating the curricula with multiple intelligences: Teams, themes, and threads.* Palatine, Ill.: IRI/Skylight.

Gamberg, R., Kwak, W., Hutchings, M., & Altheim, J. (1988). *Learning and loving it: Theme studies in the classroom.* Portsmouth, N.H.: Heinemann.

Harlin, R., Ipa, S. E., & Lonberger, R. (1991). *The whole language journey.* Markham, Ontario: Pippin Publishing.

Jacobs, H. H. (1989). *Interdisciplinary curriculum: Design and implementation.* Alexandria, Va.: Association for Supervision and Curriculum Development.

Jacobs, H. H., & Borland, J. H. (1986). The interdisciplinary concept model: Theory and practice. *Gifted Child Quarterly,* pp. 214–233. Fall.

Jones, B. F., Palinscar, A., Ogle, D. S., & Carr, E. G. (1987). *Strategic teaching and learning: Cognitive instruction in the content areas.* Alexandria, Va.: Association for Supervision and Curriculum Development.

Katz, L. G., & Chard, S. C. (1989). *Engaging children's minds: The project approach.* Norwood, N.J.: Ablex.

Kivalic, S. (1993). *ITI: The model: Integrated thematic instruction.* Village of Oak Creek, Ariz.: Books for Educators.

Lipsom, M. Y., Valencia, S. W., Wixson, K. K., & Peters, C. W. (1993). Integration and thematic teaching: Integration to improve teaching and learning. *Language Arts, 70,* 252–263.

Manning, M., Manning, G., & Long, R. (1994). *Theme immersion: Inquiry-based curriculum in elementary and middle schools.* Portsmouth, N.H.: Heinemann.

Marzano, R. J., Pickering, D., & Brandt, R. (1990). Integrating instruction programs through dimensions of learning. *Educational Leadership, 47,* 5.

National Council of Teachers of Mathematics. (1989). *Curriculum and evaluation standards for school mathematics.* Reston, Va.: NCTM.

Saul, W., & Jagusch, S. A. (Eds.). (1991). *Vital connections: Children, science, and books.* Portsmouth, N.H.: Heinemann.

Saul, W., Reardon, J., Schmidt, A., Pearce, C., Blackwood, D., & Bird, M. D. (1993). *Science workshop: A whole language approach.* Portsmouth, N.H.: Heinemann.

Strube, P. (1993). *Theme studies: A practical guide.* New York: Scholastic.

Thompson, G. (1991). *Teaching through themes.* New York: Scholastic.

Walmsley, S. A. (1994). *Children exploring their world: Theme teaching in the elementary school.* Portsmouth, N.H.: Heinemann.

Weaver, C., Chaston, J., & Peterson, S. (1993). *Theme exploration: A voyage of discovery.* Portsmouth, N.H.: Heinemann.

Wilson, L., Malmgren, D., Ramage, S., & Schultz, L. (1993). *An integrated approach to learning.* Portsmouth, N.H.: Heinemann.

CHAPTER

6

INTEGRATING THE CURRICULUM THROUGH LANGUAGE AND LITERATURE

After reading this chapter you should be able to:

1. Discuss the importance of language to learning
2. Describe the distinguishing characteristics of a whole language approach to teaching
3. Illustrate how whole language promotes curricular integration
4. Describe beliefs typically held by whole language teachers
5. Contrast a traditional curriculum with an authentic curriculum
6. Illustrate the intricacies and complexities encountered in reading
7. Describe ways in which whole language is linked to children's literature
8. Discuss the components of literacy
9. Show how children's literature can be a mainstay in curricular integration
10. Identify the various genres of children's literature
11. Discuss the benefits of using children's literature as the foundation of curricular integration in the elementary school classroom
12. Unveil myths regarding curriculum integration
13. Contrast the teaching of reading in a basal textbook setting and a whole language setting
14. Discuss the pros and cons of using textbooks in the elementary school

Learning is language borne. It commences with language as its vehicle, continues to grow and enlarge through language, and perseveres through language. Indeed, any permanence that learning attains comes about through language. Because language is such an essential to learning, the teaching of literacy is an especially good way to bring about curriculum integration. The importance of language is reiterated in this statement by Stice, Bertrand, and Bertrand (1995): "Language is a human social invention. It is pervasive in our lives. We use it nearly every waking minute, and it is also the primary means by which we think and learn" (p. 57).

Implicit in literacy instruction is that *language operates as a whole* and not in segmented, compartmentalized episodes of listening, speaking, reading, or writing, and that *children's literature is the mainstay of any literacy program.* In that regard, this chapter presents effective ways to achieve curriculum integration through whole language instruction and through children's literature.

INTEGRATING THE CURRICULUM THROUGH WHOLE LANGUAGE

Perhaps the essential belief embodied in a whole language philosophy is that *learning exists in context.* Whole language teaching provides the empowerment necessary to extend literacy across content areas, to fuse, to blend, to integrate. Whole language classrooms are child-centered and the teachers and students engage cooperatively in learning as they share in listening, speaking, reading, and writing experiences. Box 6.1 depicts beliefs, resources, and actions that distinguish the whole language teacher.

Indicating that a great amount of confusion exists regarding the meaning of the term *whole language* and that the term means different things to different people, Rubin (1995) writes:

Many beliefs put forth by the proponents of whole language are not new. Good teachers have embraced these for years and incorporated them in their teaching. Here are a number . . .

- Listen to children.
- Involve children in activities that are of interest to them.
- Have children read whole pieces of good literature.
- Have children gain an appreciation of reading.
- Integrate the language arts.
- Involve students in planning.
- Give children many opportunities to express themselves.
- Give children many opportunities to read and write.
- Have children write about things they know.
- Give children an opportunity to ask questions.

BOX 6.1   THE WHOLE LANGUAGE TEACHER'S BELIEFS,
RESOURCES, AND ACTIONS

BELIEFS

- that language is of primary importance in learning
- that children learn language by using language
- that the process in learning is more important than the product
- that teaching begins where the child is, starting with strengths
- that high expectations yield good results
- that children need your respect and trust
- that rich content is essential

RESOURCES

- a very flexible schedule
- an abundance of high-quality children's literature
- a variety of resources, including prints, pictures, audiovisual media and equipment, computer hardware and software
- a wealth of sound instructional methodologies and techniques
- effective evaluative strategies
- an environment free from risks
- a learner-centered setting

ACTIONS

- reads aloud to children every day
- provides time for children to engage in sustained silent reading every day
- provides time for children to engage in writing activities every day
- provides opportunities for children to engage in speaking activities every day
- provides daily opportunities for children to engage in careful listening
- is a co-learner with the children
- facilitates student planning, exploration, problem solving, decision making, cooperative group work, collaboration
- makes children responsible for their own learning.

- Have children work together cooperatively.
- Base materials on the needs of students.
- Engage the children in problem solving.
- Stress higher-order thinking.
- Use children's writing as a springboard for reading and vice versa.
- Organize lessons around theme units.

- Take the individual differences of students into account.
- Include parents as partners in learning. (p. 13)

Holdaway (1979) finds it intriguing that children, almost universally, learn to walk and talk with great success and satisfaction but seem to have more difficulty acquiring reading and writing skills. Walking and talking follow a process whereby acquisition is facilitated, but not forced. Reading and writing, however, often are forced rather than facilitated and don't operate in the same optimal environment afforded to the acquisition of walking and talking skills. Exploring the effective process and optimal environment exemplified as children successfully acquire talk, Cambourne (1988) describes a set of optimal conditions that form a model and an environment in which most learning can proceed very effectively. Whole language teaching provides an environment where the following optimal conditions for learning, described by Cambourne and articulated here by Cordeiro (1992), are manifested:

- **Immersion.** Under optimal conditions, the learner is immersed in what is to be learned. Children learning to speak are surrounded by their native language, and from the confusion of sounds around them, they take what they are ready for.

- **Demonstration.** Under optimal conditions, what is to be learned is demonstrated by an expert to whom the learner is bonded. Thus the learner is predisposed to want to be like the teacher to whom the child is bonded. Children learning to speak spend much time watching people demonstrate speaking.

- **Engagement.** Under optimal conditions, learners try out what is to be learned, often in private, until they feel secure in their performance. Children learning to talk often babble and play with words, practicing on their own. Cambourne points out that in order to engage, learners must see themselves as doers, must see a potential use for the new learning, and must feel that the risk involved is tolerable. Further, learners are more apt to engage with a person to whom they are bonded.

- **Expectations.** Under optimal conditions, there is an expectation that the learner will succeed. Children learning to talk enjoy an atmosphere that expects this will happen. Such an environment is "secure and supportive, providing help on call and being absolutely free from any threat associated with the learning of the task" (Holdaway, 1979, p. 23).

- **Responsibility.** Under optimal conditions, learners make decisions and choices about the learning they undertake. They are placed in a position of trust. Infants learning to talk are left to take what they need from the language flow around them and are trusted to find their own best sequence.

- **Approximation.** Under optimal conditions, learners' efforts that resemble correct form are rewarded as if they were correct. Sounds made by children learning to talk are heralded as if they were real words. Experts to whom children are bonded willingly translate and respond as if the approximation were correct. Thus, the learner is gradually led closer and closer to the proper form.

- **Use.** Under optimal conditions, learners are allowed time to "play" with and use what they are learning. This element of play permits the self-regulation necessary to a successful learning experience. Children want to perform and share successful results. Children learning to talk are eager to display newly acquired skills. This confidence is the result of much self-regulated practice.

- **Response.** Children learning to talk are given a "no-strings" response— immediate feedback that lets them begin to work with the language they are learning. This response allows children to use all their naturally occurring, self-regulating mechanisms. A learner gradually fine-tunes approximations until satisfied. Children learning to talk develop judgment about correct form through response by self-regulating.[1]

Perkins (1995) and Peterson (1992) posit a view of whole language as a curricular strategy where teachers act as facilitators in providing students with authentic opportunities to learn. Students are active participants, making choices and decisions about their learning, as they engage in authentic experiences that lead to meaningful learning. Box 6.2 depicts the contrast between a traditional curriculum and an authentic curriculum.

Perkins (1995) outlines the following strategies for teachers who want to engage their students in authentic learning transactions where critical thinking and activity-oriented, student-participatory, collaborative, and cooperative experiences lead students to meaningful learning:

- Speak less so that students think more. Try not to lecture more than 20 percent of total class time. This seems to be very difficult for teachers who view their role as transmitters of knowledge to be conveyed to their students.

- Instead of spoon-feeding surface-level information, help raise the prior knowledge of the group concerning the subject of the day to a conscious level and teach them how to read the text for themselves, actively and analytically. Focus on how to read the text stragtegically, not on reading the text for them.

---

[1] Adapted from P. Cordeiro. (1992). *Whole Learning: Whole Language and Content in the Upper Elementary Grades.* Katonah, N.Y.: Richard C. Owen Publisher, Inc. (pp. 222–223). Used by permission.

Box 6.2   Comparing the Traditional Curriculum to the Authentic Curriculum

TRADITIONAL CURRICULUM	AUTHENTIC CURRICULUM
Teachers work to achieve stated objectives.	Teachers and students work together to formulate and meet objectives that help students grow in critical and complicated ways.
Knowledge is external; students do not contribute to meaning.	Students bring meaning to an experience and construct new meaning.
Teaching is skill-based and mastery is of paramount concern.	Teaching is meaning-centered and students search for meanings and structure on a personal basis.
Skills are learned mostly in isolation and for mastery.	Skills are learned while students are engaged in student-participatory, authentic learning activities.
Curriculum is guided by standards and guides and commercial materials.	Curriculum is related to students' lives and is developed through negotiation.
Being correct is of optimal value.	It is acceptable to approximate.
Knowledge based on concepts is of primary value.	Knowledge based on concepts, feelings, and intuitions are of value.
Discipline comes through assertive techniques and reinforcement.	Discipline comes through empowering students to be responsible to themselves and to the group.
Education is viewed primarily as preparing for the future.	Education is viewed as important to make the present meaningful.
The student's cognitive needs are emphasized.	The student's cognitive, social, and emotional needs are emphasized.
Instruction is in whole groups and homogeneous subgroups.	Cooperative, collaborative, negotiative learning is the emphasis.
Teachers are accountable for student learning.	Student is accountable for own learning.
Students engage in learning plans made for them.	Students participate in planning and evaluation.
Competency is judged by testing.	Competency is judged by meanings expressed, problems solved, collaboration with others.

- Focus on fundamental and powerful concepts that form the basis for understanding, in this case literacy and learning. Have students apply and analyze the basic concepts while engaged in problem solving and reasoned application.

- Present concepts, as far as possible, in the context of their use as functional strategies for the solution of real problems and the analysis of significant issues.

- Develop specific strategies for cultivating critical reading, writing, speaking, and listening. Listen to your students. If they think a concept is difficult, it is, regardless of how easy it may seem. Let them help you point out the difficulties/complexities so that together you can investigate them in an informed manner.

- Think aloud in front of your students. Let them hear you thinking, puzzling your way slowly through problems in the subject. However, try to think aloud at the level of a good student, not a speedy professional. If your thinking is too advanced or proceeds too quickly, they will not be able to construct meaning by way of your thinking.

- Regularly question your students Socratically, probing various dimensions of their thinking; their purpose; their evidence, reasons, data; their claims, beliefs, interpretations, deductions, conclusions; the implications and consequences of their thought; and their response to alternative thinking from contrasting points of view. Look at the assumptions underlying each point of view—not just at the surface arguments.

- Have much of the time spent in class devoted to work sessions with the sharing of ideas, interpretations, and experiences an integral part of those sessions.

- Use both concrete and universal examples whenever you can to illustrate abstract concepts and thinking. Cite experiences that you believe are more or less common in the lives of your students, relevant to what you are teaching. Invite them to cite their own specific examples.

- Require regular writing for class. Too many classes require no writing except the obligatory, superficial term paper. Instead, have students write as a way of examining their own thinking during their learning/exploration process. Have them experience all aspects of the writing process by engaging in them. For example, responses to specific reading assignments are medium drafts, not scrawled on the back of a grocery sack, yet not polished for public consumption either. Respond to the content and make editorial comments only regarding recurring issues that defy convention. Teach five-minute mini-lessons in class regarding editorial issues that occur frequently. Respond to the communication intended by each student and raise questions that he or she might pursue more deeply.

- Define assessment as an integral part of the learning expected for the student. Assigning a grade at the end of the quarter or semester is but one aspect of assessment.
- Regularly break the class into small groups in which they are required to work cooperatively. Invite members of groups to report back on the process they went through as well as the task they completed and what problems occurred and how they were tackled.
- In general, design all activities and assignments, including readings, so that students must think their way through them. Lead discussions on the kind of thinking that is required.
- Keep the logic of the most basic concepts in the foreground, continually weaving new concepts into the basic ones. Talk about the whole in relation to the parts and the parts in relation to the whole.
- Spell out your expectations early in the year; explain that you are going to structure the class in such a way that students will have to contribute to the learning rather than just memorize what is put in front of them. Active learning takes active participation on the part of both teacher and student.
- Self-assessment, shared assessment, teacher assessment, and assessment of teacher by students are all feasible and important aspects of the learning that goes on in a class and should be addressed throughout the year. There should be ample opportunities to make choices about what is most important to each student at that time as well as the commitment in terms of grades for the semester.[2]

Box 6.3 shows how whole language thinking departs from traditional thinking in significant ways.

READING IN WHOLE LANGUAGE

Literacy is the ability to read and write, and in that vein reading is a major part of literacy. The intricacies involved in reading are, to say the least, very complicated. Word perception and comprehension represent major skills in the act of reading, but reading is far more complex than recognizing letters and their sounds, forming syllables and words, identifying word meanings, and adding up the word meanings from left to right. In reading instruction, a great deal of the children's time is traditionally spent on vowel and consonant letters and the sounds they represent. But sound-letter instruction, particularly the teaching of vowels and vowel sounds, is perhaps overemphasized. Simply recognizing letters, one at a time, to form words and identifying the words, one at a time, to forge a message is not reading. Instruction in reading should not be focused primarily

---

[2] Adapted from P. Perkins. (1995). *The ABC's of Whole Language.* Westminster, Calif.: Teacher Created Materials, Inc. (pp. 54–56). Used by permission.

Box 6.3   COMPARING TRADITIONAL THINKING AND WHOLE
LANGUAGE THINKING

TRADITIONAL THINKING	WHOLE LANGUAGE THINKING
Learning is driven by a format for acquisition based on textbooks and facts.	Learning is a constructivist process where meanings are generated, thinking prevails, and conceptual knowledge is emphasized.
Language is a hierarchy of skills learned in isolation using worksheets and planned exercises.	Language is a tool for learning and is learned and enhanced as a language system during the process of engaging in projects and activities.
The learner is a passive receiver of facts who engages in isolated skills practice and convergent thinking.	The learner is actively engaged, constructing understandings and making connections during divergent thinking.
The transmission of knowledge by the teacher is in lockstep sequence where meanings are reconstructed based on authoritative sources.	Transactional teaching occurs where the teacher observes, responds, and facilitates invest-igation and experimentation so the learner can construct reasoned meanings.
Reading and writing are products following specific forms and mechanics.	Reading and writing are processes propelled by meaning and self-expression.

---

on learning a hierarchy of letters and their sounds (Stice, Bertrand, & Bertrand, 1995). Consider the intricacies and complexities encountered in reading exemplified by the examples in Box 6.4.

In the first example from a well-known nursery rhyme, the word *Mary* means "a little girl," the word *had* means "owned," and the word *little* means "small in size" as well as "young." The word *lamb* suggests "a child's pet." In the second example, an alteration is made to the second line: See what happens to the meaning of the words that precede it. Now Mary is a grown woman, probably at a fancy dinner, *had* means "ate," and *little lamb* becomes "a serving of meat." In the third example, another alteration is made to the wording. This time *Mary* is a ewe, *had* means "gave birth to," and *little lamb* means "baby" (adapted from Altwerger, Edelsky, & Flores, 1987, as found in Stice, Bertrand, & Bertrand, 1995).

**Box 6.4   An Example of Complexities
Encountered in Reading**

1. Mary had a little lamb
   Its fleece was white as snow
2. Mary had a little lamb
   And she spilled mint sauce on her evening gown
3. Mary had a little lamb
   And it was such a difficult delivery that the vet
   needed a drink of water

Learning to read is a constructive process that is cognitively induced or psychogenerative. As children try to read for functional reasons, they develop an acumen, or an intuition, for how reading works. In whole language classrooms that support children making explorations, the learners are *immersed* in print that is meaningful to them. Children are encouraged to *experiment* with written language in order to understand, progress, and transcend the world around them. At appropriate junctures, the teacher *demonstrates* aspects of the reading and writing process, allowing children abundant opportunities to test and explore reading and writing in an environment that is free of risks and rich with incentives, stimuli, and motivation. Teachers promote and accept *approximations* by children as they are engaged in frequent, regular, and authentic opportunities for *using* written language. Children perceive that the teacher *expects* them to learn to read and that the ultimate *responsibility* for learning to read rests with each individual child (Stice, Bertrand, & Bertrand, 1995).

Stages in Reading Development

Ferreiro and Teberosky (1982) point to three basic insights children develop prior to actual reading:

1. Children learn to distinguish between two very fundamental types of graphic representation: drawing and writing. Drawings, they sense, have lines that depict the shape of the object being represented, while the lines in writing have no connection with the shape of the object.
2. Scribbles, strings of letters, and letterlike shapes begin to appear as patterns to children and they begin to search for these patterns.
3. Children begin to see interrelational comparisons between words and know the differences, noticing, for example, that two words are written differently from one another and recognizing the differences.

Children learn to read at varying rates and at different chronological periods during their lives, depending on their innate abilities and individual experiences. Figure 6.1 shows three stages in reading development that can be identified with most learners.

Stage 1 is the prereading and emergent reading phase. During the prereading stage, the three basic insights described by Ferreiro and Teberosky (1982) are developed by children prior to actual reading. Environmental print has been a part of the child's world since birth. Seeing signs in the environment such as those for McDonald's, Hardee's, Burger King, Taco Bell, Sears, and the like has given rise to explorations with printed symbols, which has allowed the young child to learn a great deal about reading. Children at this stage enjoy listening to stories read aloud and they often mimic the reading act from times when they have seen adults reading. Such foundations provide for emergent reading, where children construct meaning, begin to see themselves as readers, and recognize their own names in print. During this period, children memorize stories from listening to them being read and can often supply omitted words. They can describe pictures and associate them to the story. As they approach the end of the emergent reading period, children begin to recognize and point to individual letters and words with which they have become familiar.

Stage 2 is the independent reading phase. At this stage, both print cues and implied cues are used to construct the message from the author. Children focus on the letters and words in print, use the skills of word perception automatically and in concert to unlock and decode unknown words, and increasingly move toward being "on their own in reading." Reading aloud is fun and children at this stage will often read out loud to anyone who will listen. As they approach the end of the independent reading stage, children are becoming skilled readers, able to unlock unknown words competently and to skillfully comprehend literal and inferential meanings.

Stage 3, the advanced reading phase, is characterized by an efficiency in getting the meaning from the author's head to the reader's head. Children are

FIGURE 6.1 Three stages in reading development

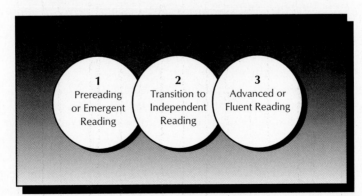

becoming successful readers in terms of being able to use reading to fulfull their needs, both in and out of school. Fluency in reading is heralded by reading orally with expression, recognizing the structure of various genres competently, and using reading both for learning and for enjoyment. Essentially, the ability to read is enhanced, improved, and optimized by reading. The more one reads, the better one becomes at reading. As readers in the advanced stage continue to read, their reading abilities will continue to improve and accelerate. In a wonderfully natural way, reading begets reading!

TRADITIONAL READING INSTRUCTION

Basal readers are series of books and related materials that help children develop and practice reading skills in each grade in the elementary school. In addition to readers for students, they include teacher manuals with detailed lesson plans, workbooks, and many other supplementary and auxiliary materials that can be used in conjunction with the basal series. Perhaps the heart of any basal reader series is the teaching plan, often called a **Directed Reading-Thinking Activity (DRTA)**. A typical plan for a DRTA has the following components:

1. *Preparation for Reading.* The teacher builds on the experience background of the students, introduces new concepts and vocabulary, and establishes purposes for the reading selection.
2. *First Reading.* Students are directed to read the selection silently to get the sense of the story.
3. *Checking Comprehension.* The teacher leads a discussion about the reading selection, answering questions, clearing up confusions through having portions of the selection retold, and asking literal and inferential questions relating to the selection (noting facts, details, main ideas, and inferences, and relating to real experiences about which the children may have knowledge).
4. *Second Reading.* The teacher leads students to read orally all or parts of the story as a means of diagnosis, checking on specific skills, developing expression before an audience, and enjoying the story.
5. *Related Skills/Abilities.* The teacher provides opportunities for students to practice skills such as word recognition (often called word perception or decoding), comprehension, and vocabulary development. This is often called "seat work" and is done with workbooks or worksheets.
6. *Extension/Enrichment.* The teacher provides opportunities for students to read supplementary materials, view films/filmstrips/videos, listen to recordings, participate in activities related to the story, and the like.

The traditional instructional emphasis embodied in a basal reading program revolves around two major skills intrinsic to the reading process: word perception and comprehension. Word perception (sometimes called word recognition, word identification, or decoding) involves skills that help students unlock unknown words. The skills of word perception typically taught in basal reading programs include phonic analysis, structural analysis, contextual analysis, and configuration. The dictionary is always available for use to readers for word perception, and picture clues are valuable aids to word perception, especially in the primary-grades reading program. Sight words (memorized words) enhance word perception because they allow the beginning reader to read a greater amount of material, thus providing more opportunities to view words in context.

Without comprehension, there is no reading. Comprehension involves getting the meaning from what is read, getting the idea from the author's head to the reader's head. Reading comprehension is a complex intellectual process centering around two major abilities: comprehending word meanings and verbal reasoning. It is, above all, a thinking process. In that regard, literal comprehension (what the words say in black and white; something that is directly stated) and inferential comprehension (interpreting something that is not directly stated) are at the forefront of teaching the process of comprehension to children. Also included as categories of comprehension are evaluation and appreciation. Most elementary teachers, however, emphasize literal and inferential comprehension, feeling that if children in the elementary school develop the ability to derive literal and inferred meanings, they will also develop reading abilities in evaluation and appreciation. Figure 6.2 shows that reading is composed of word perception and comprehension, with their subcategories.

Phonics and Whole Language

Phonics is the study of the relationships between the letter symbols of a written language (graphemes) and the sounds the symbols represent (phonemes). Rubin (1995) differentiates between explicit phonics instruction and implicit phonics instruction in the following way:

FIGURE 6.2 The traditional model for teaching reading skills

READING

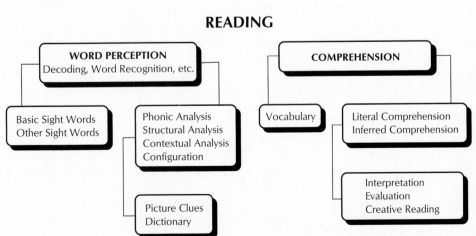

- **Explicit phonics instruction** involves sounding out or pronouncing the sounds associated with individual letters in isolation and then blending letter sounds together to sound out a word or syllable.

- **Implicit phonics instruction** involves hearing and pronouncing whole words that begin with the same sound, then seeking additional words that have the same beginning sound.

Other writers (May, 1994; Perkins, 1995) use different terms for explicit and implicit phonics, calling the isolated and intensive blending of letters into sounds (explicit, in Rubin's terminology) *synthetic phonics* and instruction where the movement is from the whole word to analysis of its parts (implicit, in Rubin's terminology) *analytic phonics.*

Perkins (1995) views the teaching of intensive letter-sound combinations to sound out words, either in explicit or implicit fashion, as a one-cueing-system view of reading. She prefers the term *grapho-phonic cueing system* for reading instruction in a whole language environment. "The grapho-phonic cueing system operates in conjunction with all of the cueing systems. It does not stand alone. Therefore, dealing with letters, sounds, and words in isolation as if they are independent of the language context in which they are embedded is misleading" (p. 17).

Indicating that phonics and other word perception techniques are a means to an end (comprehending and constructing meaning) and not an end in themselves, the California State Department of Education (1994) states:

- Phonics should not be viewed as a precursor to student interaction with authentic literature. It is not a first step to be mastered before students encounter meaningful reading and writing activities.

- Phonics is best taught within the context of reading and writing.
  (p. 2)

In a whole language or transactive view of reading, children learn to read (and to write) in the same way they learned to talk. Similar to the way they learn oral language, children should be immersed in print, have numerous experiences demonstrating how print works, and have abundant opportunities to practice the process for themselves and to make sense of it. Reading must become for children a meaning-making event in which not only the grapho-phonic (letter-sound) cueing system is used for word recognition, but the cueing systems involved with syntactics (grammar) and semantics (meaning) as well. A whole language view of reading integrates all the systems of language into authentic experiences. Whole language teaching encourages, models, and facilitates learners in making authentic inquiries and experimenting with cueing, predicting, and confirming in low-risk, supportive, enriched environments. In this holistic, transactive model of learning, children develop reading processes and strategies that will lead them to become proficient readers and writers. Such a learner-centered environment focuses on integrating language, literature, and content across the curriculum (Stice, Bertrand, & Bertrand, 1995).

Rubin (1993) depicts reading as a totally integrative process involving the affective domain of feelings and emotions, the perceptual domain of giving meaning to sensations and organizing stimuli in a field of stimuli, and the cognitive domain of involved thinking. In that regard, Rubin recommends a modified whole language approach in the teaching of reading, integrating the best of whole language with a sequential skills-development program. According to Rubin, "A modified approach would also include direct instruction, flexible grouping, standards, and the use of a variety of materials. A modified whole language approach is a balanced, eclectic one that integrates all the language arts" (p. 13).

Regardless of the approach used in teaching reading, Rubin (1995) suggests that the teacher should be proficient in the teaching of phonics so that the needs of students can be properly diagnosed and addressed. In that regard, the following developmental sequence of phonics instruction is recommended:

1. *Auditory discrimination:* hearing sounds correctly and discriminating between sounds
2. *Visual discrimination:* seeing visual symbols correctly and discriminating between visual symbols
3. *Consonants:* initial consonants; final consonants; consonant clusters such as *bl, st, str;* initial consonant clusters; final consonant clusters; initial consonant digraphs such as *th, ch, sh;* final consonant digraphs such as *ng, gh;* silent consonants such as *kn, pn, wr*
4. *Vowel sounds:* long vowel sounds; short vowel sounds; effect of final *e* on vowel; double vowel digraphs and dipthongs; vowel controlled by *r*
5. *Special letters and sounds*
6. *Phonograms*
7. *Syllabication:* syllable meaning; generalizations such as double consonant (vc/cv) and vowel-consonant-vowel (v/cv); consonant with special *le* such as c/cle or v/cle; syllable phonics including open and closed syllable; accent

Language is learned through authentic use and authentic language is holistic, therefore all of the parts and subsystems of language are learned through authentic use. Practicing on drill sheets to learn phonics rules about certain letter-sound relationships, copying spelling words over and over again for "mastery," or circling nouns in sentences on the chalkboard do not represent authentic use of language. "Instead, children learn letter-sound relationships (or graphophonemic cues) by reading real books and writing their own stories or information books; they learn how to spell through exposure to words in their reading and by trying out their invented spellings to express their own ideas in writing; they understand how nouns work by encountering those employed by authors and by using those they need in their own writing" (Pappas, Kiefer, & Levstik, 1995, p. 35).

Spiegel (1992) believes that giving a more prominent role to direct, systematic instruction in whole language classrooms strengthens literacy education and helps teachers meet the needs of more children. She proposes building bridges between traditional (direct, systematic) instructional approaches and whole language approaches so that children are provided the best opportunities to measure up to their literacy potential. Many aspects of whole language and systematic, direct instruction can be blended so that both approaches are strengthened, allowing children a better opportunity to realize their potential for developing reading and writing skills. Spiegel suggests that educators look for points of compromise and ways to blend the best of systematic, direct instruction and whole language instead of looking for points of conflict:

> I believe that bridges can and must be built between whole language and more traditional approaches to literacy instruction to enable teachers to blend the best of both in order to help every child reach his or her full literacy potential. Above all, we must avoid either/or positions that reject out of hand the possibility of blending and blind us to the value of different perspectives. Advocacy of systematic direct instruction does not mean that indirect instruction is considered of no value. Especially for many affective goals, indirect instruction is the most appropriate form of instruction. Nor does advocacy of direct instruction necessitate a skill and drill approach where skills are taught and used in isolation. On the other hand, advocacy of whole language does not mean that children are left alone in a state of benign neglect. The whole language perspective does not mean that teachers never step in to guide children's learning. Modeling and coaching are important features of whole language classrooms. If bridges are to be built, we need to think in terms of a continuum rather than a dichotomy. (p. 43)

INTEGRATING THROUGH LANGUAGE AND LITERATURE

With approximately 3,500 new children's books published each year, the potential that children's literature has to integrate and enrich the elementary school curriculum is enormous. The various genres of children's literature make learning come to life. A few minutes spent reading and discussing the poem *Harriet Tubman* by Eloise Greenfield (1978) arouses and motivates students more than toiling through a textbook account of Tubman's life. In like fashion, a little time spent reading a book such as *Nettie's Trip South* (Turner, 1987) can enlighten students about the lives of pre–Civil War slaves more graphically, descriptively, and adequately than long sessions of textbook reading and discussion on the same topic (Walley & Walley, 1995). The introduction to *Integrating Literature in Content Areas* by Walley and Walley (1995) aptly details the importance of children's literature in the elementary school:

The world of children's literature awaits all teachers who open the door and invite into their classrooms the legion of authors, poets, and illustrators ready to help them teach their students. Some of the finest writing and art being produced in our modern society is presented in children's books. When we use novels, poetry, and picture books in our science, math, and social studies classes we invite this cadre of creative and talented authors and illustrators onto our teaching team. They inspire teachers and students to learn and create. Literature adds quality to our lives and presents unique opportunities to enrich the curriculum. (p. i)

Many people refer to children's literature generally as *trade books.* Trade books include books written for children that are not textbooks. Trade books are categorized by format as either picture books or chapter books and into genres such as stories, informational books, and poems. Box 6.5 illustrates some of the categories of trade books.

A wide variety of children's literature is available today—including picture books, poetry, historical fiction, biographies, folklore, and nonfiction—that can effectively link to the curriculum. Dowd (1990) writes that picture books provide an excellent way to cultivate an understanding of both geographical and historical concepts in students in the elementary school. Even for children who are beyond the primary grades, picture books capture interest, strongly motivate, and add a dynamic extension to teaching (Farris, 1994).

Using a variety of picture books that have settings from different areas of the United States, along with a large U.S. outline map, Farris (1994) demonstrates a classroom journey that transports learners on a geography and history trip throughout the United States to other times and places. The map became an informational mural of the journey as books and their locations were added to it. Geography, history, reading, and writing were integrated in this activity, making learning interesting, fun, and effective. Such a project can be long-term, lasting several weeks or even throughout the school year.

Farris and Fuhler (1994) suggest using quality children's literature, particularly picture books, to address concepts and issues in the upper elementary and middle school grades:

Within the pages of a picture book is the potential to entice, intrigue, and motivate upper elementary and middle school readers as they vicariously experience times and places that make up their past, influence the present, and may have an impact upon their futures. Used to begin a unit of study, encourage further exploration in the middle of a unit, or stimulate extension activities at the end of a unit, picture books play a creative role in the social studies curriculum. Concepts are built and critical thinking is fostered as students compare and contrast life styles now and long ago, ponder painful issues inherent in war, or grapple with ideas presented with emotional impact in a picture book.

Box **6.5**   Categories of Trade Books for Children

Picture Books

Brief text material and pictures combine to tell a story or present information. Many informational books are published in picture-book format, as are books of poetry. Fairy tales, myths, and legends also appear as picture books. Special types of picture books, called wordless picture books, contain no text; the story is told entirely by the pictures.

Chapter Books

Longer story and informational books for elementary children written in chapter format. Can include informational books. Often have a table of contents, a glossary, and an index.

Stories

Generally, story books for younger children are in the picture-book format and story books for older children are in the chapter-book format. Types of stories include traditional literature, fantasies, realistic stories, and historical fiction.

Informational Books

These books provide information in science, math, social studies, art, music, and other topics. Some informational books present concepts like homonyms and antonyms; biographies are another type of informational book. Biographies often are written as chapter books, but some shorter biographies are done in picture-book format.

Poems

Books on poetry range from collections of poems by a single author to a compilation of poems on a single topic to anthologies, which are collections of poems written by different authors and on different topics.

Carefully chosen from the bounty of high quality books available today, picture books integrated into the social studies curriculum have the potential to bring excitement and joy to social studies learning. (p. 386)

Tomasino (1993) shows how literature provides rich and meaningful multicultural, historical, and geographical experiences for children in the elementary school. Tomasino uses the children's novel *Felita* by Nicholasa Mohr as a springboard to lead a group of fifth graders into an in-depth investigation of the culture of Puero Rican Americans and of the history and geography of Puerto Rico. "By exploring Puerto Rican foods, the children learned geography; they came to see that cultures respond to their environment. By constructing timelines, the children were able to connect Felita with Puerto Rico's history. Finally, poetry encouraged the children to respond aesthetically to their knowledge and experience. By mixing literature and social studies, children learned about Puerto Rico, themselves, and each other" (p. 9).

Literature serves as a powerful tool in an interdisciplinary social studies program. Jarolimek and Parker (1993) suggest blending literacy instruction with social studies as the most logical and significant place to begin interdisciplinary teaching. A phenomenal increase in the quantity and quality of children's trade books linked to the teaching of social studies has occurred in the last few years. This new literature is rich with detail and characterization that transports elementary students to another place and time, allowing them to identify with individuals, places, and events that make social studies meaningful and interesting (Farris, 1994). Children's trade books provide innovative and novel approaches that breathe life into the elementary curriculum. Literature possesses the magic to bring learning to life and, at the same time, bring deeper understandings and meanings to the learner.

Whole language advocates have long promoted the use of literature in the elementary classroom for the teaching of reading and writing skills (Danielson & LaBonty, 1994). Now many are applauding the potential that literature has for making content areas like social studies and science not only meaningful and interesting, but relevant to the lives of elementary school students (Ammon & Weigard, 1993; Beck & McKeown, 1991; Ceprano & English, 1990; Huck et al., 1993; Johnson & Ebert, 1992; Louie, 1993; Moir, 1992).

Literature serves as an excellent vehicle for teaching about religions of the world. "Use of literature in the classroom can help teachers point out how religions affect the way families throughout the world live within their homes and communities" (Stafford, 1993, p. 245). Literature allows religion to be approached in an academic way rather than in a devotional way. Through literature, students become aware of other religions without practicing or necessarily accepting them; trade books expose children to various religions, but no single view is imposed and no specific religion is promoted or belittled. Students are informed about different belief systems without being asked to conform to any one (Haynes, 1986). The California History/Social Science Framework (1987) calls for the use of religious literature, including poetry, novels, plays, tall tales, myths, legends, biographies, and essays, to help shed light on the ways people live their lives in various places and in different times. The role that religion has played is essential to an accurate and comprehensive understanding of humankind's story; children's literature is available at all grade levels to help tell the story in an exciting and interesting way.

Over the years, good teachers have used biographies written for children to enhance and embellish learning in the content areas. Biographies provide a natural link between literature and social studies. Children often see themselves closely connected to biographical characters. They vicariously experience the real-life circumstances of people who have made achievements and had an impact on society. These vicarious biographical encounters often leave the young reader with a positive and optimistic view about his or her own potential in life. Zarnowski (1990) describes an approach in which students collaborate to write original biographies about important historical figures. It is an effective way to take advantage of the natural curiosity children have for people, places, and events in the world. In Zarnowski's approach, small groups of children work cooperatively to investigate someone's life and then collaborate to tell the story of that person's life in an original, group-written biography. The procedure for guiding children in writing original biographies calls for the teacher to

1. help children select the person about whom they will write
2. guide students in learning about the person
3. help students keep track of what they are learning
4. help children reflect on the person's life
5. assist students in identifying key events in the person's life
6. facilitate small groups of children in the cooperative and collaborative production of their biographies

Writing and illustrating the biographies may take several directions. All groups may work on a biography about the same historical figure—Alexander the Great, for example. Each group member has the responsibility for developing and writing one chapter. Along with this strategy, the **jigsaw** technique (Aronson, 1978) might be used, where one member of each group works on the same topic, such as Alexander's early life, allowing pupils with like topics to meet together and work on their topics. Another strategy is to have groups work on different biographies altogether. One group may be investigating and developing an original biography of Christopher Columbus while another group is working on Ferdinand Magellan and still another on Simón Bolívar. In any event, the writing of the biographies should be guided by the following logical stages in the writing process:

Prewriting	Brainstorming, information gathering; generating questions to be answered
Drafting	Putting the pencil to paper, focusing on content, not mechanics; getting the information down on paper
Revising	Rereading, rewriting; making changes on the draft itself
Editing	The polishing stage, fixing errors in both content and mechanics
Final Product	The finished product, ready to be shared and viewed by others, as on a bulletin board or in a presentation

This approach provides opportunities for groups to collaborate on producing their biographies. It is a delightful way to encourage children to read, discuss, and write their way to an in-depth understanding of great people, overlapping literacy and content learning. Significant and important content is embellished by a variety of writing styles and points of view that are encountered in the literature. A medley of trade books with rich, descriptive language at a variety of reading levels allows children at different ability levels to participate equally. Facilitated by the teacher, the groups collaboratively engage in activities to

- select the individual about whom the biography will be written
- work cooperatively to collect, research, and organize information on the individual from a variety of sources
- distinguish and outline key occurrences, incidents, and events in the individual's life
- choose a presentation style for the new biography
- assemble and construct a rough draft
- create the final form of the group-produced biography

Danielson and LaBonty (1994) recommend using biographies of historical figures to develop and compose poems they designate "bio-poems." Each bio-poem contains nine elements in the following arrangement:

Element 1	First name of the biographical subject
Element 2	Four adjectives that describe the subject
Element 3	Wife, husband, siblings of subject
Element 4	Lover of (three people, places, things)
Element 5	Who feels (three things)
Element 6	Who fears (three things)
Element 7	Who would like to see (three things)
Element 8	Resident of (city, state, country)
Element 9	Last name of biographical subject

After reading *Paul Revere: Colonial Craftsman* by Regina Kelly, a fifth grade class worked cooperatively to compose the following bio-poem:

Paul
Talented, silversmith-coppersmith-goldsmith, loyal, brave
Husband of Sara Orne and, after her death, Rachel Walker
Loved his family, his craft, and his country
Who feels pride in country, pride in family,
and pride in workmanship
Who fears loss of freedom, General Gage, the English king
Who would like to see the minutemen defeat the British,
the independence of the United States, and the copper industry
of the United States equal that of Europe
Resident of Boston
Revere

After reading the biography *Juan Ponce de Leon: First in the Land* by Bernadine Bailey, a cooperative group of sixth grade students composed the following bio-poem:

Juan

Loyal, trustworthy, fair, unselfish

Son of Don Jose Ponce de Leon

Loved exploring, Queen Isabella, his loyal dog, Becerrico

Who feels capable of ruling San Juan, deserving of his knighthood,

betrayed by the Columbus family

Who fears loss of respect in Spain,

the return of Don Diego, son of Columbus,

and that people thought him to be crazy

because of the Fountain of Youth

Who would like to see La Florida developed,

differences with the family of Columbus healed,

more time with his wife, Inez

Resident of Spain and San Juan and Cuba

Ponce de Leon

Effective uses of the bio-poem scheme could include the following three approaches:

1. Use the overhead projector and let the whole class contribute to the composition
2. Facilitate children as they work in small, cooperative groups
3. Assist children in individual, noncollaborative assignments

Employing literature as a medium for teaching social studies with an interdisciplinary approach is highly recommended. Jarolimek and Parker (1993) propose two important principles to keep in mind when considering literacy instruction: Literacy instruction should connect, network, and mesh with important content information, and literacy instruction should be accomplished in an environment where opportunities for social interaction are abundant, the learning is cooperative in nature, and the expectations are high.

Shanahan, Robinson, and Schneider (1993) point out that the integration of curriculum goes beyond the cognitive and reaches into the social domain as well:

The integration of curriculum is not only cognitive; it's social, too. Reading and writing are as united by the human relationships embedded within them as they are connected by common skills, structures, and strategies. . . . Thinking about literacy separately from social connections is sort of like thinking about roses separately from the flowers. You can do it, but the essence and beauty are lost somewhere in the transaction. Reading and writing are fundamentally social activities. We use them

to communicate and to get close to each other, to maintain relationships, to emulate others, and so on. (pp. 158–159)

Strongly recommending literature to liven up and create interest in content
studies, Sanacore (1993) castigates textbooks as "uninteresting, disjointed, and
lacking in meaning, with unimaginative prose and banal content" (pp. 240–241),
and uses the chart in Box 6.6 to compare learning stimulation between textbooks
and literature-based materials.

Often thematic units are employed that use a literature-based approach to
organize the instructional materials and activities around a particular piece of
literature. Tchudi (1994), for example, described a class of second and third
graders who used Beatrix Potter's *Jeremy Fisher* and Arnold Lobel's *Frog and
Toad Together* as starting points for a study of frogs and toads.

The children's research included interviewing parents, reading trade
books, creating wall charts, finding common characteristics of frogs and
toads, verifying or refuting frog and toad mythology, and creating artistic
representations. Interdisciplinary units can be based on a social studies
topic, such as "pioneers," and include literature, science, math, and art
as a way of extending the dimensions of the topic and the children's
understanding of it. A study of space or the solar system that begins
with a science focus can lead to reading science fiction as well as
studying the history of space exploration and using math to calculate
the dimensions of space and time. (p. 32)

Barr and McGuire (1993) describe an effective and valuable way of integrating
the curriculum through a technique called *storyline.* Developed in Scotland over
the last several years, storyline uses the learner's natural enthusiasm for story making
to help develop a conceptual understanding of the social world, including places,
people, and events, by creating a story together. With objectives and a storystarter-
type beginning to generate a picture in the minds of the learners, curriculum areas
are naturally integrated as children engage in collaborative story making orchestrated
by the teacher. In this regard, the teacher is serving as a facilitator and an enabler
of learning, building on the learner's prior experience while developing important
new concepts and skills. "Storyline provides an ideal setting in which to develop
critical thinking skills, problem-tackling activities, interpersonal skills, positive
attitudes, and, at the same time, develop knowledge and understanding" (p. 7).

Another option for integrating the subjects of the elementary school
curriculum lies in the teaching of reading skills through the use of historical
novels. Studies show that pupils who are taught to read with books other than
basal readers often demonstrate superior vocabulary acquisition and reading
comprehension. Too, when teachers use biographies and historical fiction as
reading texts, pupils learn historical concepts while they enhance their reading
skills (Dobson, Monson, & Smith, 1992).

On a test project in Utah, teachers replaced basal readers with historical
novels for an entire school year. Highlights of the project were the enrichment

Box 6.6   Comparing Textbooks and Literature-based Materials

FACTORS	TEXTBOOKS	LITERATURE-BASED MATERIALS
Presentation of text	Ideas are organized in a list-like and listless fashion; a large number of concepts are introduced	Ideas are blended with poignant narration; fewer concepts and themes are highlighted and dealt with in greater depth
Short-term, long-term perspective	Immediate information is provided for classroom discussion and related tests	More opportunities are given for responding both intellectually and emotionally to the text and for developing the lifetime reading habit
Variability	One source usually dominates instruction	A variety of "real" resources (trade books, pamphlets, magazines, etc.)
Comprehensibility	Content is uninteresting and detached from readers' prior knowledge	Content is more easily personalized and understood by readers
Applicability across the curriculum	Information is vacuously linked to separate subject areas	A diversity of themes can easily be adapted to several content areas
Externally-, internally-driven curriculum	A single publisher controls the bulk of the curriculum	Students and teachers determine the focus of the curriculum
Externally-, internally-driven assessment	Chapter questions dominate quizzes and tests	Individually selected outcomes (projects, portfolios, interactions, etc.) are used to assess progress
Emulation of the home environment	Parents and children rarely read textbooks for pleasure	Parents and children are more likely to read, read aloud, and discuss "real" resources

---

BOX 6.7   BENEFITS OF USING CHILDREN'S LITERATURE

- Quality children's picture books celebrate the artistic process.
- Vocabulary and concept development are learned within the rich context of a meaningful story or genre.
- Predictable and repetitive texts give early readers confidence in their reading abilities.
- Literature allows readers to learn about other people in other settings with other perspectives.
- Literature generates interest in the real world and how people in other places live and work, as well as how things work.
- Literature involves readers and listeners with the infectious nature of language.
- Literature allows the reader to empathize with characters' problems and lifestyles.
- Literature allows reading for enjoyment.
- Literature provides models for writing.
- Literature exposes readers to multicultural issues.
- Literature spans and enriches the entire curriculum.
- Literature allows readers to do more than just read a story; it also nurtures their imagination.

---

activities that ensued in three categories: creative activities, content activities, and language activities. Creative activities included dramatic plays, presentations, writing assignments, and song writing. Content activities, enriching and focusing the students' learning of historical concepts, included debates, developing reports, inviting guest speakers, writing newspaper accounts of historical events, and producing maps of the settings in which the stories took place. Language activities centered around an appreciation for written and spoken language, employed the concept of imagery, and allowed students opportunities to work in small, cooperative groups (Dobson, Monson, & Smith, 1992).

BENEFITS OF USING CHILDREN'S LITERATURE

The benefits of using children's literature as the foundation of curricular integration in the elementary school classroom are considerable and numerous. Box 6.7 presents the major benefits derived from children's literature in the elementary school curriculum and is followed by a detailed discussion of each benefit.[3]

---

[3] Adapted from K. Danielson & J. LaBonty. (1994). *Integrating Reading and Writing through Children's Literature.* Boston: Allyn and Bacon (pp. 3-6). Used by permission.

Quality children's picture books celebrate the artistic process.   Caldecott Medal–winning books such as *Tuesday* (Wiesner, 1991), *Black and White* (Macaulay, 1990), and *Lon Po Po: A Red-Riding Hood Story from China* (Young, 1989) are visually captivating and add much to the stories they tell. There are many other picture books with outstanding illustrations in various artistic styles. *Family Farm* (Locker, 1988), for instance, is an exquisite example of impressionist painting. Egg tempera is the base of the paintings in *Good Dog, Carl* (Day, 1985), which is a wordless book that tells the story of a babysitting dog.

Other picture books include Chris Van Allsburg's *The Polar Express* (1985) and *Jumanji* (1981), both Caldecott Medal books. *Jumanji* is illustrated in pencil, whereas *The Polar Express* is rich with color paintings. Lois Ehlert uses bold colors and cutout shapes to form animal faces in *Color Zoo* (1989) and *Color Farm* (1990). Collage constructions are used in *Window* (Baker, 1991) as the changes of a young boy's life are chronicled through wordless scenes observed from the window of his room. And Ann Jonas has created books that not only create stories and illustrations right-side up but also upside down in her books *Round Trip* (1983), done in black and white, and *Reflections* (1987), done in full color.

Vocabulary and concept development are learned within the rich context of a meaningful story or genre.   Alphabet books such as *Alison's Zinnia* (Lobel, 1990) and *Eating the Alphabet: Fruits and Vegetables from A to Z* (Ehlert, 1989) show a variety of different flowers, fruits, and vegetables as they demonstrate the alphabet. These books allow students to explore new words in a meaningful manner, adding to their own knowledge. Other books develop the meaning of a concept within the context of the story. For instance, *The Principal's New Clothes* (Calmenson, 1989) uses the terms *sharpest dresser, tailors, tricksters,* and *measurements* as it tells the current-day version of "The Emperor's New Clothes." These terms are easy for children to understand once they have read the story and see how they relate to the plot and the concept of clothing. Other books develop a child's understanding of shapes, colors, and textures, such as Tana Hoban's books, *Spirals, Curves, Fanshapes & Lines* (1992), *Exactly the Opposite* (1990), *Of Colors and Things* (1989), and *Look Up, Look Down* (1992).

Predictable and repetitive texts give early readers confidence in their reading abilities.   Books such as *Moo Moo, Brown Cow* (Wood, 1992), *Polar Bear, Polar Bear, What Do You Hear?* (Martin, 1991), and *My Brown Bear, Barney* (Butler, 1989) encourage young readers to make predictions about the text and invite them to join in with the reading of the story or its refrain. Because picture clues are often given, students can make good guesses about what will be coming next in the text. There is also much repetition, which allows readers to feel confident about their abilities to read or chant along. Other good predictable and repetitive books for young readers are *I Went Walking* (Williams, 1989), *Spots, Feathers, and Curly Tails* (Tafuri, 1988), *What Do You Like?*

(Grejniec, 1992), *The Chick and the Duckling* (Ginsburg, 1972), *All I Am* (Roe, 1990), *Mary Wore Her Red Dress* (Peek, 1985), *The Jacket I Wear in the Snow* (Neitzel, 1989), *The Dress I'll Wear to the Party* (Neitzel, 1992), and *My Brown Bear Barney in Trouble* (Butler, 1993).

Literature allows readers to learn about other people in other settings with other perspectives.   Sami, from *Sami and the Time of the Troubles* (Hiede & Gilliland, 1992), lives in present-day Beirut. His story of fear and ruins contrasts with his memories of good times and helps readers think about other worlds and perspectives. *Over the Green Hills* (Isadora, 1992) tells the story of a journey in South Africa. *Hopscotch around the World* (Lankford, 1992) displays the many different ways the common childhood game is played around the world, thus expanding a reader's horizons by using a familiar experience. *On the Pampas* (Brusca, 1991) describes living on a ranch in Argentina. And the various cultural aspects of cooking rice are explored in *Everybody Cooks Rice* (Dooley, 1991), as a young girl visits the houses in her culturally diverse neighborhood during meal time and discovers how each family is cooking rice in a different manner. All these picture books are important in helping students to explore a global perspective.

Learning about history from novels is another aspect of learning about other perspectives. Readers will root for Annemarie's family to escape from the Nazi soldiers in 1943 in Lois Lowry's *Number the Stars* (1989). Readers will hope along with Anna and Caleb that the mail-order bride, Sarah, will stay with them on their early 1900's prairie farm in *Sarah, Plain and Tall* (MacLachlan, 1985). Good literature builds a perspective on history too.

Literature generates interest in the real world and how people in other places live and work, as well as how things work.   Informational books, such as the incredible *The Way Things Work* (Macaulay, 1988), leave readers with not only answers to how many mechanical things work but also questions about other marvels of our computer age. *Nature by Design* (Brooks, 1991) examines the wonder of nature, from the oyster's shell to the beaver's dam. And Gail Gibbons gives descriptions of construction in *How a House Is Built* (1990). All of these books help students to understand the processes of nature and mechanical creations. By examining the similarities and differences in food and clothing in various cultures, books such as *Hats, Hats, Hats* (Morris, 1989) and *Bread, Bread, Bread* (Morris, 1989) show the many ways that people around the world live and work.

Literature involves readers and listeners with the infectious nature of language.   *Chicka Chicka Boom Boom* (Martin & Archambault, 1989) is just such an infectious book. The refrain of this rollicking alphabet book is positively catching: "Chicka chicka boom boom! Will there be enough room?" *Is Your Mama a Llama?* (Guarino, 1989) is another "chant along" book. Readers or listeners can easily make predictions about the different animals by noting the clues and the rhyme of the contagious text. Other books with infectious lyrics are *Cat Boy!* (Lockwood, 1989), *Bears in Pairs* (Yektai, 1987), *Sheep in a Jeep* (Shaw, 1986), *Jesse Bear, What Will You Wear?* (Carlstrom, 1986), and *One Cow, Moo Moo* (Bennett, 1990).

Literature allows the reader to empathize with characters' problems and lifestyles.   Contemporary realistic fiction exposes students to many different problems that real people face. Picture books such as *Charlie Anderson* (Abercrombie, 1990), *My Mother's House, My Father's House* (Christiansen, 1989), and *Diana, Maybe* (Dragonwagon, 1987) deal with divorce and stepfamilies, helping students see the many types of families that exist. Relationships with older people are examined in the picture books *Sea Swan* (Lasky, 1988) and *Wilfrid Gordon McDonald Partridge* (Fox, 1985). Adjusting to a new sibling is addressed in the picture books *Don't Touch My Room* (Lakin, 1985), *Everett Anderson's Nine Month Long* (Clifton, 1978), *Waiting for Baby* (Birdseye, 1991), and the novel *Dear Baby* (Rocklin, 1988).

Reading difficulties are dealt with in the picture book *The Wednesday Surprise* (Bunting, 1989) and the novel *Mostly Michael* (Smith, 1987). Being homeless is dealt with in the picture book *Fly Away Home* (Bunting, 1991) and the novel *The Leaves in October* (Ackerman, 1991). Saying good-bye to a farm and moving away are dealt with in the picture book *Time to Go* (Fiday & Fiday, 1990) and the novel *Good-bye My Wishing Star* (Grove, 1988). Saying good-bye to a person or a pet after death are dealt with in the picture book *Goodbye Max* (Keller, 1987) and the novelette *Blackberries in the Dark* (Jukes, 1985). All these books give readers insight into a variety of life experiences.

Literature allows reading for enjoyment.   Students will laugh with and enjoy books such as *The True Story of the Three Little Pigs* (Scieszka, 1989). This book tells the story of the Three Little Pigs from the wolf's point of view and is a natural read-aloud book for all ages! Similar retelling of folktales with humorous results are *The Frog Prince Continued* (Scieszka, 1991) and *The Stinky Cheese Man and Other Fairly Stupid Tales* (Scieszka, 1992). Enjoyment of word play is available from *Chortles* (Merriam, 1989) and *Fighting Words* (Merriam, 1992). Literal interpretation of figurative language is another way to enjoy literature. Books such as *Amelia Bedelia Goes Camping* (Parish, 1985) and *Amelia Bedelia's Family Album* (Parish, 1988) celebrate the literal interpretations of figurative language. Fred Gwynne's books *The King Who Rained* (1970), *A Little Pigeon Toad* (1988), and *A Chocolate Moose for Dinner* (1976) are other examples of this same type of humor. These picture books invite the life-long pursuit of reading for enjoyment for all ages.

Literature provides models for writing.   Patterned language books give readers ideas for writing formats. Books such as *The Z Was Zapped* (Van Allsburg, 1987) show how an alliterative alphabet book can be written about any subject. Good writing in general gives readers models of various literary devices, such as two-level stories, unique points of view, and descriptive writing. For example, *Meanwhile, Back at the Ranch* (Noble, 1987) is a great example of a two-level story with two settings and stories told simultaneously. Different points of view are used in some picture books where animals describe things. Descriptive writing about simple things is evident in *Woodpile* (Parnall, 1990). All these books provide excellent models for readers and writers of all ages.

Literature exposes readers to multicultural issues.   Multicultural literature can be a powerful vehicle for "the underlying purpose of multicultural education, to change the world by making it a more equitable one" (Bishop, 1992, p. 51). Picture books featuring African Americans, such as *Amazing Grace* (Hoffman, 1991), *Big Mama's* (Crews, 1991), and *Aunt Flossie's Hats (and Crab Cakes Later)* (Howard, 1991), focus on common literary themes. Novels such as *The Friendship* (Taylor, 1987) and *The Road to Memphis* (Taylor, 1990) deal with the struggles of racism in the United States.

Some picture books with Asian-Pacific American characters are *The Paper Crane* (Bang, 1985) and *The Lost Lake* (Say, 1989); novels include *In the Year of the Boar and Jackie Robinson* (Lord, 1984) and *Grandfather's Journey* (Say, 1992). Native American picture books include *The Legend of the Bluebonnet* (dePaola, 1983), *Itkomi and the Ducks* (Goble, 1990), *The Story of Jumping Mouse* (Steptoe, 1984), and *Dancing Teepees* (Sneve, 1989); novels include *Indian Chiefs* (Freedman, 1987) and *Happily May I Walk* (Hirschfelder, 1986). These books are critical for inclusion in a classroom to support a celebration of diversity and pride in cultural heritages.

Literature spans and enriches the entire curriculum.   Children's books enhance the study of content areas. For instance, the mathematical concepts of multiplication and division are explored in *The Doorbell Rang* (Hutchins, 1986). Other picture books with mathematical concepts are *How Much Is a Million?* (Schwartz, 1986), *If You Made a Million* (Schwartz, 1989), *Ed Emberley's Picture Pie* (Emberley, 1984), *The Great Take-Away* (Mathews, 1980), *Fish Eyes: A Book You Can Count On* (Ehlert, 1990), *Eyewitness Books: Money* (Cribb, 1990), *26 Letters and 99 Cents* (Hoban, 1987), *Time to . . .* (McMillan, 1989), *All in a Day* (Anno et al., 1986), *Up to Ten and Down Again* (Ernst, 1986), *Ten Black Dots* (Crews, 1986), *Ten Potatoes in a Pot and Other Counting Rhymes* (Katz, 1990), and *Farmer Mack Measures His Pig* (Johnston, 1986).

For integration with social studies, *A Clearing in the Forest* (Henry, 1992) gives readers real insight into settling the frontier. Other historical pioneer fiction books include *Cassie's Journey* (Harvey, 1988), *My Prairie Year* (Harvey, 1986), *My Prairie Christmas* (Harvey, 1990), *Log Cabin in the Woods* (Henry, 1988), *Going West* (Van Leeuwen, 1992), *Lottie's Dream* (Pryor, 1992), and *Aurora Means Dawn* (Sanders, 1989); novels include *Prairie Songs* (Conrad, 1985), *Westering* (Putnam, 1990), and *Grasshopper Summer* (Turner, 1989).

No study of dinosaurs in a science unit would be complete without enjoying and learning from the poems about dinosaurs in *Tyrannosaurus Was a Beast*

(Prelutsky, 1988). Other books for use in a dinosaur unit are the picture books *Dinosaur Bones* (Aliki, 1988), *Dinosaur* (Hopkins, 1987), *Dinosaurs Walked Here and Other Stories Fossils Tell* (Lauber, 1987), and *Prehistoric Pinkerton* (Kellogg, 1987); novels include *My Daniel* (Conrad, 1989) and *The Bone Wars* (Lasky, 1988).

Literature allows readers to do more than just read a story; it also nurtures their imagination.   Readers must add sounds, tastes, smells, and individual responses to the reading process, as Gary Paulsen (1989) points out in his introduction to *The Winter Room:* "If books could have more, give more, be more, show more, they would still need readers, who bring to them sound and smell and light and all the rest that can't be in books. The book needs you" (p. 3).

Books such as *Listen to the Rain* (Martin & Archambault, 1988), *Rain* (Spier, 1982), and *Rain Talk* (Serfozo, 1990) give the reader the sights, sounds, and smells associated with rain. And books such as Chris Van Allsburg's mysterious *The Wretched Stone* (1991) stretch readers' imagination and invite them to truly experience a book with all of their senses.

In many ways, children's literature serves as a major stimulus and motivation to curriculum integration. Providing children with literature that is authentic and rich in content allows readings and investigations that integrate language and thinking that cut across all curricular areas. "Trade books are an antidote to some of the textbook's worst problems. A wealth of attractively illustrated trade books are available. Children's literature offers the promise of exciting and colorful portrayals of in-depth issues, ethical dilemmas, social models, events, persons, and places by some of the best children's authors and illustrators" (Martorella, 1994, p. 286).

Myths Regarding Curriculum Integration

Lapp and Flood (1994) point to several myths that have arisen concerning curriculum integration:

Myth 1
The first myth says that in an integrated curriculum, all children are required to listen, speak, read, and write during every lesson. In reality, it is rare for a single lesson to combine all of the language arts.

Myth 2
The second myth says that "all curriculum integration is effective," but in reality, "effective curriculum integration occurs when the content from one subject is used to enhance or enrich the content of another"; "combining subject areas just for the sake of integration is not sound educational practice" (p. 418).

Myth 3

The third myth regarding curriculum integration says that "an integrated language arts curriculum focuses on the exploration of the language arts in the content areas." However, in reality, an integrated language arts curriculum "is developed around a theme from which goals are determined and activities planned" (p. 419).

Myth 4

The fourth myth says that an integrated curriculum and a literature-based curriculum are the same. In actuality, "a literature-based curriculum ties language arts instruction to central pieces of literature; a truly integrated curriculum emphasizes language as a social and cognitive phenomenon. It emphasizes language study throughout all the academic disciplines including literature in its many forms—fiction, information, texts, poetry, and drama—but is not limited to literature" (p. 419).

Myth 5

The fifth myth says that "effective integration requires that all teachers integrate all of the subject areas simultaneously." Trying to do too much at once, however, is a primary obstacle in planning an integrated curriculum. Instead, join with other teachers who want to create an integrated curriculum. "Begin your planning with topics that naturally overlap. Design one unit of instruction that you feel confident with and use it in your classrooms. Then evaluate its success and make appropriate changes and modifications." Proceed by seeking out other appropriate themes for units and developing them accordingly. As students begin to make connections between school and the world in which they live, "they become lifelong learners" (p. 419).

TEXTBOOKS AND OTHER INSTRUCTIONAL RESOURCES

In most elementary classrooms, the textbook *is* the curriculum. Too often, teachers use the textbook as the main source of information, often the only source of information, for a subject. Teachers follow the textbook as if it were the curriculum guide for the year: It dictates what will be taught, how much of it will be taught, and what content will be emphasized. It is not unusual to hear a teacher say, "Oh, I don't think I can cover all of the material in my textbook this year. There is just too much!" Such statements indicate the influence and impact the textbook has on the elementary school program. This is unfortunate but has been true in most subject areas. In science, math, social studies, and language arts, the textbook prescribes the instructional emphasis, dictates the topics to be addressed, and directs the time spent on various tasks. Textbooks are a powerful influence on the curriculum of the elementary school.

Textbooks do have some very strong points. They are usually well researched, systematically developed, and attractively designed. Most textbooks are well organized and the photography, illustrations, and graphics are often state-of-the-art. Generally, textbooks are not written by a single author but by a team of authors and editors who are well versed in the subject area. While such multiple authorship allows for the best thinking of a wide group of experts in the field, it often produces writing that, at best, lacks inspiration and, at worst, is boring.

Perhaps the most cogent fault of the textbook, however, is that the information it contains is highly selective in terms of the events, situations, and issues addressed. Beyond the obvious desire to present content that is rich, meaningful, and appropriate, the selection of textbook content revolves around four major factors:

- Space
- Tradition
- Influence of special interest groups
- Textbook adoption practices

The *limitation on space* in a textbook impacts the selection of content. In social studies, particularly, one finds there often is not enough room in the book to present a complete picture of the events being depicted. Consequently, descriptions and portrayals of particular events, situations, and issues are abbreviated and abridged or eliminated completely.

Textbooks are *inherently traditional* in the elementary school and particularly so in science and social studies. The expanding communities model in social studies, for example, has been used traditionally by textbook authors, editors, and publishers for years. It has dominated the scope and sequence framework of elementary social studies textbooks for decades.

When it comes to school textbooks, there seems always to exist a coterie of *special interest groups* who are concerned about promoting their particular views on specific issues. These special interest groups put pressure on textbook publishers to include or exclude certain content from school texts, content that they feel either promotes or conflicts with their group's interests. Consequently, textbook publishers have shied away from confrontations with such groups and have instead adopted a neutral or otherwise bland position so as not to offend any group.

Basically, school textbooks are selected through an adoption procedure whereby committees made up of classroom teachers, supervisors, principals, and parents examine the textbooks available and adopt those that most clearly meet their needs and support their curriculum. In some states, there is a *state textbook adoption system* where the state adopts the textbooks of two or more publishers in an area like elementary social studies, and then the local school systems select textbooks from those choices. Currently, there are

22 state-adoption states: Alabama, Arkansas, California, Florida, Georgia, Hawaii, Idaho, Indiana, Kentucky, Louisiana, Mississippi, Nevada, New Mexico, North Carolina, Oklahoma, Oregon, South Carolina, Tennessee, Texas, Utah, Virginia, and West Virginia. In other areas, *local adoptions* are held, where the local school systems adopt freely from the textbooks available from all publishers.

Because textbook publishing is an expensive endeavor requiring huge outlays of funds for development, production, and marketing, textbook publishers are very careful to produce textbooks that will have the best chance of doing well in the marketplace. And in the textbook publishing business, that means getting your textbooks adopted, especially in states where there are large populations. Of the states with state adoption procedures, California is the most populous and, therefore, the state that will buy the most textbooks. The curricular design of California, then, becomes very important to textbook publishers. Because of the state's textbook-buying clout, California's curricular model may pervade textbooks and be forced on other less-populated states and local educational agencies. Texas and Florida also have large populations, and their curricular patterns could also be influential in the material chosen by publishers for inclusion in textbooks.

Textbooks can be a valuable resource to the elementary school program, but they are just that, a resource. Textbooks cannot *be* the curriculum in any subject, nor can they be the only source of information for pupils. Indeed, the authors, editors, and publishers of textbooks never intended for them to be the curriculum or the sole source of information. Textbooks, if used at all, should be interwoven with rich literature and primary-source documents where higher-order thinking is encouraged and there is a multicultural, global view of the world.

SUMMARY

Language is the vehicle of learning and, as such, can be a strong impetus for curriculum integration. Because learning exists in context, a whole language approach to teaching literacy provides the empowerment necessary to extend learning across all content areas. It provides an environment where students are immersed in language, experiment with language, and have opportunities to demonstrate the uses of language (reading, writing, speaking, and listening) in a meaningful way.

Children's literature is not only beneficial and useful in teaching reading and writing skills, but it has the potential for making social studies, science, and other content areas interesting and relevant to the lives of students. Literature has a richness that can bring learning to life and create avenues to deeper under-standing and meaning. While textbooks can be a valuable resource to teaching and learning (and remember, they are just that, a resource), it is children's literature that is the most powerful tool for curricular integration.

ACTIVITY ONE

PURPOSE

The purpose of this activity is to work cooperatively in groups to create trees depicting the genres of children's literature.

PROCEDURE

Divide into six groups. Each group is to work cooperatively and collaboratively to design a tree with branches from which actual books can hang by string. Each group is assigned a specific genre of children's literature. Each group collects children's books depicting a certain genre and hangs the books from the book tree. The groups share their book trees, briefly discussing each genre as the book tree for that genre is presented.

Each group is assigned one of the following genres:

- picture book
- poetry
- historical fiction
- biography
- folklore
- nonfiction

ACTIVITY TWO

PURPOSE

The purpose of this activity is to work collaboratively in pairs to create bio-poems.

PROCEDURE

Divide into pairs and use Danielson's (1989) approach of using biographies of historical figures to collaborate in the development and composition of nine-line bio-poems. Each nine-line poem should adhere to the following arrangement:

Line 1	First name of the biographical subject
Line 2	Four adjectives that describe the subject
Line 3	Wife, husband, siblings of subject
Line 4	Lover of (three people, places, things)

Line 5	Who feels (three things)
Line 6	Who fears (three things)
Line 7	Who would like to see (three things)
Line 8	Resident of (city, state, country)
Line 9	Last name of biographical subject

Each group (pair) should share their bio-poem with the other groups by displaying the poem on an overhead while reading it and then perhaps have the group join in a choral reading of the bio-poem.

ACTIVITY THREE

PURPOSE

The purpose of this activity is to work collaboratively with another person to create a graphic-oriented presentation for a parent-teacher meeting on the benefits of using children's literature.

PROCEDURE

Divide into pairs and design transparencies for a parent-teacher meeting to outline the benefits of using children's literature in the elementary school program. Include the pros and cons of textbooks and their appropriate uses. End the activity with a presentation of the transparencies.

STUDY QUESTIONS

1. Explain the rationale for the statement, "Learning is language borne."
2. How can literacy instruction and whole language teaching bring about curricular integration? In what ways does whole language teaching provide the empowerment necessary to extend literacy across content areas?
3. A major tenet embodied in a whole language philosophy is that *learning exists in context.* What does this mean?
4. How would you describe the environment, the teaching strategies, and the learners in a whole language classroom?
5. Describe the traditional instructional emphasis embodied in a basal reading program and explain the steps in the basal teaching plan, often called a Directed Reading-Thinking Activity (DRTA). Can and should children's literature augment the basal teaching plan? Explain.
6. Compare, contrast, and discuss the use of textbooks, children's literature, and primary-source documents for teaching content-area information.

BIBLIOGRAPHY

Altwerger, B., Edelsky, C., & Flores, B. (1987). Whole language: What's new. *Reading Teacher, 41,* 144–155.

Ammon, R., & Weigard, J. (1993). A look at other trade book topics and genres. In M. Tunnell & R. Ammon (Eds.), *The story of ourselves.* Portsmouth, N.H.: Heinemann.

Aronson, E. (1978). *The jigsaw classroom.* Beverly Hills, Calif.: Sage.

Barr, I., & McGuire, M. (1993). Social studies and effective stories. *Social Studies and the Young Learner, 5* (3), 6–8, 11.

Beck, I., & McKeown, M. (1991). Research directions: Social studies texts are hard to understand: Mediating some of the difficulties. *Language Arts, 68,* 482–489.

Bishop, R. (1992). Multicultural literature for children: Making informed choices. In J. V. Harris (Ed.), *Teaching multicultural literature in grades K–8* (pp. 37–53). Norwood, Mass.: Christopher-Gordon.

California State Department of Education. (1987). *California history/social science framework for California public schools, kindergarten through grade twelve.* Sacramento: CSDE.

Cambourne, B. (1988). *The whole story: Natural learning and the acquisition of literacy in the classroom.* Auckland, New Zealand: Ashton Scholastic.

Casteel, C., & Isom, B. (1994). Reciprocal processes in science and literacy learning. *The Reading Teacher, 47* (7), 538–545.

Ceprano, M., & English, E. (1990). Fact and fiction: Personalizing social studies through the tradebook-textbook connection. *Reading Horizons, 30,* 66–77.

Chatton, B. (1989). Using literature across the curriculum. In J. Hickman & B. E. Cullinan (Eds.), *Children's literature in the classroom: Weaving Charlotte's web* (pp. 61–70). Needham Heights, Mass.: Christopher-Gordon.

Cordeiro, P. (1992). *Whole learning: Whole language and content in the upper elementary grades.* Katonah, N.Y.: Richard C. Owen.

Crafton, L. (1991). *Whole language: Getting started moving forward.* Katonah, N.Y.: Richard C. Owen.

Danielson, K., & LaBonty, J. (1994). *Integrating reading and writing through children's literature.* Boston: Allyn and Bacon.

Dobson, D., Monson, J., & Smith, J. (1992). A case study on integrating history and reading instruction through literature. *Social Education, 56* (7), 370–375.

Dowd, F. (1990). Geography is children's literature, math, science, art and a whole world of activities. *Journal of Geography, 89,* 68–73.

Edelsky, C., Altwerger, C., & Flores, B. (1991). *Whole language: What's the difference?* Portsmouth, N.H.: Heinemann.

Farris, P., & Cooper, S. (1994). *Elementary social studies: A whole language approach.* Madison, Wis.: WCB Brown & Benchmark Publishers.

Farris, P., & Fuhler, C. (1994). Developing social studies concepts through picture books. *The Reading Teacher, 47* (5), 380–387.

Ferreiro, E., & Teberosky, A. (1982). *Literacy before schooling.* Portsmouth, N.H.: Heinemann.

Galda, L. (1990). Children's books: Our natural world. *Reading Teacher, 41,* 322–326.

Greenfield, E. (1978). Harriet Tubman. In *Honey I love.* New York: Philomel Books.

Haynes, C. (1986). *Religious freedom in America: A teacher's guide.* Silver Spring, Md.: Americans United Research Foundation.

Holdaway, D. (1979). *The foundations of literacy.* New York: Scholastic.

Huck, C., Hepler, S., & Hickman, J. (1993) *Children's literature in the elementary school* (5th ed.). New York: Holt, Rinehart & Winston.

Jarolimek, J., & Parker, W. C. (1993). *Social studies in elementary education* (9th ed.). New York: Macmillan.

Johnson, N., & Ebert, M. (1992). Time travel is possible: Historical fiction and biography— Passport to the past. *Reading Journal, 45,* 488–495.

Lapp, D., & Flood, J. (1994). Integrating the curriculum: First steps. *The Reading Teacher, 47* (5), 416–419.

Louie, B. (1993). Using literature to teach location. *Social Studies and the Young Learner, 5,* 17–18, 22.

Martorella, P. (1994). *Social studies for elementary school children: Developing young citizens.* New York: Merrill.

May, F. (1994). *Reading as communication* (4th ed.). New York: Merrill.

Moir, H. (Ed.). (1992). *Collected perspectives: Choosing and using books for the classroom.* Boston: Christopher-Gordon.

Moss, J. (1984). *Focus on units in literature: A handbook for elementary school teachers.* Urbana, Ill.: National Council of Teachers of English.

Pappas, C., Kiefer, B., & Levstik, L. (1995). *An integrated language perspective in the elementary school: Theory into action* (2nd ed.). White Plains, N.Y.: Longman.

Perkins, P. (1995). *The ABC's of whole language.* Westminster, Calif.: Teacher Created Materials, Inc.

Peterson, R. (1992). *Life in a crowded place: Making a learning community.* Portsmouth, N.H.: Heinemann.

Routman, R. (1991). *Invitations: Changing as teachers and learners K-12.* Portsmouth, N.H.: Heinemann.

Rubin, D. (1993). *A practical approach to teaching reading* (2nd. ed.). Boston: Allyn and Bacon.

Sanacore, J. (1993). Supporting a literature-based approach across the curriculum. *Journal of Reading, 37* (3), 240–244.

Shanahan, T., Robinson, B., & Schneider, M. (1993). Integrating curriculum: Integration of curriculum or interaction of people? *The Reading Teacher, 47* (2), 158–159.

Spiegel, D. (1992). Blending whole language and systematic direct instruction. *The Reading Teacher, 46* (1), 38–44.

Stafford, J. (1993). How to teach about religions in the elementary social studies classroom. *The Social Studies, 84,* 245–248.

Stice, C., Bertrand, J., & Bertrand, N. (1995). *Integrating reading and the other language arts.* Belmont, Calif.: Wadsworth.

Tchudi, S. (1994). *Integrated language arts in the elementary school.* Belmont, Calif.: Wadsworth.

Tomasino, K. (1993). Literature and social studies. A spicy mix for fifth graders. *Social Studies and the Young Learner, 5* (4), 7–10.

Walley, C., & Walley, K. (1995). *Integrating literature in content areas.* Westminster, Calif.: Teacher Created Materials, Inc.

Weaver, C. (1990). *Understanding whole language: From principles to practices.* Portsmouth, N.H.: Heinemann.

Zarnowski, M. (1990). *Learning about biographies: A reading-and-writing approach for children.* Urbana, Ill.: National Council of Teachers of English.

CHILDREN'S LITERATURE CITED

Abercrombie, B. (1990). *Charlie Anderson.* New York: McElderry.

Ackerman, K. (1991). *The leaves in October.* New York: Atheneum.

Aliki. (1988). *Dinosaur bones.* New York: Harper & Row.

Anno, M., Carle, E., Briggs, R., Popov, N., Hayashi, A., Calvi, G., Dillon, L., Dillon, D., Cheglian, Z., & Brooks, R. (1986). *All in a day.* New York: Philomel.

Baker, J. (1991). *Window.* New York: Greenwillow.

Bang, M. (1985). *The paper crane.* New York: Greenwillow.

Bennett, D. (1990). *One cow, moo, moo.* New York: Holt.

Birdseye, T. (1991). *Waiting for baby.* New York: Holiday House.

Brooks, B. (1991). *Nature by design.* New York: Farrar, Straus & Giroux.

Brusca, M. (1991). *On the pampas.* New York: Henry Holt.

Bunting, E. (1989). *The Wednesday surprise.* New York: Clarion.

Bunting, E. (1991). *Fly away home.* New York: Clarion.

Butler, D. (1989). *My brown bear, Barney.* New York: Greenwillow.

Butler, D. (1993). *My brown bear Barney in trouble.* New York: Greenwillow.

Calmenson, S. (1989). *The principal's new clothes.* New York: Scholastic.

Carlstrom, N. (1986). *Jesse bear, what will you wear?* New York: Macmillan.

Christiansen, C. (1989). *My mother's house, my father's house.* New York: Atheneum.

Clifton, L. (1978). *Everett Anderson's nine month long.* New York: Henry Holt.

Conrad, P. (1985). *Prairie songs.* New York: Harper & Row.

Conrad, P. (1989). *My Daniel.* New York: Harper & Row.

Crews, D. (1986). *Ten black dots.* New York: Greenwillow.

Crews, D. (1991). *Big Mama's.* New York: Greenwillow.

Cribb, J. (1990). *Eyewitness books: Money.* New York: Knopf.

Day, A. (1985). *Good dog, Carl.* New York: Simon and Schuster.

dePaola, T. (1983). *The legend of the bluebonnet.* New York: Putnam.

Dooley, N. (1991). *Everybody cooks rice.* Minneapolis: Carolrhoda.

Dragonwagon, C. (1987). *Diana, maybe.* New York: Macmillan.

Ehlert, L. (1989). *Color zoo.* New York: Lippincott.

Ehlert, L. (1989). *Eating the alphabet: Fruits and vegetables from A to Z.* San Diego: Harcourt Brace Jovanovich.

Ehlert, L. (1990). *Color farm.* New York: Lippincott.

Ehlert, L. (1990). *Fish eyes: A book you can count on.* San Diego: Harcourt Brace Jovanovich.

Emberley, E. (1984). *Ed Emberley's picture pie.* Boston: Little, Brown.

Ernst, L. (1986). *Up to ten and down again.* New York: Lothrop, Lee & Shepard.

Fiday, B., & Fiday, D. (1990). *Time to go.* San Diego: Harcourt Brace Jovanovich.

Fox, M. (1985). *Wilfrid Gordon McDonald Partridge.* New York: Kane/Miller.

Freedman, R. (1987). *Indian chiefs.* New York: Holiday House.

Gibbons, G. (1990). *How a house is built.* New York: Holiday House.

Ginsburg, M. (1972). *The chick and the duckling.* New York: Macmillan.

Goble, P. (1990). *Itkomi and the ducks.* New York: Orchard.

Grejniec, M. (1992). *What do you like?* New York: North-South Books.

Grove, V. (1988). *Good-bye my wishing star.* New York: Putnam.

Guarino, D. (1989). *Is your mama a llama?* New York: Scholastic.

Gwynne, F. (1970). *The king who rained.* New York: Prentice Hall.

Gwynne, F. (1976). *A chocolate moose for dinner.* New York: Prentice Hall.

Gwynne, F. (1988). *A little pigeon toad.* New York: Simon and Schuster.

Harvey, B. (1986). *My prairie year.* New York: Holiday House.

Harvey, B. (1988). *Cassie's journey.* New York: Holiday House.

Harvey, B. (1990). *My prairie Christmas.* New York: Holiday House.

Heide, F., & Gilliland, J. (1992). *Sami and the time of the troubles.* New York: Clarion.

Henry, J. (1988). *Log cabin in the woods.* New York: Four Winds Press.

Henry, J. (1992). *A clearing in the forest.* New York: Four Winds Press.

Hirschfelder, A. (1986). *Happily may I walk: American Indians and Alaska natives today.* New York: Scribners.

Hoban, T. (1987). *26 letters and 99 cents.* New York: Greenwillow.

Hoban, T. (1989). *Of colors and things.* New York: Greenwillow.

Hoban, T. (1990). *Exactly the opposite.* New York: Greenwillow.

Hoban, T. (1992). *Look up, look down.* New York: Greenwillow.

Hoban, T. (1992). *Spirals, curves, fanshapes & lines.* New York: Greenwillow.

Hoffman, M. (1991). *Amazing Grace.* New York: Dial.

Hopkins, L. (1987). *Dinosaurs.* San Diego: Harcourt Brace Jovanovich.

Howard, E. (1991). *Aunt Flossie's hats (and crab cakes later).* New York: Clarion.

Hutchins, P. (1986). *The doorbell rang.* New York: Greenwillow.

Isadora, R. (1992). *Over the green hills.* New York: Greenwillow.

Johnston, T. (1986). *Farmer Mack measures his pig.* New York: Harper & Row.

Jonas, A. (1983). *Round trip.* New York: Greenwillow.

Jonas, A. (1987). *Reflections.* New York: Greenwillow.

Jukes, M. (1985). *Blackberries in the dark.* New York: Knopf.

Katz, M. (1990). *Ten potatoes in a pot and other counting rhymes.* New York: Harper & Row.

Keller, H. (1987). *Goodbye Max.* New York: Greenwillow.

Kellogg, S. (1987). *Prehistoric Pinkerton.* New York: Dial.

Lakin, P. (1985). *Don't touch my room.* Boston: Little, Brown.

Lankford, M. (1992). *Hopscotch around the world.* New York: Morrow.

Lasky, K. (1988). *The bone wars.* New York: Morrow.

Lasky, K. (1988). *Sea swan.* New York: Macmillan.

Lauber, P. (1987). *Dinosaurs walked here and other stories fossils tell.* New York: Bradbury.

Lobel, A. (1990). *Alison's zinnia.* New York: Dial.

Locker, T. (1988). *Family farm.* New York: Dial.

Lockwood, P. (1989). *Cat boy!* New York: Clarion.

Lord, B. (1984). *In the year of the boar and Jackie Robinson.* New York: Harper & Row.

Lowry, L. (1989). *Number the stars.* Boston: Houghton Mifflin.

Macaulay, D. (1988). *The way things work.* Boston: Houghton Mifflin.

Macaulay, D. (1990). *Black and white.* Boston: Houghton Mifflin.

MacLachlan, P. (1985). *Sarah, plain and tall.* New York: Harper & Row.

Martin, B. (1991). *Polar bear, polar bear, what do you hear?* New York: Holt.

Martin, B., & Archambault, J. (1988). *Listen to the rain.* New York: Holt.

Martin, B., & Archambault, J. (1989). *Chicka chicka boom boom.* New York: Simon and Schuster.

Mathews, L. (1980). *The great take-away.* New York: Dodd.

McMillan, B. (1989). *Time to . . . .* New York: Lothrop, Lee & Shepard.

Merriam, E. (1989). *Chortles.* New York: Morrow.

Merriam, E. (1992). *Fighting words.* New York: Morrow.

Morris, A. (1989). *Bread, bread, bread.* New York: Lothrop, Lee & Shepard.

Morris, A. (1989). *Hats, hats, hats.* New York: Lothrop, Lee & Shepard.

Neitzel, S. (1989). *The jacket I wear in the snow.* New York: Greenwillow.

Neitzel, S. (1992). *The dress I'll wear to the party.* New York: Greenwillow.

Noble, T. (1987). *Meanwhile, back at the ranch.* New York: Dial.

Parish, P. (1985). *Amelia Bedelia goes camping.* New York: Greenwillow.

Parish, P. (1988). *Amelia Bedelia's family album.* New York: Greenwillow.

Parnall, P. (1990). *Woodpile.* New York: Macmillan.

Paulsen, G. (1989). *The winter room.* New York: Orchard.

Peek, M. (1985). *Mary wore her red dress.* New York: Clarion.

Prelutsky, J. (1988). *Tyrannosaurus was a beast.* New York: Greenwillow.

Pryor, B. (1992). *Lottie's dream.* New York: Simon and Schuster.

Putnam, A. (1990). *Westering.* New York: Lodestar.

Rocklin, J. (1988). *Dear baby.* New York: Macmillan.

Roe, E. (1990). *All I am.* New York: Bradbury.

Sanders, S. (1989). *Aurora means dawn.* New York: Bradbury.

Say, A. (1989). *The lost lake.* Boston: Houghton Mifflin.

Say, A. (1992). *Grandfather's journey.* Boston: Houghton Mifflin.

Schwartz, D. (1986). *How much is a million?* New York: Lothrop, Lee & Shepard.

Schwartz, D. (1989). *If you made a million.* New York: Lothrop, Lee & Shepard.

Scieszka, J. (1989). *The true story of the three little pigs.* New York: Viking.

Scieszka, J. (1991). *The frog prince continued.* New York: Viking.

Scieszka, J. (1992). *The stinky cheese man and other fairly stupid tales.* New York: Viking.

Serfozo, M. (1990). *Rain talk.* New York: McElderry.

Shaw, N. (1986). *Sheep in a jeep.* Boston: Houghton Mifflin.

Smith, R. (1987). *Mostly Michael.* New York: Delacorte.

Sneve, V. (Ed.). (1989). *Dancing teepees: Poems of American Indian youth.* New York: Holiday House.

Spier, P. (1982). *Rain.* Garden City, N.Y.: Doubleday.

Steptoe, J. (1984). *The story of jumping mouse.* New York: Lothrop, Lee & Shepard.

Tafuri, N. (1988). *Spots, feathers, and curly tails.* New York: Greenwillow.

Taylor, M. (1987). *The friendship.* New York: Dial.

Taylor, M. (1990). *The road to Memphis.* New York: Dial.

Turner, A. (1987). *Nettie's trip south.* New York: Macmillan.

Turner, A. (1989). *Grasshopper summer.* New York: Macmillan.

Van Allsburg, C. (1981). *Jumanji.* Boston: Houghton Mifflin.

Van Allsburg, C. (1985). *The polar express.* Boston: Houghton Mifflin.

Van Allsburg, C. (1987). *The z was zapped.* Boston: Houghton Mifflin.

Van Allsburg, C. (1988). *Two bad ants.* Boston: Houghton Mifflin.

Van Allsburg, C. (1991). *The wretched stone.* Boston: Houghton Mifflin.

Van Leeuwen, J. (1992). *Going west.* New York: Dial.

Wiesner, D. (1991). *Tuesday.* New York: Clarion.

Williams, S. (1989). *I went walking.* San Diego: Harcourt Brace Jovanovich.

Wood, J. (1992). *Moo moo, brown cow.* San Diego: Harcourt Brace Jovanovich.

Yektai, N. (1987). *Bears in pairs.* New York: Bradbury.

Young, E. (1989). *Lon Po Po: A Red-Riding Hood story from China.* New York: Philomel.

CHAPTER

7

INTEGRATING THE CURRICULUM THROUGH THEMES

CHAPTER OBJECTIVES

After reading this chapter you should be able to:

1. Describe a thematic approach to teaching and explain its potential for integrating the curriculum
2. List some advantages of using a thematic approach
3. Outline some appropriate considerations when selecting a theme
4. Explain how themewebs and bookwebs are used in organizing the theme
5. Explain the procedures for gathering materials and resources for a thematic unit
6. Depict the role of whole language activities in a fully functioning thematic unit
7. Describe options for implementing a thematic unit
8. Construct a sample daily teaching plan for a thematic unit
9. Address the appropriateness of religion as a thematic topic

THEME STUDIES AND THEMATIC UNITS

Theme studies and thematic teaching offer one of the most promising formats for integrating the subjects of the elementary school curriculum. **Themed teaching** utilizes a central theme around which the inquiry and learning take place. All learning activities revolve around the central theme. "A thematic approach to learning combines structured, sequential, and well-organized strategies, activities, children's literature, and materials used to expand a particular concept. A thematic unit is multidisciplinary and multidimensional; it knows no boundaries. It is responsive to the interests, abilities, and needs of children and is respectful of their developing aptitudes and attitudes. In essence, a thematic approach to learning offers students a realistic arena in which they can pursue learning using a host of contexts and a panorama of literature" (Meinbach, Rothlein, & Fredericks, 1995, p. 5).

Thematic units are instructional designs created around a central idea and lasting for an extended period of time, perhaps a few days, a week, or even longer. The thematic unit approach to teaching is not new. (See Chapter 4 and Figure 4.8, illustrating part of a unit plan associated with the project method, dated around 1928.) The unit method fell into disfavor in the 1980s but resurged in the middle and late 1990s and has become the focal point for current curriculum integration (Maxim, 1995).

Identifying thematic teaching and the study of themes as the core, substance, and nucleus of what children do in school when they engage in thematic learning, Gamberg, Kwak, Hutchings, and Altheim (1988) write this about the characteristics of a theme study approach:

> First and foremost, it involves in-depth study. A theme or topic (not reading or math or science) is the focus of attention. For a theme to qualify as deserving of study, it must fulfill several criteria: it must be of interest to the children; it must be broad enough so that it can be divided into smaller subtopics also of interest to the children; the relationship of the subtopics to the wider context must remain clean; and the topic should not be geographically or historically limiting. Throughout the study, the topic should lend itself to comparing and contrasting ideas and permit extensive investigation of concrete situations, materials, and resources. The topic should be conducive to breaking down the walls within the school—those invisible barriers that artificially demarcate knowledge from itself and place it in categories called "subjects"—so that a rich cross-disciplinary program is possible. The topic should lend itself also to breaking down the walls between the school and society that prevent children from using the surrounding world as a laboratory for their studies. It should encourage an understanding and appreciation of the community. (p. 10)

Additionally, Gamberg, Kwak, Hutchings, and Altheim (1988) explain that theme studies are exciting because they

- are successful with all children
- are child-centered
- make learning unquestionably purposeful

- make good use of class time and make learning productive
- build a bridge between school and community and help children understand the world in which they live
- encourage parent involvement
- can be done by all teachers
- provide an environment where children learn many skills and a great deal of content
- encourage children to think, solve problems, and become independent learners
- provide opportunities for children to learn to cooperate and become sensitive to others
- provide an environment where children learn to become responsible
- furnish children with opportunities to develop self-discipline
- give children self-confidence and self-esteem
- provide an educational setting where children love learning

ADVANTAGES OF THEMATIC TEACHING

An integrated curriculum really blooms through thematic teaching. Thematic approaches use a variety of materials, literature, activities, and strategies which cross curricular lines and allow children to expand their learning by exploring particular concepts and themes in depth and in all dimensions. Students are focused more on the processes of learning than on the products of learning. The barriers between subject areas are removed. The curriculum is child-centered and tailored to the needs, interests, and abilities of the children. Students become increasingly more self-directing in their learning pursuits. Thematic teaching helps children see the relationships that exist between ideas and concepts, thereby increasing their comprehension. Children are afforded realistic opportunities to build on their own informational backgrounds as they develop new knowledge. Risk-taking is encouraged and approximations are perceived as important steps on the road to reaching the absolutes in learning. Increased opportunities to participate in a wide variety of activity-oriented learning events help students develop more self-direction and independence. First-hand experiences and self-initiated discoveries are enhanced by extended time for exploration, allowing students to reflect on their learning. Box 7.1 lists these advantages.

Thematic teaching also expands opportunities for teachers because it allows them to use a variety of methods and strategies in a holistic, multidimensional, and cooperative environment. Instruction isn't crammed into artificial time periods, but rather is extended across the curriculum and across the school day. Connections between subjects, topics, and themes are logical and made naturally. Relationships are easy to observe and readily comprehensible. Learning is seen as a continuous activity, unrestricted by time, books, or the environment, and

Box 7.1   ADVANTAGES OF THEMATIC
           TEACHING FOR STUDENTS

- Focuses more on the *processes* of learning than the *products* of learning.
- Breaks down the "artificial barriers" that often exist between areas of the curriculum and provides an integrative approach to learning.
- Provides a child-centered curriculum—one tailored to their interests, needs, and abilities; one in which they are encouraged to make their own decisions and assume a measure of responsibility for learning.
- Stimulate self-directed discovery and investigation inside and outside of the classroom.
- Assists youngsters in developing relationships between ideas and concepts, thereby enhancing appreciation and comprehension.
- Offers realistic opportunities for children to build on their own individual background of information in developing new knowledge.
- Respects the individual cultural background, home experiences, and interest levels of children.
- Stimulates the creation of important concepts through first-hand experiences and self-initiated discoveries.
- Students are encouraged (and supported in their efforts) to take risks.
- Students develop more self-direction and independence through a variety of learning activities and opportunities.
- Students understand the "why" of activities and events instead of just the "what."
- Students are encouraged to make approximations of learning, rather than focus on the absolutes of learning.
- Children have sustained time and opportunity to investigate topics thoroughly and to engage in reflective inquiry.

Adapted from A. Meinback, L. Rothlein, & A. Fredricks. (1995). *The Complete Guide to Thematic Units: Creating the Integrated Curriculum* (p. 4). Norwood, Mass.: Christopher-Gordon Publishers, Inc.

often can be extended into the personal lives of the learners. Students assume a sense of ownership for their learning as teachers share control of the curriculum with the learners. Students are assisted in pursuing answers and solutions from a variety of viewpoints with an emphasis on collaboration and cooperation. Abundant opportunities arise for including children's literature and for authentic uses of all of the language arts. Teachers have numerous occasions to model appropriate learning behaviors and to provide assessment in a holistic, authentic, and meaningful way. Higher-order thinking skills are practiced through the critical and creative thinking processes inherent in collaborative problem solving. Thematic teaching provides optimum conditions for teachers to nurture and promote self-direction in their students. Box 7.2 lists these advantages.

BOX 7.2   ADVANTAGES OF THEMATIC TEACHING FOR TEACHERS

- There is more time available for instructional purposes. Material does not have to be crammed into artificial time periods, but can be extended across the curriculum and across the day.
- The connections that can and do exist between subjects, topics, and themes can be logically and naturally developed. Teachers can demonstrate relationships and assist students in comprehending those relationships.
- Learning can be demonstrated as a continuous activity—one not restricted by textbook designs, time barriers, or even the four walls of the classroom. Teachers can help students extend learning opportunities into many aspects of their personal lives.
- Teachers are able to relinquish "control" of the curriculum and assist students in assuming a sense of "ownership" for their individual learning destinies.
- Teachers are free to help students look at a problem, situation, or topic from a variety of viewpoints, rather than the "right way" frequently demonstrated in a teacher's manual or curriculum guide.
- The development of a "community of learners" is facilitated and enhanced through thematic teaching. There is less emphasis on *competition* and more emphasis on *collaboration* and *cooperation.*
- Opportunities develop for the teacher to model appropriate learning behaviors in a supportive and encouraging environment.
- Assessment is more holistic, authentic, and meaningful and provides a more accurate picture of a student's progress and development.
- Authentic use of all the language arts (reading, writing, listening, and speaking) is encouraged throughout all curricular areas.
- There is *more* emphasis on *teaching* students, *less* emphasis on *telling* students.
- Teachers have abundant opportunities for integrating children's literature into all aspects of the curriculum and all aspects of the day.
- Teachers can promote problem-solving, creative thinking, and critical thinking processes within all aspects of a topic.
- Teachers can more readily foster and promote self-direction in students.

Adapted from A. Meinback, L. Rothlein, & A. Fredricks. (1995). *The Complete Guide to Thematic Units: Creating the Integrated Curriculum* (pp. 3–4). Norwood, Mass.: Christopher-Gordon Publishers, Inc.

TEACHING THEMATICALLY

Planning for effective and successful thematic instruction requires some specialized organization. Lapp and Flood (1994) suggest the following key steps for planning a thematic unit:

Selecting a Theme

The first step in developing an integrated curriculum requires the identification of a theme. To make classroom instruction as relevant as possible, encourage students to be involved in the selection of themes. Themes should reflect students' interests and be broad enough to allow you to incorporate the skills and information required for your specific grade level into them. Remember, all of the skills and activities that are taught should be natural extensions of the theme you select. Avoid selecting a theme that is so narrow that it becomes difficult to develop worthwhile instructional activities.

Collecting Texts and Other Materials

Next, you will need to gather materials that relate to the theme that you and your students have selected. Begin by using the materials that you have in your classroom: Textbooks can be a critical part of an integrated curriculum. As you begin to develop your theme study, expand your search for materials to include computer programs, videos, games, films, and music. Remember that your school librarian is a great source for more information on a particular theme.

Engaging Students

After you have gathered materials, you need to determine the specific goals and objectives that you will want to accomplish and then plan for activities that will meet your objectives and promote conceptual learning. Brophy and Alleman (1991) suggest that activities should be educationally significant and should foster accomplishment of major goals.

Grouping Students

Now determine how each phase of your instructional plan and the corresponding activities will be carried out. Detail what portions will be done in whole group instructional formats and in other grouping patterns (small groups, dyads, individually). Involve students in various grouping arrangements. Such arrangements provide you with opportunities for content-specific instruction and minilessons focusing on specific skills within the language arts.

Expanding the Theme

Identify ways in which students will have opportunities to expand the theme. These may take the form of additional readings or even

Box 7.3   Five-Step Guideline for Designing Theme Studies

1. Selecting the Theme
2. Organizing the Theme
3. Gathering Materials and Resources
4. Designing Activities and Projects
5. Implementing the Thematic Unit

additional projects. A word of caution, however: Do not lose sight of the goals you have set for student learning in a flurry of unrelated activities. Use theme expansions as opportunities for both whole and small group minilessons regarding content area information and language arts processes.

Assessing Student Growth

As you plan meaningful, authentic activities for students, remember to plan assessment to determine if each student is making progress toward the instructional goals. Assessment may take many forms, from portfolios to class projects. Whatever form your assessment takes, it is important that it complement your designated goals and instructional activities. (pp. 417–418)

As one might expect, teaching thematically requires careful planning and organization. Box 7.3 presents a five-step guideline for designing effective and successful thematic units. Suggested by Meinbach, Rothlein, and Fredericks (1995), each step in the guideline is explained and analyzed in substantial detail below.[1]

SELECTING THE THEME

Selecting appropriate thematic topics is perhaps the most important and critical element in utilizing themes to initiate an integrated curriculum. There are many worthwhile topics for themes close at hand. Several sources of appropriate topics for initiating theme studies were developed by Martinello and Cook (1994) and are listed in Box 7.4 and described thereafter.

Children's Common Interests.   Children often demonstrate a common interest in certain topics—for example, dolphins. They will choose to read books about dolphins, talk about dolphins, draw pictures of dolphins, play with dolphin

---

[1] Adapted from A. Meinbach, L. Rothlein, & A. Fredericks. (1995). *The Complete Guide to Thematic Units: Creating the Integrated Curriculum* (pp. 9–11). Norwood, Mass.: Christopher-Gordon Publishers, Inc. Used with permission.

BOX 7.4   SOURCES FOR THEME TOPICS

- Children's Common Interests
- Children's Special Interests
- Trade Books (Children's Literature)
- Topics from Textbooks
- Artwork: Paintings, Sculptures, Drawings, Etchings, Watercolors, Murals, and More
- Things Happening in the World (Current Events)
- Special Community Sites
- The Cultural Heritage of People
- Special Expertise or Interests of the Teacher
- Real Objects and Artifacts
- Abstract Ideas

---

toys, write stories about dolphins, and so on. Because teachers know many of the common interests that children have, they can often find themes that will develop into explorations of significant ideas, concepts, and generalizations.

Children's Special Interests.   When a group of third graders found a small puddle filled with tadpoles on their way to school, their curiosity was aroused. They put as many tadpoles as they could into jars and took them to school. Because of the special interest exhibited by the children, the teacher saw the potential for a worthwhile theme study that would have highly motivated children questioning, probing, observing, reading, writing, drawing, collecting data, and entering into fervent and enthusiastic discussion. The children's special interest led them into some serious research.

Trade Books (Children's Literature).   (See Chapter 6 for a detailed discussion of the values and uses of trade books in curriculum integration.) Books such as *Hats, Hats, Hats* (Morris, 1989) and *Bread, Bread, Bread* (Morris, 1989) introduce readers to the many ways people around the world live and work. Through such trade books, children can examine the similarities and differences in, for example, food and clothing among various cultures in the world. Books depicting the lives of African Americans, such as *Amazing Grace* (Hoffman, 1991), *The Friendship* (Taylor, 1987), and *The Road to Memphis* (Taylor, 1990), give children insights and a different perspective for considering the struggles of racism in the United States. *A Clearing in the Forest* (Henry, 1992) is a wonderful book for helping children gain real insights into the settling of the frontier. The poems about dinosaurs in *Tyrannosaurus Was a Beast* (Prelutsky, 1988) and other books about dinosaurs, such as *Dinosaur Bones* (Aliki, 1988),

Dinosaur (Hopkins, 1987), *Dinosaurs Walked Here and Other Stories Fossils Tell* (Lauber, 1987), *Patrick's Dinosaurs* (Carrick, 1983), and *Prehistoric Pinkerton* (Kellogg, 1987), motivate children to make detailed explorations of prehistoric time. *Nature by Design* (Brooks, 1991) turns children on to the natural world as it examines the wonders of nature, from the oyster's shell to the beaver's dam. E. B. White's *Charlotte's Web* (1952) can propel children into an exploration of spiders, farm life, the geometric patterns in spiders' webs, and the like. Linking trade books to themes makes learning meaningful, interesting, and relevant, and can lead children to develop significant concepts and generalizations. Children's literature is self-perpetuating, in that it leads students to read and explore other books and other topics in their pursuit to know and find out.

Topics from Textbooks.   Textbooks are general, in that they are written to meet the needs of large audiences and to cover vast amounts of material. Textbooks can, however, serve as a reference and resource for children and teachers and often provide a starting point for selecting thematic topics. Textbook topics can often be developed into larger studies. Teacher's guides can also be helpful in providing ideas for topics, as well as identifying potential concepts and objectives. (See Chapter 6 for more about textbooks.)

Artwork: Paintings, Sculptures, Drawings, Etchings, Watercolors, Murals, and More.   Artwork, of course, inspired that old adage about a picture's being worth a thousand words. That may or may not be true, but in any event, artwork can certainly inspire, motivate, and stimulate, often providing excellent theme topics. A picture may lead students into extensive investigations, many times exciting their own artistic and creative inclinations. Sculptures, etchings, and other artwork with three-dimensional characteristics can appeal to the tactile nature in children, often taking learning down new pathways. Art as depicted in murals often tells a story, sometimes about an event, a culture, or a part of the world.

Things Happening in the World (Current Events).   The relevancy of the real world is compelling! Keeping up with current affairs brings the events of the real world into the school setting in a fitting way. Topics for theme studies develop naturally from events and issues reported in the media. Children are led by the teacher to identify and explore the underlying themes that are significant in the news. The O. J. Simpson double-murder trial, for example, overwhelmed the media in 1995 and brought a myriad of issues, questions, and concerns to the forefront, many of which became good topics for theme studies. The breakup of the Union of Soviet Socialist Republics (U.S.S.R.) and the changes that followed in that part of the world provided numerous theme topics. The problems in Bosnia-Herzegovina, for example, focused on a part of the world about which most Americans knew little and on problems created by cultural and religious differences that would provide a plethora of rich theme topics.

Special Community Sites. Sites in the local area have a particular relevance and immediacy for children and young people. Most schools provide for field trips to special sites in the community. It is important for students to know about the history and heritage of their community. A local site can become the central point of interest in a larger theme study, providing students with both a deeper understanding of the site itself and its relevance to the larger world.

A fifth grade interdisciplinary team selected the Fort Toulouse Historic Site near Montgomery, Alabama, as a focus for a theme study. Their central question was: Why was the fort established? This question led them to explore the theme of motivation. During their inquiry, the fifth graders became extremely knowledgeable about Fort Toulouse itself and about the motivating factors in the building of forts in general. They discovered many important ideas: water access (navigable rivers) is important to a fort, buildings are designed to meet specific purposes, building materials are limited to what is available in the area, religion has an influence in the building and design of the fort, politics has an influence in the building and design of the fort, strong convictions are apparent in those who build and occupy forts, and the like. This highly successful field trip was the centerpiece of an integrated theme study that included historical, geographical, scientific, sociological, and mathematical inquiry.

The Cultural Heritage of People. Folktales often relate the cultural heritage of a people in powerful ways. Millions of Native Americans inhabited North and South America over 400 years ago. They represented diverse populations living in literally thousands of tribes and clans spread throughout the two continents. Their cultures and traditions were reflected in the folklore that was handed down from generation to generation. Sometimes their folktales were in the form of creation myths that explained the origin of humankind. Other folktales were legends about various animals, like the eagle, the wolf, or the bear. Many folktales gave reasons for the existence of the sun, the stars, and the moon. Different tribes had their own stories to help them make sense of the world in which they lived. Their folktales tell us that Native Americans had a tremendous respect for nature and a special relationship with the animals with whom they shared their lands. Children learn a great deal about Native American clothing, food, shelter, customs, and crafts from children's trade books based on Native American folklore. Typical of excellent children's literature that invites children to explore Native American cultures are Cherry's *The River Ran Wild,* Cohlene's *Dancing Drum, a Cherokee Legend,* Hinton's *Ishi's Tale of Lizard,* Lyon and Catalanotto's *Dreamplace,* and Martin and Archambault's *Knots on a Counting Rope.*

Holiday topics are often used for special school studies and frequently include activities that overlap different areas of the curriculum. Valentine's Day, for example, was used as a basis for a theme study on friendship by one class. They discovered that people often show their feelings for one another with gifts, celebrations with food, art, music, poetry, and the like, but their celebrations differ according to their cultural practices. The meanings behind the celebrations, however, are similar.

A theme study on Kwanzaa, the seven-day holiday between December 26 and January 1 that celebrates African-American culture, can provide vivid cultural insights. Such a study might include the *nguzo saba,* or seven principles of human life, that affect everyone: unity, self-determination, collective work and responsibility, cooperative economics, purpose, creativity, and faith. Students become aware that all seven principles can be related to their own lives and that these universal and unifying principles transcend cultural differences.

The common elements of cultural heritage, like sharing similar hopes, having similar fears, and experiencing the same drives, are frequently topics found in children's literature.

Special Expertise or Interests of the Teacher. Teachers will often have a special interest or a special expertise for which they have so much enthusiasm, motivation, and interest that it becomes infectious. The interest of the students is piqued, and a very valuable theme study is likely to follow. A teacher's enthusiasm for trains and railroading, for example, was spread to his students. Acting as facilitator, he coordinated and synchronized his students' inquiry into the geography of railways, the history of railroads, the plotting of timetables, the changes in railroading over the years, and railroad folklore. The students extended the ideas and concepts they developed into generalizations:

- Transportation has an impact on people's lives.
- People's needs influence transportation.
- Advancements in technology influence transportation.

Real Objects and Artifacts. Tangible things can often be the starting point for theme studies. Studying objects that are tangible, that is, physical and concrete, allow perception by the senses. Real objects and artifacts are "readable." As an example, one can see the leather covering on a football, touch it and feel its texture, examine the pattern of its laces, find the stamp depicting the name and location of its manufacturer, examine its shape, and so on. Questions arise about each observation: Why use leather? Where does the leather come from? Are there different types and textures of leather? Why is it laced instead of sewn? What's inside the leather covering? Does the manufacturer make only footballs? How are footballs made? What tools and machinery are needed? Is there some reason for the football manufacturer to be in a particular city? Have footballs always been shaped the way they are? Must footballs be shaped as they are? Other commonplace objects can evoke similar questions. Such tangible, real objects can often become the focal points for valuable theme studies.

Artifacts are especially engaging because they are filled with the lore of the past. They have tales to tell! What stories, for example, can be found in a great-grandfather's drinking gourd found in an old barn, in a barnacle-encrusted ship's anchor half-buried in the sand on a beach, or on an arrowhead left in the deep woods by an ancient Early American hunter? They speak to us of times past, of people who are no longer living, of exotic lands, and of mysteries yearning to be solved. Artifacts provide outstanding fodder for theme studies!

Abstract Ideas. Ideas that are abstract, such as revolution, discovery, peace, freedom, and justice, can serve as sources for theme studies. Often symbolic and theoretical, abstract ideas have less specificity than other stimulators of themed inquiry and must be carefully focused before becoming meaningful for elementary students. An abstract concept like justice, for example, can have several interpretations. Teachers must consider students' ages, developmental levels, and interests in focusing on an abstract concept like justice. In primary grades, for example, justice may be defined as "being fair" or "doing what's right," and that becomes the focus. In later grades, "legality" and "lawfulness" are the terms on which the focus centers.

The topics for theme studies can come from a great many sources. Among those sources, here are a few to consider:[2]

- **Curricular topics**—Themes or topics outlined in a basal textbook or in the district's curriculum guide(s)
- **Issues**—Local concerns or topics that affect students or their families directly
- **Problems**—Concerns or questions that have a universal application or appeal
- **Special events**—A local or national celebration or holiday
- **Student interests**—Special topics that capture students' interests or reflect their hobbies and/or leisure activities
- **Literary interests**—Genres of literature, author studies, or a special collection of related books

Table 7.1 provides ideas and possibilities for consideration when selecting topics for thematic units.

ORGANIZING THE THEME[3]

Once selection of a theme topic has been accomplished, the next step is to determine the skills and the objectives for the unit as well as the activities that will be used to cultivate an understanding and appreciation of those elements. Two strategies, *themewebbing* and *bookwebbing,* are worthy of consideration for organizing the theme.

---

[2] Adapted from A. Meinbach, L. Rothlein, & A. Fredericks. (1995). *The Complete Guide to Thematic Units: Creating the Integrated Curriculum* (p. 9). Norwood, Mass.: Christopher-Gordon Publishers, Inc. Used with permission.

[3] Adapted from A. Meinbach, L. Rothlein, & A. Fredericks. (1995). *The Complete Guide to Thematic Units: Creating the Integrated Curriculum* (p. 11). Norwood, Mass.: Christopher-Gordon Publishers, Inc. Used with permission.

Themewebbing offers a planning device for the unit in the form of a **graphic organizer** that serves as an outline web. The themeweb is used to interrelate and integrate aspects of the elementary curriculum with a specific thematic topic. In planning the unit by themewebbing, students see the unit graphically. They have an opportunity to understand the universality of a topic as well as to see how the topic can be expanded and enlarged within each curricular area.

Figure 7.1 shows a unit-planning themeweb that illustrates the basic structural parts used in building a themeweb. The unit-planning themeweb serves as a blank form on which to build a themeweb by filling in the parts. Figure 7.2 depicts a fully structured themeweb entitled "The Environment" that was used by a fourth grade teacher and students to plan a unit on the environment. Note that on both themewebs there is a space to record skills to be taught during the thematic unit. Thematic teaching does not mean the elimination of skill work for students. Instead, it means that skills are taught in a more meaningful, realistic, and holistic manner. Using a thematic unit does not negate the teaching of skills, rather it offers a host of teaching possibilities

TABLE 7.1 Ideas for selecting thematic topics

Theme Topics	Primary (Grades 1–3)	Intermediate (Grades 3–6)
Curricular Areas	Animals	Body system
	The seasons	Inventors
	Dinosaurs	The environment
	Weather	Oceanography
	Plants	Life cycles
	Staying healthy	Work and energy
	The changing earth	Electricity
	Sun and moon	Sound and light
	Magnetism	Solar system
	Simple machines	The changing earth
	Light and heat	Space
	Neighborhoods	Mythology
	Communities	Geography
	Transportation	Discovery
	Growing up	Becoming a nation
	Family life	Pioneer life
	Holidays	War and peace
	Celebrations	Multiculturalism
	Sports	Careers
	Native Americans	Ancient cultures
Issues	Homework	Pollution
	Family matters	Water quality
	Siblings	Toxic wastes
	Trash disposal	Air quality
	Rules	Nuclear power

(continued)

TABLE 7.1   (continued)

Theme Topics	Primary (Grades 1–3)	Intermediate (Grades 3–6)
Problems	Energy use	Ozone layer
	Crime	Starvation
	Natural resources	Population
	The environment	Oil spills
	Food	Wildlife
		Solar power
Special Events	Birthdays	Shuttle launch
	Winter holidays	Elections
	Circus	World Series
	Field trip	Super Bowl
	Olympics	Unusual weather
	Summer vacation	Legislation
Student Interests	Dinosaurs	Computers
	Monsters	Famous people
	Sharks	Ecology
	Airplanes	Environment
	Friends and neighbors	Sport heroes/heroines
	Vacations	Sports
	Space exploration	Relationships
	Ocean creatures	Clothes
	Scary things	Vacations
Literary Interests	Nursery rhymes	Romances
	Fairy tales	Legends
	Sports stories	Mysteries
	Adventure	Autobiographies
	Mystery	Sports heroes/heroines
	Poetry	Horror stories
	Fiction	Outer space
	Books by a favorite author	Books by a favorite author

Adapted from A. Meinbach, L. Rothlein, & A. Fredericks. (1995). *The Complete Guide to Thematic Units: Creating the Integrated Curriculum* (pp. 9–10). Norwood, Mass.: Christopher-Gordon Publishers, Inc. Used with permission.

for sharing those skills with your students and assisting them in using their skills in "real-life" situations and in authentic literature.

Bookwebbing is similar to the themewebbing technique, but in bookwebbing a literature selection is featured as the focal point for the planning web. Extensions to the curriculum are tied to the material in the literature selection, providing students with opportunities to expand the book's information into many curricular areas. More and more, teachers are discovering that bookwebbing is an easy and practical way to design thematic units.

Constructing the unit begins with a single book, then two or three additional books may be linked to the initial book to create the basic structure for a thematic unit. One of the advantages of this strategy is that students are invited to actively participate in the design of the unit, particularly when they have been exposed to an abundance of children's literature and to other thematic units.

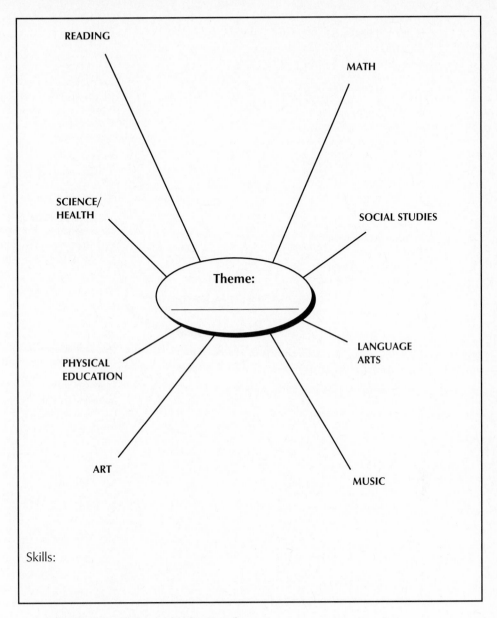

FIGURE 7.1 Themeweb planning form

Adapted from A. Meinbach, L. Rothlein, & A. Fredericks. (1995). *The Complete Guide to Thematic Units: Creating the Integrated Curriculum* (p. 16). Norwood, Mass.: Christopher-Gordon Publishers, Inc. Used with permission.

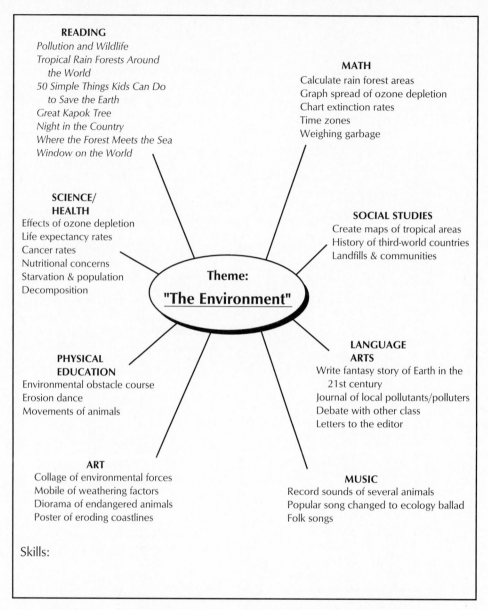

FIGURE 7.2   Themeweb planning form for a unit on the environment

Adapted from A. Meinbach, L. Rothlein, & A. Fredericks. (1995). *The Complete Guide to Thematic Units: Creating the Integrated Curriculum* (p. 12). Norwood, Mass.: Christopher-Gordon Publishers, Inc. Used with permission.

Students' contributions, in the form of ideas and related activities, help make the planning process meaningful and relevant and the eventual thematic unit a positive learning experience.

Figure 7.3 shows a book-planning web, illustrating the major parts of a bookweb. The book-planning web is useful as a blank form on which to build a bookweb by filling in the parts. Figure 7.4 shows the bookweb for *The Great Kapok Tree* and illustrates how a specific book is used in bookwebbing.

GATHERING MATERIALS AND RESOURCES[4]

Thematic units are different from textbook-based units not only in their instructional design, but also in the variety and types of materials used. The textbook-based unit approach uses the textbook as the primary resource for guiding the instruction. The thematic approach, on the other hand, knows no boundaries for materials. Thematic units encompass a host of materials and resources, ensuring that students will have abundant opportunities to experience a "hands-on, minds-on" approach to learning. A first consideration, naturally, will be the types of literature the teacher and students wish to use within a unit. After that, teacher and students work together suggesting and planning any number of materials and resources for use within the unit. When students are provided with dynamic opportunities to suggest and gather resources, they will be more inclined to use the materials throughout the duration of the unit. The following resources are possibilities for consideration when designing a thematic unit:

Printed Resources
newspapers

notices

junk mail

letters

brochures

encyclopedias

magazines

catalogues

pamphlets

travel guides

journals

maps

---

[4] Adapted from A. Meinbach, L. Rothlein, & A. Fredericks. (1995). *The Complete Guide to Thematic Units: Creating the Integrated Curriculum* (pp. 20–21). Norwood, Mass.: Christopher-Gordon Publishers, Inc. Used with permission.

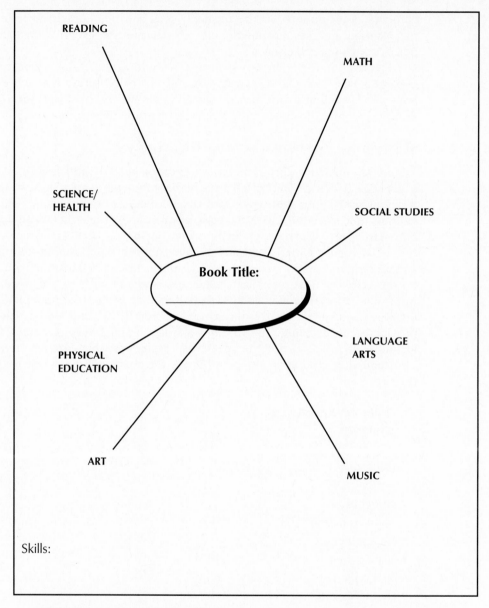

FIGURE 7.3 Bookweb planning form

Adapted from A. Meinbach, L. Rothlein, & A. Fredericks. (1995). *The Complete Guide to Thematic Units: Creating the Integrated Curriculum* (p. 16). Norwood, Mass.: Christopher-Gordon Publishers, Inc. Used with permission.

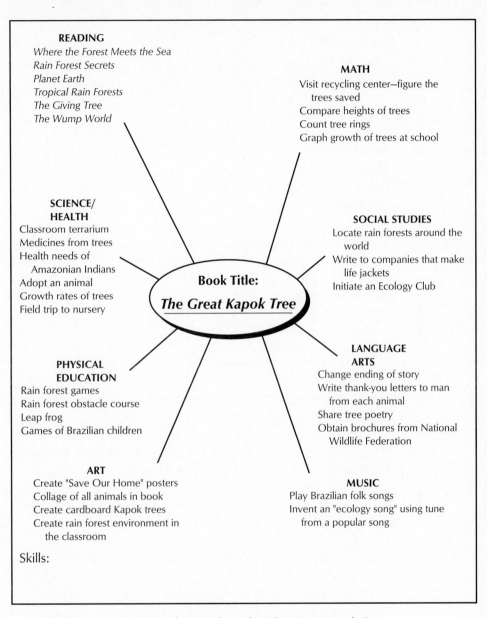

READING
Where the Forest Meets the Sea
Rain Forest Secrets
Planet Earth
Tropical Rain Forests
The Giving Tree
The Wump World

MATH
Visit recycling center—figure the
    trees saved
Compare heights of trees
Count tree rings
Graph growth of trees at school

**SCIENCE/
HEALTH**
Classroom terrarium
Medicines from trees
Health needs of
    Amazonian Indians
Adopt an animal
Growth rates of trees
Field trip to nursery

Book Title:
The Great Kapok Tree

SOCIAL STUDIES
Locate rain forests around the
    world
Write to companies that make
    life jackets
Initiate an Ecology Club

**PHYSICAL
EDUCATION**
Rain forest games
Rain forest obstacle course
Leap frog
Games of Brazilian children

**LANGUAGE
ARTS**
Change ending of story
Write thank-you letters to man
    from each animal
Share tree poetry
Obtain brochures from National
    Wildlife Federation

ART
Create "Save Our Home" posters
Collage of all animals in book
Create cardboard Kapok trees
Create rain forest environment in
    the classroom

MUSIC
Play Brazilian folk songs
Invent an "ecology song" using tune
    from a popular song

Skills:

FIGURE 7.4 Bookweb planning form for *The Great Kapok Tree*

Adapted from A. Meinbach, L. Rothlein, & A. Fredericks. (1995). *The Complete Guide to Thematic
Units: Creating the Integrated Curriculum* (p. 15). Norwood, Mass.: Christopher-Gordon Publishers,
Inc. Used with permission.

flyers

dictionaries

booklets

advertisements

Visual Resources

videos

movies

slides

films

filmstrips

CD-ROMs

overhead transparencies

computer software

Literature Resources

Eyeopeners by Beverly Kobrin (New York: Penguin Books, 1988).

"Outstanding Science Trade Books for Children," (annual March issue of *Science and Children*).

"Notable Children's Trade Books in the Social Studies" (annual April/May issue of *Social Education*).

"Children's Choices" (annual October issue of *The Reading Teacher*).

Science through Children's Literature by Carol Butzow and John Butzow (Englewood, Colo.: Teacher Ideas Press, 1989).

Social Studies through Children's Literature by Anthony D. Fredericks (Englewood, Colo.: Teacher Ideas Press, 1991).

The Literature Connection: Using Children's Books in the Classroom by Liz Rothlein and Anita Meinbach (Glenview, Ill.: Scott, Foresman and Co., 1991).

A to Zoo: Subject Access to Children's Picture Books by Carolyn W. Lima (Ann Arbor: Bowker, 1985).

Booklist Magazine, published by The American Library Association (50 Huron St., Chicago, IL 60611).

Children's Books in Print (Ann Arbor: Bowker, annual).

Children's Literature in the Reading Program by Bernice Cullinan (Newark, Del.: International Reading Association, 1987).

Fiction, Folklore, Fantasy, and Poetry for Children by S. S. Dreyer (New York: Bowker, 1986).

Best Books for Children: Preschool through Middle Grades by J. T. Gillespie and C. B. Gilbert (New York: Bowker, 1985).

A Critical Handbook of Children's Literature by Rebecca Lukens (Glenview, Ill.: Scott, Foresman and Co., 1995).

Adventuring with Books: A Booklist for Pre-K to Grade 6 by Diane Monson (Urbana, Ill.: National Council of Teachers of English, 1985).

Through the Eyes of a Child: An Introduction to Children's Literature by Donna Norton (Columbus, Ohio: Merrill, 1983).

Children's Literature from A to Z: A Guide for Parents and Teachers by J. C. Scott (New York: McGraw-Hill, 1984).

The Scott, Foresman Anthology of Children's Literature by Zena Sutherland and Myra Cohn Livingston (Glenview, Ill.: Scott, Foresman, 1984).

The Read-Aloud Handbook by Jim Trelease (New York: Penguin, 1982).

The WEB: Wonderfully Exciting Books (Ohio State University, 200 Ramseyer Hall, Columbus, OH 43210; periodical).

Book Clubs

Scholastic Book Clubs, 2931 East McCarty Street, Jefferson City, MO 65102

Troll Book Clubs, 320 Route 17, Mahwah, NJ 07498

The Trumpet Club, P. O. Box 604, Holmes, PA 19092

Weekly Reader Paperback Clubs, 4343 Equity Drive, Columbus, OH 43272

Artifacts

A variety of artifacts can be used within a thematic unit, depending on the nature and scope of the theme. For example, in designing a thematic unit on simple machines you might bring in a screwdriver, pliers, a knife, a doorknob, a small pulley, and a can opener. A unit on insects might include artifacts such as a pair of tweezers, a magnifying lens, pins, display mounts, and a microscope. Obviously, the types of artifacts appropriate for a unit will depend on the theme, or topic, of the unit. People who can assist in obtaining and selecting necessary artifacts include:

parents

computer specialists

colleagues

teachers from other schools

community members

senior citizens

community helpers

pen pals

store owners

students

relatives

social agencies

college professors

public officials

DESIGNING ACTIVITIES AND PROJECTS[5]

Whole language activities are the heart of a well-designed and fully functioning thematic unit. A thematic unit is not an arbitrary collection of random activities but a well-orchestrated assembly of whole language activities designed to help students comprehend and appreciate a specific topic or a general idea. To accomplish these goals requires an attention to the types of activities, the variety of activities, and the purpose of the activities selected. In other words, there must be a specific reason for the use of selected activities within a unit. The suggestions below will be helpful in designing activities and projects for use in thematic units.

Activities should:

- integrate the language arts—reading, writing, speaking, listening
- be holistic in nature
- emphasize a "hands-on, minds-on" approach to learning
- be cross-curricular and interdisciplinary in nature
- result from the ideas and suggestions of students
- focus on the relationship(s) between a piece of children's literature and the real world
- allow students to "tap into" their background knowledge and relate information to what they are learning
- be based in a meaningful format that engages students in productive work (as opposed to "busywork")
- be designed to last for differing periods of time (for example, one hour, one day, one week)
- be both instructional and motivational in nature
- relate to the general topic of the unit or the specific topic of a piece of literature

IMPLEMENTING THE THEMATIC UNIT[6]

Teaching thematically is not necessarily an all-or-nothing proposition. It is not necessary, for example, to use a **thematic unit** for a full day, a full week, or a full month. You have several options to consider in terms of how to present a thematic unit to your class, how much you want it to dominate your daily curriculum, and how involved you and your students want to become. Obviously, your level of comfort with thematic teaching and the scope and sequence of

---

[5] Adapted from A. Meinbach, L. Rothlein, & A. Fredericks. (1995). *The Complete Guide to Thematic Units: Creating the Integrated Curriculum* (pp. 22–23). Norwood, Mass.: Christopher-Gordon Publishers, Inc. Used with permission.

[6] Adapted from A. Meinbach, L. Rothlein, & A. Fredericks. (1995). *The Complete Guide to Thematic Units: Creating the Integrated Curriculum* (pp. 23–24). Norwood, Mass.: Christopher-Gordon Publishers, Inc. Used with permission.

your classroom or district curriculum may determine the degree to which you utilize (or do not utilize) a thematic unit. There is no one, ideal way to incorporate thematic units into classroom plans. The best wisdom, perhaps, is to consider a multiplicity of options—not only in the design of units but also in their use. The following list of options is only a partial collection; your own particular teaching situation, personal experience, and student needs may suggest other possibilities and alternatives that are more appropriate for your situation.

- Teach a thematic unit throughout a school day and for an extended period of several school days.
- Teach a thematic unit for half a day for several days in succession.
- Use a thematic unit for two or more subject areas (for example, social studies and science or social studies, science, and language arts) in combination with the regular curriculum for the other subjects.
- Use a thematic unit as the "curriculum" for a selected subject area (for example, social studies) and the regular curriculum for the other subjects.
- Teach a thematic unit for an entire day and follow up with the regular curriculum in succeeding days.
- Use a thematic unit as a follow-up to information and data presented in a textbook or curriculum guide.
- Provide students with a thematic unit as independent work on completion of lessons in the basal textbook.
- Teach cooperatively with a colleague and present a thematic unit to both classes at the same time.
- Use a thematic unit intermittently over the span of several weeks.

Because an integrated curriculum approach to teaching and learning utilizes time differently than a traditional curriculum, a restructuring in time is necessary. Seely (1995) addresses time factors in the following manner:

Time in an integrated curriculum is divided, not into one-hour segments where a different content area is taught each hour, but into blocks of uninterrupted time, depending on the nature of the theme and the activities involved. An integrated curriculum strives to have students engaged in meaningful projects and activities, rather than the current reliance on unrelated small tasks.

Blocks of uninterrupted time are achieved when the instructional day is restructured. In many instances, the day is divided into two large blocks, one in the morning and one in the afternoon. Teachers who are just beginning to integrate the curriculum might focus on language arts in the morning and math/social sciences in the afternoon. As one becomes comfortable integrating the curriculum, the boundaries between blocks of time become more permeable, enabling the various content areas to be addressed throughout the instructional day. Restructuring the school day to include larger blocks of time to integrate the curriculum promotes the authenticity of learning. Learning occurs when time is not the controlling factor. Activities and projects should not be limited to one-hour time slots. The best way to read a book, write a summary, or solve a problem is when interest and satisfaction are the determining factors. Incorporating uninterrupted blocks of time into the schedule encourages students to work on activities and projects until they are satisfied with the results and have moved on to other interests. (p. 26)

One elementary teacher developed and implemented a three-week unit on communities that allowed students exciting and dynamic opportunities to investigate all aspects of communities. The unit included explorations into such topics as:

- populations and communities of animals
- populations and communities of plants
- civic responsibilities of community members (voting, etc.)
- field trips to city hall, a senior citizen center, and the post office
- a letter-writing campaign to the local newspaper
- read-alouds by various community members, including the town mayor
- geological study of the local community
- historical study of the local community
- creation of a diorama to be exhibited in the local bank
- creation of an almanac of local weather patterns and climatic conditions over the past 100 years
- an investigation of the major industries and agricultural resources of the region
- creation of a community map for new families

The following daily plan from the unit on communities shows the details of how the teacher captured the spirit and excitement of thematic teaching for an entire day:

THEMATIC TEACHING: A SAMPLE PLAN

Theme: Communities

8:30–9:00 OPENING
As students are entering the classroom they put away their lunch boxes and continue work on any activities still unfinished from the previous day.

They may work independently or in small groups according to the nature of the activities. Activities may include journal writing, videotaping, poster creation, silent reading, library research, skit practice, or a cooperative learning venture.

9:00–9:45 REQUIRED/OPTIONAL ACTIVITIES
Group 1—Students begin to build a dual diorama (one half depicts an urban environment, the other half depicts a rural development). With plastic figures, clay, pipe cleaners, and a shoe box, the scenes are created using ideas from several selected pieces of literature.

Group 2—Students are composing a letter to a class in another state telling them about some of the information they have collected and facts they are learning (the pen pals have been established by the two respective teachers who are former college classmates). The pen pals communicate regularly about some of their activities and field trips.

Group 3—Students visit several classrooms throughout the school, collecting data about hometowns. Teachers, students, and administrative staff are interviewed about the places they have lived throughout the United States. After students complete their data collection, a large map will be constructed to illustrate their results.

Group 4—After viewing a filmstrip on some of the problems normally associated with urban life (pollution, traffic congestion, crime), students work together to draft a letter to the editor of the local newspaper, suggesting a series of solutions to address problems in their own community.

Group 5—Using a large sheet of oaktag, students create a community calendar of events. Listings in the local newspaper are added to school events and posted in a prominent place in the classroom.

Group 6—Three students are completing a reading of the book *Country Mouse, Town Mouse* by Lorinda B. Cauley and will begin work on a puppet show that will be shared with another class.

9:45–10:05 SUSTAINED SILENT READING
Students obtain books from the classroom library and scatter throughout the room. Books selected include *The Village of Round and Square Houses* by Ann Grifalconi (Boston: Little, Brown, 1986); *All About Things People Do* by Melanie and Chris Rice (New York: Doubleday, 1989); *Efan the Great* by Roni Schotter (New York: Lothrop, 1986); *The House on Maple Street* by Marcia Sewell (New York: Morrow, 1987); *We Keep a Store* by Anne Shelby (New York: Orchard, 1990); *Town and Country* by Alice and Martin Provensen (New York: Crown, 1984); and *The Little House* by Virginia Lee

(continued)

(continued)

Burton (Boston: Houghton Mifflin, 1969). Most students engage in independent reading while three pairs of students read their books to each other.

10:05–10:25 WRITING PROCESS

Journals—Several students open their journals and take on the role of an urban house. Each student writes about a day in the life of his/her house as seen through the "eyes" of that house. Students are involved in different stages of the writing process, including drafting, revising, and editing.

Reader's Theater—A small group of four students continues work on a reader's theater adaptation of *Shaker Lane* by Alice and Martin Provensen (New York: Viking, 1987). Students create scenarios about some of the events from the book. The reader's theater will be presented at a later date.

Big Book—Another group of students created an oversized book that has been cut from cardboard into the shape of a factory. Sheets of paper have been stapled inside the covers. Students prepare essays about some of the events that take place inside a factory. The completed book will be shared with several first grade classrooms.

Fact Book—A small group of students heads to the library to collect data for inclusion in a "fact book," a collection of interesting facts about urban and rural life. The final project will be donated to the school library for permanent display.

10:25–10:40 READ-ALOUD/STORYTELLING

Miss Rumphius by Barbara Cooney (New York: Viking, 1982) is read to the entire class (this book discusses the world travels of a lady and what she does when she returns home). Afterward, discussion centers on comparisons between the life of Miss Rumphius and the lives of some of the students' grandparents.

10:40–11:10 TEACHER-DIRECTED ACTIVITIES

Opening—To begin the lesson, students are asked to create a list of all the words used to describe communities. These words are recorded on the chalkboard in a vertical list. Students are told that these words are examples of adjectives.

Book Study—The book *In Coal Country* by Judith Hendershot (New York: Knopf, 1987) is introduced to students. During the oral reading students are asked to listen for adjectives used in the story. As words are noted, they are added to the list on the board.

Group Work—Students are divided into several heterogeneous groups. Each group is "assigned" four to five specific U.S. communities (urban or rural areas) and asked to generate adjectives (from the list on the board) that could be used to describe each. Each group prepares a narrative about their location, using identified adjectives. Each narrative is read to the whole class and differences and similarities in adjective use are discussed. Stories are posted on the bulletin board.

11:10–11:50 RESPONDING TO LITERATURE

Students have just completed *Farm Morning* by David McPhail (New York: Harcourt Brace, 1985).

Group 1—Students select one of the animals mentioned in the book and write about a day in the life of that animal. They draw the shape of the animal on a sheet of construction paper. They cut out the animal and, using it as a pattern, make pages and construction-paper covers for student books. Students use these materials to write their story. Students have time to share their stories.

Group 2—Students prepare a letter to the county extension agent inviting him or her to visit the classroom and share information on the care of various animals.

Group 3—Students are involved in a discussion: Which is more demanding—living on a farm or living in the city? Students establish "mini-teams" and debate the merits of each lifestyle.

11:50–12:10 RECESS/SHARING

12:10–12:40 LUNCH

12:40–1:25 SPECIAL CLASS

Students go to music, art, computer room, library, or physical education.

1:25–2:10 MATH

Group 1—Students have surveyed the adult members of their families and friends and collected data on the variety of occupations in which people have worked. The information is combined into charts and graphs that record jobs, the number of people who have worked in each job, and the number of jobs held by individuals.

Group 2—Small teams of students (with their parents) have surveyed the prices of selected food items (one pound of hamburger meat, a 16-ounce box of cereal, a quart of milk, and a jar of peanut butter) in different stores throughout the local community. The data are gathered together in class and displayed on a comparative chart. Discussion about the "cost of living" in various sections of the community is initiated.

Group 3—Students bring in recipes for cultural or ethnic foods that are prepared by their families. A Cultural Feast Day is planned, with an emphasis on the measurements used in the preparation of various dishes.

(continued)

(continued)

2:10–2:40 Teacher-Directed Lesson

Opening—Students are asked to brainstorm the various reasons why people live in different sections of a community (ethnic groups, housing costs, distance to work, etc.).

Group Work—Each student selects a reason and gets into a group identified with that reason (for example, all who believe that people live where they do because of housing costs are formed into one group). Each group prepares a written argument for its selected reason and presents its case(s) to the class. Groups research selected reasons (via interviews, library work, etc.) and share findings with the whole class.

Closure—A professor of sociology from the local college is invited to speak on the ethnic and cultural composition of the local community. Students will have prepared a list of questions prior to his or her visit.

2:40–3:00 Daily Closure

Students review daily activities. A summary statement about the day's activities is generated by the class and recorded on a large wall calendar in the front of the classroom. Each student transcribes the summary statement onto a personal calendar which is taken home and shared with parents at the end of each week.

3:00–3:15 Dismissal

Religion: An Appropriate Thematic Topic.   Religion is universal in that it is expansive, extensive, ranging, and worldwide. Certainly religion is a part of history, but textbooks often give it only scant attention, and that usually scattered and unattached. In that regard, White (1995) proposes religion as a suitable topic for thematic units. Suggesting a unit entitled "Circles of Faith," White writes:

> The unit could explore the historical development of the world's major religions. Teachers could focus on psychological, sociological, and cultural aspects of religion or include legal and constitutional questions concerning religion in America. Freedom of religion and separation of church and state in America could be contrasted to the lack of separation of church and state in other nations. Students could research and present information on elements common to all religions: beliefs, sacred teachings, worship practices, houses of worship, and holy days.
>
> Compare this approach with the chronological organization of world history textbooks and the way students encounter the information in a traditionally taught course. Judaism and the rise of Christianity typically are discussed briefly early in the book; then a few chapters later the

rise of Islam is discussed. Somewhere in this mix, a chapter on the Eastern religions may be included. Several chapters later students encounter religion again in the context of the Reformation and Enlightenment. . . . Faith then becomes identified with one specific period of history or part of the world rather than with the understanding that, throughout history, humans have sought to find meaning in their lives through faith. . . . A thematic approach to the study of religion helps students make a connection between the Eastern and Western world and the differences in the major religions of the world; more importantly, they see the commonalities among all people in their searches for meaning in life . . . a worthwhile learning outcome in itself. . . . (p. 161)

History and Geography: Other Appropriate Topics. Rocca (1994) makes the following suggestions regarding building integrated history and geography units:

One way of approaching integration is to ask questions about the places where a historical event occurred. Write down some basic questions about the places incorporating each of the five themes of geography. Use these questions to prepare an exercise or activity designed to arrive at the answer. The teacher-generated questions should focus on the activity and provide a challenge and a purpose for students. For instance, in a unit of study covering the westward movement in U.S. history, a teacher might want to use questions prompting activities that enhance a geographic perspective on the Oregon Trail. For example:

1. *Location.* Where did the Oregon Trail begin and end? Name three rivers that pioneers followed on the Oregon Trail.
2. *Place.* In what ways did the Native Americans, landforms, and climates that pioneers encountered in each portion of their journey ease the passage or make the trip difficult?
3. *Human/environmental interaction.* How did the pioneers change the landscapes over which they passed? Were all of these environmental modifications negative or were some positive?
4. *Movement.* How did rivers, deserts, and mountain ranges influence their travel route?
5. *Region.* How are the Great Plains different from Oregon's Willamette Valley, the final destination of many of the pioneers? (pp. 114–115)

SUMMARY

Focusing on a central theme around which inquiry and learning will take place, thematic teaching offers one of the most promising formats for integrating the elementary school curriculum. Having its roots in John Dewey and the

Progressive Education Movement of the early 1990s, thematic teaching is advantageous to teachers and students alike because of its multidimensional and holistic nature. Barriers between subjects are removed in a natural and logical way, and connections between topics are clear and easily identified.

 ACTIVITY

PURPOSE

The purpose of this activity is to work independently to design and create a bookweb according to the models depicted in Figures 7.3 (p. 190) and 7.4 (p. 191).

PROCEDURE

Select an appropriate children's trade book and read it carefully. Use the trade book to design a book web like the models in Figures 7.3 and 7.4. Make a transparency of the bookweb and present it to the class.

STUDY QUESTIONS

1. Describe how theme studies, thematic teaching, and thematic units offer one of the most promising formats for integrating the subjects of the elementary school curriculum.
2. Explain why it can be said that the thematic unit approach to teaching is not new.
3. What advantages does thematic teaching have for students? for teachers?
4. Planning for effective and successful thematic instruction requires some specialized organization. Identify and describe the steps needed to plan and implement an effective and successful theme study.
5. Describe the construction and use of bookwebs and themewebs. Compare and contrast the two.
6. As a leader and pioneer of thematic teaching in your school district, your superintendent has asked you to speak to fourth, fifth, and sixth grade teachers at a districtwide in-service meeting. Your topic: "Teaching thematically is not necessarily an all-or-nothing proposition." What will you say?

BIBLIOGRAPHY

Allen, H., Splittgerber, F., & Manning, M. (1993). *Teaching and learning in the middle level school.* New York: Merrill.

Barr, I., & McGuire, M. (1993). Social studies and effective stories. *Social Studies and the Young Learner, 5* (3), 6-8, 11.

Bean, J. (1992). Creating an integrative curriculum: Making the connections. *National Association of Secondary School Principals Bulletin, 16* (11), 46-54.

Bereiter, C., & Scardamalia, M. (1987). An attainable version of high literacy: Approaches to teaching higher-order skills in reading and writing. *Curriculum Inquiry, 17* (1), 9-30.

Berg, M. (1988). Integrating ideas for social studies. *Social Studies and the Young Learner, 1* (2), pull-out feature.

Brophy, J., & Alleman, J. (1991). Activities as instructional tools: A framework for analysis and evaluation. *Educational Research, 20* (5), 9-22.

Chatton, B. (1989). Using literature across the curriculum. In J. Hickman & B. E. Cullinan (Eds.), *Children's literature in the classroom: Weaving Charlotte's web* (pp. 61-70). Needham Heights, Mass.: Christopher-Gordon.

Cheek, E., & Cheek, M. (1983). *Reading instruction through content teaching.* Columbus, Ohio: Merril.

Cullinan, B. (1993). *Fact and fiction across the curriculum.* Newark, N.J.: International Reading Association.

Danielson, K., & LaBonty, J. (1994). *Integrating reading and writing through children's literature.* Boston: Allyn and Bacon.

Dobson, D., Monson, J., & Smith, J. (1992). A case study on integrating history and reading instruction through literature. *Social Education, 56* (7), 370-375.

Drake, S. (1993). *Planning integrated curriculum.* Alexandria, Va.: Association of Supervision and Curriculum Development.

Fogarty, R. (1991). Ten ways to integrate curriculum. *Educational Leadership, 49* (10), 24-26.

Fredericks, A. (1992). *The integrated curriculum.* Englewood, Colo.: Teacher Ideas Press.

Gamberg, R., Kwak, W., Hutchings, M., & Altheim, J. (1988). *Learning and loving it: Theme studies in the classroom.* Portsmouth, N.H.: Heinemann.

Gehrke, N. (1991). Explorations of teachers' development of integrative curriculums. *Journal of Curriculum and Supervision, 6* (2), 107-117.

Jacobs, H. (1989). The growing need for interdisciplinary curriculum content. In H. Jacobs (Ed.), *Interdisciplinary curriculum: Design and implementation* (pp. 1-12). Alexandria, Va.: Association for Supervision and Curriculum Development.

Jacobs, H. (1991). On interdisciplinary education: A conversation. *Educational Leadership, 49* (10), 24-26.

Jacobs, H., & Borland, J. (Fall, 1986). The interdisciplinary concept model: Theory and practice. *Gifted Child Quarterly, 30* (4), 159-163.

Jarolimek, J., & Parker, W. (1993). *Social studies in elementary education.* New York: Macmillan.

Lapp, D., & Flood, J. (1994). Integrating the curriculum: First steps. *The Reading Teacher, 47* (5), 416-419.

Lipson, M., Valencia, S., Wixson, K., & Peters, C. (1993). Integration and thematic teaching: Integration to improve teaching and learning. *Language Arts, 70* (4), 252-263.

Martinello, M., & Cook, G. (1994). *Interdisciplinary inquiry in teaching and learning.* New York: Merrill.

Maute, J. (1992). Cross-curricular connections. In J. H. Lounsbury (Ed.), *Connecting the curriculum through interdisciplinary instruction.* Columbus, Ohio: National Middle School Association.

Maxim, G. (1995). *Social studies and the elementary school child* (5th ed.). Englewood Cliffs, N.J.: Merrill.

McDonald, J., & Czerniak, C. (1994). Developing interdisciplinary units: Strategies and examples. *School Science and Mathematics, 94* (1), 5-10.

Meinbach, A., Rothlein, L., & Fredericks, A. (1995). *The complete guide to thematic units: Creating the integrated curriculum.* Norwood, Mass.: Christopher-Gordon.

Michaelis, J. (1992). *Social studies for children: A guide to basic instruction.* Boston: Allyn and Bacon.

Moss, J. (1984). *Focus in units in literature: A handbook for elementary school teachers.* Urbana, Ill.: National Council of Teachers of English.

Rocca, A. (1994). Integrating history and geography. *Social Education, 58* (2), 114-116.

Seely, A. (1995). *Integrated thematic units.* Westminster, Calif.: Teacher Created Materials, Inc.

Sunal, C. (1990). *Early childhood social studies.* Columbus, Ohio: Merrill.

Taba, H. (1962). *Curriculum development: Theory and practice.* New York: Harcourt Brace Jovanovich.

White, R. (1995). How thematic teaching can transform history instruction. *The Clearing House, 68* (3), 160-162.

Zarnowski, M. (1990). *Learning with biographies: A reading and writing approach.* Washington, D.C.: National Council for the Social Studies and National Council of Teachers of English.

CHILDREN'S LITERATURE CITED

Aliki. (1988). *Dinosaur Bones.* New York Harper.

Brooks, B. (1991). *Nature by design.* New York: Farrar, Straus & Giroux.

Byrd, B. (1972). *When clay sings.* New York: Aladdin.

Cherry, L. (1992). *The river ran wild.* New York: Gulliver Green.

Cohlene, T. (1990). *Dancing Drum, a Cherokee legend.* Mahwah, N.J.: Watermill Press.

Henry, J. (1992). *A clearing in the forest.* New York: Four Winds Press.

Hinton, L. (1992). *Ishi's tale of lizard.* New York: Farrar, Straus & Giroux.

Hoffman, M. (1991). *Amazing Grace.* New York: Dial.

Hopkins, L. (1987). *Dinosaurs.* San Diego: Harcourt Brace Jovanovich.

Kellogg, S. (1987). *Prehistoric Pinkerton.* New York: Dial.

Lauber, P. (1987). *Dinosaurs walked here and other stories fossils tell.* New York: Bradbury.

Lyon, G., & Catalanotto, P. (1993). *Dreamplace.* New York: Orchard.

Martin, B., & Archambault, J. (1985). *Knots on a counting rope.* New York: Henry Holt.

Morris, A. (1989). *Bread, bread, bread.* New York: Lothrop, Lee & Shepard.

Morris, A. (1989). *Hats, hats, hats.* New York: Lothrop, Lee & Shepard.

Prelutsky, J. (1988). *Tyrannosaurus was a beast.* New York: Greenwillow.

Taylor, M. (1987). *The friendship.* New York: Dial.

Taylor, M. (1990). *The road to Memphis.* New York: Dial.

White, E. B. (1952). *Charlotte's web.* New York: Harper.

CHAPTER 8

INTEGRATING THE CURRICULUM THROUGH AN ISSUES APPROACH

CHAPTER OBJECTIVES

After reading this chapter you should be able to:

1. Define and describe the nature of issues
2. Distinguish between real and contrived issues
3. List and describe the steps for inquiring into issues
4. Explain the use of literature sets in providing students with issues
5. Compare and contrast discipline-based approaches with integrated approaches
6. Discuss the nature of vital issues in society and their potential for integrating the curriculum
7. Characterize and give examples of global issues
8. Identify persistent-problem themes that embrace the global community
9. Characterize and give examples of cultural issues
10. Discuss ways in which religion and people's ethnocentricities provide issues for consideration and study
11. Characterize and give examples of social issues
12. Describe how current events and the media can be an issues-rich environment
13. Describe an effective way for elementary students to obtain information from a news report in a newspaper or newsmagazine
14. Depict issues that may arise regarding media influence and media ownership

15. Characterize and identify sensitive issues and explain their place in the instructional program of the elementary school
16. Discuss issues pertaining to environmental and energy factors
17. Explain sex equity and gender-specific behavior issues
18. Define and describe law-related issues and how they might be used as a vehicle for integrating the curriculum
19. Explain how issues may be controversial and argumentative
20. Discuss precautions to consider when issues are used as focal points for inquiry in elementary classrooms

WHAT ARE ISSUES?

An issue can be many things. To some, an issue is a cause, others might see an issue as a controversy, and others may see issues as problems, obstacles, predicaments, dilemmas, plights, and the like. Issues are viewed in light of one's opinions, beliefs, attitudes, biases, convictions, feelings, perspectives, sentiments, and leanings. In any event, issues provide excellent focal points for inquiries ranging across the elementary curriculum without regard for subject boundaries. Issues provide the impetus and an environment for integrating the curriculum. Seely (1995) indicates that presenting issues for inquiry in the classroom that mirror the problems in the real world promotes the authenticity and relevance of learning. "Outside of classroom doors, problems do not come in isolated, neat packages with single answers, but rather are a complex web of possible solutions" (p. 26). About the integrative nature of classroom inquiries into problem issues Ellis (1995) writes, "Problem-solving projects use methods and ideas from every discipline, combining mathematics, language, science, music, art, social studies, and anything else that might be helpful" (p. 232).

Saxe (1994) writes that issues that come about and are suitable for use in the elementary school curriculum are of three types: (1) issues as something important that has happened, (2) issues that emerge from the day-to-day activities in which the children are involved, and (3) issues that involve disputes and differences between individuals and groups of individuals.

> *Issues as something important* . . . concerns anything you or the children decide to talk about. Perhaps a child witnessed a car accident or noticed that the local fire station purchased a new fire engine. Maybe you read in the paper that someone attempted to lure a child into a car. The idea of seeing a car smashed and people hurt, watching the fire station workers wash down the new fire engine, or listening to a frightening story about an attempted abduction presents opportunities to talk about the concerns. . . .

Issues that emerge . . . concerns those that emerge during class or when children are reading, studying, practicing, and/or playing. In general, issues can materialize from any activity. For instance, perhaps Debbie was completing a project about American presidents. One of Debbie's observations was that there were no female presidents of the United States. . . . The issue that emerged from Debbie's observation was why, in the course of 200 years, no woman was ever elected president. . . .

Issues that involve disputes and differences . . . involves a dispute or difference between two or more individuals or groups of individuals. Disputes or differences may also occur between individuals/groups and institutions, individuals/groups and circumstances, or even individuals/ groups and nature . . . disputes between children offer a number of teaching opportunities and experiences to explore children's feelings, behaviors, values, and beliefs. . . . The resolution or reconciliation of conflict, differences, and disputes presents opportunities for children to practice dealing with problems. (p. 111–114)

REAL AND CONTRIVED ISSUES

Real issues are those that arise directly from the day-to-day life experiences of the students and are witnessed by them either directly or vicariously (e.g., through media reports). Real problems and issues have the potential of being highly motivational because they are a part of the ongoing, real-world life experiences of the student. Real issues are usually compelling and serve as a dynamic focal point for inquiry because the reality of the issue heightens and accentuates the investigation.

Contrived issues, on the other hand, do not arise directly from the life experiences of the students, but instead are invented and calculated situations. Contrived issues are presented for inquiry by textbooks, trade books, various kinds of instructional materials and programs, or by the teacher, in order to provide a variety of worthwhile, beneficial, and rewarding issues for study. A contrived issue can also provide a cogent, convincing, and effective impetus for inquiry, especially under the guidance and leadership of a creative and insightful teacher/facilitator.

STEPS FOR INQUIRING INTO ISSUES

Both real and contrived issues are fruitful and productive sources of inquiry in the elementary school program and provide bountiful opportunities for integrating the curriculum. Whether the issue under investigation is a real issue or a contrived issue, the following steps of inquiry on the part of students is suggested:

1. Formulate a statement that defines the issue, problem, or question to be investigated.
2. Consider, review, and choose appropriate sources of information about the issue.
3. Collect and assemble appropriate information about the issue.
4. Scour, sift, sort, and search through information about the issue.
5. Make inferences, engage in reasoned theorizing, postulate hypotheses, and draw conclusions based on the information (Ellis, 1995).

Figure 8.1 shows a web of issues suitable for study in primary grades (grades 1-3), and Figure 8.2 shows a web of potential issues for inquiry in intermediate grades (grades 4-6).

LITERATURE SETS

Zarnowski (1990) proposes the use of **literature sets**, collections of approximately 5 to 15 books that are somehow related, to provide students with interesting issues for inquiry. Literature sets are composed of books on single topics, books from a distinctive genre, or books written by a particular author. Literature sets can address important social issues of the time, like poverty,

FIGURE 8.1 Issues suitable for study in primary grades

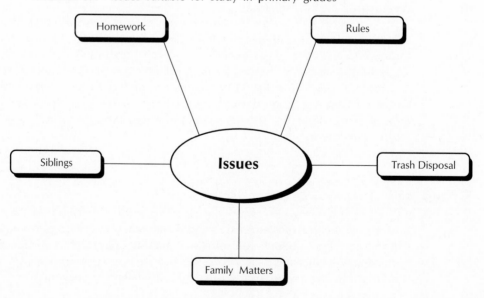

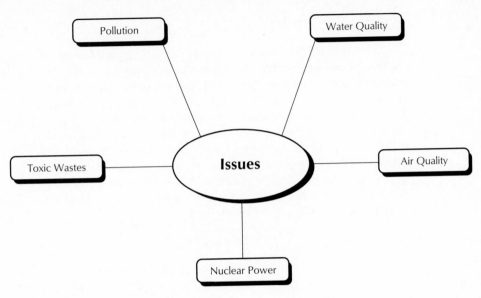

FIGURE 8.2 Issues suitable for study in intermediate grades

human rights, immigration, the environment, civil rights, the AIDS virus, and abortion. They can provide a foundation for thinking about social issues and foster children's concept development as they encounter similar concepts in various books (Hanssen, 1990). The following excerpt depicts the influence that literature sets and subsequent discussion had on the thinking and writing of one 11-year-old child about the important and complex issue of homelessness:

A book I've read, *Poverty in America* by Milton Meltzer (1986), has given me some things to think about. . . . Some people consider the homeless crazy or sick, but that's not true for most homeless people. They're just denied common resources. People who help the homeless claim the poor are poor because they lack not just an income but legal services, public amenities, basic human respect, and so on. They are deprived of ordinary activities in everyday life. They can't take a vacation, can't eat a meal in a restaurant, or give their children a birthday party.

Our homeless population is increasing rapidly. Poverty, the way I and others see it, is not an income level but a way of life. The world is breaking down slowly, and if there are no more people left to help it, besides the leaders who obviously don't care one way or another, the world will just keep on getting worse. (Zarnowski, 1990, p. 39)

Vital Issues of the Day

Contemporary social issues and problems often confront today's society. Some of these issues and problems are of vital importance to the society and become prominent. The enduring, important, and prominent issues become priorities for society because they beg for solutions. Many vital issues emerge that are so far-reaching and substantial that they are worthy of study in the elementary school program. These vital issues, moreover, do not fall into the constraints of any one academic discipline, but rather have a wide range of influence and effect that compels them to be studied in an integrated fashion. Focusing on vital issues of the day provides an excellent vehicle for integrationary studies in the elementary school. Figure 8.3 shows some current vital issues suitable for exploration in today's elementary schools.

Global Issues

Some issues span the globe in their interest, influence, and consequence and are referred to as **global issues**. They are global in the sense that they are worldwide, universal, planetary. Broad, general, widespread issues fall into the category of being global.

A thematic study of the Costa Rican rain forest is an example of a global issue that was recently investigated by a group of first grade children in Iowa. In a thematic unit dealing with the issue of natural resources, the children

FIGURE 8.3   Vital issues for inquiry

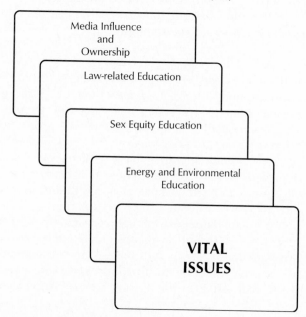

Media Influence
and
Ownership

Law-related Education

Sex Equity Education

Energy and Environmental
Education

**VITAL
ISSUES**

centered their investigation on the rain forests of Costa Rica. Their four goals were to develop *knowledge* in terms of general information on rain forests; *skills* in terms of interpersonal skills, higher-order thinking skills, and classification skills; *values* in terms of examining different points of view (those who want to make a living from the rain forest in ways that destroy it, as opposed to those who want to preserve the rain forest and avoid destructive practices); and *social participation* in terms of opportunities for action that can help solve a global problem. As an action, the children participated in a project called the International Children's Rainforest, which purchases land in the Monteverde region of Costa Rica and preserves it as rain forest by protecting it from development. By learning about recycling and then collecting soda cans to be recycled, the children earned $50, enough to purchase one-half acre of virgin rain forest in the International Children's Rainforest (Rosenbusch, 1994).

A group of elementary students in Alabama became interested in a community issue revolving around the use of safety helmets for bicycle and motorcycle riders. They worked in collaborative groups to research injuries and fatalities resulting from bicycle and motorcycle accidents. They made charts and graphs showing the differences in injuries and fatalities when riders wore protective helmets and when they didn't. They examined several types of protective helmets and obtained manufacturing data from helmet vendors, resulting in a grading system for various bicycle and motorcycle helmets. The children reproduced their data on informational posters which were placed not only in the school, but in some area businesses.

Pugh, Garcia, and Margalef-Boada (1994) cite multicultural trade books as a rich and virtually inexhaustible resource for viewing issues in a global perspective. Trade books that remind readers that they are a part of the whole world, citizens not only of their communities and particular cultures but of the planet as well, can open new windows to the world and its problems. People on earth are responsible for each other's actions and welfare because they are inextricably intertwined, as individuals, as groups and communities, and as humankind. Trade books broaden the context of concern and provide a global perspective on the whole world. A few examples:

> Focusing on an environmental and economic issue that will be of increasing importance and will constitute a major challenge for today's children in their adult lives, *Population Growth: Our Endangered Planet* by Suzanne Winckler and Mary Rodgers (1991) presents a statistical and photographic account of the worldwide consequences of unchecked population growth in the next few decades. Maxine Fisher's (1989) *Women in the Third World* focuses on the education, marriage, work, and struggles of women in developing nations as viewed from the perspective of the international women's movement. Of particular relevance to global dimensions of diversity are books dealing with world peace, such as *The Big Book for Peace,* by Ann Durrell and Marilyn Sachs (1990), which presents several metaphors for peace as they are

expressed through stories, poems, and pictures. Especially important is the emphasis placed on the concept of harmony among people of different races to encourage crossing national and cultural boundaries, surpassing prejudice and discrimination and moving toward the greater goal of global unity and understanding. (Pugh, Garcia, & Margalef-Boada, 1994, p. 64)

Parker (1991) identifies persistent-problem themes that embrace the global community and divides them into the four categories shown in Table 8.1.

Persistent problems, by their very nature, permeate every level of existence—from global to national to local—with their symptoms and causes. Moreover, the solutions to persistent problems will come both through individual behaviors taken collectively and through policy decisions taken multilaterally. Because of this, themes in this category consistently provide opportunities for students to find their role as citizens and develop their abilities for social participation in local versions of global problems or local efforts to alleviate global problems (pp. 122–123).

CULTURAL ISSUES

Some issues relate to the customs, beliefs, traditions, and doctrines of a people and are called **cultural issues**. Cultural issues also often deal with the habits, mores, and practices of people. They are tribal in the sense that they revolve around rituals, rites, ceremonies, and the like. "People create social environments and systems comprised of unique beliefs, values, traditions, language, customs, technology, and institutions as a way of meeting basic human needs, shaped by their own physical environments and contact with other cultures" (Parker, 1991, p. 121).

Apartheid is an example of a cultural issue that has been prominent in the world for a number of years. Fairly recently, the practice of apartheid in South

TABLE 8.1 Persistent-problem themes that embrace the global community

Peace and Security	National & International Development	Environmental Problems	Human Rights
the arms race	hunger and poverty	acid rain	apartheid
East-West relations	overpopulation	pollution of streams	indigenous homelands
terrorism	North-South relations	depletion of rain forests	political imprisonment
colonialism	appropriate technology	nuclear-waste disposal	religious persecution
democracy vs. tyranny	international debt crisis	maintenance of fisheries	refugees

Africa changed drastically. Apartheid, as a phenomenon of racism and segregation, was largely eliminated. It is an example of a cultural issue of tremendous magnitude to millions of people in the world. Continuing discrimination against racial and minority groups often causes serious difficulties within many communities, cities, and towns in the United States.

Indigenous homelands are the native lands, areas, and traditional home places inhabited by a particular people. The people indigenous to a homeland are bonded together, more likely than not, by culture. When the people native to a place are somehow removed or encroached upon by others, the issue of indigenous homelands appears. It is a vital, emotionally charged issue among large numbers of people in the world. The issue of indigenous homelands has often provoked confrontations and even wars among various peoples. There are almost daily news accounts of incidents, repercussions, and reverberations regarding the issue of indigenous homelands. The consequences and aftermath that follow eruptions of this highly flammable issue are often devastating. Deeply rooted in culture and religion, this issue spreads into politics and sways the entire world community. The issue of indigenous homelands is far-reaching, affecting, for example, the Palestinians, the Pakistanis, the people of Bangladesh, and Native Americans.

The issue of political imprisonment, although foreign to citizens of the United States, is a reality for some of the world's peoples. Oftentimes, the politics of an area are heavily swayed by the cultural and religious heritage of the people who live there. The unsettling conditions in Bosnia and Herzegovina in the mid-1990s exemplified uncompromising cultural and religious differences which resulted in warfare and political imprisonment. When dictatorships are established or toppled, political imprisonment often follows for opponents of the newly empowered government.

In many cultures, religion forms the cultural hearth that bonds the people together. The religious feelings run deeply and are part and parcel of the culture. In some cases, there is an intolerance for other beliefs and other religions, and religious persecution often results. Religious persecution exists even in the most civilized societies. The problems in Northern Ireland, for example, bespeak religious intolerance that leads to persecuting people because of their religious convictions. Muslims, Jews, and Christians all tie Jerusalem to their sacred teachings, and consequently this area of the world is often witness to religious persecution.

Refugees are people who have had to leave their homelands for some reason. Wars between different groups of people on the planet always produce refugees. Their homelands are captured by the enemy or have become battlegrounds, forcing the occupants to leave and thus become refugees.

SOCIAL ISSUES

Hunger, poverty, overpopulation, capital punishment, homelessness, abortion, and drug abuse are examples of **social issues** that confront humankind on a large scale.

A social issue that is becoming more prevalent in society, particularly among women, is chronic dieting. Perhaps the underlying issue here is a fixation on appearance. Beauty has been considered an essential characteristic of the feminine stereotype for centuries, and the pursuit of thinness by women is understood in that context. Such a preoccupation with appearance often leads to chronic dieting, which in turn sometimes leads to anorexia and bulimia nervosa. The intense desire for thinness extends, with anorexics, to emaciation. Bulemics endure long periods of abstinence from food followed by consumption of enormous quantities and subsequent self-induced vomiting. "Over the past twenty years, anorexia and bulimia nervosa have reached epidemic proportions within the adolescent and young adult population. This dramatic increase is directly related to the strong emphasis contemporary society places on appearance, particularly body shape" (Nagel & Jones, 1992, p. 111).

Economic issues, which are involved with the production, distribution, and consumption of goods and services, can be global or social. By and large, economic issues arise from how humankind tries to provide for infinite wants with finite resources. In like manner, political issues, which arise primarily from concerns regarding the uses of power and authority in a society, can also be global or social. Environmental issues are another example of concerns and problems that can have either a global or a social basis.

CURRENT EVENTS: AN ISSUES-RICH ENVIRONMENT

Media are a prime source for issues. Utilizing both print and nonprint media to examine the events happening in the world is a profitable experience for students and teacher alike. It is a way to bring the real world into the classroom. Studying current events adds relevancy and applicability to school work. It builds meaningful bridges between activities in school and the real world, helping students see the connections between life in school and life out of school. Exploring issues through current events instruction can help students develop clarity, for example, in distinguishing between the past and the present and in their attitudes and values. As students survey reports, dispatches, descriptions, and explanations from the media on issues such as the environment, civil rights, and sex equity, they are themselves adopting attitudes and values relative to these issues.

A myriad of diverse events and issues flow from the media on a daily basis and provide excellent sources for integrated study. For example, prevailing media reports about nutria problems in Louisiana launched a valuable study in an elementary school classroom. In Jefferson Parish, Louisiana, fifth grade students became involved in a thematic study of a persistent Jefferson Parish problem: a rodent-like animal known as the nutria. Nutria were everywhere—in bayous, ponds, lakes, rivers—and their destructive nature was a nuisance to almost everyone. The overwhelming numbers of nutria in Jefferson Parish had become a major issue and was widely discussed in the news media, by politicians, and at civic and social gatherings. The nutria issue provided the gist for a rich investigation by the fifth graders. Their inquiry led them across the subjects of the curriculum. Among other things, they learned about the nutria as an animal; investigated data regarding trapping the nutria for pelts (which led into another issue, that of animal rights and those who disavow and renounce the use of animal skins for clothing); using the nutria as a food source for humans (which led their inquiry into China, because a local entrepreneur had negotiated a deal with the Chinese government to supply nutria meat for food and nutria pelts for coats and clothing); graphing, charting, and mapping concentrations of nutria in the parish; computing mathematical problems relating to estimates of nutria damage; and compiling statistical data on the expanding nutria population.

Martinello and Cook (1994) state:

> Current events lend themselves to study in classrooms because of their relevance and immediacy. It is easy, though, simply to teach facts about an event rather than exploring the underlying themes that make it significant. Teachers can build on children's expressed interests. They can also develop children's interests in topics, events, and issues. For example, the Columbian quincentenary in 1992 was celebrated in a variety of ways. For a year preceding the anniversary date, televised presentations on Columbus and his New World discoveries were aired on the Public Broadcasting System. Replicas of the *Nina,* the *Pinta,* and the *Santa Maria* visited several American harbors. A traveling exhibit was created by the Smithsonian Institution, and articles in local newspapers and popular magazines kept the issues of interactions between the Old and New Worlds, from the fifteenth through the twentieth centuries, in the public eye. These events and activities piqued the interest of many children, causing them to bring reports of their experiences to class. Teachers were then able to build on those expressed interests by encouraging classroom discussion and by building lessons around the quincentenary. In some classrooms, where children did not initiate discussion of this anniversary, teachers were able to develop interest in Columbus's voyages by sharing conflicting accounts for their students' reactions. Additionally, through literature, audiovisual presentations, artifact study, and activities in chart and map making, teachers guided children to raise questions. Those questions became starting points for substantive theme studies. (pp. 71–72)

Stockard (1995) writes that researching current events articles is an important skill for students to acquire. In a sense, research is nothing more than looking for information. Boxes 8.1 and 8.2 present a way for students to look for information in a news article. Box 8.1 is an actual newspaper account of a helicopter crash. Box 8.2 indicates the areas of basic information that students would seek from the article: Who was involved? What happened? Where did it happen? When did it happen? How (or Why) did it happen? As students engage in reading articles and news items from newspapers, periodicals, news magazines, and other media, Box 8.2 provides a convenient guide for seeking out the basic information.

Box 8.1   A Sample News Article

'Copter hit power line in fatal crash

Beacon Staff

Federal investigators say a helicopter which crashed near Perry earlier this month, killing a Bluewater Bay pilot and a crew member, hit a power line before going down.

The National Transportation Safety Board released a preliminary report yesterday on the crash.

Jimmy Gene Tucker, 60, Bluewater Bay, was killed in the Nov. 4 crash of the LifeFlight helicopter he was piloting from Tallahassee to pick up a patient from a Perry hospital. No patients were aboard the air ambulance at the time of the crash, which occurred in a remote logging area west of Perry known as Cabbage Pond.

Also killed in the crash was Richard Thompson, 35, a Tallahassee paramedic. Another crew member, Trent Robinson, 27, a Tallahassee nurse, was seriously injured.

According to the NTSB report, visual flight rules prevailed at the time of the accident, about 11:08 a.m.

"The survivor and several deer hunters in the area stated the helicopter was flying at a low level, with high speed, when it struck a 69-kilovolt power line, broke the line, flipped and crashed," the report said. "There was an extensive postcrash fire."

The helicopter was a Blokow BO-105S operated by Omni Flight, an air ambulance company based in Dallas.

SOURCE: *The Bay Beacon*, Niceville, Florida. November 23, 1994, page A-3. Reprinted with permission.

It is difficult to shield young children from the news that flows continually from the media. Beginning in infancy, many children are exposed to a deluge of television news, much of it unpleasant. On any given evening news broadcast, children are exposed to accounts of murder, violence, corruption, immorality, as well as personal tragedies, accounts of homelessness, pollution, disaster, and the like, seemingly without end. There have been suggestions that young children should be sheltered from unpleasant events in the news, but that is an untenable and implausible position. Parents and teachers "cannot and should not try to shield children from the real world that they must confront as citizens. Rather, we should try to help them make some sense of the often frightening and confusing social phenomena around them as soon as they enter school" (Martorella, 1994, p. 267).

Exploring issues through current events helps students view noteworthy happenings on a broad basis and develop global perspectives about the people,

---

Box 8.2   GETTING BASIC INFORMATION FROM A NEWS ARTICLE

WHO?	WHAT?	WHERE?	WHEN?	HOW/WHY?
A helicopter pilot named Jimmy Gene Tucker, age 60, a paramedic named Richard Thompson, age 35, and a nurse named Trent Robinson, age 27.	A Life-Flight air ambulance helicopter, a Blokow BO-105S operated by Omni Flight air ambulance company of Dallas, Texas, crashed and killed the pilot and the paramedic. The nurse survived the crash, but was seriously injured. The helicopter was going from Tallahassee, Florida, to Perry, Florida, to pick up a patient from a Perry hospital.	A remote logging area west of Perry, Florida, known as Cabbage Pond.	About 11:07 a.m. on November 4, 1994.	The survivor and several deer hunters said that the helicopter was flying at a low level, with high speed, when it struck a 69-kilovolt power line, broke the line, flipped and crashed. There was an extensive postcrash fire. Visual flight rules prevailed at the time of the crash, according to the National Transportation Safety Board.

---

places, and things reported in the news. A very good way to display news clippings is to develop a world news bulletin board with a map of the world at the center. For younger children, use a simple, colorful world map that shows geographic and political areas (continents, oceans, countries, and some major cities) in bright colors. For intermediate and upper elementary grades, use a physical-political world map, such as the one published by the National Geographic Society. As articles are posted on the bulletin board, colorful yarn can be used to connect the article with the location on the map where the noteworthy event occurred. In addition to gaining information from the news item, students can, time permitting, also research information on the location of the event. Such strategies will often afford a great deal of curriculum integration.

ISSUES INVOLVING MEDIA INFLUENCE AND MEDIA OWNERSHIP

Media are that vast array of newspapers, magazines, periodicals, trade books, textbooks, radio, television, and the like that is often termed mass communication. Box 8.3 lists some key areas involved in the consideration of media

---

Box 8.3   Media Concepts and Key Ideas

- mass communication
- media influence
- journalism
- media industry
- media ownership
- editorial policies
- mass media

---

issues. The media are controlled by journalists who collect and report the news, by editors and producers who decide which news (and how much news) is reported, and by owners and others who dominate the communications industry and profession. Most people are influenced in some degree by the media. Many of our ideas about people, places, and events are entirely derived from the media. Concepts about individuals in the limelight, such as politicians, sports celebrities, and movie stars, are nearly always derived from media reports about those individuals. It is unusual for us to observe these individuals live, so we generally learn about them from media presentations. If the media portrayals of important people are inaccurate, then our images of these people may also be incorrect.

In similar fashion, we get our information about major events in the world from the media. Rarely if ever are we able to view major world events in person, so we depend on the media for information about the event. Media depictions of the actions, interactions, and behaviors taking place cause us to form our ideas about the events.

In many cases, it is the media that give us knowledge about particular places on the earth. Sometimes we garner such information through personal experience, but most often, it comes from the media. Our only information about the Middle East or Amazonia or Mongolia, for example, may come exclusively from the media. We have a picture in our minds of how the Middle East or Amazonia or Mongolia must look, but that picture is produced by the media.

By and large then, we are quite dependent on the media for conceptual information about people, events, and places in the world. The media have immense influence in our lives; they can color our ideas and concepts, shade our understandings, and significantly affect the way we look at the people, events, and places in the world. Media influence can have consequences on the ways we think, react, and live our lives. In large measure, the media can determine our framework for thought and action regarding issues in the world. In that regard, the media themselves may become an issue.

Because media are all-encompassing, including all of the mass communication vehicles like newspapers, magazines, periodicals, trade books, textbooks, radio, and television, they are singularly influential in our lives. It becomes important, then, to know where ownership of the media resides. Who owns what? Which newspapers and chains of newspapers have common ownership? Who owns the television stations and television networks? Who owns the radio stations? Who owns the magazines? Who owns the trade book publishers? Who owns the textbook publishers? Does ownership intrude into the editorial operations of the media? Given the significant power and influence the media have in the lives of people, ownership and control of the media is an issue of significant and increasing importance in our world and a legitimate issue for inquiry in the elementary school.

ISSUES RELATING TO THE AIDS VIRUS

AIDS (Acquired Immune Deficiency Syndrome) is one of the most deadly and treacherous diseases to confront humankind to date. It is characterized by a loss of immunity to infection, thus allowing heretofore treatable illnesses and infections, such as pneumonia and tuberculosis, to become uncontrollably fatal. It is spread by a virus called HIV (human immunodeficiency virus), which can reside in the blood of infected persons for prolonged periods and is transmitted to other persons through contacts that exchange fluids, such as sexual contact, intravenous needle sharing, transfusions with contaminated blood, and during childbirth and nursing.

The role of education here is particularly important because, as yet, there are no vaccines or drugs to effectively prevent or treat AIDS. It is only through education that the spread of this deadly disease can be thwarted. In response, many states are requiring AIDS education in their schools. Box 8.4 lists some key concepts in AIDS education. The challenge to teachers is great. AIDS is a difficult subject to teach in the elementary school because the necessary vocabulary is difficult for adults to use with children. More and more, materials suitable for use in the elementary school are becoming available to help elementary children learn about AIDS. New videos, cartoon-format publications,

---

BOX 8.4   AIDS EDUCATION CONCEPTS

- HIV
- AIDS
- virus
- immune deficiency
- epidemic
- contaminated blood
- infectious disease
- contagious

filmstrips, audio tapes, and computer software dealing with AIDS education are being developed and distributed to schools. Teachers should avail themselves of the current AIDS materials available and make plans to include AIDS as one of the vital issues for exploration in the elementary school program.

Hunt and Marshall (1994) write that children with AIDS

> must often face the unnecessary prospect of social isolation. There have been many instances in which children with AIDS have been avoided or ostracized.
>
> Although transmission of AIDS in the normal course of school activities has never been documented, many parents—and therefore their children—have an extreme fear of this condition and sometimes fight the presence of the child with AIDS in the regular classroom. When a teacher is aware of a student with AIDS, he or she must work to facilitate appropriate and normal social interaction and to educate other children in the classroom. Children with AIDS have the most difficult task of not only dealing with a painful and probably fatal illness but also of fighting for love and acceptance from the people around them. (p. 447)

The major goal of the Centers for Disease Control and Prevention is to prevent the transmission of the AIDS virus. The Centers for Disease Control and Prevention, headquartered in Atlanta, sponsors a National AIDS Clearing House which can be reached at 1-800-458-5231. The National AIDS Clearing House is the quickest and easiest way for teachers and students to get up-to-date information on AIDS and information concerning materials that are appropriate for use in the instructional program in the elementary school.

The issues surrounding AIDS bring real-life relevancy into the investigations and learning of students and may well provide information that could save their lives. Investigations into AIDS issues have a natural propensity to take learners across subject lines and provide a vehicle for natural curriculum integration.

ISSUES PERTAINING TO ENVIRONMENTAL AND ENERGY FACTORS

Living creatures, through their daily life activities, have an impact on the Earth. Living creatures affect the environments in which they live in various ways. Beavers gnaw down trees and build dams that divert the flow of brooks and streams. The activities of the aquatic rodent known as the nutria (mentioned earlier) play havoc on the ecology of ponds and bayous and lakes. Salamanders dig mazes of destructive tunnels beneath lawns, flower beds, and gardens. Locusts move in swarms over parts of the Earth, eating every patch of vegetation and leaving a barren landscape. Humans, however, seem to impact the environment the most.

Extracting the mineral resources of the Earth has often been at a high cost to the environment. For example, exploration for oil and the drilling of oil wells in parts of Louisiana and Texas in the early 1900s impacted the wetlands of the bayou country by discharging the waste products of the drilling process right into the swamps and bayous. It has taken many years for these areas to recover from this environmental scarring.

The traffic problems in many of the world's largest cities bespeak the huge numbers of automobiles in use on our planet. Fossil fuels, when burned by automobiles, machinery, and power plants, produce injurious fumes that affect the respiratory systems of humans and animals. These fumes and exhaust gases also impact forests and the growth of crops. Environmental pollution by automobiles became such a problem in California that legislative measures were taken to require pollution-controlling devices on automobiles sold in that state.

Strip-mining for coal in Kentucky and West Virginia wreaked havoc on the environment in parts of those states. The strip miners cut trees and vegetation from the mountain slopes in Appalachia, dumping the rocks and debris down the slopes in order to get to the seams of coal. The result was a landscape left with grotesque scars, soil erosion, and streams fouled by coal residues (Hennings, Hennings, & Banich, 1993).

As students pursue environmental issues, they are working in and among several academic disciplines and subjects in an integrated fashion. Biological, chemical, and earth science become a part of environmental education, as well as the social sciences of sociology, geography, economics, history, and political science. Box 8.5 offers a list of important environmental concepts.

The science of the relationships between organisms and their environments is called ecology. Sometimes scientists refer to ecology as bionomics. The branch of sociology that is concerned with studying the relationships between human groups and their physical and social environments is called human ecology. This

---

BOX 8.5   ENVIRONMENTAL CONCEPTS AND KEY IDEAS

fossil fuels	urban sprawl	world food shortage
population growth	pesticides	waste disposal
industrialization	air pollution	water pollution
biodegradable materials	reclamation	recyclable materials
noise pollution	greenhouse effect	plastic containers
endangered species	endangered rain forests	endangered wetlands
desertification	flooding and erosion	deforestation
ecosystem	balance of nature	energy
adaptation	resources	environment

often includes the study of the detrimental effects of modern civilization on the environment, with a view toward prevention or reversal through conservation. An ecosystem is an ecological community together with its environment, functioning as a unit. Students are exploring biological science when they examine the organisms making up the ecosystem, and they are engaging in the social sciences when they probe the stresses (like pollution and scarring) that human activity brings to the ecological system. In making inquiries into ecological issues, children naturally use knowledge and information from sociology, geography, economics, history, political science, and the natural and biological sciences, making curriculum integration a reality.

Energy is closely related to the day-to-day lives of most people. Extracting and consuming energy impacts the environment by scarring or polluting. Dangers to the environment stem from pesticides, disposing of solid wastes, air pollution, water pollution, radioactive substances, and overpopulation. Children easily relate to topics in energy and the environment because they are a part of their daily lives. Issues surrounding the environment and energy production naturally integrate the curriculum and provide excellent sources for pupil investigations.

SEX EQUITY AND GENDER-SPECIFIC BEHAVIOR ISSUES

Primarily in America, but to some extent in other parts of the world as well, the increasing independence of women has become one of the most significant social developments of our time. **Sex equity** deals with gender issues, particularly sex-role stereotyping, "the practice of attributing roles, behaviors, and aspirations to individuals or groups solely on the basis of gender" (Martorella, 1994, p. 262).

In the United States, sex discrimination is expressly forbidden by legislation, the best known examples being the 19th Amendment to the Constitution, the Civil Rights Act of 1964, and Title IX of the Education Amendments of 1972. Title IX concerns itself with sexual discrimination in education and opens with the following declaration:

> No person in the United States shall on the basis of sex be excluded from participation in, be denied the benefits of, or be subjected to discrimination under any education program or activity receiving Federal financial assistance. . . .

Gender plays an important role in how individuals participate in various societies of the world. In the United States, decisions based on gender begin early. Selecting a name for a new baby, choosing colors for a room, picking clothes to be worn, opting for certain kinds of toys, and the like are all gender-based. Gender issues are prominent in education, occupations, lifestyles, and hobbies.

In other societies, however, a great deal of inequality exists regarding gender roles. In Muslim countries the status of women doesn't equal the status of men. An Islamic man, for example, can have more than one wife and has rights that women don't have. Males in many Hindu societies are accorded more privileges and respect than females, even as infants. Female babies are so unwanted in some societies that they are abandoned in the wilderness. Even in some highly developed societies, there is a pervasive notion that females are inferior to males. Stopsky and Lee (1994) write, "Consider the Orthodox Jewish prayer: 'Blessed art Thou O Lord our God, King of the Universe, that I was not born a woman'" (p. 434).

For one gender group to be accorded more rights or be held more worthy or be deemed more valuable than the other is unjust. "A major overall goal of the socialization of American children is that of engendering values and attitudes based on principles of equality among human beings" (Jarolimek & Parker, 1993, p. 249). Issues relating to sex-role stereotyping, sexist language, sexist attitudes, and gender-specific behaviors are sources of meaningful student inquiry.

Recognizing the neglect of women in the teaching of American history, the U.S. Congress, declaring March as Women's History Month in America each year, notes:

> American women of every race, class, and ethnic background helped found the Nation in countless recorded and unrecorded ways as servants, slaves, nurses, nuns, homemakers, industrial workers, teachers, reformers, soldiers, and pioneers; and . . . served as early leaders in the forefront of every major progressive social change movement, not only to secure their own right of suffrage and equal opportunity, but also in the abolitionist movement, the emancipation movement, the industrial labor union movement, and the modern civil rights movement; and . . . despite these contributions, the role of American women in history has been consistently overlooked and undervalued in the body of American history. (Martorella, 1994, pp. 262, 264)

Sex equity issues cut across all curricular lines and represent ideal areas of inquiry for children in the elementary school. Issues relating to gender-specific behavior and sex equity allow students to pursue learning in an integrated fashion. Box 8.6 shows some concepts to be explored and developed in sex equity education.

LAW-RELATED ISSUES

Real and contemporary issues of law breaking and law enforcement provide relevant studies for elementary students. They can explore law-related issues through role playing, case studies, simulations, and mock trials, examining the roles of police, jails, judges, bailiffs, court reporters, prosecutors, defense counsels, public defenders, probation officers, social workers, and others (Stopsky & Lee, 1994).

Teachers have often taken the opportunity to introduce law-related education by working with children to formulate and establish the rules that will govern the class. Such issues as bathroom use, going to the water fountain, talking,

---

BOX 8.6   SEX EQUITY CONCEPTS

- equity
- sex roles
- sexist language
- reform movements
- nontraditional roles
- sex stereotyping
- feminism

---

moving about, eating, chewing gum, sharpening pencils, and borrowing from a neighbor are often regulated by rules made by the children themselves.

Another good way to present law-related issues is to take popular children's fairy tales and conduct simulated trials and hearings about the story. For example, in Cinderella, the stepmother and stepsisters could be brought to trial for their abuse and mistreatment of Cinderella. In *Goldilocks and the Three Bears,* Goldilocks could be brought to trial for breaking into the house of the three bears. Similar scenarios for law-related simulations, mock trials, and hearings are in *Little Red Riding Hood, The Three Little Pigs, Jack and the Beanstalk, The Tale of Peter Rabbit,* and many other fairy tales and familiar children's stories. Difficult concepts, such as *due process* and *justice,* become real and therefore meaningful in such interesting simulations. Box 8.7 lists some other important concepts in law.

Television programs can often enhance students' knowledge and understanding of law in our society. Dramas such as *L.A. Law* are often based on real events and are very factual relative to the law and legal processes. Court TV is available on many cable networks; it broadcasts actual video of courtroom cases with lots of commentary by lawyers and legal experts. The double-murder trial of celebrity O. J. Simpson was a mainstay on several television networks for many months in 1995 and provided a plethora of issues and concerns related to law enforcement and legal matters.

National, state, and local bar associations provide educational literature to schools and interested parties about the law. They also provide lawyers and legal experts as resource speakers for classes at all levels. Local attorneys who are members of the American Bar Association are excellent resource persons. Judges will often come to the classroom as speakers and resource persons, robes and all. Many judges welcome children to their courtrooms on field trips where they may sit on the judge's bench, in the jury box, at the prosecutor's table, at the defendant's table, in the bailiff's seat, and at the court reporter's desk. Students may even be allowed to venture into the judge's private chambers. Local politicians, like the mayor, city council members, city and county commissioners,

---

Box 8.7   Law-related Concepts

- due process
- rules
- laws
- authority
- power
- rights
- justice
- privacy
- property
- responsibility
- equal protection
- legal system

---

and school board members also make good resource people on law-related matters.

Focusing on law-related issues should help pupils:

- understand their rights in our democratic society
- understand their responsibilities in our democratic society
- understand the structure and functioning of the law and government in our democratic society
- participate as full citizens in our democratic society

PRECAUTIONS TO CONSIDER WITH ISSUES

Issues are, by their very nature, controversial and argumentative. Remember that issues have more than one side, more than one point of view. As a facilitator, the teacher needs to be careful not to inculcate closely held personal views into an inquiry involving issues. Assist and empower students to explore, probe, and investigate all aspects of an issue, but do not indoctrinate, brainwash, or otherwise condition students to your point of view. Meaningful and authentic inquiry into argumentative and highly controversial issues brings about learning that offers growth in self-direction and the establishment of a personal system of values.

Another precaution to be considered is the sensitive nature of some issues. Abortion, the AIDS virus, and homosexuality are extremely sensitive issues in the overall population and should be accorded special attention. Parents, for example, should be notified whenever an inquiry into a sensitive and emotional issue is being planned. Parental support should be sought, and parents should be asked to give assistance in supplying resources for the planned investigation. In any inquiry into issues, up-to-date data in the form of pamphlets, news reports, and magazine articles is vital; however, it is crucial to have up-to-date information for an investigation into highly sensitive issues. Critical and consequential information dealing with sensitive issues before the public is often available on a timely basis and can be of pivotal importance in the inquiry. Studies into sensitive issues, then, should be well-stocked with current and up-to-date information for use in the inquiry.

Skeel (1995) indicates that controversial issues generally fall into social, economic, political, and environmental categories and offers this counsel for teachers approaching the study of controversial issues:

> For a variety of reasons, many teachers step lightly when controversial issues arise in the news or in the classroom. . . . Certain controversial issues should be discussed in the elementary school, for children need the opportunity to study all sides of an issue and to make their own decisions. Teachers should use discretion when selecting issues for study. Several criteria should be applied:
>
> 1. Are the children mature enough to understand the issue thoroughly?
> 2. Do the children have sufficient background experiences to appraise the issue critically?
> 3. Will the study of the issue help attain the goals of the school and the community?
> 4. Is the issue of social, political, economic, or environmental significance?
> 5. Does the policy of the school permit the study of such an issue?
> 6. Will the children become better-informed, thoughtful citizens as a result of the study?
>
> The manner in which a teacher approaches the study of controversial issues is of vital importance. Teachers who have a chip on their shoulder about an issue, or those who are prejudiced, opinionated, or possess an extreme point of view and teach only one side of an issue would be wise to ask someone to assist them with the study. . . . One of the main purposes in having children research issues is to develop in them the habit of approaching any issue with an open mind, securing the facts on all sides, and then making a decision when necessary. A prejudiced teacher who permits that prejudice to show defeats this purpose. (p. 130)

Ellis (1995) uses the assassination of President John F. Kennedy and the fatal liftoff of the space shuttle *Challenger* to illustrate examples of the controversial issue of death. These events were played out on the world stage and had a shocking impact on millions of people and children in the United States and around the world. To avoid discussion of these events and of the sorrow, loss, and anxiety left in their wake would be to deny reality and create a false impression about the importance of life itself. Examining controversial issues like death brings children into the realms of compassion, empathy, understanding, and tolerance seldom reached in other ways:

> These happenings, witnessed not by a few but by the world, illustrate episodes of grief shared by us all. We can discuss them together even though our words fail to convey the depths of our emotions. But more common occurrences are a continual part of our existence. The death of a pet, a grandparent, and from time to time the loss of a parent, brother, or sister will be a part of a child's life. What kind of curriculum is too busy or too aloof to find time for such matters? This is a time for great patience and understanding on the part of a teacher. This is a signal to a child that you care and that you will do what you can to support him or her during this time of uncertainty. There are no easy answers here; but a child will generally respond to a caring, supportive adult during such a personal crisis. . . . The point is not to present yourself as an expert on these issues, but to present yourself to children as someone who has a genuine sense of humanity and as someone who genuinely cares about the deeper things in life. Therefore, the real issues regarding the examination of controversial topics are compassion, understanding, tolerance, and an undying sense of the human spirit. (p. 322)

In many cases, controversial issues are highly charged with emotion, and it is difficult for the teacher and the children to assess all sides of the issue without a display of emotion. Examples of such emotionally charged issues might include prayer in the school, the death penalty, abortion, students with HIV, and school consolidation. In such situations, the teacher should alert students to the influence emotions can have and encourage them to be as objective as possible.

SUMMARY

Issues can provide excellent focal points for curricular integration. They appear in a variety of postures, such as controversies, problems, obstacles, and dilemmas, and they are often aligned with people's opinions and beliefs. Some issues are real and derive from the actual day-to-day experiences of students, while other issues are contrived, having their sources in books and other kinds of instructional materials.

We live in an environment in which a variety of vital issues emerge constantly. There are global issues, cultural issues, economic issues, and environmental issues, to name a few. The media are prime sources for finding issues and, indeed, the media themselves, in terms of influence and ownership, can be issues. By and large, issues do not fall into the constraints of any one academic discipline or subject, but range among different subject areas making them excellent means for curricular integration.

ACTIVITY ONE

PURPOSE

The purpose of this activity is to work in a cooperative group to create a web of ideas for issues suitable for use in curricular integration.

PROCEDURE

Divide into two groups. Work cooperatively and collaboratively to brainstorm for issues suitable for grades 1–3 and issues suitable for grades 4–6. Use the webs in Figures 8.1 and 8.2 (pp. 208 and 209) as models to create webs for the ideas as they are generated. Let each group share their webs. Compare and contrast to see how the webs are alike and how they are different.

ACTIVITY TWO

PURPOSE

The purpose of this activity is to work in a cooperative group to draft a school policy for accommodating students with the AIDS virus.

PROCEDURE

You are a member of an elementary school faculty that has decided to plan for the possibility of students enrolling in your school who have the AIDS virus. Divide into three groups. Each group works cooperatively and collaboratively to design a plan for your school to accommodate children who are diagnosed with the AIDS virus. Groups should contact the Centers for Disease Control and Prevention and their National AIDS Clearing House in Atlanta (1-800-458-5231) for current, up-to-date information. Each group should address:

- strategies for educating and dealing with parents of noninfected children
- strategies for educating and dealing with noninfected children in the classroom
- ways to facilitate appropriate and normal social interaction in the classroom and in the school for the infected child

End the activity by having groups share their plans with the other groups, accompanied by discussion and critiques.

✠ ACTIVITY THREE

PURPOSE

The purpose of this activity is to work together in pairs to find gender-specific writing in textbooks used in your school.

PROCEDURE

As faculty members in an elementary school that has decided to evaluate its textbooks for gender-specific writing, you and your partner select a grade and a subject to be your responsibility. For the grade and subject selected, examine the textbook(s) used for: sex-role stereotyping, sexist language, sexist attitudes, and gender-specific behaviors. Look for passages and phrases that attribute roles, behaviors, aspirations, and the like solely on the basis of gender.

End the activity with each investigating team presenting their findings to the class. Suspect language might be shown on a transparency, with opportunities for questions, comments, and discussion from the audience.

STUDY QUESTIONS

1. Describe how issues can have many facets, thus providing potential for inquiries across the subject boundaries of the elementary curriculum.
2. Compare and contrast real issues and contrived issues. Give examples of each.
3. Give examples of some vital issues that do not fall into the constraints of any one academic discipline, but rather have a wide range of influence and effect that compels them to be studied in an integrated fashion.
4. Outline and explain appropriate steps a teacher and students might follow in making inquiries into issues.
5. Explain the nature of cultural issues, social issues, and global issues. Give examples of each.
6. In what ways can a teacher demonstrate through practice insight into gender-specific issues?
7. Because issues by their very nature are controversial and argumentative, what precautions must a teacher consider when focusing studies around issues?

BIBLIOGRAPHY

Ellis, A. (1995). *Teaching and learning elementary social studies* (5th ed.). Boston: Allyn and Bacon.

Hanssen, E. (1990). Planning for literature circles: Variations in focus and structure. In K. G. Short & K. M. Pierce (Eds.), *Talking about books: Creating literate communities* (p. 116). Portsmouth, N.H.: Heinemann.

Hennings, D., Hennings, G., & Banich, S. (1993). *Today's elementary social studies* (2nd ed.). Prospect Heights, Ill.: Waveland Press.

Hunt, N., & Marshall, K. (1994). *Exceptional children and youth: An introduction to special education.* Boston: Houghton Mifflin.

Jarolimek, J., & Parker, W. (1993). *Social studies in elementary education.* New York: Macmillan.

Martinello, M., & Cook, G. (1994). *Interdisciplinary inquiry in teaching and learning.* New York: Merrill.

Martorella, P. (1994). *Social studies for elementary school children: Developing young citizens.* New York: Merrill.

Nagel, K., & Jones, K. (1992). Sociological factors in the development of eating disorders. *Adolescence, 27* (5), 107–111.

Parker, W. (1991). *Renewing the social studies curriculum.* Alexandria, Va.: Association for Supervision and Curriculum Development.

Pugh, S., Garcia, J., & Margalef-Boada, S. (1994). Multicultural tradebooks in the social studies classroom. *The Social Studies, 85* (2), 62–64.

Rosenbusch, M. (1994). Preserve the rain forests. *Social Studies, 85* (1), 31–36.

Saxe, D. (1994). *Social studies for the elementary teacher.* Needham Heights, Mass.: Allyn and Bacon.

Seely, A. (1995). *Integrated thematic units.* Westminster, Calif.: Teacher Created Materials, Inc.

Skeel, D. (1995). *Elementary social studies: Challenges for tomorrow's world.* Fort Worth, Tex.: Harcourt Brace.

Stockard, J. (1995). *Activities for elementary school social studies.* Prospect Heights, Ill.: Waveland.

Stopsky, F., & Lee, S. (1994). *Social Studies in a global society.* Albany, N.Y.: Delmar.

Zarnowski, M. (1990). *Learning about biographies: A reading-and-writing approach for children.* Urbana, Ill.: National Council of Teachers of English.

PART 3

APPROACHES TO INSTRUCTIONAL DELIVERY

CHAPTER 9

PLANNING FOR TEACHING IN THE INTEGRATED CURRICULUM

CHAPTER OBJECTIVES

After reading this chapter you should be able to:

1. Describe the use of instructional mapping as a means of planning for interdisciplinary teaching
2. Discuss ways in which teachers can build background knowledge prior to beginning a theme
3. Plan a resource unit for an integrated theme
4. Describe techniques for instructional delivery in the integrated curriculum
5. Plan for teaching in the integrated curriculum

Teaching in the integrated program is far different from teaching in the traditional classroom. In the traditional program teachers act as directors of learning, preparing specific lessons, deciding on the sequence in which those lessons will be presented, and determining exactly how students will be evaluated. The students have little input into the content or the direction of their learning. On the other hand, the teacher working within the integrated curriculum acts as a facilitator of learning rather than a director of learning. The teacher as facilitator provides opportunities for individual learning rather than dictating what will be learned through lessons and objectives. Rather than preparing specific lessons and determining the sequence of those lessons, the teacher in the integrated classroom works with the students to plan and develop the learning experiences. And rather than determining exactly how students will

233

be evaluated, the teacher who is a facilitator works with the students to develop a representative sample of student work that demonstrates the progress of individual students.

Although the concept of the teacher as facilitator seems to mean the teacher does little planning before entering the classroom, and that the direction of the educational program is entirely dependent on the students, this is erroneous. In order to work effectively in the integrated program, the teacher must be exceptionally well prepared, and being prepared requires extensive planning. The following discussion begins after the themes have been selected for each grade level.

GENERAL PLANNING

After the scope of the program has been considered on a schoolwide and grade level basis, then the selected themes need to be developed by the classroom teachers so that units of work are outlined. The use of the word *outlined* in the previous sentence is important: It indicates that while the teacher does plan extensively, the details of the unit are left to be worked out after collaboration has occurred between the students and the teacher. Within the integrated curriculum teachers provide ample opportunity for students to plan how themes will develop, what sources of information will be used, how the class will be organized in their investigations, and how the final product or products of the investigations will be shared with others. Students in the classroom should have as much input into the direction of their learning as possible.

The amount of input from students is going to depend on the age of the students and the experiential background of those students in working with an integrated approach to curriculum. The younger the group of children and the less experience with planning within the integrated approach, the more assistance they will need. For example, kindergarten children who are considering the theme "homes" will need help in deciding what it is they want to learn about homes and the teacher will need to do a great deal of advance planning for the unit of work. Sixth graders who have had much experience with an integrated and cooperative approach to developing units of study will be more able to guide their own work when developing the theme "Olympic Games." Sixth graders who have no experience in directing their own learning, however, will probably need as much guidance as will younger children.

DETERMINING THEME DURATION

Once the classroom teacher has considered the kinds of activities possible, the means for presenting the results of the work, and the techniques to involve the children in planning for the theme, then he or she needs to consider the duration of the theme. For children at the kindergarten level, themes are generally short; a maximum of two weeks is a rule of thumb. For sixth graders a theme could last an entire school year, but six weeks is a more realistic length of time. In judging the length of time to plan for a particular theme, consider these:

1. *How substantive is the theme?* A substantive theme will be one in which students can investigate the theme from a variety of perspectives and in which there are numerous subthemes. In addition, a substantive theme will allow students to investigate questions of their own making.
2. *How is the theme related to themes to come?* A theme closely related to other themes that will be considered within the curriculum will probably use a shorter period of time than one in which the concepts will be unlikely to be revisited.
3. *How does the theme fit into the rest of the curriculum?* A primary grade theme that is related to themes at the early and later intermediate grades should receive more attention than a theme that is particular to a grade level. If concepts are to be extended at other grade levels, students should have a thorough grounding in the knowledge presented at the earlier grade levels.
4. *What interest have students already shown in the topic?* Topics in which students have previously shown interest are more likely to be sustained topics than are those in which students have shown little or no interest. However, this does not mean that student interest should be the only determinant of the length of a theme. Students may show little interest because they have not had any significant encounters with the theme. Immersion in the theme may develop interest. And students should not simply repeat the familiar but should have their understanding and their horizons broadened.
5. *How can the curriculum be balanced in terms of time spent on particular themes?* All themes should not be of the same length. This is common sense if one considers that some themes are broader and more substantive than others. However, for variety within the program, long themes should be balanced with short themes. Under no circumstances should themes be molded to "fit" the traditional curricular pattern of six-week grading periods.

Once the teacher has made some decisions as to duration of the theme, he or she begins specific planning for the integrated theme.

PLANNING IN THE INTEGRATED CURRICULUM: RESOURCE UNITS

Planning for teaching within the integrated curriculum is far more exciting than planning within the traditional curriculum. The integrated approach to curriculum allows for teaching in a dynamic and exciting classroom where children are active investigators and learners rather than passive recipients of knowledge. If that active learning is to take place, then the integrated curriculum teacher needs to abandon the dry practice of "lessons" and embrace the dynamic practice of learning.

The beginning stages of planning for the integrated curriculum were discussed in Chapter 5. In this discussion, total school brainstorming and grade level planning were considered; it was also mentioned that the next step in planning was done by the individual teacher. It is at this point, where planning by the teacher in the classroom begins, that we will begin. Planning now involves the development of a **resource unit**. A resource unit is a long-term planning tool that helps the teacher organize and identify the resources available for teaching a particular theme within the integrated curriculum. The resource unit for the integrated curriculum is different from the resource unit for a traditional curriculum.

THE TRADITIONAL RESOURCE UNIT

A resource unit for the traditional curriculum generally contains the following areas:

1. background information
2. objectives for the unit
3. unit concepts
4. classroom organization
5. prerequisites
6. activities
7. resource materials
8. evaluation methods

Each of these sections of the traditional resource unit is described below.

Background Information.   The background information consists of an overview of the topic in terms of content to be taught, the reason for teaching the unit, and any additional information that will be helpful to the individual teaching the unit. The major part of the background information is an overview of the content as a refresher for the teacher.

Objectives for the Unit.   This section contains both general and specific objectives, including the cognitive, affective, and psychomotor domains. The objectives state exactly what the students will learn in the unit and how they will demonstrate that knowledge. An example of a specific objective from the cognitive domain is: "After reading information on the pros and cons of the use of nuclear energy, each student will be able to write a paper taking one side or the other and defend that side with information from the reading."

Unit Concepts. This is a list of the concepts that will be taught through the unit. The resource unit generally includes far more concepts than could be learned by any one class. This provides the opportunity to select which concepts will be taught to a particular group. In this way the unit taught can be somewhat tailored to the class. For example, a teacher working with a class of students with high interest in arts and music might choose additional concepts in those areas.

Prerequisites. This section of the unit includes prerequisite concepts both from the discipline that is the focus of the unit and prerequisites that are a part of other disciplines. For example, a unit dealing with endangered species might have as prerequisites concepts dealing with habitat, biome, ecosystem, and other concepts from the sciences. In addition, concepts of geography and mathematics as well as the ability to produce a research paper may be listed as prerequisites.

Activities. The activities list includes a variety of possibilities for teaching each of the concepts. In general the activities are teacher developed and directed. Individual activities, small group projects, and total group instruction are included. Once the activities are listed, a list of the specific materials needed is developed. The activities list is a compilation of possible activities from which the teacher is able to select those most appropriate to the class.

Resource Materials. The section on resource materials gives a list of the written, audio, and video materials the teacher and/or the students can use in developing the content of the unit. Primary sources should be a part of the resource materials list, along with secondary and tertiary sources.

Evaluation Techniques. This section includes possible methods for evaluating the unit. It does not include the exact tests, quizzes, checklists, or worksheets that would be used in the evaluation process, but rather suggestions for how to evaluate. The evaluation techniques section may include suggestions of when to use a brief quiz or test, when an observation-based checklist might be appropriate, and when a worksheet from an activity could be used as an evaluation.

The traditional resource unit is developed by the teacher and contains all of the information necessary to plan for teaching. The concepts to be learned are specified, the activities to be used in teaching are listed, the resource materials are included, and the evaluation techniques are specified. It is true that the traditional resource unit will contain far more than will probably be used in the actual unit presented to the class, but the resource unit also contains everything that will be presented to or used by the class. The traditional resource unit assumes that the concepts selected by the teacher will be taught to and learned by all children in the class. There is generally little direct input into the development of the unit by the students.

THE INTEGRATED RESOURCE UNIT

In contrast, the resource unit developed for the integrated curriculum provides a basis for learning but not a prescription for teaching. It provides suggestions but also leaves much room for teacher and student input. The integrated curriculum resource unit may be thought of as a resource center from which the teacher may select materials for use and to which he or she may also bring additional materials for use and sharing. The integrated curriculum resource unit consists of the following sections, each of which will be discussed in detail.

1. graphic organizer
   a. semantic map
   b. tabulature
2. activities list
3. student input
4. classroom organization
5. materials and resources

DEVELOPING A GRAPHIC ORGANIZER

As school level and grade level planning occurs, one of the outcomes of that planning is a semantic map. Developed as a means for visualizing the topic, it is the basis for a graphic organizer. But the graphic organizer goes beyond the simple pictorial depiction of the semantic map.

Step 1: Developing the Semantic Map.   As a result of the grade level planning, each teacher should have a variety of themes for use in the classroom. Such a listing for the sixth grade level might include the following themes as well as others:

1. the changing Earth
2. ancient Americas
3. games
4. when worlds collide: fantasy and fact
5. getting the message across: advertising, propaganda, literature

As these themes were considered, a semantic map would have been developed. Figure 9.1 shows a semantic map developed for the theme "the changing earth."

Step 2: Developing the Tabulature.   Although the semantic map begins to develop the concepts that will be considered during the thematic unit, the graphic organizer further develops those concepts. At this point, it is helpful to leave the map format and to develop instead a tabular format. This tabular format lists the concepts that could be considered within a particular thematic unit and then provides space for details to be added to this concept. It is important for

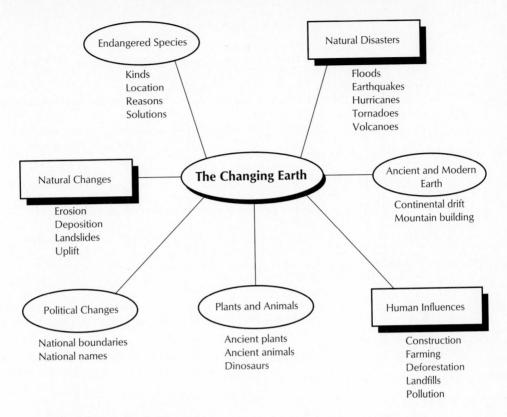

FIGURE 9.1 Earth changes

Note: Areas listed in rectangular boxes represent topics developed by the teacher. Areas listed in ovals represent topics added by the students during planning.

the teacher to remember that these concepts will not be taught directly to the children and that all concepts may not be considered by all children as they work with the unit. Instead, it is possible that a specific child will engage in projects dealing with only certain aspects of the theme and that he or she will be exposed to other areas through displays and presentations by other children in the classroom. As a consequence of this viewpoint, many more concepts may be listed than will actually be considered within the classroom. And because students have the opportunity to discuss the theme and add to the possible topics, there will be other concepts added to the tabulature after classroom discussions occur.

Once the main concepts have been listed in the table, then the subsidiary concepts leading to the main concepts can be listed. The subsidiary concepts should be listed in statement form so that it is clear which concepts are important to the particular topic. The listed subsidiary concepts should be related directly to the focal concept and should enhance understanding of that concept. Keep in mind that these concepts are tentative. They are used in planning and

"The Changing Earth"

Concept 1: Natural disasters cause changes in the Earth.
  Subsidiary Concepts: 1. Volcanic eruptions cause geological changes that affect both the living and the nonliving environment.
  2. Floods result in rapid geological changes.
  3. Hurricanes and tornadoes are storms that can cause considerable localized damage.
  4. Earthquakes occur in all parts of the Earth and can result either in extensive changes in the Earth's surface or in little change.

Concept 2: The Earth has been changed because of the actions of humans.
  1. Construction of cities and roads has changed the Earth.
  2. Farming has changed land forms through terracing, turning forest and prairie land into fields, and through changing population areas.
  3. Deforestation is causing a decrease in rain forests and in forest lands in general.
  4. Pollution is resulting in health problems, acid rain, and destruction of ancient artworks and buildings.

Concept 3: Natural geological changes are a factor in changing the Earth.
  1. Erosion and deposition operate together to cause changes in the surface of the Earth.
  2. Landslides and avalanches cause sudden changes in localized areas.
  3. Geological uplift and subsidence can result in mountain ranges and basin areas.

FIGURE 9.2 Concepts and subsidiary concepts in tabulature format

selecting possible experiences for children. Some students will be interested in pursuing all of the possibilities while others will be focused in certain areas. Additionally, as students and teachers plan together before the start of the theme, they will add to the list. Figure 9.2 illustrates the use of the table form to list subsidiary concepts as developed by the teacher.

DEVELOPING THE ACTIVITIES LIST

At this point the teacher needs to begin to give attention to the kinds of learning experiences students could use to investigate a particular theme. Some of the possibilities include:

1. *Reading* textbooks, resource books, magazines, primary source materials, or other print sources. Among other things, reading helps students gain background information, extend what is already known, and provide accurate data for construction or creative activities.
2. *Hands-on activities* in which children directly investigate some aspect of the theme, as in developing a habitat for silkworms, watching as the cocoon is spun, and then attempting to retrieve the silk from the cocoon.

3. *Constructing models* such as physical models and dioramas. In this case, children might create a model waterwheel or, in creating a diorama, show a habitat for turtles.

4. *Writing activities* in which students create their own books and poetry as well as write traditional research papers.

5. *Dramatic activities* such as writing and presenting plays and skits.

6. *Musical productions* including instrumental or vocal music as well as dance. Children can perform existing songs and dances, listen to recorded music or watch tapes of dance productions, as well as write and perform their own songs and dances.

7. *Technological activities,* as in developing video and audio tapes with tape recorders and video recorders, using computer technology to create graphics and other visual presentations and to present multimedia productions.

8. *Reality-based models,* including such things as developing a terrarium, a method for incubating eggs, or a school garden.

9. *Field trips* to locations both within the school and within the community or area. A field trip to the school cafeteria to consider the nutritional quality of food served and a field trip to a hydroelectric plant are representative of this category.

10. *Interviews* with individuals who have expertise in the area under study or who have experienced the theme firsthand. Students working on a theme dealing with civil rights could talk to persons who had been active in the civil rights movement. Students involved in a theme dealing with pre-Columbian civilizations could talk with a university professor working in that field.

11. *Craft activities* in which students replicate basket making, bead work, quilting, appliques, embroidery, native costumes, pottery, carving, and other crafts of a particular culture or time period.

12. *Firsthand experiences,* including participating in an archaeological dig, assisting with a community program such as a food bank, and working in a classroom to tutor younger children.

This list is meant only as a starting point. The theme or problem selected as well as the teacher's knowledge of the theme and of his or her students and the community will result in additional possibilities for activities. Also, the students themselves will be able to contribute to the development of activities, often suggesting possibilities that the teacher may not have considered.

OBTAINING STUDENT INPUT

Planning with the class involves cooperation between teacher and students in a nonthreatening manner and is important to the integrated curriculum for a variety of reasons. First, including children in planning allows the children involved to feel a sense of ownership of their education. They helped create it:

The curriculum is theirs. Second, it allows children to include in the curriculum those areas of interest to them as children rather than simply those ideas of importance to adults. Finally, including children in planning allows time for the children to work cooperatively, to plan within a large group setting, to engage in problem solving, and to interact with others in ways that may necessitate compromise or even a complete change of idea in the face of evidence.

At this point in planning the resource unit, the teacher needs to take a backseat to the students. The teacher needs to listen carefully to the ideas students bring to the planning session and then make decisions as to how those ideas should be used within the theme.

There are six steps to accomplishing this mutual planning. The first five deal with gaining input from the students, and the sixth focuses on the use of the input within the integrated theme.

Step 1: Brainstorming.   In step 1 of planning with the class, the teacher involves the students in a brainstorming session. In this case, the teacher tells the students the topic for the theme and gives a brief definition of it. Then the teacher asks the students to brainstorm everything they already know about the topic. This brainstorming can be done as a total class or in small groups. The teacher or other recorder should keep a record of everything that has been said. This step gives the teacher two pieces of information. First, it allows the teacher to determine what students already know about the topic. This provides an opportunity to assess background information already known to the students and permits the teacher to determine whether the students have sound knowledge, biased knowledge, misconceptions, in-depth knowledge, or shallow knowledge. Second, it allows the teacher to determine whether he or she and the students are interpreting the topic in the same way. For example, in considering the theme "the changing Earth" with a group of sixth grade students, the teacher had in mind changes within two broad categories: natural disasters, such as earthquakes, tornadoes, and floods; and human influences, such as rain forest destruction, deforestation, and the results of construction. As the students began to brainstorm, however, the teacher began to see additional concepts that could be included: dinosaurs and modern animals, old kinds of plants and current plants, moving continents, endangered species, maps and globes, and even changes in names and borders of nations.

Step 2: Determining What Students Want to Know about the Theme. Once the students have had a chance to brainstorm everything they know about a particular topic, the next step is to determine what students would like to know about the topic or what they would like to study in more depth. In general, this results in a list of questions to be researched. For example, the sixth grade classroom considering the topic of the changing earth had these questions:

1. What kinds of animals lived long ago in the United States?
2. What happened to the dinosaurs?

3. Are maps today the same as the maps used by people a long time ago?
4. What causes some kinds of animals to become endangered?
5. Were there ever any volcanoes in Alabama?
6. Are plants today like those that lived when there were cave dwellers?
7. Can continents really just float around?
8. Why do so many countries have different names today?
9. If they build a new shopping mall where there is a forest, will it cause any animals to become extinct?

Some of the questions listed here have brief and factual answers. For these, the teacher needs to help the children develop broader questions under which these questions can be subsumed. For example, rather than simply answering the question "Are maps used today the same as maps used by people long ago," students can investigate the question "How have maps changed over time?" and then use the information acquired in researching this broader question to answer the original question. In other cases, the questions will already be broad enough that no reconsideration will be needed.

Step 3: Determining What Will Be Needed to Answer the Questions.   In this step, students are assisted in listing possible sources of information that can be used to answer the questions. For example, to answer the question "What causes some animals to become endangered," the students may decide on the following sources of information: books on animals, biologists, zoo staff, films on animals, state naturalists, the Internet, and CD-ROMs. The teacher may add other sources of information with which students may not be aware.

Step 4: Deciding How to Show Others What Has Been Learned.   Once students have decided what they want to learn and the resources they wish to use, they need to determine how to communicate what they have learned to other students. For the question "What causes some animals to become endangered?" students may decide to develop a play or skit about endangered species, present a panel or roundtable discussion for other classes, create posters to show what can be done to prevent animals from becoming endangered, write their own books about various endangered species and why they are endangered, create model habitats for endangered species, or write letters to public officials urging caution when changing habitats.

Step 5: Determining the Materials Needed.   Once the students have brainstormed the questions they would like to answer as well as the kinds of projects they will complete, they will be ready to determine what kinds of materials and resources they will need as they work. It is sometimes helpful to divide the materials list into two sections: the resource materials needed—guest speakers, field trip sites, books, magazines, animals, journals—and the materials needed to produce the final products—paint, paper, poster board, pencils, costumes. By separating the items, student attention can be more focused and more directed.

Step 6: Integrating Student Input into the Theme. One area of difficulty in working with student planning in the integrated curriculum is how to incorporate the brainstorming and the questions developed by students into the planning that was previously accomplished by the teacher. The results of the teacher-student planning session can be used in a variety of ways. First, the questions brainstormed and the activities suggested by the students may already fit within those ideas and concepts developed by the teacher in his or her planning. If so, the only changes to accommodate student-teacher planning may be to emphasize those student-suggested areas more than the teacher's original planning did. Second, the results of student-teacher planning may extend some of the concepts developed in the original teacher planning. Once again, these may be incorporated easily into the theme by using them to further develop ideas selected by the teacher but extended by the students. Third, the results of the teacher-student planning session may add a new dimension to the topic under consideration. The students in the class may have interests that were not originally considered by the teacher in his or her planning. The teacher needs to include this new dimension in the theme developed within the classroom but also needs to make a decision about how to include it. Should the student-developed dimension be an addition to those concepts and activities already developed by the teacher, or should the student-developed dimension be a replacement for ideas already developed by the teacher?

In deciding the answer to this question, the teacher should take into consideration certain factors: whether or not the student-developed question is educationally sound or simply a "frill" resulting from some passing event; whether the student-developed question is broad or narrow in scope; and whether the student-developed question is likely to contribute to a broad understanding of the topic and allow for wide-ranging investigation. If the topic represents a frill, a trendy topic with little substance, then adding it to the theme as a part of what is already planned, without deleting planned material, is probably the best strategy. This same strategy holds true for student questions that are narrow in scope. Such narrow questions can be added to the already planned theme as a new twist or slightly different aspect of already present areas of study.

Broad questions developed by the students and those that will allow for broad understanding or wide-ranging investigation should probably replace a teacher-developed theme. The key to replacing a theme developed by the teacher with one developed by the students lies in the investigative procedures that will be utilized. Rather than looking to replace a teacher-developed theme with a student-developed theme because of the similarity of concepts developed, the teacher should consider whether or not to replace a topic on the basis of the degree of subject matter integration. For example, for the theme "the changing Earth" the teacher may have planned to study major destructive forces such as earthquakes, volcanoes, and intense storms. This topic can include language arts, reading, science, geography, and mathematics as well as incorporating the fine arts within various projects. This topic would probably not be replaced with a student-generated topic on how names and borders of nations have changed; the major focus there is on history. However, replacing the topic of earthquakes, volcanoes, and intense storms with a consideration of moving continents can result in the same development of reading, language, science, mathematics, and geography content.

The fourth major consideration in including teacher-student planning within the theme is whether the brainstorming session indicated that students have ample background and strong interest in particular areas. Ample background in a particular area should probably result in a discussion of how to extend the topic beyond what is already known. Students may then decide on a slightly or extensively different version of the previously considered area, which can then be effectively included within the theme. Lack of interest in a particular area may also result in discussion, but if lack of interest continues, that topic may be deleted entirely or may be modified to one for individuals to pursue.

Finally, student-teacher planning may result in the development of a problem rather than a concept to be considered within the theme. In the brainstorming session described a problem was generated: "If they build a new shopping mall where there is a forest, will it cause any animals to become extinct?" Before incorporating this into the theme, the problem may be restated as "How will the construction of a new shopping mall affect the environment?" The development of a problem by the students should result in immediate inclusion within the theme. This immediate inclusion is important because problems generally result in considerable interest on the part of the students and such interest leads to more thorough investigation. Of more importance, however, is that the development of a problem and the investigation of the solution to that problem demonstrate the application of "school learning" to the real world of the student and the community.

The teacher should always keep in mind that even though a great deal of planning has gone into the development of the theme, themes can be changed at any time during the period of study. Student investigations lead to new questions and new questions lead to new areas of study or new problems for study. The teacher and the students should always have the option of pursuing these new and interesting ideas.

CLASSROOM ORGANIZATION

Once the teacher and the students have determined the theme and contributed to its development, the next aspect of the resource unit should consider how the classroom is to be organized. The traditional system of neat desks in neat rows, with the teacher-director placed in a prominent place at the front of the classroom with chalk or overhead projector pen in hand, is not appropriate for the integrated approach to learning. Rather than organizing the classroom around which lesson is to be taught at which time, the teacher needs to consider organization in terms of (1) introducing the new theme, (2) physical location and organization of the various learning sites, and (3) conclusion and presentation of student projects.

Introducing the New Theme.   Even though the students have had a preview of the theme during the student-teacher planning period, it is still important that the teacher introduce the theme to the students. This introduction can occur in a variety of ways. The sixth grade teacher working with the theme of "the changing earth" tried to begin a new theme on Monday and so introduced the theme on Friday before the students left for the weekend. In this introduction, the teacher used the semantic web developed for the theme and including the information added by the students. She introduced the subthemes that were a part of the theme, talked about the kinds of activities in which they might be engaged, and helped the students to develop their groups for the first activities. In this way the students had an understanding of the theme, knew with whom they would be working at the start of the theme, and were ready to begin on Monday.

Another way of introducing the theme to the students is through a film or other media presentation that gives an overview of the entire theme. The teacher working with "the changing Earth" might show a film on earthquakes, volcanoes, and violent storms and then lead a discussion focusing on the idea of change. Once the attention of the students is focused on the concept of change, then the semantic map may be used to introduce additional subthemes.

A third technique to introduce a new theme is used when there is a final project to be accomplished by the class. For example, students studying "the changing Earth" may have as a final project a program for other classes or other grade levels. The teacher may then introduce the theme by describing what students will be doing at the conclusion of the theme and the kinds of information they will need to acquire in order to accomplish that project.

And themes may be introduced by totally immersing students in an environment reflecting it. In this case, the students arrive in the classroom to find that it has been set up with areas devoted to each of the subthemes. To initiate the theme, the teacher then engages the students in a class meeting where they discuss the subconcepts and the kinds of activities in which they will be involved as the theme progresses.

Location and Organization.   Any classroom using an integrated and thematic approach to curriculum is going to appear chaotic. Rather than neat rows of desks with students quietly on-task or focused on the teacher at the front of the room, there are generally groups of children interacting with one another and with materials. There are generally a variety of activities going on at the same time and the students—rather than the teacher—are directing their own learning.

Although the classroom looks chaotic, it should not literally be chaotic. Rather, the classroom should have an underlying organization that is evident in the placement of the various groups and projects. Activities and projects requiring noisy construction should be placed away from activities requiring quiet contemplation of written or visual materials. Activities requiring the use of water or materials that can result in "mess" should be placed near the source of water and in an area of the classroom where cleanup is easy. Students who will be using computers for writing, for research using CD-ROM materials, or for access to the Internet will need to be able to sit at the computers.

The use of technology can cause difficulties if there is only limited access to computers or other devices, such as VCRs, monitors, tape players, and filmstrip projectors. When such materials are limited, the teacher and students need to plan together for how those materials will be shared. Producing a plan for time-sharing cooperatively generally results in fewer problems than if the teacher attempts to dictate use and certainly far fewer problems than if no plan is made.

Planning for use of materials should also include planning for access to the library or media center. Students should be involved in how and when those sources of information will be accessed and how the teacher and class will be alerted to where users are at a particular time.

The teacher also needs to be certain that particular areas of the classroom are designated as quiet spots. These are places where individual students can read, write, draw, reflect, edit, or simply rest for awhile. Students need time to refine work, to plan, and to consider what has been done and will be done. Quiet spots within the classroom can provide this opportunity. Classrooms with lofts can designate them as quiet spots. Classrooms without lofts may use study carrels. Those totally lacking in space may even designate the hallway outside of the classroom as a quiet spot. These designated quiet spots can also be places for the teacher to conference with individual students.

There is one other location to consider. As students become engaged in research and projects they often find they lack or have forgotten certain skills. There should be a place within the classroom where the teacher can meet with small groups of students or with individual students to teach or reteach those skills that are lacking or rusty from nonuse. Such a location should be isolated enough that "lessons" will not be distracting to students not in the group, should be located so that a chalkboard or overhead is present, and when necessary should be near enough manipulative materials that they can be quickly obtained and used within the "lesson." See Chapter 4 for additional discussion of organization in the integrated curriculum.

Concluding the Theme.   Some themes come to a logical conclusion on their own. The students have investigated to the end of their interests and are ready to begin the process of showing others what they have learned. The teacher's task in concluding a theme in which the students have reached their own closure is to help organize the presentation of learning to others. These "others" may be the students in the class itself or include parents, other teachers, and administrators.

Often, however, themes do not reach so natural a conclusion. In some cases, the students simply begin to lose interest in the theme. Then it is time for the teacher to organize a class meeting in which the students and teacher cooperatively determine when the final presentations will be made. In general, these presentations will be relatively soon after the class meeting. Then there is the theme that never seems to reach a conclusion. In this case, the teacher needs to make a decision whether to allow the theme to continue or to bring it to a conclusion. This decision is not an easy one to make.

Consider once again the theme "the changing Earth." Two sixth grade classes are working with this particular theme and are still working hard after five weeks. In the first class, the students have become fascinated with the area of natural disasters as ways in which the Earth's surface can be changed. They have focused so intently on this subtheme that they are looking only at the scientific aspects of floods, volcanoes, tornadoes, tidal waves, hurricanes, and earthquakes. In this case, the narrowing of the focus is working against the concept of an integrated program as one that includes a wide variety of disciplines in an authentic manner. The class meeting held with this particular class should probably focus on either concluding the theme and moving on to another area of study or directing the theme into other areas of study.

In the second sixth grade class, however, the students working with the subtheme of natural disasters have moved beyond simply looking at the scientific aspects and into looking at how natural disasters were explained in ancient mythologies. They are writing their own myths, developing scale models to show how the map of their own community has changed over a period of time, and working with the local zoo to develop a program on endangered species for the community as a part of the festivities that will take place when a habitat for Bengal tigers is opened. The variety of concepts under consideration, the broadening of study to include mythology, and the community outreach occurring in this class probably warrants continuation of the theme.

The teacher should not base the decision on whether or not to continue the theme on how many weeks have passed since initiation, but rather on the learning that is occurring within the classroom. Time frames established at the start of a unit are guidelines, not absolutes.

MATERIALS AND RESOURCES

Once the theme has been developed and the areas of study have been chosen as well as the possible projects students may accomplish, then the teacher and the students together can begin to collect the materials that will be used. Students should assist in collecting library books and other written sources of materials, in contacting resource persons, in planning field trips, and in making certain all items whose need can be foreseen are present. Students should also be involved in collecting those materials that will be needed as the integrated curriculum theme progresses.

Although there are many kinds of resources that can be used in pursuing a theme within the integrated curriculum, the following is a list of the most common.

1. *Books.* Books, of course, are reference materials for the classroom. Books can include textbooks, fiction and nonfiction trade books, and encyclopedias. The textbook can often function as a preliminary source of information from which students can gain an idea of the scope of the topic without necessarily gaining depth. The trade book library should include both fiction and nonfiction books for the students to read as well as some for the teacher to read to the students. The encyclopedia is often the first and last source of information for the elementary level student. In the integrated approach to curriculum it should be a minor source of information, similar to the textbook as a means of getting a brief overview of a subject area before using more in-depth sources of information.

2. *Magazines, Journals, and Newspapers.* Textbooks, trade books, and encyclopedias are quickly dated. Magazines and journals, on the other hand, can provide up-to-the-minute information. For example, if students studying "the changing Earth" are investigating the changing names of some central European nations, then news magazines and newspapers will provide more up-to-date information than will books. The magazines and journals brought into the classroom should include those developed for teachers and professionals in the field, magazines especially for young learners, and general interest magazines such as *Time, Newsweek, National Geographic, Smithsonian,* and *Life*.

3. *Primary Source Documents.* Primary source documents are original written and pictorial sources of information rather than secondhand or simplified accounts developed especially for children. Included in primary source documents are diaries, court records, letters, original plans, maps, and family trees. Such documents are of particular importance when considering historical subject matter.

4. *Electronic Media.* Electronic media include such traditional items as films, filmstrips, audio recordings, and radio and television sources and newer materials such as the Internet, CD-ROM, and computer simulation materials.

5. *Maps.* Although maps can be primary source documents, especially when they show the historical development of an area, they can also be a source of information in themselves. Street maps of cities, road maps of states and nations, topographic maps, sea floor maps, planetary feature maps, and maps showing various projections can all provide information to students.

6. *Photographs.* Photographs from archival collections can show the historic development of a particular city or other area, can document an event in history or immediate time, and can provide glimpses of distant places. Vacation slides of foreign lands can be as good a source of information as the results of professional photography.

7. *Objects.* Having the real object in the classroom is a far better learning experience than seeing a picture of an object or reading about it. Shells, rocks, coral, driftwood, a shark's jaw with its rows of teeth, a saltwater aquarium, various samples of sand, and a collection of shorebird feathers can all give more information about ocean life than any video or photograph. The real object allows students to see, feel, hear, and smell, gaining direct sensory experiences rather than vicarious experiences.

8. *Resource Persons.* Although not strictly a "material," resource persons can contribute firsthand information to students as they investigate and develop the theme. Universities, local agencies, hobbyists, parents, grandparents, and many others can act as resources for students.

9. *Field Trips.* Like resource persons, field trips are not materials, but they are important sources of information. Museums, nature centers, archives, power plants, and zoos are chosen for field trips, but the school cafeteria, a local grocery store, a vacant lot, or a variety of other common locations can also serve as field trip sites for students.

10. *Other Materials.* Projects developed by teacher and students often require construction materials such as wood, paper, cardboard, glue, tape, nails, paint, and clay. Other popular materials are writing paper, pens, pencils, erasers, computer disks, drawing paper, rolls of butcher paper, and anything else that will be needed.

BUILDING BACKGROUND KNOWLEDGE

The final thing teachers need to consider is their own knowledge of the theme. In the traditional curriculum, teachers can feel secure knowing only what is in the textbook or perhaps a little more. In the integrated curriculum, the breadth of content is far-reaching and, while no teacher can be expected to know all things about all topics, each needs to have sufficient knowledge to see the implications of information, direct students into a variety of areas of study, and comment on the accuracy or inaccuracy of information. Consequently, the teacher within the integrated program needs to be certain his or her store of knowledge is sufficient to the needs of the curriculum. The teacher needs to research the content of the theme prior to initiation for a variety of reasons:

1. The teacher needs to refresh his or her memory. As anyone who has been in school knows, even though one has studied hard over a year, it is still necessary to review prior to a final exam. One can forget or only partially recall information, perhaps erroneously, after a relatively short period of time.

2. The teacher needs to be certain his or her information is up-to-date. Particularly in the area of science, new information is continuously being developed. Unless teachers remain current, they may find they

are being confronted by students who are not only far more knowledgeable but also far more current.

3. The teacher needs to acquire his or her own knowledge rather than relying on others. When teachers rely solely on others for information, errors are very likely to slip into that information. In particular, misunderstandings may be shared, biases may creep in, and errors of fact may be passed along. In order to be as certain as possible about the accuracy of information, the teacher should do his or her own learning.

4. The teacher needs to research the topic in order to determine whether differing points of view exist and where information on those differing points of view can be found. In fact, researching a topic is likely to give the teacher more information about sources in general.

5. The teacher needs to be able to present a variety of possible questions for consideration and a variety of possible means for gaining and presenting information. It is only by having a thorough grounding in the subject that teachers can be attuned to variety. With a thorough knowledge and ways of gaining knowledge, teachers can feel more confident in their teaching. More knowledge means more confidence, and more confidence means more enthusiasm.

Obviously it is important that the teacher gain knowledge before beginning to work with an integrated topic. The problem is often in knowing how to begin that quest for knowledge. There are a variety of ways for gaining information. Good starting points are often colleagues, friends, or librarians who can point the teacher to useful resources. Simply going to the public library or to a college or university library and looking up the topic in the card catalogue, whether paper or electronic, can start the teacher on the road to expertise. Often, locating one source on a topic and then going to the shelves and browsing will lead to a variety of informational sources. While at the college or university library, look into courses in the subject area or for the faculty members who teach the courses. Talking with an expert in a field can add immeasurably to the teacher's background information. In addition to libraries, societies and organizations such as the Audubon Society, the National Geographic Society, and the local historical society can provide information. Even television can help to develop background through such resources as public television, Discovery Channel, Learning Channel, History Channel, and Mind Extension University. Current events are easily researched through newspapers, magazines, and news broadcasts. One needs, however, to take care in using these sources, as biased information is often so subtle as to go unrecognized on a cursory inspection. Travel is a source of background information, whether one travels to Philadelphia to see Independence Hall and the Liberty Bell, to Egypt to view the pyramids at Giza or the temples of Luxor, or to the ends of the Mississippi to see the source and the delta. Firsthand experience is far superior to vicarious experience. Finally, an enormous source of information is the Internet.

SUMMARY

Planning within the integrated curriculum involves not only the teacher but also the students in determining the course of the theme. The beginning stages of planning involve the teacher's diagramming the theme and the subsidiary concepts of the theme. Once the teacher has done the preliminary planning, he or she then involves the students in the final stages of planning through brainstorming and discussion as well as planning for specific activities and collecting materials. The final stage of planning involves the teacher once again. The teacher must make the decision as to how to include the results of planning with the students within the theme. Finally, in order to work effectively within the integrated curriculum, the teacher must have a broad base of background information. It is up to the teacher to build that background before beginning the theme.

ACTIVITY ONE

PURPOSE

The purpose of this activity is to develop a resource unit appropriate to a particular integrated theme.

PROCEDURE

1. Select one of the following themes with which to work or select a theme developed in Activity One or Activity Two of the previous chapter.
   a. endangered species
   b. our changing community
   c. geometry in the environment
   d. exploration
   e. music through the ages
   f. holidays
   g. science fact/science fiction
   h. superstitions
   i. careers
   j. arts and crafts
2. Develop a resource unit for integrated teaching that includes:
   a. grade level
   b. suggested duration
   c. graphic organizer
   d. concepts
   e. activities list
   f. classroom organization
   g. materials and resources

✶ ACTIVITY TWO

PURPOSE

The purpose of this activity is to receive input from students and revise a resource unit to include that input.

PROCEDURE

1. Use the resource unit prepared in Activity One of this chapter as the basis for this activity. The unit does not need to be in complete form.
2. Present the topic of the resource unit to students at the grade level for which the unit is being developed.
3. Obtain input into the unit from the students following the guidelines in this text: brainstorm, determine what students want to know, determine the kinds of resources needed to answer their questions, determine how students will show what they have learned, determine materials needed.
4. Consider the draft of the resource unit in light of the input from the students. Revise the unit to incorporate that student input that is educationally sound and purposeful.

STUDY QUESTIONS

1. Five questions are listed on page 235 for determining the duration of a theme. List and discuss each of those questions, giving particular attention to how they are used in decision making.
2. Compare and contrast a traditional resource unit with an integrated resource unit.
3. Select one of the themes found under Step 1: Develop the Semantic Map and develop a graphic organizer for the theme.
4. On pages 240-241 is a list of 12 kinds of activities. Using the theme for which you developed a graphic organizer, brainstorm possible activities for as many of the types of concepts as possible.
5. Student input is important in developing an integrated program. How is student input obtained? How is it used in developing the integrated theme?
6. What factors should be considered in organizing the classroom for integrated teaching? What is the effect of each of these factors on classroom organization?
7. What are some of the kinds of materials and resources that could be used in the integrated curriculum? What other suggestions could you make for appropriate materials and resources?

8. Some themes or problems selected for the curriculum may not be familiar to the teacher. How could the teacher who is lacking in background build up his or her knowledge?

BIBLIOGRAPHY

Beyer, B. K. (1987). *Practical strategies for the teaching of thinking.* Boston: Allyn and Bacon.

Boothby, P. R., & Alverman, D. E. (1984). A classroom training study: The effects of graphic organizer instruction on fourth graders' comprehension. *Reading World, 26,* 325–339.

Caine, R. N., & Caine, G. (1991). *Teaching and the human brain.* Alexandria, Va.: Association for Supervision and Curriculum Development.

Clark, J. H. (1990). *Patterns of thinking: Integrating learning skills in content teaching.* Boston: Allyn and Bacon.

Eisner, E. W. (1994). *Cognition and curriculum reconsidered* (2nd ed.). New York: Teachers College, Columbia University.

Gagne, R. M., Briggs, L. J., & Wagner, W. W. (1988). *Principles of instructional design* (3rd ed.). New York: Holt, Rinehart, and Winston.

Hauf, M. B. (1971). Mapping: A technique for translating reading into thinking. *Journal of Reading, 14,* 225–230.

Jones, B. F., Palincsar, A.S., Ogle, D. S., & Carr, E. G. (1987). *Strategic teaching and learning: Cognitive instruction in the content areas.* Alexandria, Va.: Association for Supervision and Curriculum Development.

Mager, R. F. (1962). *Preparing instructional objectives.* Palo Alto, Calif.: Fearon.

Moore, D. W., & Readence, J. E. (1984). A quantitative and qualitative review of graphic organizer research. *Journal of Educational Research, 78,* 11–17.

West, C. K., Farmer, J. A., & Wolff, P. M. (1991). *Instructional design: Implications from cognitive science.* Englewood Cliffs, N. J.: Prentice Hall.

CHAPTER

10

INSTRUCTIONAL DELIVERY STRATEGIES

CHAPTER OBJECTIVES

After reading this chapter you should be able to:

1. Discuss the role of direct instruction in the integrated curriculum approach
2. Plan an expository lesson
3. Plan an inductive discovery lesson
4. Describe instructional mapping techniques for inductive teaching
5. Discuss techniques for developing critical and creative thinking skills
6. Define the term *metacognition* and discuss its role in the teaching and learning process
7. Utilize cooperative learning strategies for teaching in the integrated curriculum

As we have stated throughout this book, the role of the teacher within the integrated approach to curriculum and teaching is that of a facilitator rather than a purveyor of knowledge. The students in a class learn through authentic experiences rather than through "lessons" preplanned by the teacher and divorced from context. The integrated approach to curriculum, because it places the student in the role of active inquirer rather than passive recipient of information, requires that the teacher reconsider his or her role in the classroom.

The teacher in the integrated curriculum plays a variety of roles. The first of those roles has already been discussed. The teacher in the integrated curriculum is fully involved in the planning of the curriculum both separately and with the students. The second role of the teacher is that of mentor. As students work to accomplish projects, to investigate themes, to solve problems, the teacher is there as a source of support through assistance and conferencing with students. Third, the teacher is involved in presenting information to children through lessons specific to the needs of the children as they work with the theme. In developing lessons that present information to the class, small groups, or individuals, the teacher is generally involved in direct teaching through **expository teaching** or **discovery teaching**. In other cases, the teacher may utilize indirect teaching strategies. In indirect teaching, the students use materials to develop specific content information. The learning situation is directly managed by the teacher, but the students are responsible for developing the content. Cooperative learning techniques utilize this indirect approach.

DIRECT INSTRUCTIONAL STRATEGIES

Direct teaching is the type of teaching most frequently seen in the traditional classroom. The teacher is involved in presenting specific information to the students. Within the integrated curriculum, direct teaching takes place when it is necessary within the context of a student activity or project. It is most commonly found when students or teacher determines that the skills needed for completion are not present. For example, students at the third grade level are writing stories in which the characters are speaking to one another. As their writing progresses, they realize that they are not certain how to show when someone is speaking and how to show when another character begins to speak. At this point, the teacher may work with this small group of children on using punctuation to show dialogue. However, direct teaching does not have to mean the structured, textbook-based lessons so familiar to the traditional classroom. **Direct instructional strategies** may mean expository teaching or discovery teaching.

EXPOSITORY TEACHING

In expository teaching, the teacher functions as a director of instruction. The major purpose of expository teaching is to convey content information to children in a direct, concise, and time-efficient manner. In the traditional approach to teaching, lessons are presented to the children in a predetermined sequence and on predetermined schedules. Since the integrated curriculum does not have this type of predetermined sequence, the use of direct instruction must be different from that found in the traditional program. The use of direct instruction is determined by the needs of the students in the classroom rather than by the mandates of a structured and sequenced curriculum. The question then becomes how to know when direct instruction is necessary.

In general, direct instruction is necessary in the integrated curriculum when students need skills they do not yet possess or that they have forgotten due to lack of use, nonproductive teaching, or ineffectual learning. The teacher must be continually and systematically observing in order to determine when students are having difficulty, which students are in need of direct instruction, and how best to conduct the direct instruction so that it is an authentic part of the learning experience. In most cases direct instruction will be presented to individual students or to small groups of students rather than to the entire class. When the decision has been made as to who is in need of the direct lesson, the teacher needs to decide whether the skill should be presented through individual conferencing, through expository teaching, or through discovery teaching.

CONFERENCING

Definition.   Conferencing occurs when the teacher works one-on-one with a student to develop that student's skills in a particular area. Conferencing is not an opportunity for the teacher to point out errors and then show the student how to correct those errors, but rather is an opportunity for the teacher and student to work together on improving specific skills.

Using Conferencing.   Conferencing occurs when a teacher and a single student work together to develop a needed skill. The conference may occur spontaneously when a student seeks assistance from the teacher or it may be scheduled so that conferences are carried out at particular times during the day. Spontaneous conferencing is generally initiated by the student, who perceives a problem and seeks out help. In this case, the teacher may simply answer a question with information or may choose to work with the child to identify a particular problem and then work together to solve the problem In the case of planned conferences, the teacher may either work on a problem identified by the teacher or student or simply schedule weekly time for the student to work directly with the teacher.

There are two reasons to schedule a conference. It may be scheduled to allow for one-on-one interaction between a student and the teacher. In general, the purpose of this type of scheduled conference is to work on a problem area identified by the teacher. For example, the teacher may observe that although a student knows how to find an arithmetic average, his or her computation skills are weak and so errors are made when working with the addition and division aspects of averaging. A scheduled conference would be used to provide assistance in developing those addition and division skills.

Scheduled conferences are also an effective way for the teacher to keep in touch with all of the children in a class. Within the integrated curriculum classroom, students should have time each week for conferences with the teacher. These conferences can be used to discuss progress, to share successes, to consider where problems have occurred.

Whether the conference is spontaneous or planned, it should take place in a quiet area of the classroom free from interruptions. The conference should be an opportunity for the student and teacher to focus on one another. Also, the conference should take place in a cooperative manner. Even if the conference is for the purpose of remediating skills, it should be a dialogue between teacher and student and not a monologue on the part of the teacher. Finally, the conference should be nonthreatening: the student should never be ill-at-ease or placed in a defensive situation.

EXPOSITORY TEACHING STRATEGIES

Definition. Expository strategies are those geared toward direct instruction, generally within a verbal context. They include lectures, films, filmstrips, videotapes, reading from a textbook or trade book, and demonstration.

Uses of Expository Teaching. Expository teaching is generally used to present content information to students in a time-efficient manner. The effectiveness of expository teaching with children varies with the type of lesson, the age of the students, and the mode of presentation. In working with expository teaching it should always be remembered that a lecture format is less effective with children than is a presentation using visual and/or auditory materials. A demonstration lesson in which concrete materials are used to help illustrate the ideas being presented is more effective than a lecture or audiovisual presentation because the materials are present in the classroom and the students have an opportunity to question the presenter.

Problems with Expository Teaching. The age of the students will directly affect the success of an expository lesson. Young children, those at the kindergarten, first, and second grade levels, are generally in the preoperational or early concrete operational stage of development and so require concrete objects if understanding is to develop. In addition to the cognitive requirement of concrete materials, the young child understands less of the verbal material heard than the teacher expects but may not realize he or she does not understand. The verbal format of most expository lessons is therefore inappropriate for the young student. Verbal presentations do become more effective as the child matures, but most children, even through the sixth grade level, will continue to be concrete operational in their thought processes and so more concrete techniques will always be more appropriate for instruction.

The mode of presentation of an expository lesson, whether strictly verbal, using pictures or film, or using concrete materials within a demonstration, will also affect the understanding of the children. An expository presentation that uses more than a verbal format is far more effective than one that uses only a verbal format. Using pictures, diagrams, illustrations, and real objects to assist in the expository presentation increases the likelihood of understanding on the part of the students.

The degree of abstractness of the concepts presented in an expository format may also cause difficulties for the children. For the young child concepts such as patriotism and democracy and the symbolism of the flag and the bald eagle are exceptionally difficult unless couched in concrete, familiar examples. For older children, the problem of abstractness of concepts is less intense, but there is still difficulty comprehending abstract concepts without familiar examples. It is often helpful to relate new concepts to those familiar to children. For example, children who are familiar with an aquarium as an ecosystem are more likely to understand the concept of a marine ecosystem.

Overcoming Problems with Expository Teaching. The problems inherent in expository teaching may seem insurmountable, but they are not. For the most part, the difficulties in using expository teaching can be overcome by using the expository approach after involving children in more concrete learning. For example, reading in a textbook about the development of the grid system of longitude and latitude will be far more meaningful after students have had an opportunity to develop their own system for locating objects within the classroom. Similarly, students will have greater understanding of written or verbal materials dealing with the composition of types of soils found around the world if they have had the opportunity to explore the composition of different kinds of soils found in their own community. In addition to reading or listening to a verbal presentation after an activity, presenting new vocabulary terms after an activity is also a way to increase comprehension of verbal materials. For example, students can view pointillist paintings by masters of the form, looking at the characteristics of those paintings and especially noting the use of small dots of color that blend to create a mass of color at a distance. After the children have noted this technique, they can try to paint a picture in the same manner, using dots of color rather than washes. Then, after both of these experiences, the term *pointillism* can be introduced as the term for this style of painting. In this way, the concept is developed first, followed by the term used to name the concept.

A second technique to develop understanding on the part of children is the use of familiar examples to develop abstract concepts. For example, in developing the concept of government by laws, students in a sixth grade class developed their own classroom legal system, including a procedure for developing new classroom laws, a court system, and a "jail" which consisted of a time-out area in the classroom with "sentences" having a maximum term of five minutes. After the students have had the opportunity to engage in their own legal system, expository teaching can be used to expand their concept to include the more complex legal system governing a state or nation.

Understanding of an expository lesson can also be enhanced through the use of an advance organizer. Advance organizers are simply bits of information given prior to a verbal presentation that alert the listener about the important points to listen for. An advance organizer may be as simple as "While you are reading, look for the answers to these three questions" or "While you are listening to Mr. Jones, listen to find out how. . . ." These simple requests alert the students to what will be important to listen for in the presentation. It focuses attention and makes the presentation more effective in terms of learning.

Reading as Expository Teaching. Reading is one type of expository lesson and one that presents unique difficulties. Reading in the content areas, like social studies or science, is far more difficult than reading from a basal reader. One point of difficulty is vocabulary. Terms are found in the content areas that are not found in any basal reader. This presentation of new vocabulary presents a twofold difficulty: The words themselves will be unfamiliar and so must be decoded to be read, and the concepts named by the words may be unfamiliar to the children, and so simply decoding the word and pronouncing it does not help in understanding the written material. For many subject-matter-specific terms, context clues may not provide enough information to allow students to gain an understanding of new terminology. Additionally, in many content area textbooks, new terms are introduced to students at a rapid pace. A single paragraph may include more than one new term and therefore more than one new concept. For example, a paragraph dealing with photosynthesis may include the terms *photosynthesis, chemical reaction, carbon dioxide,* and *oxygen.* Such terms are rarely met outside of the science area and so will be unfamiliar in themselves. However, even more unfamiliar will be the concepts behind each of the terms. If one does not understand the concept of a chemical reaction, does not know that oxygen is an element of air, or if one is unaware that carbon dioxide is a compound containing oxygen formed through chemical reaction, then the concept of photosynthesis is not going to be developed through reading that paragraph.

As a final note in considering vocabulary in subject matter textbooks, if students do not have sufficient background experience, they may not have the knowledge that will allow them to successfully interpret the written word. For example, it is difficult for children in northern Maine to develop an understanding of a tropical rain forest because their experience with climate and environment is very different. A child living in southern Florida, however, is more likely to be able to conceptualize the conditions found in a tropical rain forest.

And, because many children do not read on grade level, the act of reading from a textbook or inappropriately selected trade book will be a difficult task. Consequently, it is important that a variety of written materials representing a variety of grade levels be available for the students in a class.

Audiovisual Presentations as Expository Teaching. Films, filmstrips, and videotapes present unique problems. Students are used to watching films for pleasure rather than as a learning device and so may view educational films in the same way. Consequently, students may see the unusual and exciting aspects of a film, filmstrip, or videotape without also gaining the concepts presented by the tape. In order to assist students to watch a video presentation, teachers can use an **advance organizer**. In this case the advance organizer allows the students to view the film, filmstrip, or videotape with purpose. An effective organizer in this case is a brief statement on what the film, filmstrip, or tape is about, followed by a few questions students should try to answer as a result of the presentation. For example, before watching a videotape on the

Civil War, students could be told: "We are going to be watching a film about the battle that took place at Gettysburg. As you watch, try to find out where Gettysburg is and why the battle was important to the Civil War, and listen for the speech made by President Lincoln at the battlefield." Students should not be asked to write the answers to the questions presented but should instead be asked to look for the answers as they watch the film. Writing the answers while the film is being shown takes the attention of the students away from the film so they miss other information presented.

Demonstrations as Expository Teaching.   The demonstration is generally the most effective of the expository strategies. In a demonstration the teacher or other individual shows how something is done or used. Demonstration lessons could consist of the teacher demonstrating how to read a topographic map, a quilter demonstrating how to create a quilt, a clog dancer demonstrating basic steps, or an archaeologist demonstrating how a grid system is used to plot the location of artifacts and aid in the systematic excavation of an area. Demonstration lessons are generally more successful than other types of lessons because the individual is directly showing objects, materials, or procedures. The demonstration is most effective when the real objects are there for the students to see, rather than photographs, drawings, or descriptions, and when the students are able to interact with the presenter by asking questions or participating in some fashion. Students who have watched a quilting demonstration should be able to try making a quilt, just as students who have watched the procedure used to read a topographic map should then have the experience of reading topographic maps themselves.

Planning for Expository Teaching.   For an expository lesson, a traditional type of lesson plan is used, including a topic, objectives, materials list, instructional sequence, and evaluation. The topic of the lesson is generally stated in a few words and arises from a difficulty students are having. The objectives for the lesson are generally written in behavioral format and state the overt behavior students will demonstrate when they have achieved that objective. The instructional sequence section of the lesson plan will show the expository format. See Figure 10.1 for a sample expository lesson plan showing the topic and the objectives for a lesson on finding arithmetic means. The sample lesson plan also shows the evaluation for the lesson and its similarity to the objectives.

Introduction.   Planning the introduction to an expository lesson is generally easy. The introduction is most likely to be an advance organizer. Recall that an advance organizer is a bit of information presented to the student prior to the presentation of information that will alert the student to the important points of the lesson. As can be seen in Sample Lesson Plan 1, the introduction is an advance organizer that tells students what to give attention to in the lesson. In this case, the organizer simply tells students the general features to attend to without giving specific names.

Topic: Finding the arithmetic mean of a set of data

Grade Level: Sixth

Objectives:

    1. As a result of the lesson, each student will be able to find the arithmetic mean of a set of data.
    2. As a result of the lesson, each student will be able to orally define the term *average* as it applies to an arithmetic mean.

Materials:

tape measures
pencils
paper
chalkboard and chalk or overhead projector and pens

Procedure

Introduction

    1. Remind the students that they have been trying to determine how much a plant grows in a week. The problem was that each of the plants they measured grew a different amount in the same period of time.
    2. Tell them that they will be learning a way of finding out how fast plants grow using a technique known as finding an average.

Body

    1. Ask the students what they think of when they hear the word *average*.
       a. Record their responses on the chalkboard or overhead.
       b. If students list "earned-run average" or "average points per game," ask them to describe what is meant by those terms.
    2. Tell the students that they will be learning how to find the same kind of average being considered in "earned-run average."
    3. Have the students measure their hand spans.
       a. Show how to find the average hand span by adding together all of the measurements and dividing by the number of measurements taken.
       b. Have the students review the steps for finding an average and list those steps on the board or overhead.
    4. Have the students measure the circumferences of their heads and find the average circumference of a sixth grader's head.
    5. Discuss how the technique of finding averages could be used to determine how much a plant grows in a week.

Summary

    1. Ask the students what steps are followed in finding an average.
    2. Ask the students to define in their own words the term *average*.

Evaluation

    1. As students return to the problem of how much a plant grows in a week, observe to see if they find an average with accuracy.
    2. During the summary step, ask each of the students to define the term *average*.

FIGURE 10.1 Sample Lesson Plan 1

Body.   The body of an expository lesson is geared toward the presentation of content information in the clearest, most efficient manner. This means that the major problem of the planning of an expository lesson is in sequencing the presentation so that it builds not only on the previous knowledge of the students but also on the previous points made by the lesson itself. In Sample Lesson Plan 1, the first step is to recall the problem the students were having that resulted in the lesson. In this case, the teacher reminds the students that they were trying to determine how much a plant grows in a week but that when they measured their plants, they found that all had grown different amounts.

Once the reason for the lesson has been recalled, the teacher asks the students if they have heard the word *average* and asks for their definitions. When some of the students bring up such ideas as "earned-run average" and "average number of points per game," he or she asks the students what those terms mean.

Once the students have discussed the meaning of the term *average,* the teacher has them measure their hand spans and shows how to determine the average hand span of a sixth grade student. Teacher and students outline the procedure used in finding averages (arithmetic mean). At this point the students measure the circumference of their heads and find the average head circumference.

Summary.   The final part of the lesson's body is the summary section. As can be seen in the lesson plan, the summary section simply reviews the main points covered by the lesson. In this case, the teacher has the students recall the steps used in finding averages and also has them define the term *average* in their own words. In other cases, the teacher will conduct the summary without the assistance of the children.

The expository lesson is one in which information can be presented to students in an efficient manner. Although children can be engaged in the use of thinking skills within an expository lesson, the use of those skills is generally somewhat limited. In order to include greater depth in terms of thinking skills, students should be engaged in a different type of direct teaching lesson. The kind of lesson used to develop thinking skills more fully is discovery teaching.

DISCOVERY TEACHING

INDUCTIVE DISCOVERY

Inductive discovery strategies begin with specifics and move toward the development of a generalization. For example, in an inductive lesson on the common characteristics of insects, students begin by making observations of a variety of types of insects: ants, grasshoppers, butterflies, dragonflies, and beetles. After the students have had an opportunity to observe, the teacher collects the observations on the chalkboard or overhead projector. From those observations, the teacher helps the students to determine the characteristics they observed in all of the different types of insects. Students then draw the conclusion that all insects have three body parts, wings, two antennae, and six legs. The students move from collecting *specific* observations of the insects to a *general* conclusion about the characteristics of all insects. In real life, children generally learn through induction. They see at home and in their neighborhoods different kinds of animals, all called dogs, and from those examples develop the ability to recognize any example of dog. Induction is a familiar means of learning for children.

Teaching through Inductive Discovery. Learning through induction generally requires three steps. First, students collect observations from activities or scan written materials for details. In this first stage, students are gathering information through the senses. Second, students classify those observations or details into categories or concepts that help to explain the information collected. In this step students are making inferences and attempting to determine commonalities. Finally, students draw conclusions that describe the facts and observations, generally in causal terms. These conclusions are generalizations. When the generalizations are drawn, the teacher should keep in mind that the final product of induction is probable answers rather than *right* answers. That is, the conclusions drawn by the children should fit the observations and should be defensible. Inductive strategies are used, then, to construct a view of the world.

Although induction does result in conclusions based on evidence and conclusions defensible according to that evidence, errors can be made in inductive thinking. The first kind of error is in *sampling:* If not enough information is collected or if the information is biased, then the generalization may be erroneous. The second kind of error is in *estimating probabilities:* In this case, predictions based on information may be faulty because trends shown by one set of information may not be reflected in other sets of information. *Abstracting* may also result in difficulties if the generalization is too broad or too narrow to suit the information; it is also possible that the students will stop at the level of making inferences and not develop a generalization at all. Another error can occur in *hypothesizing.* In order to maintain flexibility in inductive thinking, it is often necessary to keep more than one hypothesis in mind at a time. Unfortunately, our usual thinking patterns cause us to favor one hypothesis over another and so we tend to seek out information that will support our favored hypothesis and to ignore or overlook information that does not support that hypothesis.

Using Graphic Organizers in Induction. A graphic organizer is a visual device students can use to represent relationships among facts, between facts and inferences, and among facts, inferences, and generalizations. Two types of graphic organizers are particularly appropriate for working with induction: **circle diagrams** and **tower diagrams**.

Circle Diagrams.   Circle diagrams are essentially Venn diagrams used to show relationships between parts and the whole, between the specifics and the generalizations. These diagrams can also be extended into a matrix format, which can then be used to summarize and review information.

Developing a circle diagram requires the following steps:

1. Collect the observations for a pair or series of events.
2. Place the observations for each series of events into separate circles.
3. Review the observations in each circle for areas of overlap.
4. Draw a new circle diagram showing the overlapping areas.
5. Place into the diagram the observations collected.
6. Use the diagram as a basis for drawing a conclusion or making a generalization.

See Figure 10.2 for an example of a completed circle diagram as a graphic organizer.

The circle diagram can also be organized into a matrix that can function both as an organizing pattern for study of a unit and as a review matrix at the conclusion of a unit. The matrix is essentially constructed from the circle diagrams for a variety of information included in a single unit. Because there is a greater wealth of information in the matrix diagram it can be used to facilitate higher-order thinking through the use of questions that ask students to apply, analyze, synthesize, and evaluate information.

Tower Diagrams.   Tower diagrams are extensions of circle diagrams but allow for greater use of inference and generalization. The tower diagram begins as does the circle diagram, with observations. In this case the observations are kept separate by placing each into a circle of its own. These observational circles are placed on the bottom level of the tower. The second level of the tower begins

FIGURE 10.2 Graphic organizer using a circle diagram showing a comparison of two planets

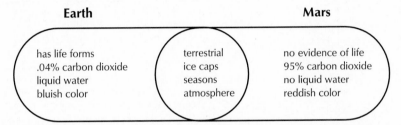

Earth   **Mars**

has life forms	terrestrial	no evidence of life
.04% carbon dioxide	ice caps	95% carbon dioxide
liquid water	seasons	no liquid water
bluish color	atmosphere	reddish color

The area where the circles overlap shows commonalities between the two planets. Of course, much more information could be included, but the circle diagram should be kept fairly simple when used with elementary school children.

the transformation of the observations into inferences as students try to relate the observations; this generally results in a variety of inferences. If there are a variety of inferences on the second level, a third level may be used to transform those inferences through identification of relationships into new, broader inferences. Finally, at the highest level, the inferences are related into a single generalization. It is possible that more than two levels of inferences will be developed or that only one level will be needed. The diagram, however, begins with observations, relates those observations into a variety of inferences, and then finally caps the tower with a single generalization that relates the observations and inferences. Figure 10.3 is an example of a tower diagram.

Planning an Inductive Lesson. The inductive lesson is planned as all lessons are planned, with a topic, objectives, materials, procedure, and evaluation. The statement of the topic is the same as in all lessons, as is the

FIGURE 10.3 Graphic organizer using a tower diagram: chemical change

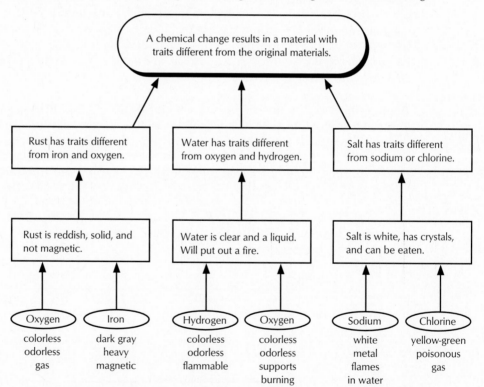

In developing the circle matrix diagram, the process is begun at the lowest level, where the specific information about the elements is shown. The process proceeds upward to the highest level, where a conclusion is drawn.

materials list. Although most objectives for an inductive lesson will be similar to those of other lessons, there is one place where a difference can occur.

Objectives.   In an inductive lesson, the conclusion drawn or the inference made cannot be judged on the basis of a predetermined correct answer. The conclusion drawn from an inductive lesson must be consistent with the data on which it is based and must be defensible on the basis of that data. If the data collected are unbiased and sufficient to the development of a conclusion, then that conclusion will probably reflect what has been previously found. The objective for an inductive discovery lesson should reflect this *probability* of conclusion. Consequently, an objective for a discovery lesson may be stated:

1. As a result of the lesson, each student will participate in a small group discussion that draws a conclusion consistent with the data collected.
2. As a result of the lesson, each student will be able to defend the conclusion drawn by the small group using examples from the evidence collected.

The objectives for an inductive lesson should reflect the nature of the induction process as well as emphasize the need for a conclusion consistent with the data collected.

Procedure.   Once the objectives have been written, the body of the lesson plan is developed. As with an expository lesson the procedure is divided into three parts: introduction, body, and summary. Figure 10.4 outlines this procedure in a sample lesson plan.

The introduction to an inductive lesson is designed to arouse curiosity on the part of the children or to alert them to the purpose of the lesson. The difficulty is in arousing curiosity or developing the lesson's purpose without also telling the students what is going to be learned in the lesson. Consider an inductive discovery lesson for sixth graders in which the students are to develop the idea that living things have certain common characteristics: cellular structure, growth, metabolism, movement, responsiveness, homeostasis, and reproduction. It would be inappropriate to begin a lesson for these students by telling them that they are going to be learning that living things have six characteristics in common, then having them look at a chart that lists those six characteristics. An appropriate introduction would be to place the words *living things* on the chalkboard or overhead and have the students brainstorm the words they associate with the term. Then the teacher might tell the students they will be finding out which of those characteristics scientists have discovered all living things have in common. In this way, the children are alerted to the topic, prior knowledge is elicited in the context of a free association, and the nature of the new lesson is not revealed.

Inductive Teaching

Topic: Punctuation using quotations

Grade Level: Third

Objectives:

After discussing examples of the use of quotations marks in writing dialogue, each student will be able to use quotation marks, commas, and periods appropriately in punctuating sentences within their own writing.

Materials:

Examples of literature in which dialogue is recorded.
Student work in which dialogue is included in the written sample.

Procedure:

Introduction:

Remind the students of the problem that arose as they were writing stories in which they needed to show that the people in the stories were speaking to one another. No one was really sure of how to show when the characters in the story began speaking, when they finished speaking, or when a new character started to speak.

Body:

1. Have the students select a partner with whom to work.
   a. Give each partnership four examples from literature of dialogue.
   b. Tell the students that it is their task to find out what marks were used to show people talking, how those marks were used, and how the authors showed when someone else was beginning to speak.
   c. Give the students time to work with the materials to find the answers to the questions posed.
2. Bring the group back together.
   a. Discuss each aspect of showing dialogue separately:
      (1). How do the authors show when someone is speaking?
      (2). What punctuation marks are used to show that someone is speaking?
      (3). How do the authors show that a new person is beginning to speak?
   b. From the answers to the questions, develop a list of rules for punctuating dialogue.
3. Have each student edit his or her own writing sample for punctuation when dialogue is taking place.
   a. As students finish their editing, conference with each student to see that the rules for punctuation of dialogue are being applied.
   b. When students have difficulty, discuss the rules developed and compare the student's writing to the rules developed.

Summary:

Review with the group how punctuation is used to show dialogue.

Evaluation:

Evaluate the objective through the conferencing with students as they edit their own writing samples.

FIGURE 10.4 Sample Lesson Plan 2

Body.   In the body of the lesson the students are given the materials from which they will collect the data on which they will base the final conclusion or generalization. Frequently working in small groups, the students are helped to collect the data and then to organize it in terms of a circle diagram or a tower diagram. Once the small groups have had the opportunity to develop their diagrams, the teacher continues the lesson by leading a class discussion of the small group diagram. The result of this discussion is a class circle or tower diagram from which generalizations are made. It should always be kept in mind that different small groups may reach different conclusions and that there may not be a consensus on a single generalization for the class once the circle or tower diagram for the group is constructed. This should not be seen as a weakness of the lesson or a problem with induction but as an opportunity for discussion and for critical thinking as students analyze and evaluate the different conclusions.

The conclusions or generalizations developed by the students may differ from standard knowledge on a particular topic. This generally occurs if the data and examples are not selected appropriately. If the generalization differs from the commonly accepted conclusion, then students can use textbooks or other materials to read the common conclusion. At this point, the teacher leads the children in a discussion, not of why they came to a "wrong" conclusion, but of why their conclusion differed from what is generally accepted. In this way, critical thinking skills are used by the children in a purposeful manner.

Summary.   The summary of an inductive lesson should return to the generalizations derived from the discovery lesson and reinforce those generalizations. If the generalization developed by the students was different from what is typically found, then the summary should also review the reasons determined by the students for differences in outcome. If a circle diagram or a tower diagram was used in developing the lesson, the summary should include a review of the diagram as well as of the generalization.

DEVELOPING CRITICAL AND CREATIVE THINKING SKILLS

Much of the learning that takes place in the traditional elementary school classroom is designed to add to the store of factual knowledge or to the development of skills. This type of learning is frequently considered low level, that is, concerned with names, dates, and definition of terms. Children are frequently asked to memorize information out of context and with the goal in mind of passing the test on Friday. Memorizing the definitions of a series of science terms falls into the category of information memorized out of context. It would, however, be impossible to remove from the classroom, whether traditional or integrated, all of the attention to factual material. There is some information—for example, basic facts in arithmetic, standard spelling, and names of presidents—that is most efficiently, if not most effectively, learned through memorization. However, being able to recite multiplication facts or record standard spellings or name presidents is important only when that information is later applied in some meaningful task. When students apply their knowledge to other situations, when they begin to analyze, synthesize, and evaluate, then they begin to think at higher levels. This thinking at higher levels than mere memorization is known as critical thinking and, in many cases, as creative thinking.

DEFINITION

Thinking is often described as *a search for meaning.* This definition is based on the assumption that meaning does not simply exist in a set of data, but rather that the meaning in a set of data must be determined by the individual. As individuals try to determine the meaning in a set of information, they use a variety of mental operations including analyzing, conceptualizing, decision making, distinguishing relevant from nonrelevant information, problem solving, reasoning, and synthesizing. Because the integrated curriculum seeks to place learning in context, thinking becomes a major aspect of learning. This emphasis on thinking occurs because the integrated curriculum is geared not only to gaining knowledge but also to the application of the knowledge acquired. Within the integrated curriculum, subject matter gives purpose to the teaching of thinking and the teaching of thinking gives purpose to the learning of subject matter. This balance between subject matter as a purpose for teaching thinking and thinking as a purpose for subject matter means that emphasis must be given not only to what is learned but also to how students use information and how they react in situations where they do not immediately know an answer. Students who consider thinking as a part of the learning of subject matter will be more likely to try to find answers for themselves than will students who consider subject matter an end in itself. The student who has been taught to think will actively seek out information. The student who has been taught to memorize will wait to be given the answer.

Thinking can generate excitement in a classroom. Students who are actively attempting to solve problems, to locate sources of information, and to determine how to present what is learned are far more excited about learning than are those students who listen to the teacher, read from the text, and respond to multiple-choice test items. However, simply because thinking generates excitement does not mean that teaching thinking will be easy. A major problem encountered when trying to teach thinking is interference from the teacher's own concepts and attitudes. When the teacher's concepts and attitudes are too prominent, the result is often praise for results that agree with the teacher's own idea and opposition to results that do not agree. Consider for a moment a sixth grade teacher who was leading a discussion on getting glasses that was used as an introduction to a basal reader selection about a child who had to get glasses. The teacher asked a group of sixth grade girls how they would feel if they had to get glasses. All of the comments from the seven girls in the group were negative. The teacher listed them on the overhead projector, then asked if they could draw a conclusion from the discussion. The conclusion these girls drew was "Getting glasses would be terrible." After recording that conclusion, the teacher turned to the girls and lectured them for the next fifteen minutes on how *wrong* they were to feel like that and that the *right* way to feel about getting glasses was pleased. She had been pleased when, in the sixth grade, she had had to get glasses. The teacher then drew a line through the students' conclusion and wrote the *correct* conclusion on the overhead: "Getting glasses would be a wonderful experience." Later the teacher could not understand why her students did not want to contribute to other discussions!

Other problems teaching thinking include the feeling that lessons that focus on thinking take too much time, the belief that the topic could be taught more effectively through direct experiences in which students are told information, and the noise that is often generated. Students who are discussing and debating, who are excited by the learning experience, are not as quiet as those who are reading or listening and absorbing information presented to them. Noise generated by the thinking process, however, should be considered productive noise.

Thinking should be taught across all subject matter areas and all grade levels; however, remember that thinking is a developmental process. The structures and contexts of any thinking operation and of thinking as a whole become more complex, more sophisticated as students develop and grow, as they accumulate experiences. A teacher cannot expect the same type of thinking or the same depth of thinking at the first grade level as at the sixth grade level, and so thinking requirements should be geared to the age and experiential background of the children. Teaching thinking adds a sense of excitement to the classroom as children learn to use information, to think critically, and to think creatively.

Whether thinking is taught to first graders or to sixth graders, three general assumptions hold true. First, the teacher should begin with the assumption that all students can learn to think. In the past it was believed that children from impoverished backgrounds have such deficits in academic skills that their education should focus only on the acquisition of information. This idea is erroneous. Children from all socioeconomic and ethnic backgrounds and all geographic areas need to learn thinking skills as well as content information.

Second, teachers should keep in mind that students can think better when they are taught how to think. Often teachers say: "These kids can't or don't or won't think." And they are often correct. That does not mean, however, that children cannot learn to use thinking skills well. Just as children must be taught to read or write or multiply, they must be taught to think using appropriately developed lessons and appropriate teaching techniques. No one expects a child to come into the world knowing the names of the continents or the location of the various European nations. No one should expect children to come into the world knowing how to think.

Closely related to the first assumption is the third, that teaching is for children of all intellectual levels and not simply for those who have been identified as intellectually gifted. In the past, thinking development programs have been part of programs for the gifted child. These children were generally pulled out of the regular classroom, given specific lessons in critical thinking, problem solving, and creative thinking and then returned to the classroom to continue with the daily routine. Such an approach is indefensible when it is acknowledged that children of all intellectual abilities are challenged to make decisions every day and so should be given the tools needed to make those decisions appropriately.

Once the teacher is committed to teaching thinking, there is a need to differentiate between two types of thinking: critical thinking and creative thinking.

CRITICAL THINKING

In its simplest form, critical thinking is knowing when to question something as well as the inclination to question. In more sophisticated terms, it is teaching students how to recognize and/or construct sound arguments, apply the principles of formal and informal logic, and avoid fallacies in their reasoning. As such, critical thinking includes not only the production of ideas but also the evaluation of those ideas. Critical thinking is the means by which assertions and arguments are analyzed and evaluated in the light of available evidence. Critical thinking can also involve problem solving and the evaluations of solutions to problems. Critical thinking means judging the authenticity, worth, or accuracy of a piece of information, a claim, or a source of data.

When it comes to critical thinking, the evaluation of the outcomes of the thinking process is equally important as the development of outcomes. Even when solutions are eminently practical based on flawless reasoning and the latest evidence, other people will not necessarily perceive the results as reasonable or sound. Therefore, each outcome of critical thinking and problem solving should be evaluated according to evidence and not opinion.

Critical thinking includes certain skills. The following list is not meant to be comprehensive but is illustrative of the range of critical thinking skills children should learn to use. Children should learn to:

1. Determine the strength of an argument or claim
2. Determine when a problem exists and what the problem is
3. Determine the credibility of a source
4. Identify ambiguous claims and arguments
5. Identify unstated assumptions
6. Distinguish between verifiable facts, opinions, and value claims
7. Distinguish relevant from irrelevant information, claims, and reasons
8. Determine the factual accuracy of a statement
9. Detect bias
10. Identify logical fallacies
11. Recognize logical inconsistencies in a line of reasoning

CREATIVE THINKING

Critical thinking tends to focus on a single end point, a concept or piece of information that has been evaluated in terms of its accuracy and its credibility.

Creative thinking, on the other hand, is divergent, generates something new, and often violates accepted principles. Creative thinking focuses on the creation of something original, something not previously developed or thought. It relies on both flexbility and diversity. Creative thinking attends more to purpose than to results, stretches competence beyond previously established levels, and is driven by originality. It often involves looking at something familiar, analyzing its parts, and then forming new, original relationships among and between those parts. Creative thinking takes the old and creates the new. It is problem solving applied to creative ends.

Creative thinking begins with creativity. The more a student takes for granted, the less likely he or she is to think in a creative manner. Creative ideas often come from associating things not commonly associated or from actively bringing together antithetical elements. The beginning of creative thinking is the disposition to be curious, to wonder, and to inquire. The more likely a student is to fear failure, the less likely he or she is to work creatively. Because fear of failure can act to inhibit creative thinking, the teacher should not judge ideas as they are being developed. Instead, a brainstorming format in which ideas are generated, collected, and recorded prior to any attempt at evaluation is far more effective.

There are six general principles of creative thinking. The more these principles guide one's thinking, the more likely one is to think creatively.

1. Creative thinking depends as much on being objective as on being subjective. Creative people consider different viewpoints; set final or intermediate products aside and come back to them later, so they can evaluate them with more distance; seek intelligent criticism; and subject their ideas to practical and theoretical tests.

2. Creative thinking depends on attention to purpose as much as to results. Creative people explore alternative goals and approaches early in an endeavor, evaluate them, and remain ready to change the approach or redefine the problem as necessary. As naturalists attempted to explain the cause of shells and marine fossils on mountain tops, the solutions proposed changed with new information and with new and creative interpretations of that information.

3. Creative thinking depends on mobility more than fluency. When difficulties in creative thinking arrive, creative thinkers do not generally attempt to find more ideas but instead attempt to make the original problem more abstract or concrete, more general or specific, or more practical or fanciful. Reformulating the problem is more productive than brainstorming additional problem solutions.

4. Creative thinking involves aesthetic as well as practical standards. Creative people try to develop something original; however, the original may not be practical or elegant. The Ptolemaic geocentric solar system with its orbits within orbits to account for the observations made of the night sky was indeed creative, but it became

impractical as an explanatory force. The Copernican system was both creative and elegant in its simplicity and practicality.

5. Creative thinking depends on working at the edge more than at the center of one's competence. Creative people maintain high standards and accept confusion, uncertainty, and the high risk of failure as a part of the process of thinking and creating.

6. Creative thinking depends on intrinsic more than extrinsic motivation. Creative people believe that they, rather than other people, choose what they will do and how they will do it. They tend to view the task they have undertaken as worthwhile in itself and not just as a means to an end. They enjoy the activity, the context, and the setting.

METACOGNITION

In its essence, **metacognition** is thinking about thinking. It involves not only thinking about one's own thinking processes but also the ability to know what one does or does not know, and so it is the cognitive ability that monitors other thinking processes. It is the ability to plan a strategy for producing needed information, to be conscious of one's own strategies during an act of problem solving, and to reflect on and evaluate the productiveness of one's own thinking. Because metacognition is a key attribute of formal operational thought, it is sometimes thought to be more appropriate to introduce metacognitive strategies at the sixth grade level than at earlier grades. However, there is evidence to show that metacognitive strategies can be introduced in a simplified form even at primary grade levels.

Although the concept of metacognition can be introduced at virtually any level of the elementary school, it should be kept in mind that teaching metacognition directly may not be beneficial to students. When strategies of problem solving are imposed by the teacher rather than generated by the students themselves, their performance may become impaired rather than enhanced. When students experience the need for problem-solving strategies, induce their own strategies, and discuss and practice them to the degree that they become spontaneous and unconscious, their metacognition seems to improve.

As with critical thinking and creative thinking, metacognition has certain components: developing a plan of action, maintaining that plan in the mind over a period of time, and reflecting back on and evaluating the plan on completion. These components provide the foundation for the basic teaching strategies to develop metacognitive strategies in children.

First, prior to an activity, take time to develop and discuss strategies and steps for attacking problems, rules to remember that can be used in problem solving, and the directions to be followed. This assists students in thinking about how they will solve a problem rather than simply jumping in and beginning to develop a solution. Also, students should develop, with the assistance of the teacher, a time frame for working on the problem, the purpose of the activity, and the rules under which they will be operating.

Second, during the lesson students should share with one another the progress they have been making, their thought processes, and their perceptions of their own behavior. The students can also be encouraged to talk about how they reached the current place in their strategy and what they intend to do next in solving the problem. After the activity has been concluded, have the students evaluate how well they did in solving the activity problem. This strategy can also be extended to exploring the consequences of the choices as well as the decisions made by the students. In this way students are exploring not only the solution but the results and ramifications of the solution selected. As students explore their decisions, they should analyze the cause-and-effect relationships in the choices they made, the actions they took, and the results of those actions and choices.

Third, students should also be encouraged to pose their own questions rather than simply rely on questions posed by the teacher. Questions can be viewed as problems for solutions, with students discussing how they can solve the problem and then using their strategies to do so.

Fourth, the teacher can apply differentiated evaluations to the actions and solutions of the students. This concept of evaluation applies to student action rather than teacher action. It asks students to reflect on and categorize their actions according to two or more sets of evaluative criteria. Students may evaluate solutions to problems on the basis of like–didn't like, helpful-hindering, practical-impractical, creative-ordinary. They may also use similar criteria to evaluate the activities in which they engage.

Fifth, through his or her own actions the teacher can assist students at all grade levels to develop their thinking, particularly metacognitive, abilities. First, the teacher can help students to reduce and eventually eliminate the statement "I can't" by helping students to identify what they know and do not know and how their knowledge relates to the problem at hand. Once what is not known has been identified, the teacher can help students determine what information, materials, or skills are needed. Once the needs are identified, students can proceed to answer the question or solve the problem. Second, the teacher can assist in the development of metacognitive strategies by helping to paraphrase or reflect back on student ideas. In this case, the teacher can invite the students to restate, translate, compare, and paraphrase one another's ideas so they begin to listen to their own thinking and that of others. The important point is that the students be doing the paraphrasing and restating rather than the teacher. Third, the teacher can assist in the development of metacognitive strategies by helping students to clarify the terminology they use. Students should be asked to clarify value statements. For example, students may say the race to put a man on the Moon was good. "Good" is a value, and students should be asked to clarify what is meant by the term. The teacher needs to ask students why the race to put a man on the Moon was "good." Conversely, if students decide the development of atomic energy was "bad," they need to be challenged to give their reasons for this conclusion. Students should also be asked to specify their source of information. "They said" or "it said" should not be enough: Students should clarify who "they" are and what "it" is so that they become more definite in their statements and use of supporting evidence. Students should also be encouraged to use **operational definitions** of terms. In general, an operational definition is one developed by the students to clarify a particular term as it is being used in a particular instance. For example, students discussing immigration may want to define the term *immigration* in their own words so that all members of the class are thinking of the term in the same way. The use of operational definitions is also important when a term can be defined in a variety of different ways. For example, the word *chemistry* has a variety of interpretations, from the study of the chemical makeup of the universe, to the development of new compounds for consumers, to the study of the structure of the atom, to the interaction between people who fall in love. Until a definition is agreed on, students may be discussing different concepts under the same umbrella term. Fourth, the teacher can encourage role playing and simulations within the classroom. For older children role playing and simulations can require the student to take the point of view of another person, one in opposition to his or her own point of view, and so results in thinking about one's own thinking. In the primary grades, consideration of other viewpoints can be better accomplished during group discussions in which the teacher can assist in the identification of contradictions and in the development of differing points of view. Fifth, teachers in all grade levels can encourage students to use journal writing. Journal writing provides an opportunity to revisit and think about what was already done and to compare what was known previously with what is now known. Finally, teachers can engage in a powerful form of teaching known as modeling. In modeling the teacher uses the techniques of metacognition as a part of his or her own thinking skills. As students observe the teacher using the strategies, they begin to use the strategies themselves. However, it is important that the teacher use the strategies naturally and not in a manner that is forced or designed to call particular attention to those strategies.

TEACHING CREATIVE AND CRITICAL THINKING SKILLS AND STRATEGIES

In teaching creative and critical thinking skills, the first step is to select the proper skill or strategy, and the first thing to take into account is the age and developmental level of the children involved in the lesson. Young children, kindergarten through second grade, can be taught thinking skills and can apply those skills provided the task selected is appropriate and the required cognitive skills are present. For example, a first grade class heard about children in Africa who were hungry. They decided they wanted to do something to help. With the assistance of the teacher, these children listed four possible courses of action: send the children in Africa their lunches, send the children in Africa canned foods, send the children in Africa seeds to grow their own food, and collect money and send it to Africa to help the children buy food to eat. Once the list was made the teacher asked the children to decide which of the ideas was the best. They ruled out sending lunches because they recalled what had happened when one of the children in the class had left his lunch in the classroom over a weekend; they were not certain how long it took to get to Africa, but they were certain it would take more than a weekend. Suggestion 1 was ruled out because of past experience with lunches. Suggestion 2 was also ruled out after a lengthy conversation about what the children themselves liked to eat. They discovered that not all of them liked the same food, and since they did not like the same things they were not certain whether children in Africa would like the same things. They decided not to send canned goods because of the possibility of sending food the children did not like. The third idea, sending seeds, seemed to have a great deal of support until some of the children remembered how much difficulty they had growing seeds. Many simply did not grow. Again there was the problem of what kinds of seeds to send so the children in Africa would have something to eat that they liked. Finally, these first graders decided to simply collect money and send it to Africa. With the teacher's help they developed a program to present to others in the school and began their collection. At the end of the two-week time period they were ready to send the money to Africa. The teacher was about to ask what address to use when one of the children asked who they were going to send the money to. The child had identified the problem for herself. Finally, after collecting more information, the children identified an organization and sent the collected money to that organization. These first graders were engaging in higher-order thinking skills, particularly analysis and evaluation, and did so successfully. The reason for the success was that the children were able to relate the problem and solutions to what was familiar to themselves. In selecting thinking skills activities, the first step is to make the activity appropriate to the children.

In addition to the selection of an appropriate activity, the selection of thinking skills involves the consideration of certain questions:

1. Can an understandable form of the skill or strategy be mastered relatively easily by the students, given their degrees of readiness and experience?
2. Does the skill or strategy have frequent, practical applications in the students' everyday, out-of-school life?
3. Does the skill or strategy build on previously taught thinking operations or lead to the development of other, more complex operations?
4. Does the subject matter in which the operation is taught lend itself to teaching the operation?
5. Does the skill or strategy have frequent, practical applications in a number of subject matter areas?

Once the thinking skill or strategy has been selected, the task becomes to teach the children to use that skill or strategy in a way that allows them to gain the ability to apply the skill or strategy rather than simply follow a series of preprogrammed steps in one situation. The approach described here is an inductive strategy for the teaching of thinking skills and consists of five steps.

Step 1.   The teacher introduces the new thinking operation in the context of the subject matter being studied. The introduction of the thinking skill may be initiated whenever the teacher sees a need for the skill. This introductory phase focuses directly on the skill or strategy and how it is used in the particular context of the subject matter. At this level students are expected to gain basic knowledge of the skill or strategy but are not expected to become proficient in its use. In introducing the skill the teacher generally states for the children that learning the skill is the objective of the lesson and then gives the name of the skill and synonyms for the name that may be more easily understood by the students. Once the name of the skill or strategy is given, the teacher gives the students a working definition. At this point the students are asked to state some ways in which they have used the skill or strategy: personal experiences, school activities, or in the subject matter being considered. Finally, the teacher with the students should explain why the skill or strategy is useful and worth learning. The goal of this introductory step is to define the skill or strategy and to demonstrate to students its usefulness.

Step 2.   Students are asked to use the thinking skill or strategy to the best of their current ability in a task presented by the teacher. The task selected at this stage in the development of the thinking skill or strategy should use subject matter familiar to the students and appropriate to the unit or topic under consideration. It is also possible at this stage to use subject matter from the experiences of the students. In executing the skill or strategy, students should work in pairs or small groups to foster interaction and discussion of the thinking skill.

Step 3.   The students reflect on what they did during their attempt to execute the skill or strategy. The students should participate in a large group discussion in which they report on their thinking processes while using the skill or strategy; identify the steps or rules they used, including the sequence of steps; and clarify the procedure and any criteria that were used during their work in pairs or small groups.

Step 4.   Students are given a second task using the thinking skill or strategy. As in step 2, the students again work in pairs or small groups. This time, however, the students have more information about the skill or strategy and seek to apply what was discussed in step 3 to the new task. The content used for this new task should be appropriate to the unit or topic and should be in the same format and in the same medium as the task used in step 2.

Step 5.   This should be considered a review step, for its basic purpose is to review the skill or strategy that has been used in the task. During this step, the students again report on their thought processes as they used the skill or strategy, review the steps or procedures that are a part of the skill or strategy, and review the rules that direct the use of the skill or strategy as well as when it is used. This discussion is generally conducted in a large group format. In addition to the discussion of the use of the skill or strategy by the students, the teacher should help to develop the relationship of the skill or strategy to other skills or strategies, review or revise the skill definition, and state where the skill or strategy can be used in personal or out-of-school situations.

In summary, the basic format is to introduce the skill or strategy, execute it, reflect on what was done, apply the skill or strategy to a new task, and review the skill or strategy, extending it to new areas.

Consider a fifth grade class involved in a theme dealing with communication. As a part of this theme, the teacher wants to help the children develop the ability to determine the strength of an argument or claim. Because children are so familiar with television, the teacher begins by asking the students to describe the commercials they see on television. After making a list of commercials on the board, the teacher asks the students to work in small groups to separate the list into two groups: those the students think are accurate and have evidence to support what they are saying, and those they think do not. After the groups complete the task, the teacher has the students discuss each advertisement and place it into one of the two categories. As they try to decide which advertisements belong in each group the teacher asks them to tell their reasons. Finally, she tells the students that they are learning how to judge the strength of an argument or claim. She asks the children what they think that means. As the children offer answers, the teacher records their ideas:

1. It means being able to tell if something is true.
2. It means looking at a commercial and deciding if what the commercial says is right or wrong.
3. It means figuring out if the commercial is lying.
4. It means that when you think the commercial is true that you ask yourself how true it really is.
5. It's figuring out if they have any information to back up what they say.

Once the students had decided on the meaning for the new thinking skill, the teacher again asked the class to divide into groups. This time, she gave each group a collection of advertisements taken from magazines. She then asked the students to look at the advertisements and read the text that went along with the pictures. Once they had considered the advertisements, the students then applied their understanding of the thinking skill to the advertisements.

The groups were asked to report on their decisions about the advertisements. Each group's spokesperson was asked not only to give the group's decision, but also to tell why they made their judgment. Students reported their thought processes:

1. It says that more doctors recommend this, but then another ad says more doctors recommend their product than any other. Both of them can't be true. We need to know how they got that information.
2. This makes it look as if all you have to do to be popular is use this kind of toothpaste. We think they need to show how that happens.
3. This car says it is the safest of its kind on the road. It shows the people who tested it and the results of the tests and it also shows that some magazines rank it as really safe. We thought this was pretty good.

Finally, the teacher helped the students in the class to summarize how they used the new thinking skill and what they looked for in judging the advertisements. Only after the students seemed comfortable using the new thinking skill did she ask them in what other areas they thought they might need to use the skill. The group unanimously decided it would be very helpful in deciding whether toys and other things they saw advertised on television were worth the money, but also went on to discuss how they probably should look for supporting information when they were reading books and magazines.

Once the new skill or strategy is taught it must be practiced in a variety of ways. At first, the practice of the new skill or strategy should be guided. In this type of practice the students are given a number of lessons in which they use the skill under guidance from the teacher. These lessons should all use the same kind of subject matter, the same medium, and the same type of data. As the students progress through the guided practice phase, the amount of guidance should gradually be decreased. When the students show the ability to use the skill or strategy with some ease and effectiveness, they should begin to use it independently. At first, the independent practice of the skill or strategy should use the same subject matter, data, and medium as the tasks used for guided practice. The students would have many opportunities for the use of the new skill or strategy in an independent manner over the next few months. When students show the ability to use the skill or strategy with ease in an independent manner, then the teacher should help the students to generalize the use into other settings and other subject matter. As students move toward using the skill or strategy in other settings, the teacher should show students how to apply it in those new settings rather than simply assume transfer will occur. Also, the tasks that are used for transfer to additional areas should allow the skill or strategy to be used in more complex and sophisticated ways. Each time the skill or strategy is introduced into a new setting or into greater complexity, the students should be given some guided practice in the use of the skill or strategy to be certain it is being used accurately and effectively.

KNOWING WHEN CRITICAL AND CREATIVE THINKING SKILLS ARE DEVELOPING

The proof of learning creative and critical thinking skills is found in the use of those skills by the students outside of specific lessons on thinking. Certain indicators demonstrate that students are indeed learning from their instruction in thinking skills.

Students who are beginning to use thinking skills outside of the instructional sequence will show greater perseverance in working at problems where the solution is not immediately known. Rather than looking to the teacher or the textbook for an immediate answer or for guidance in how to solve a problem, students will try to find their own solutions and their own procedures. This perseverance will also manifest itself as a decrease in impulsivity. Papers will show fewer erasures. Students will be less likely to blurt out answers to questions as they begin to reflect on their answers before relating them to the class and the teacher. And, students will begin to gather information, ask questions about directions to be certain of understanding, and plan a strategy before they begin to work at that strategy.

Along with increased perseverance, students will also begin to show increased ability to listen to others, both those with similar points of view and those with differing points of view. As they listen more effectively to one another, students will also begin to build on the ideas of others.

As students become more persevering and more apt to consider a variety of points of view, they will also begin to demonstrate more flexibility in thinking; they will look for several ways to solve the same problem. As many possible ways are developed for looking at the same problem, they will begin to evaluate the merits and consequences of two or more alternative courses of action. And they will also change their minds in the face of new evidence.

Additional evidence of the growth of problem-solving skills will be found in the questions asked by the students and in the problems they pose to the teacher and others in the class. Students who are developing the ability to use thinking skills will find their own problems, and so the teacher will see a shift from teacher-originated problems to student-originated problems. As students approach and solve these problems, there will be an increasing tendency of the students to draw on past knowledge and experience. They will start to call on their store of knowledge and experiences as sources of data to support their ideas, to develop theories to explain their observations, and to develop processes to solve each new problem-solving challenge. Within their development of problems and the solution strategies for those problems, students will begin to use language more precisely. More descriptive words, more use of correct terminology, more criteria to be used in making value judgments, more supportive evidence, and more elaboration of ideas in order to clarify their statements will begin to be evidenced.

Finally, students will show an increase in cooperative thinking. Because problem solving and critical thinking tend to occur best in small groups, students will begin to show increased ability to work and to think with others. There develops a greater use of consensus, more empathy toward fellow students, and an increase in altruism.

GROUPING AND COOPERATIVE LEARNING

Discovery teaching strategies, critical and creative thinking strategies, and discussion strategies for values teaching all have in common two things: the need for thinking rather than for memorization and the use of small groups for optimum use of the strategies.

Use of grouping in teaching in the integrated curriculum can mean simple partnerships between two students, larger groups of three, four, or five students, or **cooperative learning** groups. In general, groupings fall under the categories of heterogeneous groupings or homogeneous groupings.

HETEROGENEOUS GROUPING

Heterogeneous groupings contain students with a variety of interests, backgrounds, and abilities. When students are grouped heterogeneously, they interact on the basis of their different stores of information. This has an advantage in discovery and problem-solving situations in that what is not known to one member of a group may be known to another and so additional information may be applied. In other cases, such as when children are working on an integrated curriculum project, a heterogeneous group will allow children with varying artistic, language, research, and motor skills to work together to the satisfactory completion of the project. The disadvantage of heterogeneous grouping lies in the possibility of group domination by a single student with a strong background or strong personality.

HOMOGENEOUS GROUPING

Homogeneous groupings occur when some common factor is used to select the students for a particular group. Ability, achievement, and interest are some of the factors that may be used in selecting students for a group. For example, students who are most interested in art may be assigned to a group in which the research paper written by the group focuses on the art of a particular culture. Similarly, students who have an interest in mathematics may be assigned to a group that will develop and interpret the results of a survey. Homogeneous groups are particularly effective in the integrated curriculum, where students are able to pursue topics of interest and may wish to pursue their investigations by working with other students with similar interests. The major problem with homogeneous grouping is that the students may be so alike that there is no diversity of ideas to assist in discovery or problem solving.

COOPERATIVE LEARNING

Cooperative learning is a type of group learning in which students work together in small groups to achieve a particular goal or complete a particular task. In some types of cooperative learning, the group works together on a single task, while in others the members of the group work individually, then pool the results of the work when they are finished. Cooperative learning appears to raise the academic performance of students because they help and support each other rather than competing against each other. In addition to this support, students also have the opportunity to learn from one another. Cooperation and learning from one another are especially important for students who are of low ability and who have been turned off by school. Cooperative groups allow the student of lower ability to work with and learn from students of higher ability. Additionally, students who are unable to succeed in a competitive situation are able to succeed in a cooperative situation, thus giving the turned off student a chance to turn on again. Finally, cooperative learning can improve relationships between ethnic groups. If students from varying groups work together, they begin to learn about and appreciate each other's strengths and begin to develop friendships. Three models of cooperative learning will be described here.

Student Teams-Achievement Divisions (STAD).   **STAD** is made up of five components. The first of these components is *class presentation.* The class presentation is a teacher-directed presentation of the concepts, skills, or processes that the students are to learn and generally occurs in the form of expository teaching. The second component, *teams,* is the most important aspect of STAD. Working in teams composed of four or five students grouped heterogeneously, the students together use prepared study materials. Worksheet and workbook pages can be used along with study questions developed by the teacher. Within each team, students should work together to answer each question. This may involve the students working in pairs within the team and then pooling the answers at the end. Teams should be encouraged to make certain that each member of the team can answer each question correctly, to try to answer the questions within the team rather than going outside the group to the teacher, and to explain their answers if the questions are in multiple-choice format. Once the questions are answered it's time for the third component, the use of *quizzes.* After the student teams have answered the questions presented to them, the teacher gives a quiz on the work in order to measure the amount of learning that has taken place. Those quizzes are not given as a cooperative effort; instead, the students work on them individually. The fourth component is the *individual improvement score.* For this the teacher establishes a minimum score for a quiz for each student; the improvement score is how much the student exceeded the minimum score. Team scores can then be computed by adding the improvement scores for each team member. The final component, *team recognition,* is when the teacher recognizes the work of each team through a newsletter that announces the team scores and the ranking of each team within the class. Outstanding individual performances are also reported.

Jigsaw.   The second model of cooperative learning to be considered here is called jigsaw. In this model, students become experts on a part of the material they are learning about. The expert on that part then teaches the other members of the team. In this way the students become responsible for their leaning. Three elements of jigsaw are of particular importance. First, the teacher begins by preparing the learning materials. An expert sheet and a quiz for each topic within a unit is developed. The expert sheets tell the students what they should do in order to gain the information and outline the topic in the form of questions. Once the planning is completed, the students are divided into expert groups and learning teams. The expert sheets are distributed to each learning team with an explanation for those who will become an expert on some aspect of the topic everyone is studying. Expert groups generally have five or six students. The students within the expert groups are given time to work on their topics prior to meeting within their expert groups. When the students have researched their topics they move to the expert groups to discuss the information collected and to combine the information. The third phase is the *reports and quizzes* phase, in which students return to their learning teams. Each of the experts now has the task of teaching the topic to the other members of the group. After the experts have taught their groups, a brief class discussion or question-and-answer session should be held, with the teacher encouraging the experts to answer any questions that arise from the other students. Finally, a quiz is administered on an individual basis. As with STAD, quizzes are scored on the basis of improvement, with a team score based on the improvement scores.

Group Investigation.   For **group investigation**, the students are first divided into small groups of five or fewer students. Each group plans their strategy for what topic they will study and how they will study it. Individuals or pairs select subtopics and decide how they will pursue them. They then report on their progress and the results of their work in the small group. The small groups discuss the individual reports and then prepare group reports to be presented to the whole class.

There are six stages in group investigation. *Topic selection* is the first stage; the students choose specific topics within a general problem area. They are then organized into two- to five-member groups. In the second stage, *cooperative planning,* the teacher and the students work together to plan specific learning procedures, tasks, and goals that will be consistent with the subtopics of the selected problems. In stage three, *implementation,* the students carry out the plans formulated in stage two. This learning phase should involve a wide range of activities and skills and should also lead students to different kinds of sources, both inside and outside the school. The teacher's role at this stage is to offer assistance to the groups as needed and to monitor their progress. At the *analysis and synthesis* stage, the students analyze and evaluate the information they have gathered and plan how they will summarize that information for an interesting class presentation. In stage five, *presentation of the final project,* the groups present their topics. They should try to give the most interesting presentation possible. The role of the teacher at this point is to coordinate the presentations. In stage six, *evaluation,* the students and the teacher together evaluate each group's presentation and contribution to the work of the class as a whole. The evaluation can include individual or group assessment or both.

STAD is the easiest form of cooperative learning to implement as it utilizes the most common forms of instructional materials in a new, cooperative manner. Slightly more difficult to use is jigsaw, as it places more responsibility on the students for their learning. The most difficult form of cooperative learning discussed here is group investigation, as it places maximum responsibility for learning on the students. They are responsible for identifying what to learn, how to learn it, where to learn it, and how to present it most effectively

SUMMARY

Within the integrated curriculum, the teacher needs to give attention not only to sound planning for the total theme, but also to presenting lessons to students who have not developed a particular set of skills, to developing critical and creative thinking skills, and to developing the ability of children to engage in metacognition. Determining when formal lessons are needed is based on interactions with the children. Formal lessons are presented when students show a need for particular skills. In working directly with students to present skills, the teacher may use conferencing, expository teaching, or inductive discovery teaching depending on the number of students involved and the type of information to be conveyed.

Critical and creative thinking, along with the development of metacognition, require that the teacher interact with the students in an open manner where ideas can freely flow, where students and teacher are asked to defend their conclusions with facts, and where creativity is rewarded along with the acquisition of knowledge.

In the integrated curriculum in general, grouping becomes important. Students may be grouped heterogeneously so that different students bring different interests and skills to a group, homogeneously so that similar interests can be used to focus on a concept, or in cooperative learning groups with more formalized structures.

ACTIVITY ONE

PURPOSE

The purpose of this activity is to plan and carry out an expository lesson pertinent to the needs of a small group of children.

PROCEDURE

1. Through consideration of student work, observation, and discussion with the children or with the teacher of the children, determine a specific problem the children are having in one of the subject matter areas: science, mathematics, social studies, language arts.
2. Plan an expository lesson that addresses the specific problem the students are having.
3. If you are not currently teaching the identified children, discuss the lesson plan with the classroom teacher before carrying out the lesson.
4. Teach the lesson to the identified group of children.
5. Critique the lesson taught. Make any changes necessary to improve the lesson. If you are not currently teaching, be certain to get input from the classroom teacher as part of the critique.

ACTIVITY TWO

PURPOSE

The purpose of this activity is to plan and carry out an inductive discovery lesson pertinent to the needs of a small group of children.

PROCEDURE

1. Through consideration of student work, observation, and discussion with the children or with the teacher of the children, determine a specific problem the children are having in one of the subject matter areas: science, mathematics, social studies, language arts.
2. Plan an inductive discovery lesson that addresses the specific problem the students are having. Include in the lesson the use of a graphic organizer.
3. If you are not currently teaching the identified children, discuss the lesson plan with the classroom teacher before carrying out the lesson.
4. Teach the lesson to the identified group of children.
5. Critique the lesson taught. Make any changes necessary to improve the lesson. If you are not currently teaching, be certain to get input from the classroom teacher as part of the critique.

ACTIVITY THREE

PURPOSE

The purpose of this activity is to plan and carry out a lesson that focuses on the development of either critical or creative thinking in the classroom.

PROCEDURE

1. Decide whether the lesson will focus on critical thinking skills or on creative thinking. Select a particular grade level.
2. Select a concept being developed within a theme currently in use in a classroom setting. If you are not currently teaching, discuss the theme with the classroom teacher and get his or her input into selecting a concept.
3. Plan a lesson around the concept that will help students to develop either critical thinking skills or creative thinking.
4. Present the lesson to the class.
5. After the lesson is taught critique it and make any changes necessary on the basis of the critique. If you are not currently teaching, be certain to get input from the classroom teacher as part of the critique.

ACTIVITY FOUR

PURPOSE

The purpose of this activity is to plan and carry out a cooperative learning strategy within the classroom setting.

PROCEDURE

1. Consider the current instruction within the classroom. Plan to introduce a cooperative learning sequence to the class. If you are not currently teaching, discuss with the classroom teacher when and how he or she would want to include cooperative learning.
3. Select the type of cooperative learning that would best fit the classroom situation.
4. Plan a cooperative learning experience and present the experience to the class.
5. After the class has participated in the cooperative learning experience, critique the experience and make any changes necessary to make the experience more productive for the students involved. If you are not currently teaching, be certain to get input from the classroom teacher as part of the critique.

STUDY QUESTIONS

1. What is the role of direct instruction within the integrated curriculum? When might a teacher decide to use direct instruction in the classroom?

2. What is conferencing? Give a specific example of how conferencing would be used in an integrated program.

3. You are a fourth grade teacher in an integrated program. When might you use expository teaching strategies? What problems could occur in the use of expository teaching?

4. Plan an expository lesson focusing on a specific arithmetic or language arts skill.

5. How does inductive discovery teaching differ from expository teaching?

6. Turn the expository lesson developed in question 4 into an inductive discovery lesson.

7. Discuss the use of graphic organizers in inductive discovery teaching. How does a circle diagram differ from a tower diagram?

8. Compare and contrast critical thinking skills and creative thinking skills.

9. What can the teacher in the classroom do to foster creative and critical thinking skills?

10. Develop a lesson that could be used to teach a specific creative or critical thinking skill.

11. You are a sixth grade teacher. Develop a checklist you could use to determine whether your students are developing critical or creative thinking skills.

12. Compare and contrast heterogeneous grouping with homogeneous grouping. How do these types of groupings differ from cooperative learning groups?

13. What techniques for cooperative learning have been considered in this chapter? How are those techniques organized for use in the classroom?

BIBLIOGRAPHY

Beyer, B. K. (1987). *Practical strategies for the teaching of thinking.* Boston: Allyn and Bacon.

Boothby, P. R., & Alverman, D. E. (1984). A classroom training study: The effects of graphic organizer instruction on fourth graders' comprehension. *Reading World, 26,* 325–339.

Caine, R. N., & Caine, G. (1991). *Teaching and the human brain.* Alexandria, Va.: Association for Supervision and Curriculum Development.

Cantlon, T. L. (1991). *Structuring the classroom successfully for cooperative team learning.* Portland, Oreg.: C&M. Education Consultants.

Ciborowski, J. (1992). *Textbooks and the students who can't read them: A guide to teaching content.* Boston: Brookline Books.

Clark, J. H. (1990). *Patterns of thinking: Integrating learning skills in content teaching.* Boston: Allyn and Bacon.

Collins, C. (1992). Thinking development through intervention: Middle school students come of age. In C. Collins & J. N. Mangieri (Eds.), *Teaching thinking: An agenda for the 21st ccentury* (pp. 120–125). Hillsdale, N.J.: Laurence Erlbaum.

Collins, C., & Mangieri, J. N. (Eds.). (1992). *Teaching thinking: An agenda for the 21st century.* Hillsdale, N.J.: Laurence Erlbaum.

Costa, A. (1992). An environment for thinking. In C. Collins & J. N. Mangieri (Eds.), *Teaching thinking: An agenda for the 21st century* (pp. 20–24). Hillsdale, N.J.: Laurence Erlbaum.

Costa, A. (Ed.). (1985). *Developing minds: A resource book for teaching thinking.* Alexandria, Va.: Association for Supervision and Curriculum Development.

Dishon, D., & O'Leary, P. W. (1994). *A guidebook for cooperative learning.* Homes Beach, Fl.: Learning Publications, Inc.

Eisner, E. W. (1994). *Cognition and curriculum reconsidered* (2nd ed.). New York: Teachers College, Columbia University.

Forgan, H. W., & Mangrum, C. T. (1989). *Teaching content area reading skills: A modular preservice and inservice program* (4th ed.). Columbus, Ohio: Merrill.

Gagne, R. M., Briggs, L. J., & Wagner, W. W. (1988). *Principles of instructional design* (3rd ed.). New York: Holt, Rinehart, and Winston.

Hassard, J. (1990). *Science experiences: Cooperative learning and the teaching of science.* Menlo Park, Calif.: Addison-Wesley.

Hauf, M. B. (1971). Mapping: A technique for translating reading into thinking. *Journal of Reading, 14,* 225–230.

Johnson, D. W., & Johnson, T. R. (1991). *Learning together and alone: Cooperative, competitive, and individualistic learning* (3rd ed.). Englewood Cliffs, N.J.: Prentice Hall.

Jones, B. F., Palincsar, A. S., Ogle, D. S., & Carr, E. G. (1987). *Strategic teaching and learning: Cognitive instruction in the content areas.* Alexandria, Va.: Association for Supervision and Curriculum Development.

Lapp, D., Flood, J., & Farnan, N. (Eds.). (1989). *Content area reading and learning: Instructional strategies.* Englewood Cliffs, N.J.: Prentice Hall.

Mager, R. F. (1962). *Preparing instructional objectives.* Palo Alto, Calif.: Fearon.

Mason, E. (1972). *Collaborative learning.* New York: Schocken Books.

Moore, D. W., & Readence, J. E. (1984). A quantitative and qualitative review of graphic organizer research. *Journal of Educational Research, 78,* 11–17.

Ruggiero, V. R. (1988). *Teaching thinking across the curriculum.* New York: Harper & Row.

Shepherd, G. D., & Ragan, W. B. (1992). *Modern elementary curriculum* (7th ed.). Fort Worth, Tex.: Harcourt Brace Jovanovich.

West, C. K., Farmer, J. A., & Wolff, P. M. (1991). *Instructional design: Implications from cognitive science.* Englewood Cliffs, N.J.: Prentice Hall.

PART 4

APPROACHES TO

ASSESSMENT

CHAPTER

11

ASSESSING LEARNER OUTCOMES

CHAPTER OBJECTIVES

After reading this chapter you should be able to:

1. Define the terms *traditional assessment* and *authentic assessment*
2. Discuss the differences between traditional assessment and authentic assessment
3. Discuss the underlying principles of portfolio use
4. Discuss the kinds of portfolios that can be used in the classroom
5. Discuss the development of a portfolio
6. Discuss the use of the portfolio in the assessment of student progress

In the traditional classroom where subject matter areas are kept separate, where all children are expected to participate in the same lessons, learn the same concepts, and gain the same skills all at exactly the same time, assessment is generally in the form of tests and quizzes. It is easy to determine whether or not a child has learned the basic facts of addition by giving a written test in which all of the basic facts appear and the child must show the answers. Then, when all of the children have completed the test it is easy to collect and grade the papers. And finally, it is easy to assign a grade. Children who respond correctly to all 100 basic facts receive an A-plus, those who have 90-99 correct receive an A, those with 80-89 correct a B, and so on until the child who scored 27 out of 100 receives an F. Once mathematics has been assessed, the teacher and the children can move on to assessments in other subject matter areas.

Traditional assessment is based on certain premises. First, it is assumed that there are specific bits of information that all children should know. Once these are identified, it is relatively easy to develop a test to determine whether they have been acquired. Second, traditional assessments are based on the premise that all children will learn specific skills or concepts at the same time; therefore, all students can be assessed on the acquisition of those skills at the same time. And traditional forms of assessment are based on the idea that there is a certain level of achievement that all children should reach by a particular time.

In schools and classrooms where discipline-centered curricula are in use and where hierarchies of skills and concepts drive the curriculum, these premises may be inherent to the program. That does not, however, mean that they form a firm foundation for evaluation.

The major problem is simply that all children are not ready to learn the same things at the same time. As a consequence of differences in cognitive-developmental level, environment, or content and skill background, different children learn at different rates and times. A child who has had the opportunity to travel in Mexico is going to have a distinct advantage understanding differing cultures presented in social studies over the child who has never been further from home than the school building or the local shopping mall. A child who has plenty to eat and a safe place to sleep is going to have an advantage over a child who goes to bed hungry in an unsafe building. Consequently, differences in scores on tests of skills may be as reflective of the child's background as of the child's learning.

In addition to the problem of differences in background, there is also the problem traditional assessment has in taking into account the child's prior learning as it may be reflected in scores. Consider a science lesson in which children are asked to learn the names of the nine planets in order of distance from the sun. Janice has been interested in astronomy ever since the first night she looked into the sky and saw the stars. She came to the lesson not only knowing the names of the planets in their order but also knowing that at this point in time Neptune is actually farther from the Sun than Pluto. On the unit test she lists all of the planets correctly and with ease. Mike, on the other hand, was surprised to learn that there were other planets than the Earth. On the test he listed five planets in no particular order. Janice passes because she was able to write the names of the planets in correct order while Mike fails because he was not able to do so. And yet, in terms of learning, Mike gained a great deal more than Janice.

Another problem with traditional forms of assessment is that such forms are most often based on errors, mistakes, and failures to learn particular ideas or skills. Students' problems are identified and remediation to eliminate those identified problems is developed. The emphasis of traditional forms of assessment is on what the child has not learned rather than on what the child has learned.

Traditional forms of assessment also tend to be divorced from the learning process. The child works with hands-on science activities Monday through Thursday, but on Friday the hands-on science stops and the pencil and paper science test starts. Children write stories as a part of their language arts class, but they are evaluated on whether they can identify the nouns in sentences on a worksheet. And, for the clearest indication of how traditional evaluation is divorced from learning, consider standardized achievement tests. Not only are the tests developed outside of the school and school system, but the rest of the educational program stops when the standardized achievement tests are given.

Finally, traditional forms of assessment generally are based on divisions between subject matter areas: one tests for science, mathematics, social studies, language arts, or reading concepts and skills. All one needs to do is look at standardized achievement tests to know this is indeed standard. There is little, if any, opportunity to demonstrate how one's knowledge of mathematics is important to science or how knowledge of history can help one understand art or music. The application of information is generally not as important as the recall of disconnected bits of factual information.

Traditional forms of assessment tend to reflect the traditional curriculum. However, if one considers the integrated curriculum in which separation of subject matter areas is not appropriate, where students may be investigating different concepts at different times, and where hierarchies of skills and concepts give way to learning in authentic situations jointly developed by teacher and class, then traditional forms of assessment are inappropriate. The integrated curriculum requires a different form of assessment. This type of assessment is generally termed authentic assessment and the major form it takes is the **portfolio**.

AUTHENTIC ASSESSMENT

According to Ryan (1994, p. 1), "Authentic assessment is the process of gathering evidence and documenting a student's learning and growth in an authentic context." In essence, authentic assessment involves evaluating students by the work they do in the classroom, in authentic learning situations, and in a continuous manner. Authentic assessment does not take place when Friday comes around and everyone takes a test on science vocabulary words. Authentic assessment does take place when the teacher and child collaborate to collect evidence of science activities and experiments, discuss that evidence, and then look for progress on the part of the child. The attention is on the growth of the individual child rather than on comparison of the child with predetermined standards or with other children. In authentic assessment there is no discontinuity between teaching and assessment, between learning and assessment.

Authentic forms of assessment are more appropriate to the integrated curriculum than are traditional forms of assessment. First, within the integrated curriculum, emphasis is on learning rather than on teaching. Therefore, assessment that focuses on what the child has learned is more appropriate than assessment that focuses on what the teacher has taught. Second, the integrated curriculum promotes learning in an authentic setting. Children learn to construct coherent paragraphs not because it is the next lesson in the book but because writing a paragraph is needed in order to effectively communicate the results of research to other children. Authenticity in learning demands authenticity in assessment. Third, the integrated curriculum focuses on collaborative learning opportunities rather than on individual effort. Traditional forms of assessment tend to look only at the work of individuals on individual tasks. Authentic assessment incorporates the work of collaborative teams into the assessment process. Finally, in the integrated curriculum process is equally as important as if not more important than product. The development of an idea for a story, the production of a rough draft, the editing, the illustrating, and the binding of the story into a book are as important in learning as the final product. Traditional forms of assessment consider only the final product. Authentic forms of assessment consider the intermediary steps to the final product as well, thus showing the child's progress from start to finish.

One way of incorporating authentic assessment into the classroom is the use of a portfolio as the basis for assessment.

PORTFOLIOS

Portfolios are probably the most common method of authentic assessment in the classroom. According to Paulson and Paulson (1991, p. 295), a portfolio is "a purposeful, integrated collection of student work showing student effort, progress, or achievement in one or more areas. The collection is guided by performance standards and includes evidence of students' self-reflection and participation in setting the focus, selecting contents, and judging merit."

This definition points out the five factors that underlie the construction and use of portfolios in the integrated curriculum. First, portfolios are collaborative in nature. Students share with the teacher the responsibility for developing the portfolio and determining the standards on which the portfolio will be evaluated. Students share with the teacher such decisions as what will be included in the portfolio, how much will be included, how the portfolio will be used, and what criteria will be used in evaluating the contents. Second, portfolios are longitudinal and multidimensional in nature. They include not only a variety of student work, but also a record of work over time. The portfolio demonstrates the variety of approaches used in learning and shows the diversity of learning that has taken place. As no two students learn in precisely the same manner or at precisely the same rate, no two portfolios will be identical. This diversity in demonstrating knowledge is opposed to the view that knowledge is demonstrated only through answering questions on tests constructed by teacher, text, or educational testing company. Third, portfolios are a way of viewing the process and not simply the product of learning. Through the inclusion of beginning, intermediate, and final products both teacher and student gain insight into how progress has occurred. The portfolio shows learning as a series of starts and stops, or successes and difficulties, rather than as a single continuous line toward a final product. Fourth, the portfolio allows students to explore a variety of perspectives. This multiplicity of perspectives demonstrates the variety of learning styles that exist within a classroom and also helps to dispel the idea that there is only one way to reach a particular goal. This multiplicity of learning styles and techniques also gives the teacher an opportunity to reflect back on his or her instructional strategies and so improve the quality of instruction received by the students. Finally, the portfolio allows for self-reflection by both the teacher and the students. Students are able to examine their work and to make judgments on their progress, to see their strengths and identify their weaknesses. The teacher also has the opportunity to reflect on the effect on student learning of his or her instruction, project selection, and general class-room strategies.

While portfolio assessment is appropriate for all children in a classroom, it is particularly useful for children from culturally different backgrounds, children with learning problems, and gifted children. Children from cultural backgrounds different from the mainstream are often unable to demonstrate their actual levels of learning through traditional forms of assessment. Those who use English as a second language or who have little or no command of English find pencil and paper tests particularly daunting. In addition, children from culturally diverse backgrounds, even those for whom English is the native language, often feel greater dread in testing situations than those from the cultural mainstream. This increased level of test anxiety results in lower scores and so does not result in an accurate reflection of the culturally different child's level of learning. Portfolio assessment, on the other hand, allows the child, whether from the mainstream culture or from a culturally different background, to include in the portfolio items that demonstrate the child's actual learning. Children who do not do well on written assessments may include artwork, project results, photographs, and other nonverbal items to demonstrate true levels of achievement.

As with the culturally different child, the portfolio can give a more accurate basis for assessment of the child who is mentally retarded or learning disabled. For the child who is mentally retarded, the portfolio can demonstrate learning based on the individual child's starting point rather than on some criterion established for average children. In situations where individualized educational programs (IEPs) are a part of the mainstreamed child's educational program, the portfolio provides for documentation of progress toward the child's individual goals. Drawings, audiotapes, videotapes, and construction projects provide opportunities for the mentally retarded or learning disabled child who does not use language effectively or easily to demonstrate learning.

Gifted children in the regular classroom often have little opportunity to demonstrate that their learning has progressed beyond that of the average child, that they have gained a greater depth or breadth of knowledge than others in the classroom. With the portfolio, the gifted child has an opportunity to show areas of outstanding achievement in any of the intelligences. The child who is gifted with bodily or musical intelligence has a unique opportunity, as the portfolio allows the child to include a videotape or still photography record of a dance, instrumental, or athletic performance. Gifted children with strengths in other intelligences also have the opportunity to include the portfolio examples of their accomplishments.

In essence, the portfolio allows all students in the classroom to demonstrate their progress in appropriate and authentic ways, that is, through reports, artwork, constructions, and other items completed as a part of the learning process.

Once the decision has been made to use portfolios as a means of assessment, the next decision is the type of portfolio that will be used.

TYPES OF PORTFOLIOS

Valencia and Calfee (1991) identified three types of portfolios in common use about a decade ago. Since that time a fourth type has been added. All of these portfolio types and their uses and limitations are discussed here.

Showcase Portfolios.   The **showcase portfolio** consists of examples of work showing the best efforts of a particular student. Both the teacher and the student are involved in collecting the items to be included in the portfolio. Such a portfolio is used to demonstrate the best work completed by a student for parents, other teachers, and other students. The showcase portfolio is similar to the portfolio constructed by an art student applying to art school: he or she selects examples of the best work produced in order to demonstrate his or her best ability.

This selection of only best work brings up the first of the limitations of portfolio use. Because only final products, and the best of those final products, are chosen, the evaluator cannot determine the amount of progress made by the student. The intermediate steps are not included in the portfolio, and so the evaluator has no idea how the final product was produced or where the student started in the learning process. This is analogous to the science fair projects many schools have students complete. The final project is put on display with its computer-generated graphs and charts of final results, its conclusion neatly shown. Unfortunately, there is no indication in that final product as to how much the child learned, how much the child actually did, or how much struggle went into its completion. It is a final project that has no antecedents. Science fair projects, like showcase portfolios, have an additional limitation. By the time the science fair projects reach regional or state competitions, all of the projects displayed are of exceptionally high quality. It is very difficult to establish standards for evaluating the best of the best. This is also true of the showcase portfolio. The teacher is presented with the best of the child's best efforts and evaluation is difficult.

Documentation Portfolios.   **Documentation portfolios** document the entire learning process rather than simply the final result. The documentation portfolio is a systematic collection of information from rough draft to finished product. In this type of portfolio, the teacher has more input than the student into what is included in the portfolio but the student is not omitted from the selection process. The documentation portfolio is used to demonstrate the child's progress to parents and students. It may even be used in making placement decisions during the child's educational career.

Because the documentation portfolio includes not only finished products but also works in progress, the collection of material is large. One of the limitations of this type of portfolio is the sheer quantity of material included, with the concomitant problem of how to interpret that information. The second limitation lies in the workload of many teachers. With so much to do in a classroom, teachers are often less than systematic in their collection of information. Consequently, the portfolio may not have the necessary intermediate items that will allow for an accurate view of student progress over time.

Evaluation Portfolios.   The **evaluation portfolio** is closest in nature to traditional evaluation. The materials included are the result of preselected tasks that all students are required to complete. Students not only complete the same evaluations, but they are then judged according to predetermined criteria. In mathematics, all third graders may be evaluated at different times during the year on their knowledge of basic addition, subtraction, multiplication, and division facts. Each child's test paper is included in the evaluation portfolio. Students who receive a score of 90 percent or above are not required to repeat the assessments, while those scoring below that level do repeat the tasks until they reach the required evaluation level. The evaluation portfolio is dominated by tasks and activities that are predetermined by the teacher; the standards children are required to meet are often determined not by the teacher and students in collaboration but by school, district, or state mandates.

The evaluation portfolio as a method for assessment has the same limitations found in traditional assessment forms. In addition, two more limitations are inherent in the evaluation portfolio. First, it lacks authenticity. Rather than demonstrating the child's learning through his or her work, the evaluation portfolio divorces evaluation from learning. Second, the evaluation portfolio does not include items selected for inclusion by the student; consequently, the student feels no sense of ownership of the portfolio and its contents.

Process Portfolios.   The **process portfolio** is used to document work that is part of a larger project. Its purpose is to demonstrate the learning process a student engages in through the various projects that take place during the school year. The process portfolio differs from the demonstration portfolio in that the samples of work collected are always a part of a much larger final project. Returning to the analogy of the science fair project, the process portfolio would focus only on the project and documentation of how the child decided on the project, drafts of hypotheses and procedures that would be used to test those hypotheses, and design possibilities for the organization of the final project. In the process portfolio, the student selects the materials to be included in the portfolio and engages in a great deal of self-reflection on them. The process portfolio allows the teacher to assess student progress at intervals rather than continuously and so to individualize instruction to suit student needs.

The major limitations of the process portfolio fall into two areas. First, it is difficult to establish standards. Because the items included lead to a particular final project, the difficulty of establishing standards is related to the difficulty of evaluating intermediate efforts. Second, the items included in the portfolio are selected by the students. Therefore, there is no opportunity for other points of view to be included.

Of the four types of portfolios described here, probably the most appropriate to the integrated curriculum is the documentation portfolio. Through this type of portfolio the teacher is able to document the child's progress over a long period of time and to show through the collection of rough drafts and intermediate work as well as final products the degree of learning that has occurred. This type of portfolio is particularly helpful in discussing with parents the child's progress, as the teacher can demonstrate concretely the child's range of learning and total progress.

Although it is helpful to know the types of portfolios that exist, simply selecting a type of portfolio to adopt and deciding to use it in the classroom is not enough if the teacher is going to use portfolio assessment effectively.

BEGINNING TO USE PORTFOLIO ASSESSMENT

Once the decision has been made to use portfolio assessment, the teacher has a number of other decisions to make:

1. What is the purpose of the portfolio?
2. Which type of portfolio best suits this purpose?
3. Who is the audience for the portfolio?
4. What standards and criteria will be applied?
5. What format will the portfolio take?

PURPOSE

There are three basic purposes for the use of the portfolio. First, the portfolio can serve to document student growth and development; this is probably the most common purpose for using portfolios in the classroom. In essence, the portfolio is the means for evaluating student progress in the educational program. The second purpose of portfolios is as a means of enhancing and developing autonomous learning on the part of students. As students become more autonomous, they also develop a greater sense of ownership of the educational program. Although assessment is a part of this purpose for portfolio use, the major reason for keeping the portfolio is to have students reflect on their work and make decisions as to the direction and course of their learning. The third purpose for using portfolios in the classroom is to allow the teacher to reflect on instructional practices. In this way, the portfolio is not used to evaluate the growth of individual students, but rather to evaluate the overall program and to assist in making decisions.

None of these purposes are mutually exclusive, but they do have slightly different focuses and so the types of materials collected would be slightly different. For example, if the purpose of the portfolio is to document student learning, then samples of work in progress and completed work over a long time period will be needed, with student and teacher collaborating on the materials completed. If the purpose is to foster autonomous learning, then the items will be selected by the student with a view to demonstrating the independent learning and the decisions on how learning will occur. If the purpose is to make curricular decisions, then the documents collected will reflect the total program and emphasize both the breadth of content and the breadth of teaching strategies; the major influence in selecting the materials will come from the teacher.

TYPE OF PORTFOLIO

Once the purpose of the portfolio is determined, the type of portfolio is chosen. As most portfolio use in the classroom is geared toward documenting student progress, the most commonly selected type of portfolio is the *documentation portfolio.* However, if the purpose is to make curricular decisions, then standardized information from a variety of classes may be desired and the *evaluation portfolio* might be the better choice, or, if the desire is to show the curriculum in its best light, perhaps the *showcase portfolio* would be the most appropriate.

AUDIENCE

The third decision revolves around the audience for the portfolio. Who is to see the portfolio? Who is to use it? If the primary audience is the teacher, the student, and the parents, then the portfolio is going to include materials selected by both teacher and student, and, when possible, input from the parents. If the portfolio is to be used to demonstrate for the general public or for state or local educational officials the total school program and to focus on the quality of the program, then the items selected will focus more on the final products of the educational process. If the main audience is the child, then items selected for reflection and analysis by the student and teacher may be selected.

STANDARDS AND CRITERIA

Without a set of standards on which to base judgments and without criteria to elucidate those standards, the portfolio is simply a collection of items. The first decision about standards and criteria is a broad decision: Will the portfolio be quantitative or qualitative?

Quantitative portfolios are based on the quantity of items included. This does not mean that the child with the thickest portfolio gets the highest grade, but rather that the child has included all of the items required. In general, the child is provided with a list of the required materials and checks off each item as it is placed in the portfolio. The student is, in essence, evaluated on the completeness of the portfolio. The **qualitative portfolio**, on the other hand, is based on the quality of the items rather than on simply the presence of the items. In this case it is necessary to develop standards by which the items in the portfolio will be evaluated.

Standards for portfolio evaluation are established by the teacher and the students working in collaboration. The general pattern for the standards used in the portfolio is in the form of a **rubric**. Rubrics are simply sets of criteria which students see prior to the start of a task or activity. Rubrics may be either **analytic** or **holistic**. When a holistic rubric is used, the total piece of work is judged for such things as overall organization, creativity, and expression of ideas. This type of evaluation is often applied to art projects, where it is the overall effect of the project that is important rather than specific aspects. When specifics are to be judged, an analytic rubric is generally used. It usually has three to six categories of response, and each category has certain descriptors that allow the rubric to be applied consistently. For example, using an analytic rubric to evaluate a science activity, the rubric may read:

1. *Excellent Achievement:* Develops and tests a hypothesis with all variables controlled.
2. *Above Average Achievement:* Develops a hypothesis and a procedure to control identified variables, but some variables are not identified.
3. *Average Achievement:* Develops a hypothesis but only some variables are identified and controlled in the experimental design.
4. *Below Average Achievement:* Develops a hypothesis but is unable to control factors in developing the experiment.
5. *No Response:* Unable to write a hypothesis or develop an experimental procedure.

In evaluating portfolio items, both types of rubrics are often applied to the same piece of work and two scores are given. In the example of the art project, the holistic rubric might be used to judge the overall effect of a painting, while an analytic rubric might be used to judge the use of perspective, or color, or line in the painting.

FORMAT

One of the biggest problems teachers have in the classroom is space. Consequently, it is important to decide what shape the portfolio will take. Looseleaf notebooks, expandable files, artist's portfolio folders, even boxes have been used for portfolios. If the major component of the portfolio is paper, then a notebook or expandable folder may be sufficient. If larger objects are to be included, then boxes may be necessary. The teacher needs to make a decision as to how much space can legitimately be devoted to the storage of portfolios. This becomes a major problem if the portfolios are used as a cumulative record over the course of the child's elementary school education.

A technological alternative to the notebook or box portfolio is a *laser disk portfolio* in which the contents of the paper portfolio are transferred to a single laser disk. The laser disk can be used to record anything from scanned images of a student's written work to videotapes of the student reading aloud, working in a cooperative group, or creating a mural. Large amounts of data can be added to or retrieved from a disk with great ease. The disk itself, however, is so small that it can be stored with far more ease and efficiency than can a paper portfolio. The use of computer technology can allow for the development of a truly cumulative record that is also easy to handle, store, and update over many years of schooling.

CONSTRUCTING THE PORTFOLIO

Since one of the purposes of the portfolio is to show growth over a period of time, the portfolio must be developed over a long period and demonstrate not a single theme but a broad range of themes. The portfolio should show the child's growth over a school year and should contain information that can be used by the teacher in the next grade and built upon in subsequent grades to show the child. The best portfolios will not only reflect a long period of development but will also include a wide variety of types of work. The kinds of materials that can be represented in the portfolio include, but are not limited to, the following.

WORK SAMPLES

Samples of student work should form the bulk of the portfolio. These include writing samples, both rough drafts and finished products; drawings; photographs of projects, including photos of students at work on those projects and of the finished project; photographs of students working in heterogeneous, homogeneous, or cooperative groups; copies of reports, papers, and journal pages; and tape recordings or videotapes of students reading or presenting their work. In a documentation portfolio, work samples should include not only finished products but works in progress so that original copy, editings, and final products are all represented. In a showcase portfolio, only finished products of the highest quality will be included.

SYSTEMATIC OBSERVATIONS

During group discussions and problem-solving activities as well as during project work, observations made by the teacher using checklists and rating scales can provide a record of the children's accomplishments, particularly with respect to group interaction, group problem solving, and social activity. In order to assure the accuracy of the observations, teachers should make and record their observations while the child works. It is important that the teacher be as discreet as possible in making observations so that children do not change their behavior patterns as the result of teacher behavior. Going to the desk, getting a clipboard, and beginning to make notes is going to alert the children to the fact that they are being observed; no longer will the behavior be an accurate reflection of the child's work. In addition to using discretion, the teacher should make observations at various times during the day, in various settings, and over a long period of time. This will allow the widest possible picture of the child's behavior in the classroom. **Checklists** are one way of assuring that observations will be systematic.

The use of checklists is in part determined by the grade level of the children being evaluated. Teachers of kindergarten and primary grade children may use checklists more frequently than teachers at the intermediate grades. At the kindergarten level, the checklist will be of particular importance. Because kindergarten children are not yet able to record ideas effectively in written or drawn form, the teacher will want some way to determine how a child reacts to a particular type of activity or investigation. The checklist is based on teacher observation, but is standardized so that the same items can be observed over a period of time, thus demonstrating a child's progress in particular areas. In using a checklist, the teacher lists the items that are most likely to be demonstrated in the situation and then uses the checklist to systematically observe the child's progress toward those items. See Figure 11.1 for an example of a checklist.

FIGURE 11.1 Preschool-kindergarten checklist

CHILD'S NAME:

ACTIVITY:

Place a check next to each item observed beneath the date of the observation.

DATE:

1. Planning
   a. Helped to identify problem
   b. Helped to define problem
   c. Helped to determine how to solve the identified problem
2. Participation
   a. Worked with small group
   b. Worked with one other child
   c. Worked alone
   d. Left the activity without participating
   e. Developed alternative activity dealing with problem
   f. Developed alternative activity unrelated to problem
3. Discussion
   a. Contributed to discussion of the activity
   b. Listened to the discussion of the activity
   c. Did not participate in the discussion of the activity

At the primary grades, checklists are not as important in the assessment of children as they are at the kindergarten level. First, second, and third grade children are making great strides in literacy, documented best through samples of their written work. However, it should be remembered that primary grade children, like kindergarten children, are likely to be preoperational in developmental level and will not yet use symbols effectively in all situations. Checklists can provide supplemental information for the portfolio. Once again, the checklist should be used over a period of time to show progress toward those items identified as important in certain activities or projects.

For children at the intermediate grade levels, checklists are no longer necessary for basic evaluation. At this level, children can provide far more appropriate indications of learning than can be demonstrated by teacher observation. There are, however, three instances where the checklist remains a vital part of the evaluation procedure. First, the checklist can be used to evaluate the mechanics and format for a written report or paper. The checklist can help the teacher determine how well a sixth grader is able to follow the standard format for writing a research paper and how his or her skill in writing such

FIGURE 11.2   Checklist for evaluating a research paper

CHILD'S NAME:

AREA: TITLE OF PAPER:

1. Topic
   a. Topic is appropriate to the unit of study
   b. Topic is well-defined
   c. Topic is clearly stated
2. Writing Style and Mechanics
   a. Full sentences are used
   b. Punctuation is accurate
   c. Grammar is accurate
   d. Spelling is accurate
   e. Paragraphs are used appropriately
   f. Sentences are well written
   g. Entire paper communicates clearly
   h. Paper is written in student's words
3. Content and Presentation
   a. Content is accurate
   b. Paper is consistently on the topic
   c. Paper does not show bias in content
   d. Paper is neatly done
   e. Illustrations are used to clarify content
4. References
   a. One outside reference
   b. More than one outside reference
   c. Textbook used as only reference
   d. Encyclopedia used as only reference

Additional Comments:

CHILD'S NAME:

AREA: DATE OF ASSESSMENT:

1. Distinguishes between fact and opinion
2. Distinguishes between facts and value statements
3. Distinguishes relevant from irrelevant information
4. Checks on factual accuracy of information
5. Asks for supporting evidence for arguments or claims
6. Supports own statements with information
7. Identifies bias in statement or text
8. Identifies errors in logical reasoning
9. Reasons logically
10. Determines when a problem exists
11. Develops a plan for solving a problem
12. Determines whether a source of information is credible
13. Uses credible sources of information

FIGURE 11.3 Thinking skills checklist

papers develops over time. The second appropriate use of a checklist at the intermediate grades is in evaluating growth in the use of thinking skills. Finally, checklists can be used in evaluating group projects. These should allow for evaluation of both the process used by the group and the final project. Naturally, children should be made aware from the beginning of group project work that they will be observed to see how well their group works as well as how well they develop their final project. See Figures 11.2 and 11.3 for examples of a checklist to evaluate a research paper and a checklist to evaluate use of thinking skills.

CONSTRUCTING APPROPRIATE EVALUATIONS FOR THE CLASSROOM

CONSTRUCTING A CHECKLIST

The first consideration in constructing a checklist for use in the classroom is its purpose. Checklists are used to standardize observations, so the teacher must decide what to observe. Is the purpose of the observation to see how well young children interact with one another? Is the purpose of the observation to determine the accuracy of the mural developed by a third grade class to show the history of their town? Is the checklist to determine how effectively sixth graders are able to use semantic or network mapping strategies in reviewing information before a test? Determining the exact purpose of the checklist allows the teacher to focus on that purpose for the evaluation and usually results in the deletion of extraneous items from the list.

Once the purpose of the list has been determined, the second step is to analyze the process or product that is to be evaluated to determine its major aspects. For example, a teacher using a checklist to evaluate the accuracy of a relief map of Eurasia made by fifth grade students would focus on accuracy within the checklist rather than on cooperation among the students developing the map or neatness of the final product. If cooperation is a major goal of the project, then the purpose of the checklist should be extended to include cooperation.

The next step in the development of the checklist is to analyze the task to be evaluated, breaking the task into components that can easily be observed. For example, the task analysis for the relief map of Eurasia might include the following items:

1. Outline of European continent is accurate
2. Map should include the Alps, Pyrenees, and Ural mountains
3. Map should correctly locate the Alps, Pyrenees, and Ural mountains
4. Map should show the Loire, Seine, and Rhine rivers
5. Map should accurately place the Loire, Seine, and Rhine river systems
6. Map should show the boundaries of the European nations
7. Map should correctly locate each of the European nations
8. Map should clearly show the varying elevations of the European continent through the thickness of the map's medium

Once the task has been analyzed into its components, the final step is to organize the checklist itself. The final checklist is shown in Figure 11.4 on p. 308.

ANECDOTAL RECORDS

Anecdotal records, particularly for younger children, should be included in the portfolio. Once again, these should be recordings of factual, nonjudgmental observations of a child participating in an activity or lesson. Anecdotal records can be especially effective in documenting how a child interacts with other children during group activities or in documenting the child's spontaneous questions, researches, and investigations.

The anecdotal record relies on the observation of the teacher to gain information, but rather than consider the lesson as a whole, the teacher focuses on specific children.

In developing an anecdotal record it is important for the teacher to record observations rather than inferences based on the observations. This distinction between an observation and an inference is an important one. Observations are descriptions of the child's behavior at a particular time. Inferences are interpretations of that behavior, often assumptions of the meaning of the child's behavior. For example, a valid observation of a kindergarten child would state:

1. Outline Eurasian continent
   a. Outline is accurate
   b. Outline is partially accurate
   c. Outline is inaccurate
   d. Outline has no resemblance to Eurasian continent
2. Inclusion of the Alps, Pyrenees, and Urals
   a. Map shows all three mountain ranges
   b. Map shows two of three mountain ranges
   c. Map shows one of three mountain ranges
   d. Map does not show any mountain ranges
3. Accurate location of the Alps, Pyrenees, and Ural mountain ranges
   a. Map shows all three mountain ranges accurately
   b. Map shows two of three mountain ranges accurately
   c. Map shows one of three mountain ranges accurately
   d. Map does not show any mountain ranges accurately
4. Demonstration of the Loire, Seine, and Rhine rivers
   a. Map shows all three river systems
   b. Map shows two of three river systems
   c. Map shows one of three river systems
   d. Map does not show any river systems
5. Accurate placement of the Loire, Seine, and Rhine river systems
   a. Map shows all three river systems accurately
   b. Map shows two of three river systems accurately
   c. Map shows one of three river systems accurately
   d. Map does not show any river systems accurately
6. Map shows the boundaries of the European nations
   a. Map shows all nations
   b. Map shows some nations
   c. Map shows no national boundaries
7. Map correctly locates each of the European nations
   a. Map accurately shows all nations
   b. Map accurately shows some nations
   c. Map shows no accurate national boundaries
8. Map clearly shows the varying elevations of the European continent through the thickness of the map's medium
   a. Map demonstrates various elevations through thickness
   b. Map demonstrates some differences in elevation through thickness
   c. Map shows no variations in elevation

FIGURE 11.4 Checklist for evaluating a project

Joanne sat in the reading corner looking at the picture books for 20 minutes. When Kevin joined her she showed him the book *The Hungry Caterpillar* and told a story to go along with the pictures.

This statement indicates how much time Joanne spent looking at books and how she reacted to the arrival of Kevin in the reading corner.

On the other hand, a teacher might make the statement:

Joanne enjoyed looking at picture books and liked telling a story to Kevin about the pictures in *The Hungry Caterpillar.*

A child who passes 20 minutes looking at books in the reading corner probably did enjoy it, but she could have stayed in the reading corner for that length of time because she saw nothing more interesting, because the other areas of the room were crowded, or even because she did not feel well and the quiet center was a refuge for her. As for enjoying telling Kevin the story, she may have enjoyed doing it or she simply may have acquiesced to Kevin's request for a story.

In keeping anecdotal records, the teacher should take care to write objectively. The interpretation of anecdotal records is a second aspect of record keeping, and interpretation should be based on fact.

RUBRICS

Rubrics can be included in the portfolio when a behavior has several different aspects or components. Each behavior is rated on a continuum from the lowest to the highest level and is assessed at certain points along the scale. Three to six points along the scale are defined and descriptors are written so that assessment can be standardized. Rubrics are most effective if used with similar types of work over a period of time and if attached to the work sample so that the progress can be documented. Figure 11.5 shows a rubric for a mural.

FIGURE 11.5   Rubric for evaluation of a mural

1 Outstanding
Mural shows a high level of artistic quality using a wide variety of media and presents the subject matter with accuracy. The mural shows a high level of creativity. The artistic aspects and the subject matter hold equal roles.

2 Proficient
Mural shows more than average artistic quality using a limited variety of media. The subject matter is shown accurately but the artistic aspects of the mural are of greater importance than the subject matter. Some creativity is shown in the presentation.

3 Satisfactory
Mural shows average artistic quality using only a single medium. The subject matter is partially accurate. The artistic aspects of the mural are of far greater importance than the content accuracy. Limited evidence of creativity is shown.

4 Needs Improvement
Mural is lacking in artistic quality. Content shown is inaccurate. No evidence of creativity is shown.

TESTS AND QUIZZES

Teacher-constructed tests and quizzes can be included as a component of the total portfolio. These traditional forms of evaluation, however, should not become the only items in the portfolio or even the predominant items in the portfolio. They are a measure of only one aspect of a child's progress and should be treated as such. If children are learning in cooperative groups, the test taken by those groups can be included. Also included should be reflection on those tests by the members of cooperative groups, as these reflections can provide feedback about the contributions of individuals to the test items. If evaluation is to be authentic, then tests and quizzes make up a less than appropriate inclusion in the portfolio.

PEER REVIEWS

As students progress through the grades, they should become more able to listen to and provide feedback to their peers. When students give reports, peers can provide written reviews of the reports. When students work in heterogeneous, homogeneous, or cooperative groups, the children can reflect on and review not only the work done by individuals within the group but also the work of the group as a whole.

GROUP REPORTS AND PROJECTS

Students working in groups, whether cooperative or otherwise, often produce group reports or group projects. If the product of the group's work is a written document, copies can be placed in each member's portfolio. The inclusion of a group report will be most helpful if it is accompanied by peer reviews that discuss the work of individual and group members while working on the report. If a project is the result of the group work, then photographs or tapes of the project can be most effective in documenting the work.

COMPUTER PRINTOUTS

For students who use computer technology in the classroom, examples of their work and of their work in progress as documented by computer printouts should be included in the portfolio.

STUDENT REFLECTIONS ON THEIR WORK

The development of the portfolio is accomplished through joint participation of the student and the teacher. As a part of this development, the student should have the opportunity to review the examples of work included in the portfolio and to reflect on the work. This reflection should result in another component of the portfolio. Students should be encouraged to develop an ability to self-assess. For the young child, this may simply be a comment that one picture is better than another or that one written story is better than another. Also effective for young children is an interview in which the child talks about his or her work;

the record of that interview is then included in the portfolio. For the older student, the self-assessment should ask the child to indicate why he or she views one piece of work as better than another. Additionally, the child should have the opportunity to comment on work that is not successful and to comment on why it is unsuccessful.

VIDEOTAPES AND AUDIOTAPES

Some types of projects involving performance, such as plays, musical productions, or other visual presentations, will not lend themselves to static products. When such activities are a part of the work of students the use of audio or video recordings can provide a record of both product and process. A play or skit can be recorded visually, from the selection of actors through the rehearsal process and to the final production.

PHOTOGRAPHS

Many kinds of integrated curriculum activities involve group work. Photographs of children at work can help to document the work of groups and the work of individual children in groups. In addition, photographs can provide a record of field trips and of final products that may be too large to include in the portfolio.

When most effective, the portfolio is an ongoing assessment of the child's progress that develops continuously over the child's school career. It is a record of the child's growth from topic to topic, project to project, year to year. It is the ultimate in cumulative records for the child's educational career.

USING THE PORTFOLIO IN EVALUATION

The portfolio, unlike traditional forms of evaluation, can be used not only to determine student achievement and communicate that to parents, but also to evaluate the effectiveness of teaching strategies and the total integrated curriculum. In the latter cases, the portfolio gives the teacher an opportunity to view the results of his or her teaching, to see if it was effective or ineffective. Because the portfolio is a longitudinal record, it gives an opportunity to assess the development of research skills, group work skills, and thinking skills over time. It gives an opportunity to assess the effectiveness of the activities and procedures selected for teaching in terms of the effect of those procedures and activities on student learning. This ability to evaluate the success of teaching strategies and activities results in more reflective thinking on the part of the teacher and in a greater likelihood that the teacher will become aware of needed changes in presentation of a unit of work.

The portfolio is also used to evaluate the achievement of an individual child. The most appropriate use of the portfolio is in making comparisons between the student's current work and his or her earlier work. It is generally inappropriate to use the portfolio to compare one child to another. However, such comparisons may be used in special cases, as when a child has been recommended for placement in a program for gifted students or referred for placement in a remedial situation. In this case, comparison of portfolios may add strength to the recommendation or referral.

In order to assess the child the teacher should look at the examples of work in the portfolio and note areas of strong progress and areas of little or no progress. The teacher should then use checklists and anecdotal records along with the work samples to determine whether the child is participating fully in activities that will allow for strengthening of the areas of demonstrated weakness. It is important that the teacher be systematic in his or her observation of students. If the teacher determines that the child is participating in classroom activities that address the areas of weakness, then the teacher might use systematic observation of the child during those activities as well as interviews with the child to determine why there are difficulties. If the child is not participating in activities that will strengthen areas of weakness, then the teacher needs to encourage such participation. At times, the teacher will discover areas of weakness on the part of a student that are not being addressed by the current grade level program. When this is the case, the teacher may wish to develop some independent projects for the child so that he or she can develop in a particular area. When areas of weakness are found among children from culturally different backgrounds, the teacher should develop materials and projects that are culturally appropriate as well as a means of remediating areas of difficulty. And when there is weakness in an area among the majority of class members, the teacher needs to assess his or her teaching strategies in that area in order to develop more appropriate and effective methods of teaching. It may also be necessary for the teacher to develop remedial teaching materials that will allow the children to develop those skills and concepts that are lacking.

The teacher should not only evaluate the portfolio for his or her own benefit, but should also discuss the work in the portfolio with the child. Children benefit from reviewing work they have done over a long period of time. It gives them a chance to see how much they have learned, to receive praise for their accomplishments, and to develop an understanding of why certain areas are being emphasized in current work. Children need to know why they are being asked to perform certain tasks, particularly when those tasks are remedial in nature.

Of course, the teacher should discuss the portfolio with the parents as a means of demonstrating the child's learning over a period of time. The first task in portfolio assessment with parents is to be certain they understand the use of the portfolio in assessment. Most parents are not familiar with the idea of a portfolio, and their concept of assessment is likely to be grades, tests, and passing or failing. Parents will need to be educated in the use of a portfolio. When discussing the portfolio with parents, the teacher should use the work samples to demonstrate areas of strength, areas of weakness, and progress over time. The samples of work should be discussed so that parents understand the purpose of the activity within the program, the strengths and weaknesses shown in the work samples, and the reasons the teacher has for indicating that growth in a particular area is showing strength or weakness. The work samples should also be shown to the parents within the context of the goals and objectives of the integrated curriculum. For example, if a goal of the program is to develop in children an understanding of the multicultural nature of their own community, then parents should be told that goal and then shown examples of work that contribute to that goal.

When presenting the assessment portfolio to parents, the portfolio's contents should not be used to compare one child to another. The purpose of the portfolio is to demonstrate an individual child's growth in the program over time. The purpose of the portfolio is not to demonstrate that one child is progressing faster or slower than another child in the program.

Besides being useful to the current teacher and the parents of the child, the contents of the portfolio should be discussed with the teacher who will have the child at the next grade level. The child's portfolio can be used to demonstrate effectively the achievement and progress made at the current grade level and can assist the teacher at the next grade level in developing appropriate learning materials for the child. If used appropriately, the portfolio can add yet another dimension to the planning from one grade level to another and can enhance the cohesiveness of the total school program. When the portfolio is used appropriately, it will be added to continuously as the child progresses through school.

SUMMARY

The integrated curriculum is based on the concept of authenticity in learning. Children develop and complete a variety of projects during which they often pursue topics of interest to themselves and so of their own choosing. Consequently, the type of assessment used in the integrated curriculum should also be authentic and as such should reflect what it is that the children have accomplished.

Portfolios are the primary method of providing authenticity in assessment. Portfolios are more appropriate to the integrated curriculum than traditional forms of assessment because they provide samples of the child's work in progress and the finished product, rather than artificially constructed tests of information.

To use the portfolio, the teacher must first decide its purpose, then what type of portfolio to use. For the classroom and the integrated curriculum, the most common type of portfolio in use is the documentation portfolio. Once the type of portfolio is selected, the teacher then determines who will view the portfolio: other children, parents, other teachers, administrators, and/or the public. The purpose of the portfolio is, of course, to assess student progress; consequently, the next step in the use of portfolios is determining the standards for its assessment. In this case rubrics are often helpful. Finally, the teacher needs to determine the form of the portfolio: notebook, expanding folder, file, and/or box.

ACTIVITY ONE

PURPOSE

The purpose of this activity is to present a panel discussion among individuals favoring traditional forms of assessment and individuals favoring authentic means of assessment.

PROCEDURE

1. At least a week prior to the discussion, three persons should be selected to represent each side in the discussion and a moderator should also be chosen. Those persons presenting each side in the discussion should research their position before participating in the discussion itself.
2. The others in the class will form the audience.
3. The discussion should proceed according to the following:
   a. One person from each side presents the main arguments for his or her side. Only ten minutes should be allowed for each side's presentation.
   b. Once the presentations have been made, the members of the panel are permitted to ask questions of the other side.
   c. When the panel members have finished with their questions, audience members may also ask questions of the panel members.
   d. The moderator is present to ensure that the groups maintain their time limits, to ensure each side speaks, and to call on audience members for questions.

ACTIVITY TWO

PURPOSE

The purpose of this activity is to prepare a position paper to convince proponents of traditional assessment forms that the portfolio is a more appropriate form of assessment for an integrated approach to curriculum.

PROCEDURE

1. Your school system has decided to use portfolio-based assessment rather than traditional forms of evaluation. However, your school board is opposed to such a change, saying it will lower standards in the schools. You have been asked to appear before the school board to present an argument that will change their opposition to support.

2. Write the paper you will present to the board. You have only fifteen minutes in which to speak, so your arguments must be clear, concise, and compelling.

ACTIVITY THREE

PURPOSE

The purpose of this activity is to prepare and use an anecdotal record, a checklist, and a rubric in assessing a lesson or project.

PROCEDURE

1. Select an activity appropriate to the integrated curriculum. This may be a specific lesson or a project.
2. Prepare a checklist to evaluate the lesson or project, then prepare a rubric to evaluate the same lesson or project.
3. While the students are participating in the lesson or working on the project, make an anecdotal record of the actions and reactions of five of the children.
4. Use the checklist to evaluate the lesson or project, then use the rubric to evaluate the lesson or project for the same five children.
5. Compare the results for each of the means of assessment used. Which form of assessment gave the most valuable information in this particular setting?
6. Critique the checklist and the rubric. Make any changes needed to make it a more valuable and appropriate form of assessment.

ACTIVITY FOUR

PURPOSE

The purpose of this activity is to prepare appropriate forms of assessment for a resource unit.

PROCEDURE

1. Return to the resource unit developed in Chapter 9.
2. Review the resource unit, including the student input.
3. Develop appropriate forms of evaluation for the resource unit, including in your evaluation:
   a. appropriate uses of anecdotal records
   b. checklists for assessing lessons or projects

    c. rubrics necessary for assessing or projects

    d. suggestions for other appropriate kinds of assessments for the unit: tests or quizzes, group reports or projects, video or audio tapes, computer work, photographs, etc.

STUDY QUESTIONS

1. What is meant by the terms *traditional assessment* and *authentic assessment*? How do these two forms of assessment differ from one another?
2. Why is authentic assessment more appropriate to the integrated curriculum than traditional assessment?
3. What is portfolio assessment? How is it used in the integrated curriculum?
4. Compare and contrast the four types of portfolios. Where would each type be most appropriately used within the integrated curriculum?
5. You are a teacher who has decided to begin using portfolio assessment in the classroom. What decisions will you have to make prior to beginning the use of portfolios?
6. Develop a checklist to evaluate a project completed in an integrated program.
7. What kinds of materials could be included in a portfolio? How would you decide which materials would be included in a particular child's portfolio?
8. How does a checklist differ from a rubric? Develop a rubric to evaluate a project completed in an integrated program.
9. How should portfolios be used in assessing the integrated curriculum?

BIBLIOGRAPHY

Campbell, J. (1992). Laser disk portfolios: Total child assessment. *Educational Leadership, 49,* 69–70.

Collins, A. (1992). Portfolios for science education: Issues in purpose, structure, and authenticity. *Science Education, 76,* 451–463.

Correro, G. (1988). Understanding assessment in young children. *Developing Instructional Programs K-3.* Jackson, Miss.: Mississippi Department of Education.

Dorr-Bremme, D. W. (1983). Assessing students: Teachers' routine practices and reasoning. *Evaluation Comment, 6,* UCLA Center for the Study of Evaluation.

Engle, B. (1990). An approach to assessment in early grades. In C. Kamii (Ed.), *Achievement testing in the early grades: The games grown-ups play.* Washington, D.C.: National Association for the Education of Young Children.

Farnan, N., & Kelly, P. (1991). Keeping track: Creating assessment portfolios in reading and writing. *Reading, Writing, and Learning Disabilities, 7,* 255–269.

Goodman, K. S., Bird, L. B., & Goodman, Y. M. (1992). *The whole language catalog supplement on authentic assessment.* New York: Macmillan.

Goodman, Y. (1991). Informal methods of evaluation. In J. Flood, J. Jensen, D. Lapp, & J. Squire (Eds.), *Handbook on research on the teaching of the English language arts.* New York: Macmillan.

Grace, C., & Shores, E. F. (1992). *The portfolio and its use: Developmentally appropriate assessment of young children.* Little Rock, Ark.: Southern Association of Children under Six.

Graham, B. (1993). *New directions in portfolio assessment: Assessing the assessors.* Report No. 143. Winnipeg, Canada. ERIC Document Reproduction Service No. ED 355 537.

Haney, W., & Madus, G. (May, 1989). Searching for alternatives to standardized tests. *Phi Delta Kappan,* 684.

Harp, B. (Ed.). (1993) *Assessment and evaluation in whole language programs.* Norwood, Mass.: Christopher-Gordon Publishers.

Hart, D. (1994). *Authentic assessment: A handbook for educators.* Menlo Park, Calif.: Addison-Wesley.

Herman, J. L., Aschbacher, P. R., & Winters, L. (1992). *A practical guide to alternative assessment.* Alexandria, Va.: Association for Supervision and Curriculum Development.

Jasmine, J. (1993). *Portfolios and other assessments.* Westminister, Calif.: Teacher Created Materials.

Jasmine, J. (1994). *Middle school assessment.* Westminister, Calif.: Teacher Created Materials.

Johnson, P. H. (1993). Assessment and literate "development." *The Reading Teacher, 42,* 264-265.

Maeroff, G. I. (December, 1991). Assessing alternative assessment. *Phi Delta Kappan, 278.*

National Association for the Education of Young Children. (1988). *Statement on standardized testing of young children 3 through 8 years of age.* Washington, D.C.: National Association for the Education of Young Children.

National Association for the Education of Young Children and Early Childhood Specialists in Departments of Education. (1987). *Guidelines for appropriate curriculum content and assessment in programs serving children age 3 through 8.* Washington, D.C.: National Association for the Education of Young Children.

Paulson, F. L., Paulson, P. R., & Meyer, C. A. (1991). What makes a portfolio a portfolio. *Educational Leadership, 48,* 802-806.

Paulson, P. R., & Paulson, F. L. (1991). Portfolios: Stories of knowing. In P. Dreyer (Ed.), *Knowing: The power of stories.* Claremont, Calif.: Claremont Reading Conference.

Perrone, V. (Ed.). (1991). *Expanding student assessment.* Alexandria, Va.: Association for Supervision and Curriculum Development.

Ryan, C. D. (1994). *Authentic assessment.* Westminister, Calif.: Teacher Created Materials.

Seely, A. E. (1994). *Portfolio assessment.* Westminster, Calif.: Teacher Created Materials.

Smith, J. (1994). Standardized testing vs. authentic assessment: Godzilla meets Winnie the Pooh. In L. Morrow, J. Smith, & L. C. Wilkinson (Eds.), *Integrated language arts: Controversy to consensus.* Boston: Allyn and Bacon.

Southern Association on Children under Six. (1990). *Developmentally appropriate assessment.* Little Rock, Ark.: Southern Association on Children under Six.

Tiernet, R. J., & Desai, L. E. (1991). *Portfolio assessment in the reading-writing classroom.* Norwood, Mass.: Christopher-Gordon Publishers.

Tippins, D. J., & Dana, N. F. (March, 1992). Culturally relevant alternative assessment. *Science Scope,* 51.

Valencia, S. (1990). A portfolio approach to classroom reading assessment: The whys, whats, and hows. *The Reading Teacher, 43,* 338-340.

Valencia, S., & Calfee, R. (1991). The development and use of literacy portfolios for students, classes, and teachers. *Applied Measurement in Education, 4,* 333-345.

Wolf, D., LeMahieu, P., & Erish, J. (1992). Good measure: Assessment as a tool for educational reform. *Educational Leadership, 49* (8), 8-13.

Wolf, D. P. (1989). Portfolio assessment: Sampling student work. *Educational Leadership, 46,* 36-38.

CHAPTER 12

ASSESSING TEACHER
EFFECTIVENESS

CHAPTER OBJECTIVES

After reading this chapter you should be able to:

1. Describe some benefits of teacher evaluation
2. Characterize the assessment in terms of processes and focuses
3. Describe important teacher attributes in the evaluation process
4. Depict elements that denote teacher competence in evaluation
5. Describe important observer attributes
6. Explain the clinical supervision model
7. Describe ideal supervisory behavior

BENEFITS OF TEACHER EVALUATION

Performance appraisal presents both opportunities and obstacles for the teacher seeking to grow into the role of a teacher-as-facilitator through curriculum integration. The public believes that school systems should recognize effective teachers and retrain or dismiss ineffective teachers. Public funds are increasingly linked to some form of quality control and thus teacher evaluation. Box 12.1 presents some of the benefits derived from teacher evaluation.

Teacher evaluation serves to improve teaching and learning in the classroom. However, there is another context for teacher evaluation and that is for the purpose of accountability. This accountability purpose is a legal context to help

---

Box 12.1 Benefits of Teacher Evaluation

- Improved communication between administration and teachers
- Improved consensus on instructional goals and school goals
- Enhanced teacher competence, confidence, morale, and professionalism
- A firmer basis for personnel decisions and actions
- Increased public confidence in the schools
- Opportunities for better relations between school districts and teacher organizations

---

Box 12.2 Assessment Processes

- Specifying what is expected or desired in the teaching performance
- Gathering evidence on the specifications
- Formulating judgments and reaching decisions

Box 12.3 Assessment Focuses

- Teacher competency
- Teacher performance
- Teacher effectiveness

Box 12.4 Sources of Evidence

- Interviews with the teacher
- Observations in the classroom
- Achievement of students
- Teacher-made products for teaching

is put on fair and uniform procedures rather than the more individually designed strategies of evaluation to improve teaching and learning. Box 12.2 shows three closely related assessment processes.

The performance appraisal of teachers depends on the purposes of the evaluation as well as on the administrative philosophy of the school system. In any event, appraisal almost always concentrates on the focal points in Box 12.3, with a much heavier concentration on performance and effectiveness and less emphasis on competency.

Two elements of teacher appraisal are gathering evidence and formulating judgments. Box 12.4 presents the major options available for the sources of evidence in teacher appraisal.

DEVELOPMENTAL SUPERVISION

The ultimate aim of most supervisors is for teachers to become reflective about teaching and learning, allowing them to become increasingly autonomous. If possible, the modern supervisor wants to facilitate the autonomous development of teachers through nondirective supervisory techniques. However, because many teachers are functioning at entry and developmental levels of teaching and are incapable of realistic self-direction, the supervisor may not function in a nondirective capacity. Initially, perhaps, the supervisor will use collaborative or directive informational supervisory behaviors to move the teacher toward self-direction. In rare instances, the supervisor may resort to direct control behaviors in order to move the teacher along. In any event, the initial supervisory approach is based on individual situations and the teacher's level of development and expertise.

Glickman, Gordon, and Ross-Gordon (1995) indicate that, ideally, the practice of supervision today should be eclectic, with the ultimate objective of returning control to teachers so that they may decide collectively on instructional improvement. While such ideal supervisory behaviors are often unrealized, the movement from supervision as collaborative experimentalism to supervision as nondirective existentialism is worthy of pursuit. Supervisory practices, in other words, should always strive to shift control to the teachers. Supervisory practices that are directive, collaborative, and nondirective are all valid if they propose shifting control to teachers. In this regard, supervisors should use a variety of practices emanating from various philosophies as long as they result in more teacher self-control. Increased teacher autonomy results in teachers becoming more reflective, altruistic, and committed to improvement. Glickman, Gordon, and Ross-Gordon (1995) make the following key points regarding supervision:

- All participants in instructional improvement efforts have knowledge to contribute to the supervisory process.
- Supervision should engage participants in reflective inquiry leading to professional growth and renewal.

- Successful supervision produces organizational growth through a synergy of individual and group efforts.
- Successful supervision fosters both common purpose and alternative means to contribute to that purpose; effective supervision recognizes teacher and student diversity.
- Successful supervision integrates various supervision functions into a comprehensive whole.
- Successful supervision is a long-term process; it balances the importance of completing the immediate task with the need to maintain positive long-term interpersonal relationships.
- Successful supervision is built on trust, openness, and mutual respect.
- Successful supervision creates an environment conducive to experimentation and risk taking.
- Successful supervision adapts to changing contexts and cultures within and outside of the school.
- Successful supervision fosters a critical examination of educators' beliefs about teaching and learning as well as movement toward congruence of beliefs and practice.
- Successful supervision requires a wide range of knowledge as well as technical and interpersonal skills.
- Successful supervision takes into consideration principles of adult learning and knowledge about adult and teacher development. (pp. 102–103)

CLINICAL SUPERVISION

There are, of course, many ways of observing teachers, but the model for executing observations is comparatively standard and accepted, and has a respectable base in research (Sullivan, 1980; Adams & Glickman, 1984; Pavan, 1985; Nolan, Hawkes, & Francis, 1993). **Clinical supervision** provides, in both concept and structure, a model for supervision that provides for:

- instructional improvement
- deliberate intervention into the instructional process
- an orientation to both personal and school goals
- an assumption of a professional working relationship between teacher and supervisor
- a high degree of mutual trust
- a systematic yet flexible and changeable approach that bridges the gap between the real and the ideal
- an assumption that the supervisor is knowledgeable about the analysis of teaching and learning
- a requirement for continuous inservice on effective approaches.

Supervision experts have defined clinical supervision in various ways. Upon examination, however, the experts' definitions tend to have several common elements: gathering classroom data, observing the teaching act, and improving teaching. Morris Cogan (1973), clinical supervision's developing pioneer, defined clinical supervision as

> the rationale and practice designed to improve the teacher's classroom performance. It takes its principal data from the events of the classroom. The analysis of these data and the relationship between the teacher and supervisor form the basis of the program, procedures, and strategies designed to improve the students' learning by improving the teacher's classroom behavior. (p. 9)

In rather similar fashion, Sergiovanni and Starratt (1988) write that clinical supervision

> refers to face-to-face contact with teachers with the intent of improving instruction and increasing professional growth. In many respects, a one-to-one correspondence exists between improving classroom instruction and increasing professional growth, and for this reason staff development and clinical supervision are inseparable concepts and activities. (p. 304)

Acheson and Gall (1987) have a similar definition of clinical supervision:

> Clinical supervision has as its goal the professional development of teachers, with an emphasis on improving teachers' classroom performance. It is supervision to help the teacher improve his or her instructional performance. (pp. 1, 11)

Presenting the same general concept but with a different twist to the definition, Flanders (1976) defines clinical supervision as

> a special case of teaching in which at least two persons are concerned with the improvement of teaching and at least one of the individuals is a teacher whose performance is to be studied. . . . [Clinical supervision] seeks to stimulate some change in teaching, to show that a change did, in fact, take place, and to compare the old and new patterns of instruction in ways that will give a teacher useful insights into the instructional process. (pp. 47–48)

Seasoned supervision practitioners Lovell and Wiles (1983) define clinical supervision as

> a problem solving approach to instructional supervision in which objective observation and analysis of teaching is the basis for feedback as frameworks for change and improvement of performance. (p. 69)

Oliva (1989) writes:

> Clinical supervision is the provision of supervisory help to the individual teacher to improve instruction. The typical clinical model calls for a one-to-one, face-to-face relationship between the teacher and supervisor. Clinical supervision focuses on the events that take place in the classroom. (p. 503)

Goldhammer, Anderson, and Krajewski (1993) sketch clinical supervision in this way:

> As we see it, then, clinical supervision (CS) is that aspect of instructional supervision which draws upon data from firsthand observation of actual teaching, or other professional events, and involves face-to-face and other associated interactions between the observer(s) and the person(s) observed in the course of analyzing the observed professional behaviors and activities and seeking to define and/or develop next steps toward improved performance. (p. 4)

The clinical supervision model is structured into five sequential steps:

1. A preconference between the teacher and the supervisor to determine (a) the motive and reason for the observation, (b) the focal point of the observation, (c) the procedure and pattern of observation to be used, (d) the time for the observation, and (e) a time for the postconference.
2. Classroom observation to follow up on the planning of the preconference, including descriptions of events and interpretations of the descriptions.
3. Analysis and interpretations of the observational data and deciding on the approach to be used in the postconference with the teacher.
4. Postconference with the teacher to discuss the analysis of the observation and to plan for instructional improvement.
5. Critique of the preconference, observation, analysis, and postconference by supervisor and teacher together, allowing the teacher to feed input into the supervisory process and the supervisor to gain feedback from the teacher pursuant to the supervisory practices employed.

IMPORTANT ATTRIBUTES OF THE TEACHER

The teacher, of course, is the most critical factor in teacher evaluation. Just like all adults, teachers too go through various stages of development. Teachers have individual interests, individual abilities, individual values and beliefs, and, of

---

Box 12.5 Important Teacher Attributes

- Instructional competence
- Personal expectations
- Openness to suggestions
- Orientation to change
- Subject knowledge
- Experience

Box 12.6 Teacher's Instructional Competence

- Diagnosing the needs of students
- Planning, designing, and implementing lessons
- Presenting information to students
- Using questioning strategies to promote learning
- Assessing student learning
- Managing the classroom effectively

---

course, individualized and varied experiences. Probationary teachers, for example, deal with the evaluation process differently than a more experienced, tenured teacher. By and large, however, six teacher attributes, shown in Box 12.5, exert an influence on the process of evaluation.

Teacher knowledge about the elements of effective instruction is part and parcel of instructional competence. Teachers need to remain current in their profession and keep up with new insights regarding effective instructional delivery strategies. Keeping abreast of new pedagogical developments, instructional approaches, evaluation techniques, and classroom management techniques is vital. The competencies depicted in Box 12.6 are fairly basic in assessing the instructional competence of teachers.

The personal expectations of the teacher are of major importance as an attribute. There are some teachers who expect to be effective with all students, while other teachers feel it is not possible to be successful with everyone. Generally, teachers who demand a great deal from themselves, feel they still have many things to learn and can continually grow, benefit the most from the evaluation process. Box 12.7 shows some ways that teachers reveal their personal expectations.

The openness with which teachers receive suggestions is an important attribute. Successful and effective teachers glean information from a variety of

Box 12.7 Teacher's Personal Expectations

- How the teacher accounts for student success
- What the teacher does when a student fails to achieve
- How the teacher approaches setting professional goals
- How the teacher reacts to opportunities for professional development

Box 12.8 Teacher's Openness to Suggestions

Gleaning information from:

- Supervisors
- Fellow teachers
- Students
- Specialists
- Teacher aides
- Volunteers
- Parents
- Teacher educators
- Researchers

Box 12.9 Teacher's Orientation to Change

- Teacher's expectations of success when trying something new
- Teacher's need for success
- Teacher's amount of commitment
- Teacher's perception of support during change process
- Teacher's reservoir of ideas about how to change

Box 12.10 Teacher's Subject Knowledge

- Knowledge of the subject matter content to be taught
- Knowledge of the school district's assignment of that content within the system's curriculum plan

---

Box 12.11 **Teacher's Experience**

- Record of success with students
- Reputation for classroom control
- Previous evaluations and relationships with supervisors and administrators
- Feedback from parents and peers
- Seniority in the school system

---

useful sources. Box 12.8 shows some of the people from whom teachers derive useful suggestions.

Evaluation often precipitates change. There are always new strategies, methods, approaches, ideas, and the like for testing in the classroom. In a way, teaching and learning in the elementary school classroom is a continuous process of hypothesis testing. The most effective teaching is characterized by constant experimentation and calculated risk taking. Teachers who are open to change often benefit greatly from the evaluation process. Box 12.9 illustrates factors associated with a teacher's orientation to change.

Having technical knowledge about instructional techniques and strategies is one thing, but content knowledge is quite another dimension as a teacher attribute. The amount of knowledge a teacher has about his or her subject can greatly influence the effect of the evaluation process. Box 12.10 shows two important elements regarding teacher's subject knowledge.

A teacher's general professional experience is an important teacher attribute and can play a major role in how the teacher handles the evaluation process. The teacher's responsiveness to evaluation may be affected by the experiential factors shown in Box 12.11.

Important Attributes of the Observer

The interaction between the teacher and the person who observes and evaluates the teaching performance is critical. Like teachers, supervisors bring different attributes to the evaluation process. In that regard, Box 12.12 indicates six important observer attributes that may affect the quality of the teacher evaluation experience.

Unless the teacher feels that the supervisor has credibility, it is unlikely that the evaluation will be taken seriously. Credibility is a major attribute of an effective supervisor. Box 12.13 depicts some of the functions that denote credibility.

While credibility is likely to be the most significant attribute of the evaluator, alone it is insufficient. Good evaluators are persuasive: They are able to persuade teachers to alter their approaches when appropriate. Another valuable attribute of an evaluator is patience. Change is gradual, and good evaluators allow teachers

---

Box 12.12 IMPORTANT OBSERVER ATTRIBUTES

- Credibility
- Persuasiveness
- Patience
- Trust
- Track record
- Modeling

Box 12.13 CREDIBILITY OF THE OBSERVER

- Knowledge of the technical aspects of teaching
- Knowledge of subject areas
- Years of classroom teaching experience
- Years of experience in the school district
- Recency of teaching experience
- Familiarity with the teacher's classroom and students

---

time to evaluate feedback and react. Giving a teacher time and space to reflect on the feedback that has been provided is an important attribute in an effective supervisor. Another key attribute for the supervisor is to gain the trust of the teacher. To change teacher behavior, the ability to inspire trust is invaluable. The subsequent experiences and events in the performance of the supervisor reflect the track record. Previous suggestions that proved valuable, for example, will do much to enhance the supervisor's track record. Modeling or demonstrating new ideas or techniques is one of the most effective ways for an evaluator to make suggestions to a teacher. It is of exceptional value for the teacher to see what the recommendation looks like in practice. Also, supervisors who model and invite the teacher to critique the demonstration have provided an openness to the teacher that should make the process of evaluation even more valuable.

SUMMARY

The fundamental purpose of appraising the performance of teachers is to improve teaching and learning in the classroom. In that regard, supervisors seek to have teachers become reflective about teaching and learning in their classrooms and to determine, independently or through collaboration, where and how improvements can be made. For the most part, modern supervision is primarily nondirective and assists teachers in becoming increasingly autonomous; having increased self-control. Clinical supervision, a supervisory technique that is widely followed today, is a strategy for giving teachers direct help in the classroom by way of a preconference, observation, analysis, postconference, and critique.

Attributes of teachers that are important in the teacher appraisal process include instructional competence, personal expectations, openness to suggestions, orientation to change, subject matter knowledge, and prior experience. Attributes of supervisors that are important in the teacher appraisal process include credibility, persuasiveness, patience, ability to model, ability to create trust, and track record.

ACTIVITY

PURPOSE

The purpose of this activity is to role-play a postvisitation conference between teacher and supervisor.

PROCEDURE

Divide into pairs where one person plays the part of a new faculty member in an elementary school and the other person plays the role of the supervisor conducting a postvisitation conference. During the course of the conference, the following points should be addressed.

- orientation to both personal and school goals
- specific ideas for instructional improvement
- creating an atmosphere of a professional working relationship between teacher and supervisor
- developing a high degree of mutual trust
- an approach that bridges the gap between the real and the ideal
- an agreement for continuous inservice on effective approaches

At the end of the conference, have participants change roles and role-play another postvisitation conference. Conclude with a discussion where each role-playing pair reports on the pros and cons encountered in their conferencing sessions.

STUDY QUESTIONS

1. Explain how performance appraisal presents both opportunities and obstacles for the teacher seeking to grow into the role of a teacher-as-facilitator through curriculum integration.

2. Contrast developmental supervision with clinical supervision.
3. As an experienced teacher in your school, you have been given the assignment of explaining to new teachers the five sequential steps of the clinical supervision model. How would you explain the process to new teachers?
4. Describe the six teacher attributes that tend to exert an influence on the process of evaluation.
5. What attributes does a teacher look for in a supervisor that lend credibility to the evaluation process?

BIBLIOGRAPHY

Acheson, K., & Gall, M. (1987). *Techniques in the clinical supervision of teachers: Preservice and inservice applications* (2nd ed.). New York: Longman.

Adams, A., & Glickman, C. (1984). Does clinical supervision work? A review of research. *Tennessee Educational Leadership, 11* (11), 38–40.

Cogan, M. (1973). *Clinical supervision.* Boston: Houghton Mifflin.

Duke, D., & Stiggins, R. (1986). *Teacher evaluation: Five keys to growth.* Washington, D.C.: National Education Association.

Flanders, N. (1976). Interaction analysis and clinical supervision. *Journal of Research and Development in Education, 9,* 47–48.

Glickman, C., Gordon, S., & Ross-Gordon, J. (1995). *Supervision of instruction: A developmental approach* (3rd ed.). Boston: Allyn & Bacon.

Goldhammer, R., Anderson, R., & Krajewski, R. (1993). *Clinical supervision: Special methods for the supervision of teachers* (3rd ed.). Fort Worth: Harcourt Brace Jovanovich.

Lovell, J., & Wiles, K. (1983). *Supervision for better schools* (5th ed.). Englewood Cliffs, N.J.: Prentice-Hall.

National Association of Elementary School Principals. (1984). *Teacher incentives: A tool for effective management.* Reston, Va.: National Association of Elementary School Principals.

Nolan, J., Hawkes, B., & Francis, P. (1993). Case studies: Windows into clinical supervision. *Educational Leadership, 51* (2), 52–56.

Oliva, P. (1989). *Supervision for today's schools* (3rd ed.). New York: Longman.

Pavan, B. (April, 1985). *Clinical supervision: Research in schools utilizing comparative measures.* Paper presented at the annual meeting of the American Educational Research Association, Chicago.

Sergiovanni, T., & Starratt, R. (1988). *Supervision: Human perspectives* (4th ed.). New York: McGraw-Hill.

Sullivan, C. (1980). *Clinical supervision: A state of the art review.* Alexandria, Va.: Association for Supervision and Curriculum Development.

GLOSSARY

Academically Challenged. Children who are mildly retarded and have learning problems affecting both the academic and social areas.

Accountability. Taking responsibility for learning and providing documentation of the teaching-learning process that has taken place in the classroom setting.

ADD/ADHD. ADD refers to Attention Deficit Disorder and ADHD to Attention Deficit-Hyperactivity Disorder. Both disorders are characterized by distractibility, impulsivity, and hyperactivity.

Advance Organizer. A brief piece of information given prior to a verbal presentation that alerts the listener to important points within the presentation.

AIDS. Acquired Immune Deficiency Syndrome. One of the most deadly and treacherous diseases to confront humankind to date. It is characterized by a loss of immunity to infection, thus allowing heretofore treatable illnesses and infections to become fatal.

Analytic Rubric. A means of evaluation used to judge specific aspects of a single piece of work.

Anecdotal Record. A means of evaluation in which a record of nonjudgmental and factual observations is made of an individual child during the learning process.

Approximation. Learners' efforts that resemble correct form.

Arithmetic. The aspect of the quantitative curriculum that includes computation, counting, and measuring. The purpose of arithmetic is to use numerical manipulations to arrive at a particular outcome.

Aural-Oral. Using both hearing and speaking.

Authentic Assessment. The process of gathering evidence and documenting a student's learning and growth in the context of learning. Authentic assessment generally includes work done in the classroom in authentic situations and in a continuous manner.

Authentic Inclusion. Occurs when the concepts and skills of science, mathematics, language arts, reading, social studies, art, and/or music are used as a purposeful means for gathering, presenting, or understanding information related to a theme or problem.

Autonomy. Self-directed behavior.

Basal Readers. Series of books and related materials that help children develop and practice reading skills in each grade in the elementary school.

Behaviorism. Actions and conduct during the act of learning. Learning that deals only with observable (overt) behavior.

Block. An extended instructional period used to organize particular aspects of an integrated approach to curriculum.

Bodily Intelligence. One of Gardner's eight forms of intelligence in which the individual lives and learns primarily through the physical body. Movement is of great importance in learning.

Bookweb. A children's literature selection is featured as the focal point for a planning web to integrate instruction.

Brainstorming. A method of generating ideas in a nonjudgmental atmosphere.

Cause and Effect. The ability to attribute to some event a certain result. Cause and effect does not fully develop in children until ten years of age or later.

Centration. The tendency of the preoperational child to consider one characteristic of an object, even to the exclusion of all others.

Checklist. A device for evaluation used to make detailed observations of a specific child or a specific activity.

Circle Diagram. A type of graphic organizer in which a Venn diagram is used to show relationships between parts and the whole, between specifics and generalizations.

Classification. Placing of objects into groups or sets on the basis of one or more characteristics.

Clinical Supervision. A collaboration between supervisor and teacher to gather classroom data, observe the teaching act, and improve teaching.

Collaborative Learning. Learners assist one another as they collude, coincide, and concur in a learning exploration.

Concept. A broad, organizing idea that is idiosyncratic to each individual and is often developed through classification.

Conceptualization. The development of concepts around and within which factual information can be organized.

Concrete Objects. Real, three-dimensional objects used for learning. Does not include pictorial or model representations of objects.

Concrete Operational Stage. The second stage in development, according to Piagetian theory, in which the child becomes able to apply logical thought to concrete problems. Characterized by the development of conservation, reversible thought, decentration, and decreasing egocentricity.

Conferencing. Working one-on-one with a student to develop that student's skills in a particular area.

Constructivist Approach. An active, student-participatory approach in the learning process in which children compose, form, devise, trailblaze, and the like.

Conservation. Understanding that when the appearance of an object changes, the quantity of the object does not change. Forms of conservation identified by Piaget include conservation of number, substance, area, weight, length, volume, and time.

Constraints. Restrictions that harness and restrain curricular integration.

Content Rich. Instructional materials that provide abundant depth and a stimulating environment; usually describes children's literature used in a content setting.

Contrived Issues. Issues that do not arise directly from the life experiences of the students, but instead are invented and calculated situations.

Conventional Level. The second stage in Kohlberg's theory of moral development, in which behavior is based on living up to the expectations of people close to the individual and in which relationships are based on gratitude, loyalty, respect, and trust rather than on fear of punishment.

Cooperative Learning. A type of group learning in which students work together in small groups to achieve a particular goal or to complete a particular task.

Creative Thinking. A type of thinking that generates something new. Creative thinking often violates accepted principles and is generally looking toward the development of original ideas. Creative thinking is divergent in nature.

Critical Thinking. A type of thinking that is oriented toward the production and evaluation of ideas, including recognition and construction of sound arguments, application of principles of logic, and the avoidance of logical fallacies. Critical thinking includes knowing when to question ideas as well as the inclination to question. Critical thinking is generally convergent in nature.

Cultural Issues. Issues related to the customs, beliefs, traditions, and doctrines of a people.

Curricular Integration. A synthesizing, blending, and combining of instructional planning and instructional delivery among and between content subjects in a natural and harmonious way. *See* Integrated Curriculum.

Curriculum. A means for organizing the planned learning experiences within the school setting.

Departmentalized. An organizational plan where various subjects are taught by different teachers. In grade two, for example, Teacher A teaches reading/language arts and Teacher B teaches social studies/arithmetic/science.

Developmental Supervision. Supervisory strategies that move the teacher toward self-direction.

Directed Reading-Thinking Activity (DRTA). The teaching plan at the heart of any basal reader series. A typical DRTA includes preparation for reading, silent first reading, checking comprehension, oral second reading, related skills and abilities, and extension and enrichment.

Disabled Children. Those children who have special learning needs because of mental, physical, language, or emotional disabilities.

Disciplines. The underlying areas of study. Social studies, for example, is composed of the disciplines of geography, history, anthropology, sociology, economics, and political science.

Discovery Teaching. A teaching strategy in which students engage in active learning through activities that allow the development of concepts and conclusions. Discovery learning frequently includes hands-on activities using concrete materials.

Documentation. Providing proof of the teaching-learning process for specific skills, concepts, or projects.

Documentation Portfolio. A type of portfolio that documents the entire learning process from first draft to finished product.

Double Seriation. A form of ordering in which objects of one set are matched to the objects of a second set so that the object in the first set having the greatest amount of a given characteristic is matched to the object in the second set having the least of the given characteristic.

Egocentricity. The tendency on the part of the preoperational child to see all things from his or her own point of view. This leads the child to be unable to consider other points of view and to assume that everyone knows exactly what he or she knows.

Egocentric Speech. (1) To Piaget, egocentric speech is the representation of a child's egocentric thought. (2) To Vygotsky, egocentric speech provides coordination between thought and action.

Empowerment. To enable and sanction children to pursue learning.

Evaluation Portfolio. A type of portfolio that contains the results of preselected tasks all students must complete. Judgment of each of the tasks is by predetermined criteria. The evaluation portfolio is similar to traditional forms of evaluation.

Exhaustive Sorting. The ability to classify all objects into groups. Prior to about six years of age, children do not tend to use exhaustive sorting.

Explicit Phonics Instruction. Sounding out or pronouncing the sounds associated with individual letters in isolation and then blending letter sounds together to sound out a word or syllable.

Expository Teaching. A means of direct instruction in which the teacher functions as a director of instruction and the major purpose of the instruction is to convey content information to the students.

External Organization. Refers to factors affecting the manner in which a curriculum is implemented at the classroom, school, or district level.

Facilitator. A teacher who provides a learning environment where children are enabled and sanctioned to pursue learning in a process-oriented, constructivist way.

Formal Operations. The fourth period in cognitive development according to Piagetian theory. This stage is characterized by the ability to reason abstractly, to reflect on one's thinking, and to solve problems through systematic consideration of many possibilities.

Genres. Categories of children's literature.

Global Issues. Issues that span the globe in their interest, influence, and consequence.

Graphic Organizer. A visual means for organizing information.

Group Investigation. A type of cooperative learning in which small groups plan and carry out a strategy for learning.

Heterogeneous Grouping. A type of grouping practice in which the resulting groups have students with a variety of interests, backgrounds, and abilities.

Heteronomy. Behavior that is directed by influences external to the individual.

Higher-order Thinking. Generally, divergent rather than convergent thinking.

Holistic Rubric. A means for evaluation that develops a system for judging a total work, including overall organization, creativity, and expression of ideas.

Homogeneous Grouping. A type of grouping practice in which the resulting groups have students with a common factor, such as ability, achievement, or interest.

Immersion. Complete envelopment in a topic or skill; to cover in depth; to encompass; to enfold. Under optimal conditions, the learner is immersed in what is to be learned.

Implicit Phonics Instruction. Hearing and pronouncing whole words that begin with the same sound, then seeking other words that begin with the same sound.

Inclusion. Serving children with disabilities in the regular classroom setting whenever possible.

Inductive Discovery. A form of discovery teaching/learning in which learning proceeds from the specific to the general.

Integrated Curriculum. An approach to curricular organization in which the lines separating subject matter areas from one another are erased and distinct and discrete subject matter areas disappear.

Interdisciplinary. An approach to curricular organization in which there is an intermingling and merging in and among subject matter areas and disciplines.

Internal Organization. Factors that influence the organization of the subject matter within the curriculum.

Interpersonal Intelligence. One of Gardner's eight forms of intelligence, in which the individual shows a high level of ability to understand the feelings, desires, or ideas of others.

Intrapersonal Intelligence. One of Gardner's eight forms of intelligence, in which the individual shows a high level of awareness of himself or herself. These individuals tend to be introspective and self-starters.

Issues. Issues have many faces, including controversies, problems, obstacles, predicaments, dilemmas, and plights. Issues deal with people's persuasions in that they are viewed in light of one's opinions, beliefs, attitudes, biases, convictions, feelings, perspectives, sentiments, and leanings. Issues provide excellent focal points for inquiries that range across the elementary curriculum without regard for subject boundaries.

Jigsaw. A type of cooperative learning in which students become experts in a specific part of the total information to be learned and then teach other members of the team that information.

Learning Style. The most effective means of learning for an individual. Includes oral, aural, and kinesthetic modes.

Linguistic Intelligence. One of Gardner's eight forms of intelligence, in which the individual focuses on the elements of language, including language itself as well as the message communicated through language.

Literacy. The ability to use language effectively and efficiently in communication.

Literature Sets. Sets of books on single topics, books from a distinctive genre, or books written by a particular author.

Logical Intelligence. One of Gardner's eight forms of intelligence, in which the individual shows strength in developing systems to organize and classify information and to develop logical conclusions according to systematic sets of rules.

Mainstreaming. A child with a disability is mainstreamed if he or she spends any part of the day in the regular classroom setting.

Many-to-One Correspondence. The ability to match a number of objects from one set to a single object in a second set. A child uses this form of correspondence in mathematics when ten ones are regrouped into one ten.

Mathematical Intelligence. One of Gardner's eight forms of intelligence, in which the individual excels in thinking about the physical world and its properties and then in encoding the information gained in numbers and symbols.

Mathematics. That aspect of the quantitative curriculum concerned with conceptualization of mathematical concepts.

Media. The vast array of newspapers, magazines, periodicals, trade books, textbooks, radio, and television that is often termed *mass communication*.

Metacognition. Thinking about thinking. Metacognition includes knowing what one does or does not know as well as the cognitive ability that monitors other thinking processes.

Musical Intelligence. One of Gardner's eight forms of intelligence, in which the individual demonstrates a high level of ability to think in terms of musical sounds.

One-to-Many Correspondence. The matching of one object in a set to many objects in a second set. This form of correspondence is used in arithmetic when one ten is regrouped as ten ones.

One-to-One Correspondence. The ability to match one object in a set to one object in a second set. This form of correspondence is used in counting.

Operational Definition. A definition developed by students to clarify a particular term as it is being used in a particular instance.

Performance Appraisal. Teacher evaluation. Major components include gathering evidence and formulating judgments.

Phonics. The study of relationships between the letter symbols of a written language (graphemes) and the sounds the symbols represent (phonemes).

Physically Disabled. A child is considered physically disabled if he or she has functional limitations such as difficulty with body control, hand use, or mobility or has a medical condition affecting strength, a heath disorder, or missing limbs.

Portfolio. A purposeful, integrated collection of student work showing student effort, progress, and/or achievement in one or more areas. Students participate in both the development and the evaluation of a portfolio.

Prenormative Stage. A stage in Kohlberg's theory of moral development, in which moral reasoning is based on obedience to authority out of fear rather than on obedience based on mutual respect.

Preoperational Stage. The second stage in development as described by Piaget, which is characterized by lack of reversible thought, egocentricity, inability to conserve, and reliance on direct experience with concrete objects in learning.

Problem. A real-world situation into which students must bring content information from a wide variety of sources to the solution of that situation.

Process Portfolio. A type of portfolio that documents the learning process a student engages in through the various projects that take place during the school year.

Qualitative Portfolio. A type of portfolio in which assessment is based on the quality of the items included rather than on the simple presence of items in the portfolio.

Quantitative Portfolio. A type of portfolio in which assessment of the portfolio is based on the number of items included as itemized in a list.

Real Issues. Those that arise directly from the day-to-day life experiences of the students and are witnessed by them either directly or vicariously (e.g., through media reports).

Reasoning. The use of past information in a new situation and in a logical manner.

Resource Unit. A long-range planning tool that helps the teacher organize and identify the resources available for teaching a particular theme.

Reversibility. The ability to follow a process in both the forward and reverse directions. According to Piagetian theory, preoperational children are unable to reverse their thought processes.

Rubric. An evaluation device consisting of a set of criteria which students see prior to the start of a task or activity.

Semantic Map. A graphic organizer that shows interrelationships among concepts and ideas in a theme. Semantic maps can also be used to assess the knowledge held by students prior to a theme.

Sensory Disabled. A child is considered to be sensory disabled when hearing or visual problems are not fully corrected by devices such as glasses or hearing aids.

Seriation. Placing objects in order on the basis of some characteristic, as in ordering straws from longest to shortest.

Sex Equity. Gender issues, particularly sex-role stereotyping and equity concerns between genders.

Showcase Portfolio. A type of portfolio in which the included work samples demonstrate only the best efforts of the student.

Social Issues. Issues that confront humankind on a large scale such as hunger, poverty, overpopulation, capital punishment, homelessness, abortion, and drug abuse.

Spatial Intelligence. One of Gardner's eight forms of intelligence, in which the individual demonstrates a high level of ability in interacting with the environment through forms and images. This individual learns most effectively through visual images.

STAD. (Student Teams-Achievement Divisions.) A type of cooperative learning made up of five components: class presentation, teams, quizzes, individual improvement scores, and team recognition.

Tabulature. A method used in developing a graphic organizer in which the concepts that could be considered within a particular thematic unit are shown in table form.

Thematic Units. Instructional designs created around a central idea and lasting for an extended period of time, perhaps a few days, a week, or even longer.

Theme. A broad area that provides a focus for teaching and learning in the integrated curriculum. A theme has substance and is worthy of exploration.

Themed Teaching. The utilization of a central theme around which the inquiry and learning take place.

Themeweb. A planning device for units in the form of a graphic organizer that outlines the major components of the unit. The themeweb is used to interrelate and integrate aspects of the elementary curriculum with a specific thematic topic.

Thinking. The search for meaning within a set of information that apparently has no meaning.

Topic. A narrowly focused and subject-matter-specific area of study.

Tower Diagram. A type of graphic organizer that extends a circle diagram and allows for greater use of inference and generalization.

Traditional Assessment. The most commonly used form of grading in the classroom setting. Traditional evaluation procedures are based on the assumption that there are specific pieces of information all students should learn at the same time.

Transductive Reasoning. A form of reasoning generally used by preoperational children and containing two aspects: reasoning that draws a conclusion from something connected perceptually to an occurrence but not connected causally, and reasoning from specific to specific without the development of a generalization.

Visual Organizer. A visual means for organizing information. *See* Graphic Organizer.

Whole Language. An approach to literacy in which all elements of communication through language are developed simultaneously and in authentic situations. Perhaps the essential belief embodied in a whole language philosophy is that *learning exists in context.*

Zone of Proximal Development. According to Vygotsky, the distance between the actual developmental level as determined by independent problem solving and the level of potential development as determined through problem solving under adult guidance or under the direction of more capable peers.

INDEX